RETHINKING NA 3279453300
CULTURE, IDEO

RETHINKING NORTHERN IRELAND

Culture, Ideology and Colonialism

Edited by
David Miller

Longman
London and New York

Addison Wesley Longman Limited
Edinburgh Gate
Harlow
Essex CM20 2JE
England
and Associated Companies throughout the world

Published in the United States of America
by Addison Wesley Longman Inc., New York

Visit Addison Wesley Longman on the World Wide Web at:
http://www.awl-he.com

© Addison Wesley Longman Limited 1998

First published 1998

ISBN 0582 30287 0

British Library Cataloguing-in-Publication Data
A catalogue record for this book is available from the British Library

Library of Congress Cataloging-in-Publication Data
Rethinking Northern Ireland : culture, ideology, and colonialism/
    edited by David Miller.
        p.   cm.
    Includes bibliographical references and index.
    ISBN 0-582-30287-0
    1. Northern Ireland–Civilization. 2. Northern Ireland–Politics
and government. 3. Northern Ireland–Social conditions.
I. Miller, David, 1964-
DA990.U46R47 1998
941.6–dc21   98-28732
                                                                               CIP

Set by 30 in 10/11 Pt Palatino
Printed in Malaysia, PP

For Caitlin and Lewis
and the silenced and repressed

The moment the very name of Ireland is mentioned the English seem to bid adieu to common feeling, common prudence and common sense and to act with the barbarity of tyrants and the fatuity of idiots.

Sydney Smith, English clergyman and essayist, 1771–1845

A desire to expiate what are seen as past sins, and a genuine surprise at the appalling record of much of British government in Ireland is understandable . . . but it must be questioned whether it gets us any nearer understanding. Innocent and sometimes naively hilarious works of piety about the Fenians or Young Irelanders, written by amateur historians on the British left fall into a much cruder category. They are joined by half-baked 'sociologists' employed on profitably never-ending research into 'anti-Irish' racism, determined to prove what they have already decided to be the case.

Roy Foster, Carroll Professor of Irish History, Oxford University, 'We Are All Revisionists Now', *Irish Review*, 1986, p.3

My Dear Mosley,
I have just returned from Northern Ireland. I was disappointed to hear that in some semi-official organ of the Blackshirt Movement there had been attacks upon the North of Ireland government. I think this is a very grave mistake. In the North of Ireland you might find the most valuable recruiting ground of anywhere in the United Kingdom. I am intensely interested in that country, as perhaps you know. My forebears came from there. I do not want my enthusiasm for your cause to be diminished by such an unnecessary and unfair attack . . .

Yours faithfully,
Rothermere.

Lord Rothermere, proprietor of the *Daily Mail*, to Oswald Mosley, 12 April 1934, copied to Blackmore, Cabinet Secretary to the Unionist Government, in PRONI, CAB9F/123/7

Contents

Notes on Contributors

James Anderson is a political geographer with interests in nationalism and transnational integration, and territorial and non-territorial forms of political community and democracy. He has worked on various aspects of European integration, and published extensively on Ireland's partition, the conflict between Irish and British nationalisms, and cross-border linkages, particularly in the context of the European Union. A recent professorial appointment at the University of Newcastle upon Tyne, he was previously with the Open University where he chaired the Faculty of Social Sciences Foundation Course.

Desmond Bell was born in Derry and studied philosophy and sociology at the University of Warwick where he gained his doctorate. He is the author of *Acts of Union: Youth Culture and Sectarianism in Northern Ireland* (Macmillan, 1990) as well as numerous academic articles dealing with culture, the media and politics in Ireland. He is also a documentary film-maker and directed *We'll fight and no surrender*, *Redeeming History*, *Out of Loyal Ulster* (all screened on Channel Four television) and *Dancing on Narrow Ground* (Cultural Traditions). He is currently Professor and Head of the Department of Photography, Film and TV at Napier University, Edinburgh.

Ronan Bennett is the author of three novels, *The Second Prison*, *Overthrown by Strangers* and *The Catastrophist*. His television credits include *Love Lies Bleeding* and *A Man You Don't Meet Every Day*. His feature film, *Face*, starring Robert Carlyle and directed by Antonia Bird, was shown at the Edinburgh, Venice and Toronto Film Festivals, and on general release in 1997. Another film, *A Further Gesture*, starring Stephen Rea and directed by Robert Dornhelm, was released in 1998. His other books are: *Stolen Years: Before and After Guildford*, written with Paul Hill, and *Double Jeopardy: The Retrial of the Guildford Four*, originally a long essay in the *London Review of Books*. His work for radio includes *Fire and Rain*, his memoir of the 1974 burning of Long Kesh, which was broadcast on BBC Radio Four in October 1994 and won a Sony Radio Award Gold Medal. A radio play, *Marked for Place*, was broadcast in November 1994 on Radio Four and nominated for a Writers' Guild award. He is a regular contributor to the *London Review of Books*, the *Guardian*, the *Independent*, the *Observer*, *New Left Review*, *Sight and Sound*, *Il Manifesto*, *Linea d'Ombra*, *Red Pepper* and *Labour Briefing*. Ronan Bennett holds a PhD in history from the University of London.

Pamela Clayton taught for ten years in Belfast and is currently Research Fellow at the Department of Adult and Continuing Education, University of Glasgow. She is the author of *Enemies and Passing Friends: Settler Ideologies in Twentieth-Century Ulster* (Pluto, 1996).

Carol Coulter worked as a freelance journalist before joining the *Irish Times* in Dublin in 1986. In 1990 she won the National Media Award for campaigning journalism. She is the author of *Web of Punishment* (1991) and *Ireland Between the First and Third Worlds* (1989) both published by Attic Press; *The Hidden Tradition: Women, Feminism and Nationalism in Ireland* (Cork University Press, 1993); 'Feminism, Nationalism and the Heritage of the Englightenment' in *Gender and Colonialism* (edited by Foley *et al.*, Galway University Press, 1995) and 'Hello Divorce, Goodbye Daddy' – Sex, Women and Gender in Ireland's Divorce Debate' in *Gender and Sexuality in Modern Ireland* (edited by Anthony Bradley and Maryann Gialanella Valiulis, University of Massachussets Press, 1997). She is a founder and the general editor of the magazine *The Irish Reporter*.

Sarah Edge is a lecturer in Media Studies at the University of Ulster in Coleraine. She teaches the theory and practice of photography and feminist cultural theory. Her most recent research is published in *Feminist Review* (no. 50, Summer 1995) and the *Irish Journal of Feminist Studies* (vol. 1, no. 2, 1996). She is co-editor of *Gendered Narratives: Irish Cultural Identities and Political Divisions* (forthcoming, 1999). She is a member of the editorial board of the *Irish Journal of Feminist Studies*.

Douglas Hamilton is currently undertaking a PhD in the Department of Geography, University of Newcastle on 'The Political Economy of North–South Co-operation and Development in Ireland'. He was previously Senior Economist at the Northern Ireland Economic Council in Belfast and has worked in local government in England and undertook economic research at the University of Strathclyde. He has written extensively on economic and industrial development issues in Ireland, both North and South, with a wide range of publications in official reports, academic journals and books.

Robbie McVeigh is Research Officer with the West Belfast Economic Forum. He also teaches racism and anti-racism part-time at Queen's University, Belfast and University College, Dublin. He was formerly

Research and Publications Officer with the Centre for Research and Documentation. He is author of *The Racialization of Irishness: Racism and Anti-racism in Ireland* (Belfast: CRD, 1995). He is also active in a number of human rights organisations working on racism and sectarianism.

David Miller is a member of the Stirling Media Research Institute. He is author of *Don't Mention the War: Northern Ireland, Propaganda and the Media* (London: Pluto, 1994), editor (with Bill Rolston) of *War and Words: The Northern Ireland Media Reader* (Belfast: Beyond the Pale, 1996), co-author (with the Glasgow Media Group) of *The Circuit of Mass Communication: Media Strategies, Representation and Audience Reception in the AIDS Crisis* (London: Sage, 1998) and co-author (with Greg Philo) of *Cultural Compliance: The Dead Ends of Media/Cultural Studies and Social Science* (Glasgow: Glasgow Media Group, 1998).

Ronnie Munck is currently Senior Lecturer in the Department of Sociology at Liverpool University, having previously worked in South Africa and the University of Ulster. He has written extensively on development issues, both in Ireland and Latin America. Books include *The Irish Economy – Results and Prospects* (London: Pluto Press, 1993), *Ireland – Nation, State and Class Struggle* (Boulder, CO: Westview Press, 1985), *Politics and Dependency in the Third World: The Case of Latin America* (London: Zed Books, 1984), *The Difficult Dialogue – Marxism and Nationalism* (London: Zed Books, 1986), *Latin America: The Transition to Democracy* (London: Zed Books, 1989).

Liam O'Dowd is Professor of Sociology at Queen's University, Belfast. He has recently co-edited *Ireland: Sociological Perspectives* (Dublin: Institute of Public Administration, 1995), and edited *On Intellectuals and Intellectual Life in Ireland* (Belfast/Dublin: Institute of Irish Studies/Royal Irish Academy, 1996).

Bill Rolston is a senior lecturer in Sociology at the University of Ulster. His books include *Northern Ireland: Between Civil Rights and Civil War* (CSE Books, 1980 with Liam O'Dowd and Mike Tomlinson); *Drawing Support: Murals in the North of Ireland* (Beyond the Pale, 1992); *Abortion in the New Europe: A Comparative Handbook* (Greenwood, 1994, with Anna Eggert).

Joseph Ruane lectures in sociology and anthropology at University College, Cork. He has published extensively on Irish development and on the Northern Ireland conflict. He is co-author (with Jennifer Todd) of *The Dynamics of Conflict in Northern Ireland* (Cambridge University Press, 1996).

Jennifer Todd lectures in politics at University College, Dublin. She has published extensively on political theory and on the Northern Ireland conflict. She is co-author (with Joseph Ruane) of *The Dynamics of Conflict in Northern Ireland* (Cambridge University Press, 1996).

Mike Tomlinson lectures in social policy and criminal justice at the Queen's University of Belfast. He is co-author of *Northern Ireland: Between Civil Rights and Civil War* (London: CSE Books, 1980) and *Unemployment in West Belfast* (Belfast: Beyond the Pale, 1988), and co-editor of several books including *Whose Law and Order? Aspects of Crime and Social Control in Ireland* (Belfast, SAI, 1988). He is a regular contributor to Statewatch and has written widely on the political economy of the security industry in Northern Ireland.

Preface

I first became interested in Northern Ireland in the early 1980s, because I noticed that the British left appeared to be reluctant to discuss the conflict on its doorstep, yet at the same time were willing to wax lyrical about far-away revolutions in Nicaragua, South Africa, Namibia or even Palestine. I wondered why there was this difference and started reading. I also remember hearing anti-Irish jokes about the hunger strikers (and particularly Bobby Sands) in 1981/2 and had – in around 1979 – purchased a copy of (in my view!) one of the finest albums of the period, *Inflammable Material* by Belfast outfit Stiff Little Fingers. After a while, it seemed to me too, that the least we needed was an 'Alternative Ulster'.

In research on the media and Northern Ireland conducted between 1988 and 1994, I was struck by the paucity of good critical accounts of the conflict and in particular by the lack of any single volume which contains a sustained critique of the dominant popular, academic and political wisdom. Although writing on the media and the conflict is somewhat underdeveloped, the concern with issues of balance and objectivity as well as the critical current in media studies has meant a recognition that there are a number of contending explanations for the conflict. Furthermore there was a widespread recognition that British journalism was systematically oriented towards the British government perspective. I suppose I had assumed that academic work would not replicate such inadequacies, since it was not so dependent on official sources for its routine information or conceptualisations. Having just written a chapter in this book on academic representations of the conflict, I now think that was a rather naive view. On reflection the media, for all the major inadequacies in their coverage, come out of a comparison with academic production rather well.

In any case, this book was conceived as an attempt to give its readers a reasonably broad critical introduction to the Northern Ireland conflict. It is intended as an intervention and as an attempt to contribute to the reorientation of understandings of the Northern Ireland problem. As I write this preface, the media are full of reports about, alternately, a historic deal at the talks in Belfast and the impossibility of a deal. In recent years with the emergence of the peace process the critical view on Northern Ireland has become newly respectable. No longer is talk of injustice or of Irish republicans as representing a valid constituency regarded as fellow-travelling with terrorism, and much academic and journalistic production over the last three decades and more looks naively parasitic on the official line. Nevertheless, the changes in perception of the Irish conflict still leave very many issues of justice, equality and democracy unresolved. It is my hope that this book can play some part in keeping these issues alive.

David Miller
Glasgow
10 April 1998

Acknowledgements

Thank you to all the contributors for producing their chapters and for associated advice and help. Thanks to all those who helped in pointing me to useful sources, in suggesting people who might write chapters and in giving me information: Raymond Boyle, Catherine Couvert, Paddy Hillyard, Oliver Kearney, Mark McGovern, Gerry McLaughlin, Robbie McVeigh, Willy Maley, John Naughton, Mike Ritchie, Terry Ritchie, Bill Rolston, Mike Tomlinson, Margaret Ward. Thanks to Michael Goodall of the Public Record Office of Northern Ireland for all his help, also to the Committee on the Administration of Justice, Ciaran Crossey at the Linenhall Library, the Fair Employment Commission, the estimable *Irish News* web site, and everyone who posts material on the US-based Ireland List news group. Thanks especially to all the students and lecturing staff at universities in the North, who over the last decade have spoken to me about academic politics there. Unfortunately, the reason I cannot name any of them is the nature of academic politics in Northern Ireland.

Thanks to the anonymous referees who provided reports on the outline of this book. I hope it does not disappoint. At Stirling thanks to my colleagues in the Stirling Media Research Institute for assorted help and patience and for some small financial assistance to this book. Thanks to Philip Schlesinger for discussions and for not discouraging my work on Ireland. Thanks to Rita Lago for references, associated help and for compiling the index. Thanks also to Will Dinan and Deirdre Kevin for going to the library, good humour and putting up with me. Thank you to Karen Hotchkiss for word processing and photocopying and to Emma Miller for Stakhanovite late-night copy-editing and bibliographic work. Thank you to my colleagues at Glasgow University for conversations and arguments and especially to Greg Philo for numerous discussions and for supporting my interest in Ireland from the beginning. Also, a mention to Jacquie Reilly for valiantly trying to curtail my tendency to inflate 'short-hand' descriptions of the 'six ....'

Thanks to Emma for support, arguments and criticism and to Caitlin and Lewis for being.

Lastly, thank you to everyone who has made my too infrequent trips to the North interesting and enjoyable, especially those who have kindly put me up and put up with me in assorted homes, pubs, cafes, libraries and streets, on demonstrations and at festivals.

Acknowledgements

Thanks to the Deputy Keeper of Records at the Public Record Office of Northern Ireland for permission to quote from official papers. Thanks to Brian Moore for permission to reproduce the Cormac cartoon in Chapter 9 and to Laurence McKeown for premission to quote from his poem 'Hardlines'. We have tried to trace other copyright holders without success and would appreciate any help that would enable us to do so.

Introduction: Rethinking Northern Ireland

David Miller

The standard of academic, media and popular commentary on the Northern Ireland conflict remains abysmal. Specifically, British propaganda, unionist ideology and revisionist 'scholarship' inform most contemporary discourse. In those spaces where this is not the case, traditional nationalist discourse retains something of a grip. This book is conceived as a major challenge to the shibboleths of contemporary debate on Northern Ireland. It is intended to raise critical, empirically informed objections to the way in which Northern Ireland is discussed across the range of public debate. From the heights of academic theorising (whether postmodern or not) to the routine misinformation of the tabloids, from hard news to television drama and mass circulation novels, and from art, poetry, theatre, literature and museum installations to government documents and politicians' speeches, the similarities in debate and representations are more striking than the variations. The predominance of notions of tribal conflict and irrational or self-interested violence gives a seriously misleading and distorted view of the conflict in Ireland and in the process hampers the chances for a lasting and just peace.

This book is divided into three fairly loose sections which deal with explanations, ideologies and strategies; structures, spaces and struggles, and culture and representation. Section 1 deals with explanations for the conflict in Ireland, and the ideologies and strategies of the three major players. In the first chapter I examine the reluctance of academics to discuss the conflict in Ireland or later Northern Ireland in terms of colonialism and a corresponding unwillingness to make use of the wider literature on colonialism in analysing the conflict. The argument is that this reluctance, as well as being an abdication of the responsibilities of intellectuals, is explained partly in terms of fear, danger and coercion, but also partly in terms of the class, national and occupational interests and ideologies of academics.

Pamela Clayton criticises those who advance theories of ethnic conflict or religion to explain the conflict. Showing a considerable grasp of the history of the development of the settlement colony in Ireland as well as the history of doctrinal disagreements she argues that such explanations by themselves are at best inadequate. Turning to an examination of the development of 'settler ideology' she makes the case for treating Northern Ireland as an example of settler colonialism. Joseph Ruane and Jennifer Todd examine the extent to which it can be said that Irish nationalism is the cause of the conflict. Against those who would argue that the backwardness and bloodlust of Irish nationalism is the key problem in Ireland, they point out that since the conflict in Ireland precedes the emergence of nationalism as an ideology we have to look elsewhere for causative agents. Without denying the contemporary role of Irish (and British) nationalism in the conflict they seek to situate the conflict in a more adequate structural and cultural context. They argue that even were a form of postnationalism to emerge – and this is doubtful – that this would not resolve the conflict. What is needed in their view is an 'emancipatory' approach to the conflict which would' moderate and differentiate the dimensions of difference ... undo the structure of dominance, dependence and inequality and ... weaken the forces producing communal polarisation' (1996: 307). This is an approach with which several of the authors here would concur.

Liam O'Dowd examines the extent to which 'new' unionism is part of this emancipatory process, or at least part of the actually existing peace process. His conclusions are bleak for those anticipating the emergence of a unionist De Klerk. He detects few signs here that important elements of unionism may be coming to the public realisation that the game is up. In many respects this suggests that perhaps it is not, at least not yet. The reconstitution by unionist intellectuals of their project as a higher form of civilisation featuring universal and progressive values is a case, O'Dowd argues, of old British nationalist wine in new bottles. Tomlinson also seems less than optimistic about the likelihood of British policy moving towards an emancipatory approach. His chapter is also a strong rebuke to those who would study Northern Ireland without being able to focus properly on the role of the British. Of those few who have explicitly examined British policy most seem unable to conceive that the role of the British state might have been more significant than that of the occasionally misguided and clumsy neutral umpire. Based throughout on empirical evidence Tomlinson argues clearly that such approaches are both inaccurate and conceptually naive. In studying state killings and collusion with loyalist paramilitaries he goes where most analysts of British policy fear to tread. He emphasises that these are important issues, not just in terms of lives lost, but in the tendency of British policies in this area to worsen rather than ameliorate conflict in the North of Ireland. Nowhere is this more apparent than in the pressing issue of demilitarisation in the peace process, where a key consequence of British policy in the last twenty years has been to arm legally the Protestants (in the police and army), giving them what Tomlinson refers to as their 'ultimate power base'.

In the second section of the book, Spaces, Structures and Struggles, Anderson and Munck and Hamilton explore changing notions of sovereignty and political space and economic development respectively. Anderson is critical of those approaches which point (approvingly or disapprovingly) to fundamental changes in the sovereignty of nation states. We are not about to leave nation states behind and move into the Europe of the regions next Monday or come the millennium. However, he does note the impact which European transnationalisation has had and is having on concepts such as sovereignty, particularly in the context of some globalising tendencies. To understand these tendencies properly he argues for a rejection of traditional unionist and nationalist approaches and their homes in 'realist' and liberal 'functionalist' theories of international relations. Instead he stresses a critical approach which emphasises the struggles and conflicts which fit the contradictory nature of international developments more adequately. In similar vein Munck and Hamilton tackle the debate about the economy of Northern Ireland in the context of an all-Ireland economy. Rejecting more of the same as a viable policy, they also attack a technicist emphasis on purely economic integration, as inadequate for the task of peace. Instead they propose a more radical alternative, which takes the colonial context seriously and would involve democratic development for Ireland in which conventional economic analysis was turned on its head in a human-centred analysis. Both Anderson and Munck and Hamilton conclude by proposing variants (or analogues) of the emancipatory approach of Ruane and Todd in the specific circumstances of political spaces and economics.

Emancipation is also very much central to the analyses of Coulter and McVeigh. She is concerned with the struggle of women for emancipation, but sees this in the context of other structures of domination, in particular both class and colonial structures. Her argument is, therefore, more complex than a feminist analysis of women's subordination under capitalism or democratic conditions and she sees in some western feminist analyses the traces of the societies from which they emerged. In practical politics, she argues, it is possible to discern the influence of colonialism on feminism in Ireland, both in the past at the time of the suffrage movement and in the present in the debates which have divided feminists in Britain and Ireland and within Ireland. Although not arguing for a form of cultural relativism, she does insist that feminist struggles need to be understood in the specific historical circumstances of the force fields of class, colonial and gender power. McVeigh also wants to locate his discussion of sectarianism and racism in their specific historical circumstances. In Ireland this means understanding sectarianism as a structuring phenomena which makes the analysis of racism and class relations additionally complex. McVeigh sees many more similarities between sectarianism and racism than most analysts who want to keep them analytically separate. Crucially he sees sectarianism, like racism, as bound up with colonial history and with power and interests. Nevertheless he argues in favour of an analytical separation between the two, both on the grounds that the racism suffered in the North by Chinese, Asian and other ethnic minority peoples, is identifiably different to that suffered by Catholics at the hands of Protestants or the Irish at the hands of the British. But the similarities between the two are indeed striking and McVeigh calls for more comparative analysis of racism in Britain and elsewhere with sectarianism in the North of Ireland.

The final section of the book examines culture, conflict and representation. These are among the most neglected areas of study on Northern Ireland and four chapters are included here. Ronan Bennett examines British, Irish and unionist culture in Northern Ireland. Ranging across theatre, the arts, film, novels, television drama, music, poetry, community festivals and commemorations and demonstrations, he shows the reluctance of official culture to mention the war, the richness and diversity of oppositional cultural work and, sadly, the culturally confined world of 'unionist' culture. Here, as most unionist intellectuals will acknowledge, unionism has been less than proficient at fostering convincing myths and stories to tell to itself and the world. The acknowledgement by unionist and Protestant leaders that sectarian marches through Catholic areas are key parts of their culture is seen by Bennett, and by Edge, Bell and Rolston, as symptomatic of the poverty of a stranded culture.

Edge, however, is more concerned with changing portrayals of gender in recent audio-visual production. She discerns a trend towards the humanisation of men engaged in political violence in recent film and television productions. The psychopathic or irrational 'terrorist' gives way to the representation of caring masculinity. This is significant, Edge argues, because of the historical period in which it occurs, namely coincident with the peace process. But she also notes that this is paralleled in some representations with new portrayals of women as peace-makers. Ironically some of the new representations can be read as positive from a feminist perspective. But for Edge, this opens up a new problem which is that changing representations of gender are being used in the service of particular strategies designed to marginalise dissent by the state. Feminism is being used against nationalism as if the two were intrinsically opposed. This takes us back to Coulter's argument about the necessity for understanding gender subordination in the context of the structures of class and colonialism. Edge criticises the misrepresentation of the audio-visual work of Irish feminists as intrinsically critical of nationalist and republican politics and calls for a move beyond essentialist nations of both gender and national identity.

Des Bell also adopts a non-essentialist position on identity, in the context of a discussion about cultural heritage and tradition. He examines attempts to represent Irish history in museum installations. Focusing especially on the Tower Museum in Derry, his home town, Bell argues that there are parallels between the museum's exhibits and the cultural policy of the British government. When he compares the installation in Derry with the new Famine Museum in the Republic, some of the difficulties of representing history which was only recorded by the powerful become apparent. Nevertheless, Bell concludes that the key watchword of heritage presentation is tolerance, as if being nice to each other was enough to undo the heritage and effects of colonialism.

Rolston brings the volume to a conclusion with a mammoth survey of the origins and transformations of multiculturalism. Tracing the idea back to the USA in the 1960s and Britain in the 1970s, he provides a critique of its liberal and culturally relativist contentions and then examines its importation into Ireland in the name of community relations. Rolston analyses multiculturalism in the context of British government policy in education, development and culture. But he also points out that it has directly political uses in justifications for Orange marches through Catholic areas. The book ends, then, where it started with a recognition that to understand and rethink Northern Ireland centrally involves recognising the economic, social and cultural inequalities which underlie the conflict, which have their origins in colonialism and their current form as a result of that legacy and the actions of the participants in the conflict.

Rethinking Northern Ireland requires that the inequalities brought about by colonialism in Ireland be recognised for what they are. Tackling them is the only way to a lasting and just peace, since they are the key reasons for conflict. Failing to recognise the relations of power and ideology at the heart of the conflict can only leave commentators in the academy, the media and public life more generally seriously unable to comprehend the reasons for the conflict and vulnerable to regurgitating the official versions of the conflict provided by British government propagandists, Ulster unionists and traditional Irish nationalists.

Part One

Explanations, Ideologies and Strategies

CHAPTER 1

Colonialism and academic representations of the troubles

David Miller

According to the vast bulk of literature on the topic Northern Ireland is not a colony of Britain and the conflict there is not colonial in nature. Many analysts are willing to admit that there used to be a colonial relationship between Britain and Ireland (although a substantial portion see this as of little significance and some even appear to deny that Ireland was a colony). When we come to the present, hardly a whisper is heard about the colonial relationship between Britain and Northern Ireland. Most historians do refer to relations between Britain and Ireland as colonial for the years between the late medieval period and the eighteenth century (see Ruane 1992). But after that colonialism as an explanation seems to vanish – reference to it by historians becomes 'unusual' (Ruane 1992: 296). Economists, sociologists and anthropologists have tended not to analyse the political, economic or cultural development of Ireland in colonial terms. Political scientists – especially in Ireland – and geographers have analysed the relationship between Britain and Ireland in terms of colonialism at least at some stage in history. But as we move nearer to the present references to colonialism become rarer. According to Ruane no anthropological study has referred to Northern Ireland as a colonial situation (1992:303). This is at best curious.

Amongst those who acknowledge a colonial relationship or dimension in the past, there is little which identifies the precise date or historical period when Northern Ireland ceased to be a colony. If all Ireland was a colony of Britain, did it stop being so with the Act of Union in 1801? Did the North stop being a colony in 1920 with the Government of Ireland Act? Or perhaps in 1921 with the ending of the war of independence and the withdrawal of British forces from the 26 counties of the Free State? Was it before that with the alleged emergence of a separate 'nation' in the North in the nineteenth century? Was it when the British state ceased to have economic interests in Ireland which some argue was after 1945? Or was it when unionist one-party rule was ended in 1972 and Westminster imposed direct rule? Or when British strategic interests became less important in the 1970s and 1980s and decisively so after 1989? The date is not specified and the discussion on this matter severely underdeveloped. As one leading analyst (who himself does not describe the North of Ireland as a colony) has observed, those authors who do not use a colonial model 'simply remain silent on the subject, and do not actually argue the case against employing it' (Whyte 1990: 178). Similarly, Ruane states 'the language of colonialism simply stopped with the advent of the nineteenth century, without explicit discussion or justification' (1992: 318).

The argument here is that none of the above dates is of any significance for describing the colonial relations between Britain and Ireland and later between Britain and Northern Ireland, since they refer to arguments about changes in British (or Irish) interests or to arguments about settler identity which do not relate to the structural and historical realities of the contemporary situation. Nor would such arguments be accepted in analyses of other settler colonial societies. No one now suggests that Northern Ireland is really part of 'Great Britain' and the mouthful which is the name of the state reflects this – the 'United Kingdom of Great Britain and Northern Ireland'. When people in Northern Ireland claim to be British they justify this in imperial and ideological terms since they don't actually live in Britain. Ulster is British in the sense that it is a colonial possession which the British state has tried to present as an integral part of the state. Not even Margaret Thatcher really believed that Northern Ireland was, in her own phrase, 'as British as Finchley', as her memoirs show (Thatcher 1995:385).

This chapter will examine how academics in Britain, Ireland and beyond have responded to the conflict in Northern Ireland. First it will examine the inadequacies of a wide variety of academic work which has dealt with Northern Ireland, ranging across both the social and human sciences, from history, political science, sociology, international relations, economics, economic history, psychology and geography to philosophy, literary criticism, art history and media and cultural studies. This section will highlight how such studies deal with the question of colonialism, and with their characterisations especially of unionism.

Academic explanations of the conflict

If Northern Ireland is a colony the question arises, how could so many academic 'experts' get their analyses so comprehensively wrong? Whyte seems somewhat perplexed by the failure to argue about colonial explanations in the literature, tending to treat academic explanations of the conflict at face value rather than as emanating from and contributing to the ideological contest over definition of the conflict.[1] This chapter sets contemporary Northern Ireland in its colonial context and argues that colonialism and its associated propaganda, information and cultural enterprises are part of the reason for the systematic inadequacy of much writing on Northern Ireland. In other words it directs attention to the class, national and ethnic backgrounds of intellectuals and academics, their sectional interests, and their role in hegemonic contest (see O'Dowd 1996b). But before we go on to assess some of the reasons for this, let us turn to some of the arguments for and against colonialism as an explanation.

Northern Ireland as a colony

Northern Ireland is a colony of 'Great Britain'. But this does not necessarily mean that the conflict is 'colonial' in exactly the same way as all other colonial conflicts. For a start, as Pamela Clayton argues (this volume, 1996; see also Lustick 1993; MacDonald 1986; Weitzer 1990) Northern Ireland exhibits many of the characteristics associated with settler colonialism. Apposite parallels include Rhodesia, Palestine and especially French Algeria. South Africa also exhibits some of the same features, though matters are made more complex by two competing groups of settlers. Northern Ireland, by contrast, shows less parallel with colonial situations such as India under the Raj, any of the other British non-settler colonies, or with the resistance against repressive third world regimes such as those in Nicaragua under Somoza or Chile under Pinochet. The colonial relationship between Britain and Ireland also makes the conflict different from other armed struggles in Western Europe, such as those waged by the Rote Armee Fraktion in West Germany, by the Combatant Communist Cells in Belgium or by Action Directe in France. The situation in Euskadi (the Basque country) does bear more comparison (in the strategies of the state and the insurgents and arguably in the facets of relations between the Spanish state and the Basque country which have colonial parallels), but the specifically settler dimension of the conflict in Northern Ireland does mark it out as different.

However, the designation settler colonialism cannot by itself explain everything. We must also take into account how settler colonies differ and the specific historical circumstances and contests which shape every conflict. Not all settler societies resolve the tensions which tend to arise between settlers and natives in the same way and consequently the process of decolonisation (where it occurs) varies.[2] The declaration of UDI by the white settlers in Rhodesia is one variation (Weitzer 1990). Although there have been some stirrings amongst Ulster unionists on this matter, it is not more than a minority demand. More fundamentally, one key way to avoid conflicts between settlers and natives over territory and resources – by exterminating them – did not happen in Ireland as it did in, for example, North America. Today, few unionists publicly advance the extermination of natives as a policy goal – although in 1984 DUP Belfast city councillor, George Seawright, did propose that the council purchase an incinerator to burn Catholics and their priests (Johnson 1984). Loyalist paramilitaries also seem to have this as part of their military strategy, expressed in slogans in wall murals such as 'Kill All Irish' and 'Any Catholic Will Do'.

Ireland is also different in that it was ruled by 'Britain' for a long time prior to the processes generally identified as colonialism and imperialism and some writers have referred to Ireland as a whole as an integral part of British attempts at nation-building. This is one key way in which Northern Ireland is different from some other colonies. Ireland was Britain's first colony, but there was also an attempt to integrate it into the national territory. This strategy failed with the creation of the Irish Free State. Today Northern Ireland is officially a part of the 'UK' state. It is not, however, part of 'Great Britain'. In a sense then, Northern Ireland is a less integral part of Britain than Algeria was as a *departèment* of France. But Northern Ireland is to some extent integrated into the UK state and political system, albeit not to the extent that Scotland and Wales are.

To be fair, settler colonialism does seem to be a fairly widespread characterisation of the *origins* of the conflict in Northern Ireland. It has recently been partially endorsed by the leading political science commentators (O'Leary and McGarry 1993; McGarry and O'Leary 1995). However, many such commentators are reluctant to follow the point through and describe the current conflict as colonial in the same terms. Reading McGarry and O'Leary (1995) one is left feeling – contrary to evidence they quote elsewhere – that the conflict is simply about the playing out of historical wrongs as if it had been frozen in political stasis since the plantation. They argue that settler colonialism fits the experience of 'historic Ulster' (1995: 334) and that dispossession of the natives left a 'legacy of bitterness' (1995: 334). This is quite true, but it is surely not meant to suggest that this is the key motivator of the current conflict, nor could such a factor account for the significant periods of peace in Northern Ireland between the 1920s and 1960s. Although McGarry and O'Leary also note that the role of Britain is important they say only that it showed 'a lack of will' to solve the conflict. Britain is henceforth referred to as the 'sovereign power' with the colonial dimension mysteriously slipping out of view.

Imperialism

Nor does maintaining a settler–colonial position require one to subscribe to the crude parodies of vulgar Marxism available in the literature or to the crude analyses of vulgar Marxism itself. Much of the debate on the left in social science seems to have been over the question of imperialism. Left writers are criticised by non-Marxists for a crude and conspiratorial conception of the interests of British imperialism (Whyte 1990; McGarry and O'Leary 1995) and by revisionist Marxists for overestimating the homogeneity of the Protestant community and underestimating the progressive potential of the Protestant working class (Morgan 1980; Bew *et al.* 1980; Patterson 1980b). We will return to the substantive issue of Protestantism, unionism and loyalism below. For present purposes we can note that the interests of the British state do not affect the characterisation of the problem as colonial, since whether the colonial power wants to retain a territory or not, the important point for analysis is whether it does or not. To be fair, to designate the Northern Ireland problem as one of imperialism can tend to imply the pursuit of interests. In general Marxist writers from the varying revisionist camps (in common with non-Marxists) tend not to say explicitly why they do not describe the conflict in colonial terms. Some stress internal factors in producing conflict, and others the role of the state in mediating ruling class interests.

The most well known example of the latter, and the most widely cited, is that of Paul Bew and his colleagues (Bew *et al.* 1979, 1980; Bew and Patterson 1985). They attack approaches which emphasise the material interests of the participants in the conflict as economistic and reductionist. Their approach – drawing partly on Althusserian Marxism (and on Poulantzas) – emphasises the relative autonomy of the state from the ruling class since it must be able to broker contradictions in ruling class interest. The chief problems with this type of work at a theoretical level are its functionalism and lack of agency. In the end it is as reductionist as its opponents in seeing state actions as a necessary function of bourgeois (and therefore capitalist) interests (Althusser 1970, 1971). The 'glacial grip' (Eagleton 1996b:3) of Louis Althusser on their theoretical conception of the state is related to their inability fully to comprehend the sectarian nature of class relations in Northern Ireland. For them sectarianism is a superstructural phenomena, relatively autonomous of economic determination. Pre-1972 Northern Ireland was, they say, in many ways an 'ordinary bourgeois' state (1980:155). This is a rather breathtaking misdescription of the actual situation, which sees the colonial marker of difference and domination as somehow an epiphenomenon of deeper structural processes. As Paul Stewart has put it

> Unless one recognises that the process of class rule depended upon ... Catholic subordination, the notions of 'ordinariness' and 'normality' merely serve to reinforce the 'Alice in Wonderland' optic which was the prevailing way of viewing Northern Ireland from Westminster between 1920 and 1968.
> (Stewart 1991: 199)

The advantage of a conceptualisation involving settler colonialism, is that it requires that we analyse colonial/sectarian relations as well as class relations in explaining the conflict.

One of the few academics to address the colonial argument explicitly argues that his own 'preference, when it comes to contextualising the Irish experience, is for a European comparative perspective' (Kennedy 1996: xv). This can certainly be illuminating as can comparison with non-European countries, but Kennedy adopts a severely empiricist argument which fails to capture structural relationships in its haste to castigate Irish nationalism (and to a lesser extent Ulster unionism). He advances the rather patronising thesis that Irish nationalists claim to be 'Most Oppressed People Ever (MOPE)'. This framework, Kennedy argues, 'speaks as much to emotion as to reason' and results in 'a flourishing of the wilder forms of fanaticism, feeding off their mutual atavisms' (1996:222). He proceeds to demolish the arguments of Irish exceptionalists by reference to slaughter and genocide elsewhere; since proportionately more Algerians died in their struggle for independence than died in Ireland, the colonial comparison breaks down. But the argument that the pools of blood in Ireland were historically not so deep as those in Germany, Russia, North America or Algeria seems rather incidental to both normative and conceptual questions.

Kennedy also attacks those who bewail British colonialism in Ireland by noting that Ireland 'was relatively advantaged by its mild climactic conditions' having more rain and fewer 'hot, dry summers' (p. 188) than even some other European countries. It is as if the relationship of conquest and domination between Britain and Ireland are all a fiction of the fevered imagination of the 'atavistic' Irish brought on by insufficiently rigorous application of British torture and killing and by a lack of sunny weather.

Ironically much of Kennedy's energy is devoted to attacking that brand of cultural analysis known as postcolonial studies, which, he reasons, must – when it refers to Ireland – see colonialism as at least a historical experience. Sadly, he is mistaken. Postcolonial studies originate with the study of literature in societies emerging from colonial domination. As with much contemporary cultural theory in its obsession with 'discourse' (see Philo and Miller 1998), a fair proportion of such work has very little grasp of empirical, economic or political realities in postcolonial societies and has very little account of postcolonial misery (Eagleton 1996c). Furthermore, some exponents find it difficult to avoid the temptations of colonial ideology when discussing Ireland. In one study, which includes even the USA, Canada and Australia in the postcolonial, Ireland (together with Scotland and Wales) is excluded, because:

> while it is possible to argue that these societies were the first victims of English expansion, their subsequent complicity in the British imperial enterprise makes it difficult for colonised peoples outside Britain.to accept their identity as postcolonial. (Ashcroft et al. 1989: 33)[3]

As Luke Gibbons notes:

> this extraordinary statement (which does not appear to include Ireland as one of those countries 'outside Britain') only makes sense if one identifies the Irish historically with the settler colony in Ireland ... thus erasing in the process the entire indigenous population. (Gibbons 1996: 174)

Furthermore as one observer has pointed out:

> The term 'post-colonialism' is, in many cases, prematurely celebratory: Ireland may, at a pinch, be 'post-colonial', but for the inhabitants of British occupied Northern Ireland, . . . there may be nothing 'post' about colonialism at all. (McClintock 1994: 294)

We should have to say no more than Liam O'Dowd's neat summary that 'attempts to contain and marginalise the legacy of British colonialism in Ireland end up sustaining it politically and culturally – even if its old economic base has become attenuated' (1990: 31). Yet the literature on Northern Ireland and its parallel discourse in the media and the world of politics, forcefully remind us of the persistent and wilful forgetting which dominates discussion of Northern Ireland to this day.

Understanding unionism

One of the key areas of dispute in conceptualising the Northern Ireland problem as colonial, and indeed one of the most common themes for work on the Northern Ireland problem since the late 1970s, has been about how to think about the unionists of Northern Ireland. The call for academics to 'understand' unionism was issued and since then a great deal of research has been done on the unionist community (See e.g. Aughey 1989; Bew and Patterson 1985; Bew *et al*. 1979, 1980; Bruce 1986, 1992, 1994b; English and Walker 1996; McAuley 1994; Nelson 1984; Porter, 1996; Shirlow and McGovern 1997). There has been a good deal of valuable work in this tradition which has helped refine understandings of aspects of the political economy of unionism, Ulster identities, struggles within unionism and amongst different class factions and religious factions. However, one key problem is that some social scientists have been unable to distinguish between understanding a social phenomenon and identifying with it. Moreover, some academics, usually with backgrounds in unionism have taken on a missionary function for the interests of unionism (O'Dowd, this volume).

Early work by left writers such as that by Bew *et al*. (1979, 1980), was in response to traditional nationalist and anti-imperialist left analyses which, it was argued, portrayed Ulster unionists as dupes of British imperialism or viewed the Protestant working class as manipulated by the Protestant bourgeoisie into an all-class alliance against Irish nationalism. Not only was the allegiance of many Protestants to the British state 'genuine', but there were important elements of class consciousness and class politics in sections of the Protestant industrial proletariat in the North. This argument called into question the role of Irish nationalism in causing and/or prolonging the conflict (see Ruane and Todd, this volume) and suggested that the most important issue was not colonialism, but respectively, ethnic division or class unity. We will examine questions of heterogeneity amongst Protestants now and then consider questions about ethnicity and identity.

Divisions among Protestants

Much of the work in this area has agreed that it is a mistake to see Protestants as a unified bloc, and has encouraged appreciation of the fractures and tensions within the 'whole Protestant community'

(Brown 1985). It is undoubtedly correct to argue that the Protestant 'community' is not a monolith and that there are a number of contending and competing currents within the class alliance which is known as unionism (as is accepted by most commentators, see O'Dowd, this volume).[4] Some theorists see this as pointing to the possibility that progressive forces might emerge from the Protestant working class which – so they argue – would enable some forms of class politics to prosper. Most obviously, this would allow Catholic and Protestant workers to come together as _workers_, rendering the national question at least secondary and at most irrelevant. Such wishful thinking neglects the material fact of sectarian division, which is the result of colonialism. Such theories have long been recognised as misguided by theorists of colonialism. As Fanon put it, thirty years ago:

> In a colonial country, it used to be said, there is a community of interests between the colonized people and the working class of the colonialist country. The history of the wars of liberation waged by colonized peoples is the history of non-verification of this thesis.   (Fanon 1970a: 92)

On the other hand the search for class consciousness (and in parallel the search for feminist commitment) among Protestants has had a rather narrow focus and has tended to ignore those Protestants who have become radicalised in other ways, such as those who reject unionism. As Flann Campbell has argued 'a curious aspect of Irish historiography has been the fact that so little has been published, at least up until recently, about the dissenting aspects of Ulster Protestantism' (Campbell 1991:1). Campbell also notes that the 'failure to draw attention to the democratic, as distinct from the conservative Protestant tradition' (p.1) and another critic argues that the role of Protestants in nationalist politics has been 'overlooked, minimised or misrepresented' (McLoughlin 1984 cited in Campbell 1991: 2).

Nevertheless the dominant tradition amongst Ulster Protestants is the unionist one. And the extent to which there are strong socialist currents present within the Protestant working class is clearly limited (cf. Stewart 1991). Furthermore, as Bew _et al._ and writers such as Bruce recognise, the class-alliance of unionism is at its strongest whenever it is perceived that there are threats to Protestant interests – namely when constitutional reform is suggested. This in itself suggests that the strength of Protestant identity and unionist politics varies with material conditions. Yet, many authors discuss Protestant identities as if they are set in stone

Ethnicity and identity: construction and change

Protestant ethnicity is claimed to be one of the keys to the conflict by writers such as Bruce (1986, 1992, 1994b). Bruce argues that 'much thinking about Northern Ireland is neither here nor there because it fails to appreciate the strength of ethnic identification, the power of ethnic divisions' (1994b: vi). Northern Ireland is an 'ethnic conflict' in which religion is an important element. Nationalists and Marxists, he argues, fail to appreciate that unionists will not magically become 'Irish' if the British withdraw. It is certainly the case that 'Ulster Unionist' identities are not the result of ideological manipulation and nor do they mask the 'true' (class or national) interests of Protestants in Ireland. Indeed it is quite possible to see unionist ideology as an efficient means of pursuing Protestant interests. Although Bruce does acknowledge that identities are not natural or inevitable and are subject to change, the weight of his case pulls in the opposite direction suggesting that they are too difficult to change and that they are the products of 'perceptions' rather than being linked to material and ideal interests. Several other authors have claimed that Protestants object to a united Ireland, because of their irreducible sense of Britishness. McGarry and O'Leary (1995) and Whyte (1990) emphasise the identifiably separate identity of Protestants as if this were some sort of fundamental criteria which rules out serious constitutional reform.[5]

Such arguments assert an essentialist notion of identity, as if identities were not historically contingent and constructed by human beings in the context of social, political and economic processes. The questions of how and why they came to regard themselves as 'British' tend to be neglected. Before partition many 'Ulster Unionists' referred to themselves as Irish. They became more clearly 'Ulster' unionists when it became obvious that some form of home rule was likely, leading to a split with unionists in the South (and to some extent in the West of Ulster). A key part of this process was the Ulster Unionist Convention of 1892 which was organised with the recognition amongst the Protestant business class that there was a distinct northern 'cause' (Gibbon 1975: 130). Although we should remember the extent to which unionists at the time saw themselves as key players in the British imperialist project, nevertheless the Convention was a key moment in the emergence of 'Ulster' identities.

> The star of 'Unionism' which rose with the convention, proved to be the signal for the birth of a new being, the 'Ulsterman'. His birth was greeted with the provision for him, by an array of publicists, of a unique 'character', 'heritage' and destiny. (Gibbon 1975: 136)

After partition the Ulster Unionist Party put much effort into the creation of an 'Ulster' identity as distinct from Irish identity in its propaganda and publicity campaigns (MacDougall 1996). These emphasised (among other things) the number of American presidents with Ulster origins and the hard-working, entrepreneurial character of 'Ulster people'. But also crucially important in the construction of new identities was an emphasis on the connection with Britain. In some unionist circles, the name of the state 'Northern Ireland' left too much to chance since it sounded more Irish than British. Indeed in 1959, the Unionist government's Cabinet Publicity Committee considered a long memo from the Director of Publicity, Eric Montgomery which recommended changing the name of the state to something more British-sounding.

I believe it was a great mistake ever to have included the word Ireland in the title of our new state when it was set up in 1921. It links us forever with the south and with a stage-Irish interpretation of our character of which we feel ashamed ... If only it were practicable, one of the biggest steps we could take towards clearing up permanently this confusion over our separateness from Eire would be to change the title of our state to something that would exclude the word Ireland. This would enable us to propagate our own picture of the Ulster character and of our modern industrial state ... 'Ulster' is such a title and is already widely known and used though, could it but be found, there would be many advantages in using a name that would also imply a connection with Britain. I say this in part because it would emphasise our 'oneness' with the mainland (whereas the word 'Ulster' still implies a province of Ireland). (Montgomery 1959)

'West Britain' might have been a solution, but it was not suggested. Montgomery's proposal was rejected by the Cabinet Publicity Committee. It was thwarted by the twin factors of imperial and capitalist power. The power to change the name lay with Britain and a name change would not be in the commercial interest of the linen and whiskey industries which marketed themselves as Irish. By 1968 as many as 20 per cent of Northern Protestants still thought of themselves as Irish. With the impact of the conflict from 1969 this declined to 8 per cent in 1978 and 3 per cent in 1986 (Whyte 1990: 67-9).

Meanwhile, those Protestants in the South who had been attached to the union moved in the opposite direction, gradually coming to think of themselves as Irish. In his study of the fate of Protestants in an independent Ireland, conducted in the 1970s, Bowen points to

the growing irrelevance – indeed the absence – of the constitutional and ethnic issues of the past in Irish political life ... In this new climate, the British ethnic allegiance of the minority finally seemed to die away. With the exception of a small proportion of upper-class 'West-Britons', all [interviewees in the study] insisted that they regarded themselves as simply Irish Protestants. (Bowen 1983: 70)

Ulster Protestants will not magically be converted to a united Ireland by argument or even by the fact of a 32-county republic or any other serious constitutional change. It is likely that there would be a long-term problem of Protestant accommodation to a united Ireland, until and unless their material interests change, or until 'the conditions that produce conflict and give power its compelling meaning' are dismantled (Ruane and Todd 1996: 324). In some respects a serious constitutional reform would itself change the material interests of some Protestants, but it would not by itself produce accommodation. We need only look at the varying ways in which settler populations in Africa (South Africa, Zimbabwe, Algeria) have fared, the ways in which their politics have evolved and the considerable extent to which they have maintained some economic privileges to appreciate this point. The dispute between the British and Zimbabwe governments over land ownership by Whites in late 1997 is one indication of the long-term nature of such problems. Nevertheless, there is a fairly extensive world-wide experience in how such problems play themselves out, not to mention the closer experience of changes in identity to be found just over the Irish border.

The point is that identities are formed and continually alter in relation to material circumstances and, crucially, interests. This does not make them any less real nor are they liable to wither away until the conditions which sustain them change. Apart from neglecting the dynamic nature of identities and their formation in relation to material and ideal interests, the basis upon which identities are said to be fundamental would need some very explicit grounding. As things stand this smacks of a cultural relativism which would in practice leave cultural (and political and economic) hierarchies intact in the name of identities forged in a mythical past. It is as if the 'identity' of Protestants was formed in a political, economic and indeed cultural void and just happens to be their politically neutral sense of place. This can no more be maintained for White supremacists than Orange parades for 'Flower of Scotland', 'God Save the Queen' or 'The Soldier Song'. There is no reason why the argument should stop with where people currently are.

Bruce argues that there are two possible outcomes (rather than solutions) to the conflict. The first is to 'accept the ethnic fault lines where they lie' and back a side and the second is to try to 'reduce the salience of ethnic identity' (1994b:147). In his view such efforts as there have been from the British government to do the latter have actually hardened loyalist identities. Bruce concludes, that divisions are now 'beyond manipulation'. Therefore, we should back a side. Bruce's preference as 'a relatively disinterested observer' is that on the grounds of their greater number 'doing the will of the majority leads one to the unionist rather than the nationalist position' (1994b:153). Because Protestants see every attempt to ameliorate sectarianism as a gain for Catholics, he argues that 'political changes are seen by loyalists as all loss and no compensation' (1995b: 148-9). Therefore, since, in his view, there is no prospect of getting Protestants to accept justice, the best solution is to back the dominant group, one of the key agents in the gerrymandering of the state in the first place. Supposing the apartheid regime had succeeded in its policy of moving Black South Africans into 'homelands', leaving a White majority in South Africa 'proper'. By the same logic we could find ourselves supporting White South Africans who felt that attempts to reform South Africa meant all loss and no compensation for them or that their 'cultural identity' was being devalued or 'swamped'. As Terry Eagleton writes:

> justice, unlike the society it hopes to create, is a necessarily one-sided affair. It is this which the middle class liberal pluralist finds so hard to stomach ... To foster a tolerantly multiracial society means intransigently opposing fascism ... The narrative of political justice, and the narrative of cultural diversity, are related but distinct, and one must beware of those who recount one but not the other. (Eagleton 1996a: 272)

Unionism, is founded on the material and ideal interests of 'Protestants' in Northern Ireland. The evidence of continuing supremacism in Northern Ireland is there for all to see in the publications of the Fair Employment Commission, in the experience of ordinary Catholics at the hands of the 'security forces' and in everyday sectarian harassment in public and social life. Such experiences are not confined to the working classes, but infect broad sweeps of public life in the private and public sectors (see e.g. Fair Employment Commission 1996). Sectarianism also structures employment patterns in the Northern Ireland Civil Service. A Fair Employment Agency report concluded in 1983 that the numbers and proportions of Catholics at senior level are 'very small' (p.13). Moreover, such surveys tend to concentrate on numbers and recruitment policies, rather than the atmosphere of workplaces. It is clear that the recruitment pattern parallels the sectarian mindset of many NIO officials. This can on occasion be expressed openly in what are thought to be secure conditions. In the early 1980s Liz Drummond was Chief Press Officer at the Northern Ireland Office in London. She later became Director of Information at the Scottish Office and was sacked by the incoming Labour government in 1997. She reports a meeting with a senior member of the Belfast press office, Billy Millar, now retired. Over lunch on her first visit to Belfast the conversation turned to football:

> I told him my father was a professional footballer and he said 'Oh, who did he play for?' and I said 'Scotland and Glasgow Rangers', which of course meant that I was perfectly all right – I was a bluenose. He then took me back to Stormont to look at the press office and as we were approaching it he turned to me and said 'Of course, we've got two of *them* working here'. I said 'Two of what, Billy?', and he said 'Catholics!' and he said it with such venom I was shocked – I was appalled. I had never seen such blind prejudice. I could not believe that this man in a senior position in a responsible civil service job could hold that kind of view. I was a Protestant, I was a patriot, but I was so appalled ... That was a bad start, and I just hated it. There were just so many little incidents of bigotry, prejudice, ignorance, I thought I want out of it.   (interview with the author, February 1998)

She lasted one year in the NIO. Since the Labour landslide on 1 May 1997 three Catholics have been appointed to the rank of Senior Information Officer and some in the civil service see this as symptomatic of an erosion of Protestant power. However, Andy Wood, the sacked English Director of Information, has recently been replaced by a Northern Protestant, Tom Kelly (Barker 1998). In addition, the proportion of Catholics in the Information Service at higher levels remains low. Only one third of Senior Information Officer's is Catholic, there is only one Catholic among the eight Principal Information Officers and there are no Catholics amongst the three most senior (grades 5 and 3) positions. Catholic information officers report that colleagues in the civil service at Stormont still pass derogatory comments and make 'jokey' sectarian comments, which allow them to get a measure of the changing culture of the civil service.[6]

Alternatives to colonialism

A wide variety of contemporary authors explain Northern Ireland as the result of backwardness, extremism, myths, religion, tribal conflicts, irrationality, atavism, emotional attachment to self-serving versions of history, etc. 'Revisionist' historians seem to be particularly prone to such approaches (see Boyce and O'Day 1996; Brady 1994). Such explanations tend to fail to register that the conflict is about the pursuit of interests, and most tend incorrectly to leave the role of the British state as a party to the conflict out of consideration or to see it in terms which accord well with the propaganda of the Northern Ireland Office as holding the ring (see Tomlinson, this volume, on the role of the British state).

The most common approach to the conflict in Ireland is to see it as some sort of internal conflict. Whyte calculates that around 60 per cent of writing on the conflict since 1968 has conceptualised the problem in this way. It is extraordinary that the dominant account of the conflict given by academics could ignore the obviously central roles of the British state and the Irish Republic in the conflict, not to mention the impact of the world system of international relations (Cox 1997).

There are *recent* text books on Ireland which attempt to explain the troubles by reference to the 'backwardness' of Northern Irish politics, culture and economics, as Sabine Wichert has it (1991: 2).[7] Additionally some 'Marxist' analysts view the project of British imperialism as bringing progress to the backward colonies and as helping to 'modernise' Ireland (Bew *et al.* 1979). Conversely, according to economic historian Liam Kennedy, it is the relatively advanced nature of economic development and the relatively high levels of GNP in Ireland as a whole compared to both other European colonies and even some European countries at the turn of the century which makes the colonial parallel inappropriate (Kennedy 1996).

On the other hand the conflict can be explained as a product of the 'myths' of Irish nationalism (Hughes 1994) or by theories of 'ethnic conflict' in which ethnic identities are so deeply ingrained as to be little affected by political initiatives (Bruce 1992, 1994b). The ethnic conflict paradigm appears to go from strength to strength with its characterisation of 'the conflict of two [Irish] nationalism's' (Kennedy-Pipe 1997: 180). Meanwhile John Darby, one of the most experienced analysts of the conflict, opens his most recent book for the Minority Rights Group with the following: 'Any divided community is like a bottle containing two scorpions. If the scorpions cannot be persuaded to mate, or at least co-habit in a civilised manner within the same space, it may be better to recognise the fact, and to look around for another bottle' (1998: 1). According to the blurb, this is supposed to be a 'thought-provoking' statement. It can also be described as misleading in giving no indication that one scorpion is dominant and in suggesting that there are only two scorpions, thus leaving the British role out. More fundamentally, Darby doesn't ask who put the scorpions in the bottle in the first place. It is an indication of the problems of 'dispassionate' analysis that the book's title metaphor condemns the people of Northern Ireland (all except the 'objective' academics presumably) as uncivilised poisonous invertebrates. For Theodore Hoppen, the 'divisions' in Northern Ireland are 'in many crucial respects quite literally religious ones'. Apparently academics should remember that they are not like the tribes on whom they seek to comment and it is therefore 'a mistake (tempting above all for intellectuals with no religion themselves) to seek to explain this away' (1989: 252).

Unfortunately, academics are more likely to succumb to the temptation to condescend to their research subjects and treat them as repositories of the irrational and emotional. Implicitly (and sometimes explicitly) they draw a contrast with themselves and their like who are – their books infer – rational, unemotional and not subject to the myths of history. Yet, their writings are not value-free, but profoundly committed to particular ways of seeing the world, the bulk of which are complicit with the official British (colonial) view. This mode of writing says more about the class position, national identity and ideology of intellectuals and academics, than about the conflict in Ireland. Moreover, given the appalling mess that is the Northern Ireland conflict, a lack of emotion on the part of the analyst suggests a serious lack of humanity.

British academia and Northern Ireland: The silence of the lambs[8]

How has British academia responded to the colonial conflict on their doorstep? It has been suggested that 'it is quite possible that, in proportion to size, Northern Ireland is the most heavily researched area on earth' (Whyte 1990: viii). However, this picture of 'an explosion' of research (1991: viii), obscures the extraordinary neglect of the Northern Ireland conflict by academics outside Ireland. British academics especially have tended to steer clear of Northern Ireland in spite (or perhaps because) of the continual crisis of the last three decades. Although there clearly are a number of individuals who have become specialists on Ireland and there are an increasing number of centres for Irish Studies, there has been a very marked silence within social scientific disciplines on the significance of the war for social theory and its impact on the British political and legal system. Moreover, some accounts show great difficulty in even acknowledging the existence of the conflict in Ireland. Anthony Giddens is the doyen of British sociology. His textbook *Sociology* is a typical example of the genre. In 815 pages there is one index reference to Northern Ireland. This refers to a single paragraph in the midst of a discussion of the sociology of religion which states that religious differences are more marked in Northern Ireland than in Britain (Giddens 1989: 44).[9] The third edition fares slightly better, quantitatively, with three references to Northern Ireland in 625 pages (Giddens 1997) One of the additional references is worthy of note because it is empirically untrue and conceptually naive.[10] The entire reference reads as follows:

> In Northern Ireland, Protestants and Catholics keep alive a set of divided religious loyalties established for centuries, while the most activist members of each denomination engage in open warfare against each other. (1997: 465)

Firstly, the 'war' in Northern Ireland involved more than 'Protestants' and 'Catholics'. As is well known British forces inflicted and had inflicted upon them a large proportion of the casualties (Sutton, 1994). Secondly, the 'open warfare' has not been simply between religious denominations, since more than half of all killings by the IRA have been of 'security force' personnel, and it is them, rather than 'Protestants' which the IRA claimed to be at war with.[11] Leaving the British out implies their role has been theoretically insignificant. Perhaps they simply 'keep the peace' between the two warring factions – as British government propagandists have tried to suggest (Miller 1993b, 1994).

Let us turn now to one of the major criminology textbooks, *The Oxford Handbook of Criminology* (Maguire, Reiner and Morgan 1994), a 'massive textbook consisting of 1240 pages and 25 chapters and over 400,000 words. From all accounts, it has sold extremely well and is now a standard text for criminology courses at both A level and undergraduate level' (Hillyard 1995: 5). The editors note that the focus of the text is not international but specifically on the British system of justice. Yet, there is not a single chapter on Northern Ireland, nor are there any significant accounts of the differences between the criminal justice system in Northern Ireland and Britain or the significant impact of the Northern Ireland conflict on the British system. As Hillyard notes, there are only two references to Northern Ireland in the entire book. The first is a minor note on the difference in the juvenile justice system in Northern Ireland. The second – at a page long – relies almost entirely on a single source (O'Leary and McGarry 1993). The thirteen-page reference list includes only two references to publications on Northern Ireland, one for each of the index entries.

The most serious point emerging from this is that the conflict in Northern Ireland seems not to have made much of an impact on mainstream social science. Given that this is a serious armed conflict within the national territory of the 'UK', this is at best somewhat surprising. One consequence is that many social science accounts of UK politics and governance must be inadequate. A more fundamental result is that British social scientists have been denied insights on the impact of the conflict on the political system. Another is that the writings of predominately Irish social scientists, who have examined the conflict have been undervalued. Conversely, much writing on Northern Ireland has proceeded in ignorance of and isolation from trends on social and cultural theory in Britain and elsewhere, some of which might be productive – though we should beware of transferring models of conflict, sectarianism and ethnicity wholesale as if they were automatically relevant to the contemporary Irish experience (McVeigh 1995c).

The British left and Ireland

The neglect is not confined to social science, but is even replicated by some of the sternest critics of the state on the British left. Contrary to the impression fostered by writers as diverse as Declan Kiberd (1996) and Edna Longley (1994b), the left in Britain has not made major common cause with the Irish struggle. And whatever deficiencies there are or have been on the 'British' left in their analyses of Ireland (and there have been many: See for example the minimal products of the CPGB, and the more extensive output of the various Trotskyist factions such as the SWP (Bambery 1987), RCP (Irish Freedom Movement 1983) and RCG (Reed 1984; see also Evans and Pollock 1983) it has not been the 'labourist left' which has been guilty of being 'greener than green' (Kiberd 1996: 647) They have been as good at ignoring Ireland as the best of them (Bell 1982; Moore 1991).[12] Furthermore a large part of the greenery of the Labour and trade union movement was and is supplied by the Irish Diaspora, especially in London, Liverpool and Glasgow. Examined in comparative terms, the engagement of the British left in the conflict in Northern Ireland has been cursory and reluctant. John Arden – one of the few who tried to raise the profile of the Irish question – put it in a more adequate comparative perspective in 1979:

> For Zimbabwe, Chile, Vietnam and the massacred leviathans of the deep there are lobbies, factions, pressure-groups of political significance and intellectual weight: they draw upon both Oxbridge and Redbrick for their knowledge of public affairs ... and yet – save ... for a few intrepid agitators – all these worthy Britons have steadfastly refused to mobilise to extricate their nation from its incapacitating moral cramp created by the oppression of Ireland.   (1979:57; see also Arden 1977, Arden and D'Arcy 1988)

For example, between November 1970 and October 1994 the journal *New Left Review* did not publish a single article on Ireland (Porter and O'Hearn, 1995).[13] The response of the British left echoes that of the French left towards Algeria in the 1950s. Such similarities, though, seem to be difficult for contemporary academics to perceive and they tend to ignore the literature thrown up by colonial conflicts elsewhere, such as the account of French intellectuals and the left given by Fanon, in his 'French Intellectuals and Democrats and the Algerian Revolution' (1970b: 86-101; see also Fanon 1970a and Memmi 1990).

Colonial hegemony and academic production

In Britain and Ireland, even (or perhaps especially) in academia, the boundaries of the thinkable are tightly drawn around a collection of 'acceptable' views. These are subject to a hierarchy of credibility and seriousness at the top of which is the notion that academics should, in similar vein to the alleged role of the British state, be 'above' the conflict. In practice this means a replication of and/or cross-fertilisation with official views, giving representations of the war in Ireland the 'hallucinatory character' which Fanon (1970a: 127), argued was fostered by some European intellectuals writing on Algeria. Some commentators would prefer tighter strictures on researching the conflict. Brenda Maddox objects to the very idea of studying Ireland in a holistic way under the rubric 'Irish Studies'. For her this is a manifestation of 'aggressive ethnicity' and 'narrow nationalism'. 'There is' she writes 'something unlovely about young people seeking academic degrees in how the world has done them wrong' (1996: 21).[14] Presumably, we should be happy to study only within the systematic distortions on Ireland supplied by colonial history and government propaganda? Naturally enough Maddox also dislikes media studies, a discipline which, whatever its faults (on which see Philo and Miller 1998), can provide space to examine the construction and dissemination of misinformation by governments and their adversaries.

Approaches to studying the conflict

We saw above that British social theory has been largely insulated from the empirical and theoretical questions thrown up by the conflict in Ireland. This finds parallels in the way that the British state has tried to 'contain' the conflict within the borders of Northern Ireland (or more precisely within certain localities within Northern Ireland (Rolston 1991b). British academics seem to have produced more work on the conflict in the 1970s. By the 1980s writing about Northern Ireland was largely dominated by Irish academics, or those working in Irish universities. Of course, there has been a great deal of research on the conflict in Ireland. One observer has referred to 'a factory of books' (Cox 1989). Yet the vast bulk of such work has managed to avoid incorporating the colonial into its analyses and as a result has been severely limited in explanatory power. However, such work is not always pointless. To the extent that it is useful in administrative or propaganda terms to the British state, it has its purpose.

Amongst those who do research the conflict we can identify, in very crude terms, five traditions. The first is counter-insurgency theory – that brand of security analysis which concentrates on 'terrorism' and 'responses' to it by the state. The bulk of this school is openly partisan on behalf of the state (see, Clutterbuck 1981; Evelegh 1978; Hooper 1982; Kitson 1971, 1987; O'Ballance 1981, 1989; Wilkinson 1986, 1996). In practice, though, such writing tends to be aligned with key elements of the military/security apparatus of the state and not always with the state as a whole (see George 1991, Herman and O'Sullivan 1989, Schlesinger 1991: ch. 4). In fact, to the extent that state policy changes – for example, in suing for peace – or there are divisions within the state, the influence of counter-insurgents varies. Counter-insurgency theorists tend to be associated with the military and tend not to work in Northern Ireland.

The second broad category are neutrals, those academics – whether British or Irish, or working in Britain or Northern Ireland – who see themselves as 'above' the conflict as neutral or disinterested commentators, able to provide dispassionate and explanatory commentary if not always to offer solutions. This group is clearly the largest, contains a wide variety of divergent views, and draws on a very wide range of disciplines. This is in contrast to the counter-insurgents who come fairly narrowly from military or strategic studies type disciplines and tend not to be in arts departments or in anthropology, geography or history departments. Their commonality with official views is their similarity of outlook as supposedly disinterested. In practice, as we saw in some of the examples above, such writers see the conflict as variously, tribal, irrational, outdated and see the participants as at best misguided and at worst as evil. Naturally the British state is not thought to be one of the participants but is seen as enlightened if sometimes arrogant and clumsy in its handling of the sectarian tribes. McVeigh notes that universities in Northern ireland are heavily populated by academics from Britain (up to 68 per cent of staff at the University of Ulster in Coleraine are from outside Northern Ireland, mostly British (McVeigh 1995c: 112)). But neutrals can also be found amongst Irish (Protestant and Catholic) staff in the North and populate academic departments across Britain and elsewhere.

The third category we can call unionists. These are mainly but not exclusively from Northern Ireland and are disproportionately Irish Protestants. David Trimble the leader of the Ulster Unionist Party was formerly lecturer in Law at Queen's. Detailed commentary on unionist academic output can be found in the chapters in this volume by Anderson, O'Dowd, and by Munck and Hamilton.

Fourth is research of a broadly Irish nationalist orientation, tending, unsurprisingly to be written mostly by Irish people. According to Whyte traditional unionist and nationalist writings accounted for around 10 per cent each of writing on Northern Ireland in the period between 1968 and the end of the 1980s (Whyte 1990: 202).[15]

We can also identify a fifth approach to the conflict, which might be called the critical approach. This draws variously on critical theory and on empirical social science. It is concerned with public issues and how they might be understood, explained and changed. Such an approach is drawn upon in differing ways and to differing degrees by all of the chapters in this book. However, this kind of approach is not unified and some of the criticisms made in this chapter are of work which might be regarded as critical or would self-identify as such.

The vast bulk of research on Northern Ireland is either supportive of the military actions of the British state or sees it as some form of neutral umpire. Some elements of this orientation speak of more than the self-evident superiority of the British case. Academic writing on Northern Ireland cannot be fully explained without some theory of the production of consent to dominant views (Gramsci 1971, 1985). The British view on Northern Ireland is dominant and might be described as hegemonic. Hegemony refers to the dominance of the state in the circulation of ideas in civil society, by means not simply of coercion but by winning consent. However, in a situation like Northern Ireland, we must immediately qualify any account which rested on hegemony, since it is apparent that key elements of the production of consent in Northern Ireland rest and have rested since its formation on coercion. The restriction of 'normal' democratic freedoms have taken their toll on academics both in dissuading research and analysis and making it difficult to do. Furthermore, a second qualification to the use of hegemony in the Northern Ireland context is that the key reason why coercion has been more important in the Northern Ireland case than in Britain has been because of the counter-hegemonic project of Irish nationalism/republicanism (and arguably that of loyalism). This suggests a role for the concept of ideology in analysis of Irish nationalist and unionist academic production as well as in relation to hegemonic production.

But our explanations cannot stop with the state and ideology, since we also need to account for the concrete form and context in which academic production takes place. We need to examine the role of universities themselves in hegemonic contest. Of prime importance here are the universities in Northern Ireland, where a great deal of the research that has been done on Northern Ireland has taken place. These institutions are indelibly marked by the history and contemporary development of the conflict. This implies overlaying any understanding of intellectuals in democratic states with an analysis of the impact of colonial relationships on academia in the North.

One result of colonialism is to make it harder to conduct critical research in Northern Ireland universities than in Britain, where the conflict is geographically, politically and emotionally further away. However, critical research is a relatively rare commodity in British universities in general, not just in relation to Northern Ireland, although this does seem to be one of the most sensitive points for research. As a result of these factors researching Northern Ireland is constrained, by the 'consensus' which sees the state as neutral. We will examine some of the difficulties of conducting research on Northern Ireland in the following sections. We start by examining state attempts to manage academic production by winning consent and by coercion. Then we will deal with the management, recruitment practice and culture of universities in the North, going on to look at the impact of both state and academic pressures on research practice.

Research and the state

First of all it is difficult and can be dangerous to do research on a conflict situation like that in Northern Ireland. In particular, state agencies tend not to be keen on research which they judge might not depict them in the most favourable light (Taylor 1988: 129–34). The Royal Ulster Constabulary has recently adopted a policy for research access which requires an extremely restrictive contract to be signed by prospective researchers. As Superintendent B. D. Wilson of the Force Research Branch writes 'we welcome requests ... to conduct research which may prove to be of benefit to the force' (Wilson 1997). The RUC has written to research establishments asking them to 'ensure that any requests for research go through Force Research Branch, where a database of applications has been established and where all research projects will have an appointed RUC liaison officer.' The contract provides that a 'full project specification' be submitted and agreed, that the RUC are kept informed of research progress and any changes to the research. Data from any such research can only be disclosed to 'authorised' persons. The ownership and copyright of all data remains with the Chief Constable. Finally all output (whether published or not) must be approved by the RUC. Researchers are required:

> To submit the text of any proposed report, thesis, or other publication in connection with the research to the RUC – giving them the opportunity to comment on, and seek modification of any part of the text derived from official sources. This is to enable the RUC to ensure that nothing published would be likely to cause embarrassment ...   (RUC 1997)

Researchers must also:

> Consult with the chief constable of the RUC, prior to the publication or communication in connection with the research through any channel of publicity, with regard to content, format and timing of any such publication.
>   (RUC 1997)

This policy was put in place after the attempts by PhD researcher Graham Ellison to gain access to the RUC, which were rebuffed:

> With the benefit of hindsight I was perhaps rather naive in framing the content of my proposal in terms of ... the prevalence of 'sectarian attitudes' amongst rank and file officers, given that the sensitive nature of the issue would inevitably set alarm bells ringing within the organisation. Indeed after months of delay and numerous letters from the Force Information Office stating that my request was still 'under consideration' it soon became clear that there was no possibility of me being granted any kind of formal access to the organisation, and certainly no possibility whatsoever of being granted permission to conduct interviews with rank and file officers.
>   (Ellison 1997: 96)

As a result of this dead end Ellison almost gave up the project completely, only reconsidering when he coincidentally met a serving RUC officer at a party who offered to be interviewed. Later he secured an interview with a senior officer who he knew personally. 'By this stage', he writes:

> I had refined my research proposal to an examination of the official dis-
> course of professionalism articulated by the RUC ... I was acutely aware
> that if I was to be successful my proposal should be framed in a 'neutral'
> manner and not make any explicit reference to what the force hierarchy
> would regard as sensitive or controversial issues.   (1997: 98)

By these means he was able to interview a number of senior officers,
but he continued to meet rank and file officers without going through
the hierarchy.

The Northern Ireland Office too has set out a research agenda for
community relations work which rules out conceptualisations which
do not accept the inevitability or desirability of the Northern Ireland
state (Central Community Relations Unit 1991). More restrictively, in
one publicised case the Fair Employment Agency intervened in
research on sectarianism in the civil service. The FEA rewrote the independent consultants' report to suggest that past patterns of inequality
were improving. The consultants' analysis had suggested they were
getting worse and were affecting recent appointments (Miller, 1986).
Later the FEA threatened to sue an academic journal if it published an
article by the consultant (Taylor 1988: 131).

One step away from the central state are the Research Councils. In
30 years of the troubles, the relevant British research council, the ESRC,
has funded one modest initiative on Northern Ireland, the priorities of
which were drawn up with the NIO. Its terms of reference ruled out
the investigation of the war as a research question and it funded no
projects which examined either the impact of conflict or the contemporary experience of discrimination (Wainwright and Miller 1986, 1987;
Miller 1988).

However, the research policies of state institutions are perhaps the
least of the problems of critical researchers. The Official Secrets Act and
especially emergency legislation such as the Prevention of Terrorism
Act (PTA) affects what can be disclosed and is used by state organisations to refuse access to, or seize, perfectly anodyne material. But it is
direct contact with the police, army or special branch which can most
hamper research. Academic researchers are vulnerable to the emergency legislation. Many (including the author) have been stopped,
held and questioned under the PTA (see also Butler 1995). Doing
research on the ground also brings potential danger from the actions of
the security services. Harassment is 'a way of life' for residents of
nationalist areas (McVeigh 1994), and so researchers can be subject to
harassment too.

Sluka records that the house where he was staying was raided
shortly after he left and the occupant asked questions about his where-
abouts. After he left Belfast he was threatened by loyalists (1989: 39,
32). Rona Fields, records being 'gassed along with the people of the
Bogside and Creggan in Derry' (1973:26) as well as being brought in
for IRA 'interrogation'. Perhaps one of the key reasons why so few
researchers venture into empirical research on the security forces or in

nationalist or loyalists areas is that it can be dangerous. Sluka refers to the 'general atmosphere of oppressiveness' in West Belfast, by which he means the constant watchfulness for army patrols or other danger:

> During my stay in Belfast I got away to London for a week. While there I noticed how relaxed life felt. My friends and I laughed when one of them said 'Isn't it great not having any Brits around!' And this in the heart of London. Of course what he meant was that there were no soldiers to watch out for. I found that, like my Irish companions, I too had been keeping my eyes open for Army patrols. (1989: 35)

Added to this general atmosphere Sluka reports a:

> feeling of never being quite safe. There was always that slight fear when encountering a patrol that it might be the one that arrests you. And then there was always the possibility that something might go wrong and you might get a visit from the IRA or INLA. Living in the Lower Falls also meant accepting the possibility of sectarian attacks by Loyalist assassins, of being caught in a bomb blast, or in cross fire during an ambush or gun battle. It means getting used to constant surveillance and being stopped and questioned on the streets by heavily armed soldiers. And it means getting used to having guns pointed at you and having soldiers peering at you through the sights of their rifles. (1989: 35)[16]

However, it can also be the case that once researchers living or operating in nationalist areas become known to the 'security forces' that their treatment can become quite cordial. Both Fields and Sluka note the familiarity of local army patrols with their work and Fields suggests the changing pattern of treatment showed 'there had been some order given that I was to be treated courteously' (Fields 1973: 23).

Fields reports that a dozen rolls of exposed film were confiscated from her students by the army (1973: 23). This points to the need that academics doing research on controversial areas have to take precautions that their research data is not confiscated or allowed to fall into the hands of state personnel. Apart from hampering research and potentially laying researchers open to the extremely wide provisions of emergency legislation which impose a proactive duty to report information to the police, such data can also have a harmful impact on research subjects in terms of surveillance and intelligence-gathering. Some researchers therefore take the precaution of immediately copying data and lodging both the copies and the originals with trusted sources outside Northern Ireland (e.g. Feldman 1991: 11; Ellison 1997).

Researchers who have displeased the RUC have found that displeasure can turn to harassment. Graham Ellison, himself from a Protestant background in Northern Ireland, found that on one occasion an interview with an RUC officer in a Co. Fermanagh pub led to violence and threats

> the respondent took exception to my line of questioning and stormed off, stating that I was 'asking too many personal questions'. I became rather nervous when I saw my respondent chatting to three or four men and pointing over in my direction. At this stage I decided that it was probably better to leave the pub as quickly as possible. To get to the exit I had to walk past my respondent and his friends who were standing along a narrow passageway. As I walked past, one of them turned sharply around and 'elbowed' me in the face. I became even more concerned when I saw my respondent and his friends following me from the pub. As I was making my way to a public phone box at the other end of the street to call for a taxi, a car drew up alongside me and a voice shouted 'fuck off you fenian IRA bastard'.   (1997: 105)

One researcher even found himself on the receiving end of crank phone calls from the Chief Constable of the RUC.[17] More important than harassment, perhaps is the targeting of researchers by the powerful in public attacks. Critical academics can be attacked by state officials and effectively dismissed as propagandists, as in the statement by Les Rogers, chair of the Police Federation of Northern Ireland who has complained of 'parasitic and irrelevant academics' who 'lionise' paramilitaries (*Irish News*, 7 June 1995, cited in Rolston, forthcoming). Even studies of apparently innocuous topics, such as unemployment and investment, can draw responses from government ministers which smear academics as supporters of Sinn Féin. This happened to Bill Rolston at the hands of Northern Ireland Economy Minister Richard Needham, thus potentially putting his life in danger (cited in Rolston, forthcoming). Graham Ellison's study of sectarianism in the RUC also drew responses from the RUC hierarchy. Following the appearance of a short 'and heavily edited' extract from the research in the *Irish News* in October 1996:

> the initial reaction of the RUC was to suggest to a journalist (who subsequently contacted me) that I had not actually conducted the research at all. It was at this point that I faxed the journalist copies of official correspondence I had received from the RUC over ... a number of years (I also faxed copies to the RUC Chief constable and the RUC's Information Office ... I added that unless the innuendo stopped I would be forced to contact the University of Ulster's legal department) ... Nonetheless, while the RUC made no official comment, nor has anything appeared in writing, I have been informed by a number of reliable sources that certain members of the RUC hierarchy have privately attacked the methodology of the study, branding it 'unrepresentative' and 'anecdotal'.   (1997: 103)

We should note here that both paramilitary organisations and nationalist and unionist communities can be suspicious of social researchers as either agents of the state or as carrying out research which might be of use to the state or distort their experiences. This can also lead to refusal of access, non-co-operation and on occasion threats against researchers (see Taylor, 1988b).

Academic hierarchies and interpretative frameworks

Although the state can be a serious limitation on critical research, more serious pressure comes from within disciplines and academic institutions in Britain and Ireland. Universities in the North are clearly the most pressured, since they are closest to the conflict. Although the universities are supposed to be havens of tranquillity, where politics are left at the door, there is a sense in which the conflict is also played out in academic institutions. The very structure and organisation of the universities in the North reflects particular balances of power and privilege. Sectarianism remains a serious issue. The hierarchy and senior appointments at Queen's University remain dominated by Protestants (Taylor 1988b). Although there has been something of a change in the balance in recent years (Fair Employment Commission 1989; Queen's University 1993), the latest figures for Queen's do show a continuing bias in employment towards Protestants, and in some cases, such as in the medicine faculty, there was actually a decline in the proportion of Catholics in relation to Protestants between 1987 and 1992 from 19.9 to 11 per cent (Smyth 1994: 49).

More importantly, however, there are continued cases of alleged discrimination, as the cases taken by the Fair Employment Commission against Queen's and the University of Ulster show. In the year to 31 March 1997 there were at least three separate cases where Catholics settled claims in their favour against Queen's University receiving payouts of between £6,500 and £30,000 (FEC 1997). These settlements were all made by Queen's without accepting liability, which was allegedly condemned by an internal report as 'chequebook diplomacy' – 'paying out damages ... in advance of a hearing to avoid unfavourable publicity' (*Irish News*, 28 July 1997).

Other recent happenings include; the disciplining of a porter at the University of Ulster after a complaint that he was harassing students by whistling the 'Billy Boys', which includes the delightful line 'We're up to our necks in Fenian blood, surrender or you die' (*Irish News*, 5 September 1997) and a booking for a dinner of the Queen's Masonic Lodge (with 165 people) at Queen's University made by a Professor of Chemistry (the booking cancelled after being revealed in the *Irish News* (27 February 1997)). Other sources tell of an application for a course from an ex-republican prisoner being deliberately 'lost' (as well as the documented attempts to disallow applications from ex-prisoners (Smyth 1994)), and a well known senior academic, whose penchant for anti-Catholic and anti-Irish jokes during lectures is legendary. Unsurprisingly his work in the field of geography suggests that discrimination against Catholics is not a significant factor in their secondary status.[18]

Academic staff applying for posts, particularly in some parts of some Northern Ireland universities, can find appointments slipping out of their grasp as less qualified candidates, who happen not to have origins in the nationalist community or to have any record of critical work on Northern Ireland are appointed. In such cases academics who might in other circumstances be discriminated against – such as feminist scholars – can be thought a safer bet providing they are not Irish.[19] Religious and political discrimination also have a marked impact on internal promotion procedures, both at Queen's and the University of Ulster. At the time of writing Queen's alone has 60 cases outstanding against it (McGill 1998).

Most controversially the removal of bilingual signs from the students union following a report by Capita Management Consultants (*Irish News*, 20 August 1997) was met by a three to one student vote in favour of their reintroduction (*Irish News*, 9 December 1997). Queen's University's ruling Senate refused to re-erect the signs for what they tried to suggest were equal opportunity reasons 'the presence of the signs may constitute a chill factor for the majority of Protestant students, and as such run counter to the policy of providing a neutral working environment for its staff, student and visitors' (*Irish News*, 17 December 1997). In the Orwellian world of Northern Ireland public life 'neutral' here means the continued dominance of the sectarianism implicit in British/Protestant universalism.

These anecdotal cases do seem to be part of a larger pattern, if the evidence of the Fair Employment Commission investigations into Queen's and the University of Ulster are anything to go by (see McVeigh 1995c). Queen's has been in the forefront of the fair employment crisis in the North, with three of the five most senior Catholic administrators taking cases against the university (Smyth 1994: 14). The extent to which a similar picture exists at the University of Ulster is unclear, because less academic research has been conducted on it. Any account of the University of Ulster would have to take into account the separate and much shorter history of the institution compared with Queen's. As things stand Protestants proportionately outnumber Catholics among the staff and especially at senior academic level and the university has yet to acknowledge an Irish dimension to the institution. Unlike Queen's, there have never been Irish language signs in the Jordanstown students' union and such matters are routinely ruled off the agenda for discussion.[20] The situation is more complex than can be explained by a simple Protestant conspiracy theory or by assigning blame to 'prejudiced individuals', as some Irish nationalists and the past and present Queen's hierarchy respectively attempt. There are clear examples of bigotry, sectarianism, Orangeism and conspiracy, but Cathal Smyth provides a more sophisticated analysis which emphasises the shared culture and assumptions of the university hierarchy and many academics. As Smyth argues in his perceptive and devastating critique:

> From an equal opportunities perspective those with real power to take decisions within the university are male, Protestant and share a similar, relatively narrow background and outlook, making them not only unrepresentative of wider society but ill-equipped to understand or effectively deal with the fair employment agenda. (1994: 22)

The impact of the dominant culture in the universities and in wider public life in Northern Ireland is such that political and religious discrimination is not always or only the responsibility of Northern Ireland Protestants. There are cases where staff with origins in the nationalist community or of British origin have been party to political discrimination. There are even cases where academics who have in the past written work which might be regarded as critical on Northern Ireland have become involved in such actions. Defending against such cases can also mean threatening colleagues by invoking 'loyalty'.[21] This does show the extent to which what is being discussed here is neither a few isolated examples or a widespread pattern of Orangeism in the universities, but is a more fundamental structure of power which can win the active consent of even non-Protestant staff. In their crisis the Queen's University hierarchy have stuck to denial, blaming prejudiced individuals or the victims of discrimination, leading to a 'defensive reluctance' in dealing with the issue. The university view is summed up by Smyth:

> The discrimination that did take place, mostly indirect, occasionally direct ... has been processed and will be recorded as mere 'procedural irregularity', the FET cases similarly as 'taking advantage of sloppiness in documentation'.
> (1994: 37)

The new Vice Chancellor, George Bain, exemplifies this approach rather than challenging it, when he tries to explain the large number of cases against Queen's in terms of personal prejudice – people he would 'sack ... they should be dealt with extremely harshly' and in terms of taking advantage of the procedures: 'some people take cases because they are disappointed or because they hope to get a settlement' (McGill 1998).

Impacts on research

This kind of atmosphere has knock-on effects on the types of research which are deemed possible or acceptable and on the public role of intellectuals. Taylor (1987) notes three responses for liberal academics – turning inwards, ineffectual involvement and conscious retreat. He also notes that those who have taken public stands on civil liberties issues have experienced 'difficulties gaining acceptance by Protestant elements in [Queen's] University' (1987:32).

Such pressures also impact on the topics which are thought legitimate for both students and academics to study. An early example is the pressure put on Bernadette Devlin as a student to alter the focus of her psychology thesis:

> In 1969 she had wanted to do her psychology thesis on police methods in minority communities and was met with the objection that she could not do such research in Northern Ireland because it would not be 'valid objective research'.
> (Fields 1980: 18)

Although there have been many changes in the universities and in research culture in the last thirty years, such problems still seem to occur. In talking with undergraduate and postgraduate students as well as lecturing staff (working or formerly working in Irish or British universities), I have come across recurrent patterns of such discouragement. All the following are recent (in the last ten years) cases known to me. Some students are pressurised to tackle less contentious PhD topics, in one case studying Irish landscapes was suggested in preference to politics and propaganda. Writing about the North, drawing on their own experiences and making use of colonial conceptualisations can all be frowned upon, even by lecturers whose origins are in the nationalist community. In some British universities (including those in Scotland and Wales) such work can be severely penalised or even failed by unsympathetic lecturers or external examiners. Involvement in work on Northern Ireland can in the view of some senior British academics hamper career development and promotion prospects. One senior academic (in a friendly caution to the author) reports that writing about Northern Ireland had, over the years, brought the sound of 'slamming doors' to his ears. In other cases the development of PhD or research projects can be seriously diverted, to such an extent that the relevant researchers leave academia or change supervisors.

It is important to recognise that it is not simply the lingering of Orangeism in the Northern Ireland university hierarchies that hampers critical research. The contribution of liberal objectivity is a more important factor. Objectivity meant either ignoring the conflict or adopting views which had an elective affinity with state policy. As Rolston puts it:

> In the name of cosmopolitanism and objectivity the university in its staffing practices and academic approach to the social and human sciences retreated from the local. It was all done in the spirit of academic impartiality, but became in effect the rewarding of those whose origins and concerns were as far removed as possible from what was seen as the archaic quagmire of Northern Ireland politics. (Rolston forthcoming)

Indeed McVeigh has argued that academia in the North is still run on colonial lines:

> At its worst ... academia in Ireland is still like a colonial Big House. Serviced by Irish labourers, an intellectual ascendancy theorises the real concerns of the world. Most of the time this means what is going on across the water or in the US or in Europe, or anywhere other than Ireland. (McVeigh 1995c: 116)

This means that the pressing social issues of contemporary Ireland are ignored or under-theorised and that fundamental issues such as the structuring forces of sectarianism and especially of colonialism are played down or simply invisible in teaching practice or research monographs.[22] It can also mean that Irish researchers can disappear altogether from future presentations of their work by their supervisors. Thus, sociologists such as John Brewer can write a critique of the ethnographic method based on an ethnography undertaken by his research assistant. Although, readers of his piece in *Sociology* are told that he didn't carry out the research himself (Brewer 1994), in the text he refers to 'my ethnography' (1994: 237) and reference to the original book appears as authored by 'Brewer' rather than in its original form 'Brewer with Magee' (1991).

The reluctance of many academics to tackle Northern Ireland stems in part from the high proportion of British academics in university departments in the North of Ireland and a corresponding closure around theorising colonial and sectarian relations. Liam O'Dowd recalls of his return to Ireland and Queen's University in the 1970s:

> I was Irish, most of my colleagues at the University were English. While I saw the conflict against a backdrop of historical colonial conflict in Ireland, they knew little of that history and were seldom interested in it. Our students from both communities had suffered a kind of enforced intellectual marginality. The conflict in which their families and communities were embroiled was being represented to them by the media as irrational and incomprehensible, as a struggle between secular humanism and religious fanaticism, between peace and violence, even between good and evil. They had experienced an education system which, if it taught them any history, generally denied them their own. They were ill-prepared to understand what was happening against the background of British and Irish history, and even less able to relate it to the world beyond the British Isles.
>
> (O'Dowd 1990: 36–7)

Since academics tend not to live in the nationalist or loyalist ghettos, they tend not to experience routine harassment in everyday life. Bill Rolston recalls his own experience as a student:

> I lived in a working class area where political violence was an everyday occurrence and felt increasingly passionate about the politics with which I was confronted every day. As a human being, I could not escape from the 'troubles'. On one occasion I remember trying to leave my home as members of the British paratroop regiment searched every house in the street. I remonstrated with one sandy-haired, very angry paratrooper who pointed a rubber bullet gun at me and assured me that he would not hesitate using it if I did not get back in the house. Twenty minutes later the same soldier fired a rubber bullet at a neighbour, Emma Groves, blinding her for life. But as a student I was expected to leave these experiences behind. With the exception of a few lectures on social mobility, there was little reference to the society in which I lived and even less reference to the 'troubles'.
>
> (Rolston forthcoming)

The lack of interest in and experience of the conflict by academics and, therefore, the lack of empirical studies which situate the conflict in relation to other similar conflicts feeds through into a vacuum in teaching practice and fails to enlighten students except in terms already anointed by official sources and the media. Bill Rolston recalls his return to Belfast in 1970 and his decision to go to Queen's to study sociology:

The Social Studies department at Queen's University, offering an Honours sociology degree, was established in 1969. When I joined it as an undergraduate student, it was still in its infancy. In my naiveté I believed that my timing was impeccable. Here was a political conflict begging for serious commentary and research, an emerging base within a discipline which could critically examine the conflict, and me willing and eager to put these two elements together and become immersed in critical social research . . . but as time went on, it became clear to me that those issues which interested me, which I regarded as crying out for research and interpretation, were not in the mainstream of my discipline at least as it was developing in Ireland. None of the lecturers in the Department were local and few had specific knowledge of the North. (Rolston, forthcoming)

Such a state of affairs increases the difficulty of doing empirically based research in the first place. O'Dowd recalls the sensation of scales falling from his eyes when he first read Memmi's *The Colonizer and the Colonized* in the mid-1970s:

Reading Memmi was to induce a shock of recognition. His book was a reminder that the most militant protagonists of the Irish conflict spoke the language of the 'colonizer and the colonized'. This made them appear less an anachronism than a part of the wider history of twentieth century decolonization ... Even if the conflict was not 'purely colonial', Memmi raised the question of why so many of those not directly involved in the struggle were striving to deny it any colonial dimension. (O'Dowd 1990: 38)

In British universities studying Ireland is discouraged especially if such study leads the student to look beyond the narrow horizons of much contemporary social science and see 'inappropriate' parallels with other conflicts. Even university departments with a liberal/radical reputation appear to suffer from this. South African political refugee Mercy Zani-Merriman studied for a masters degree in the Peace Studies Department at Bradford University. In conversation with fellow students she pointed out to 'her new liberal acquaintances – eager for tales of oppression in South Africa – rather awkward similarities between her country and Northern Ireland.' She reports that they said 'It's so different' and she says that 'Even my supervisor discouraged me' (cited in Beckett 1996). While some work on Ireland has been done at Bradford (e.g. von Tangen Page 1996; Jacobson 1997), adverts for the department which make a feature of research on 'regions in conflict' mention 'especially former Yugoslavia, the Middle East, Africa and Latin America', but not Ireland.[23] Discouraging work which locates Ireland and Northern Ireland in their colonial context is quite routine in British and Irish universities as can be seen from examining almost any text book or monograph on Northern Ireland.[24]

Impacts on conceptualisation

The ideological exclusion zone also works to distort the research that is done on the North. In conducting his ethnography of the BBC, Philip Schlesinger refers to his own inability during his early fieldwork to formulate proper research questions on the significance of Northern Ireland. He refers to this process as one of captivation by the organisation which he was researching:

> I became partially socialised, and this explains why at one point it became so difficult to generate problems for investigation ... When the fieldwork first began the BBC had been assailed by the British government for screening *The Question of Ulster*, and a debate was under way concerning the censorship of news from Northern Ireland. I realised that this was of importance, but certainly had no strategy for investigating the BBC's handling of Northern Ireland coverage, other than wishing to talk to people about it ... Quite rapidly it ceased to be a matter for investigation ... I began to steer away from the subject because I had to some extent adopted the Corporation's view of it as taboo.   (Schlesinger 1980: 353-4)

This illustrates the way in which frameworks of understanding and information gathering are closely bound up with one another and also crucially with censorship and information control. Schlesinger did in the end write a separate chapter on Northern Ireland:

> When, finally, I came to write a separate chapter on Northern Ireland in Autumn 1976, I found that the suppression effect had led me to under-utilise material gathered in my earliest field notes.   (Schlesinger 1980: 354)[25]

Apart from the dangers of captivation by any organisation on which detailed research is carried out, the lack of an alternative framework for understanding either the conflict in Northern Ireland or the role of the media in a semi-colonial situation at that time made even *thinking* constructively about Northern Ireland difficult.

This has knock-on effects on the type of methods adopted for conducting research on the troubles. The problem for political scientist Paul Arthur was who to speak to. His worries betray the dominant ideology for researching the troubles:

> Should we lend credence to terrorist organisations by interviewing and publicising spokesmen for their front organisations?

This revealing formulation, accepts the official definition of 'terrorism' and, more importantly, appears to regard the function of research as to lend credence to its subjects. However, Arthur gives no indication that he also worried about lending credence to the British government by interviewing and publicising statements by their officials. More revealing still is Arthur's answer to his own question:

> At an early stage of my research I made a value judgement that I would not talk to anyone from Provisional Sinn Féin but that I would interview a spokesman for the UDA. The decision was based on the well-publicised position of Sinn Féin that it unequivocally supported the armed struggle of the IRA, whereas the UDA appeared to be entering a political phase by probing the potential support for Ulster independence. Time will tell whether the latter was no more than a smoke screen to gain respectability so as to avoid proscription by the authorities. Subsequently I decided to use their material only as 'background'. In either case one is erring on the side of caution and is open to the charge of self-censorship.   (Arthur 1987: 214)

It seems to me that one is open to a great deal more than the charge of self-censorship. Arthur clearly operates a hierarchy of legitimate voices, at the top of which is the British state. Somewhere below are loyalist paramilitaries and at the bottom is Irish republicanism. It is methodologically inadequate to examine a conflict by reference only to one side of the conflict (British state personnel). It is doubly inadequate to confer only with actors the analyst regards as legitimate, since this categorisation already betrays an inability to analyse the conflict dispassionately. Were a researcher to have investigated the conflict in Apartheid South Africa by interviewing only state personnel and (on background terms) members of the Afrikaner resistance (AWB), while leaving out the ANC or PAC, we would want to accuse the researcher of more than self-censorship and judge their findings accordingly. We might also remember that this piece was written and the research practice it describes undertaken some years before broadcasters were banned from transmitting the sound of Sinn Féin interviews (Miller 1995). Thus, some academics were pre-empting state censorship by a number of years.

On the very next page Arthur goes on to contend that the researcher:

> needs to be aware that he is not used as a megaphone to convey others' prejudices. Perhaps the only means to overcome this is to interview as widely as possible.   (1987: 215)

Bizarrely, he appears already to have forgotten his admission that he himself had limited his interviewing for political reasons. Unsurprisingly when we turn to Arthur's published work such as his text book *Government and Politics of Northern Ireland* (1980) we find that it is almost entirely confined within the dominant paradigm, containing references to the importance of the 'ghosts of history' (p.15) and stating that 'any solution will have to be found *within* Northern Ireland' (p.141, his emphasis) a suggestion that openly takes sides and is now not regarded as a sensible proposition by any serious observer.

However, Arthur is to be commended for openly admitting his research practice. Others feel able to write extensively on the activities of the republican movement without so much as speaking to a single member of Sinn Féin or the IRA and then neglect to mention this in their published work, as is the case with counter-insurgency writer Joanne Wright (1990).[26]

Researching Northern Ireland

The most striking feature of the mainstream writing on Northern Ireland is that it tends to ignore inconvenient empirical data and research. In particular, the lack of attention to the repressive apparatus of the state and the literature on it is instructive (e.g. Ackroyd *et al.* 1980; Bloch and Fitzgerald 1983; Faligot 1983; Hillyard 1993; Lindsay 1981; O'Connell 1993; Watson 1978). There is very little research on the role of the British Army in Northern Ireland. Hockey's (1986) ethnography touches on the North, and Arthur's (1987) interviews with soldiers who have done tours of duty there are two examples. Some of such research has itself been limited in its ability to focus effectively on the levels of policy or even on routine sectarianism in the RUC (Brewer with Magee 1991). Admittedly, such research has itself been the poor relation of research on 'terrorism', for some of the reasons outlined above. Furthermore, although some of this literature might have limitations in data or conceptualisation, these of themselves are not reasons for ignoring the topic altogether. Perhaps more strikingly for liberal scholars in other parts of the world, obvious topics such as civil liberties and human rights and sources such as Amnesty International (e.g. 1994) and the Committee on the Administration of Justice (e.g. Dickson 1990, 1993; see also Human Rights Watch 1991, National Council for Civil Liberties 1993) which are – by and large – easily available tend to be ignored or even, in the well-worn pattern adopted by oppressive regimes everywhere, dismissed as partisan.

More widely, there is a very large amount of literature and empirical data on conflicts which are broadly comparable in some respects to Northern Ireland, whether these be communal conflicts or domestic revolutions where colonialism has played a more minor role in recent times (Nicaragua, El Salvador, Chile) or those where colonialism is more important such as South Africa (e.g. Naidoo 1989) or Palestine (Said 1981, 1993; Said and Hitchens 1988). Yet such work is rarely cited in discussions of Northern Ireland. Although the broader literature on colonialism and imperialism has itself neglected Ireland (Clayton, this volume), this could also prove enlightening. Closer to home, there is space for revisiting the work of past Irish theorists and activists. Connolly is one of the most obvious and one of the most disdained, but the political and cultural writings of other key figures in decolonisation also deserve more respect than they currently receive. For my money McSwiney's brief writings on aesthetics, theatre and propaganda remain more sophisticated than much of the current obsession with style which informs postmodernism (e.g. McSwiney 1964).

Some work requires not so much revisitation but new acquaintance. In 1973 Penguin published Rona Fields's *A Society on the Run*. A psychologist, Fields had empirically examined the 'psychic damage brought on by political, military and social violence'. She included material on the impact on the British Army, on internees, on women and on children. She was the first and only mental health researcher to gain access to Long Kesh internment camp and her book is one of the few to have examined such things from the perspective of psychology. It provides an interesting parallel with Fanon's work on the impact of colonialism on mental health (Fanon 1967). Such parallels have not been widely taken up. Fields's chapter on the impact of the war on women was pathbreaking in both attention to the topic and in her conclusions where she compares feminists in the North to 'their peers in the history of the women's movement in Ireland, Britain, USA, China and Vietnam' (1973:164). However, Fields's work is rarely referred to in books on psychology and the North or in books on Northern Ireland in general. A key reason for this is that the book was first censored and then withdrawn and 10,000 copies pulped as a result of what Fields called 'a massive effort on the part of the governments involved to suppress my findings' (Campaign for Free Speech on Ireland 1979: 27). Although it was later published by an academic publisher in Philadelphia, it has remained obscure and is not cited in the major surveys of the literature on the North (McGarry and O'Leary 1995; Whyte 1990).

The ideological exclusion zone which has affected Northern Ireland has meant that British social science has not learnt enough from the conflict in Ireland. Equally, it has meant that discussions of Northern Ireland have not learnt enough from broader developments in social theory. Of course whether recent developments in social theory would necessarily enrich understandings of the troubles, elevate them to the rarefied atmosphere of high theory or founder on the rock of uncomfortable empirical realities, is a somewhat separate question. Clancy *et al.* observe that postmodernism has had relatively little influence on Irish sociology (Clancy *et al.* 1995). It had been more popular in textually based disciplines such as literary criticism and – as Des Bell observes (this volume) – in the service of revisionist relativism (see e.g. Kearney 1997). The few examples of studies on Northern Ireland making use of the cultural and discursive turns in social science illustrate the limitations of some recent developments in social and cultural theory. One study taking up Althusserrian notions of ideology as interpellation (somewhat belatedly it has to be said) illustrates the problems of importing theory and grafting it on the conflict (Finlayson 1996). The high unintelligibility factor of much left-bank theory also sadly affects two pieces of participant observation research (Arextaga 1997; Feldman 1991). Although both authors do show a strong commitment to explaining the conflict and to grounding their work in the empirical, the tendency is for it to become preoccupied with the elaboration of theory rather than the object of study. They can become lost in post-structuralist or Foucauldian mists, unable any more to discern clearly the wood of the conflict for the trees of conceptualisation. Much contemporary social and cultural theory has lost itself in arcane language games and theoreticist speculation (Philo and Miller 1998) and the desirability of applying this to the Northern Ireland conflict (or anywhere else) seems to me less than compelling.

In conclusion

The colonial dimension is a fundamental part of the conflict in Ireland and this has been ignored by the vast majority of academics writing on Northern Ireland, especially those from a British or unionist background or from a certain segment of Northern or Southern society. But the problem is more general than this and is difficult to explain without recourse to some version of the theory of hegemony. The dominant (in the sense of most numerous and in the sense of powerful) explanations of the Northern Ireland conflict are indelibly marked by colonial and neo-colonial ideology. That is the use of evidence and what counts as evidence is filtered by a model which discounts colonial explanations, fundamentally distorting most writing on the subject. This means that inconvenient data or studies are ignored or dismissed as 'half-baked' (Foster 1986:3).

This state of affairs relates both to the winning of consent by the state and to the material and cultural interests of academics. But in the specific case of Northern Ireland it also relates to state coercion and to the continuing existence of sectarianism as a structural factor in Northern Ireland, some of which manifests itself in the universities in the North, in terms of employment practice, sectarian harassment, managerial culture and the ethos of social and human sciences.

The argument here has concentrated on the outcome of academic production and tried to give a sense of some of the varying and complex factors which underlie the rarity of colonial models. At present there is very little research on academic production on and in Northern Ireland. As O'Dowd points out, the argument that there is a divorce of intellectuals from centres of political and economic power is convenient for intellectuals: 'The positing of such a divorce may be self-serving, by enabling intelligentsia's to avoid confronting and analysing the material conditions of their own existence' (1996b: 21). Extensive empirical research would be useful and could open up repressed questions of ideology (Ruane 1992) and hegemony and the extent of their usefulness in a colonial situation more fruitfully.

The material fact of partition has severely impacted on the fact and tone of commentary and has *de facto* deepened divisions between what we now call 'Ulster unionists' (rather than Irish Protestants) and the rest of the Irish. The most important argument of this chapter is that writing on Northern Ireland has been fundamentally distorted by the colonial relationships which are of major importance in the origins and current form of the conflict in Ireland.

Notes

1. In some passages he appears to assume that ideas and theories are the simple motors of academic developments rather than accepting that changes in academic production relate to changes in ideal and material

interests. Thus he argues that traditional nationalist, unionist and Marxist analyses attract the allegiance of only a minority of students of the conflict, as if the popularity of ideas in academia related simply to their intrinsic worth.

2. Discussing Northern Ireland as a colony does not *necessarily* lead to decolonisation as a policy prescription, although, given the history of most settler colonies in the twentieth century (where the natives were not more or less exterminated), it would not be a surprise for it to be raised as a possibility.

3. The later 526-page *Post-colonial Studies Reader* (Ashcroft *et al.* 1995) does include one three-page excerpt on Ireland, which discusses Shakespeare's *Henry V* (from Cairns and Richards 1988). But there is no mention of the literature or literary criticism of Ireland during decolonisation, after British disengagement, or of the North.

4. We should also note that the same holds true, arguably to a greater extent amongst Catholics, although nationalists in the North seem to have been researched much less heavily than unionists (Ruane and Todd, this volume, 1996; see also Phoenix 1994; O'Connor 1993).

5. Some writers on the left have even advanced the argument that unionism constitutes a nascent brand of nationalism. Tom Nairn, for example, argued that the development of an 'Ulster nationalism' was the only way out of sectarianism for unionism (1977). In his more recent work he has returned to the question, asserting that new unionist politicians from the UUP, DUP and PUP sound collectively like the voice of 'a new civic nationalism' compared with Sinn Fein's new version of 'assimilative nationalism' (Nairn 1997:165). Indeed, some commentators have seen hopeful signs in the emergence of the PUP on a stated 'political socialist and unionist' platform (for a discussion see Price 1995). However, the problem with Nairn's analysis is that it pays little attention to the actual policies of the main unionist parties (UUP and DUP), or to their continued sectarian make-up. If it is civic nationalism, it is a civic nationalism which mysteriously excludes non-unionist, or 'disloyal' opinion.

6. Information from Northern Ireland Information Service source, March 1998.

7. Apparently, according to the blurb on the back, 'this book is special: the approach is distinctively that of an historian, rather than a political scientist or a journalist; and the author is uniquely well-placed to write with insight, authority and compassion'. This is because Wichert is 'both an outsider and an insider: herself a German national, she has lived in Northern Ireland for 20 years'. Although this study prides itself that it is more 'objective' and more empathetic (rather than sympathetic) than those of political scientists or journalists Wichert shows little awareness of her inability to understand the conflict and the closest she gets to objectivity is a lack of interest in the conflict. Her much vaunted historical viewpoint involves no real sense of the history of the relationship between Britain and Ireland or of the more general history of imperialism and colonialism. She starts the book arguing that her analysis is better than those of journalists and social scientists because she recognises that the conflict 'included a great deal of "irrational" behaviour and assumptions' (p. 3) and closes it by bemoaning the failure of the Irish to 'subscribe to democratic and constitutional modes of politics' (p.203). This is no Olympian detachment or understanding and empathy. It is patronising, victim-blaming and wrong about Northern Ireland.

8. The subtitle for this section is taken from a paper by Paddy Hillyard (1995). The contents of this section also draw heavily on Hillyard's paper.
9. For the record here is the paragraph:

> In terms of their consequences for day-to-day behaviour, religious differences are much more marked in Northern Ireland than anywhere else in Britain. The clashes between Protestants and Catholics which occur there only involve a minority from either faith, but are often acute and violent. The influence of religion in Northern Ireland is not easy to disentangle from other factors involved in the antagonisms there. The belief in a 'united Ireland', in which Eire and Northern Ireland would become one state, is generally held among Catholics, and rejected by Protestants, in the North. But political considerations and ideas of nationalism play an important role alongside religious beliefs. (p.474)

Hillyard notes that of more than 1000 references in the back of the book, there is not a single one on Northern Ireland (1995: 3). To be fair Giddens does also include a paragraph on 'Irish immigrants in England' (pp.263–4) and has a section on 'Terrorism' (pp.361–8) which, however, relies almost entirely on counter-insurgency writers for references, rather than on sociological work.
10. The paragraph on religion noted above is still there (p.462), the section on 'terrorism' has been removed and is not replaced with anything more sociological. The other reference, in full, is as follows: 'grammar schools are still usual in Northern Ireland' (p.406).
11. Of 1,755 killings by the IRA between 1969 and 1993, 1,006 or 57.3 per cent were members (or former members) of British forces (471 British Army, 227 UDR, 285 RUC and 23 prison warders). Even subtracting all former members of the security forces (59) leaves serving British forces as 54 per cent of IRA killings. The IRA were also responsible for killing 33 civilians working for the security forces, 24 Loyalist military activists and 9 loyalist political activists, together with 133 sectarian killings of Protestant civilians. Collectively these killings constitute 11.3 per cent of their victims. Of 357 killings by British forces 141 (39.5 per cent) were republican military activists, of which 123 were killed by the British Army (as opposed to the UDR or RUC). British forces were responsible for killing 194 civilians in this period (54.3 per cent of their total victims) (see Sutton 1994: 195–205).
12. Moore concludes: 'Within British Labour circles, Ireland clearly is an issue apart' (1991: 79).
13. See also the responses to this piece by Hazelkorn and Patterson (1995) and by Blackburn (1995).
14. Incidentally, she is wrong to identify Irish Studies as simply following a 'narrow nationalist' agenda as a perusal of the academic journals in the area will testify.
15. Although Whyte also identified 17 per cent as Marxist, a category which he judged divided two to one 'revisionist' to 'traditional'. Some of the revisionists would fall into the unionist or neutral camp in the categories here and some of the traditional Marxist analyses would fall into the nationalist camp. However, a proportion of both might be included under the rubric of critical research.
16. Lee also briefly notes the 'stress' of living in and researching the North (1992:138).
17. Information from source at the university concerned, January 1998.
18. Information from former lecturer, Queen's University, February 1998.

19. Information from former and current lecturers, University of Ulster, and candidates allegedly discriminated against, 1994–8.
20. Information from students' representatives, March 1998.
21. Information from well-placed sources at a university in Northern Ireland. Strangely enough, in the recent published work of such people ethnic conflict is preferred to colonialism as an explanation of the 'troubles'.
22. It is also the case that it is extremely difficult to teach adequate courses on colonialism or sectarianism since there can be pressure from a variety of sources, not least from some students. This raises the deeper and more intractable issue, which has been emphasised to me by some academics working in the North. This is the question of how to teach adequately about a conflict in the middle of the conflict. Clearly even raising the issue of studying the conflict can be painful for people with first-hand experiences of the conflict and nerve endings can sometimes be raw. However, rather than tackle such issues head-on, discuss the matter openly and give guidance to staff, the universities in the North have tended to retreat behind the façade of neutrality.
23. See the advert in *Guardian Higher Education* 3 February 1998, pxxxv.
24. Of course, this is also due to the reluctance of academic publishers, in Britain especially, to take on Irish books, partly for 'market' reasons, but also partly because they are seen as potentially controversial and legally tricky (Rolston and Miller 1996).
25. The chapter on Northern Ireland is in his *Putting 'Reality' Together: BBC News* (2nd edn, 1987), London: Methuen (first published by Constable in 1978).
26. Wright claims to have carried out some of her research at the Linenhall Library, itself only a ten-minute taxi ride from the Republican Press Centre which was then in the Falls Road.

CHAPTER 2

Religion, ethnicity and colonialism as explanations of the Northern Ireland conflict

Pamela Clayton

Introduction

Northern Ireland is not only a problem because of the conflict and lack of political progress; it is also a problem about which theoretical questions can be asked and which explanatory framework sought. People have accordingly asked questions, and from a wide range of disciplines, including economics, history, political science, psychology, social psychology, social anthropology and sociology. Each of these, furthermore, incorporates different tendencies and schools of thought. So there is a wide range of explanations on offer (for works reviewing these see Lijphart 1975, Martin 1982 and Whyte 1990). What these largely have in common is that they are very different from popular notions that the conflict is 'religious', 'tribal', mere gang-warfare driven by 'hard men', or in other ways anachronistic, mindless or merely reprehensible.

Given the well-known division between 'Protestants' and 'Catholics' (terms which will be retained here largely because they are widely used both within and beyond Northern Ireland), the idea that the conflict is religious deserves careful consideration. It is, however, very much a minority view among sociologists, and indeed participants, that the religious divide is both the cause of the conflict and the fount from which Protestant fears spring. The other two explanations examined here propose that the divisions are founded on, respectively, settler colonial history and ethnic difference. These are not mutually exclusive.

Northern Ireland as a religious conflict

A term frequently used in the Northern Ireland context is 'sectarianism', used to mean mutual dislike between Protestant and Catholics. That the hostility in the religious sphere, where it exists, is mutual is not in doubt; but the term suffers from the handicap that the inferior social, economic and political state of the members of one sect, Catholics, is not obvious from the term.

Nevertheless it is not surprising that the ethnic division most frequently highlighted both in the academic literature, as well as in the media and 'commonsense' perceptions outside Northern Ireland, is between actors in their roles as Catholics and Protestants. Aughey's (1989:4) observation that Northern Ireland is a society 'permeated with religious imagery and sectarianism' may appear extreme; but the very frequency of the labels 'Protestant' and 'Catholic' used by insiders themselves points to the importance of religion, which is indeed one of the features distinguishing the region from the rest of the United Kingdom. Virtually everybody if pressed identifies him/herself with a religious grouping and identifies other people in the same way (Rose 1971:248; Whyte 1990:20). Much of the academic literature takes religious affiliation as a line of cleavage for the study of disadvantage in Northern Ireland (for example, Aunger 1975, Boyle 1977, Compton 1976, Osborne 1981) or attitudes and value systems (for example, McKernan and Russell 1980; Rose 1971; Stringer and Robinson 1991). Even public housing policy is constrained by the religious divide (Singleton 1982:78–81), and a majority of people in urban areas live in towns that have had high rates of segregation since at least 1911 (Poole 1982:292, 300).

The sociologist best-known for propounding that Northern Ireland's conflict is religious is Steve Bruce, a sociologist of religion. In a debate held at the Queen's University Belfast following the publication of a number of books on Northern Ireland, including his *God Save Ulster!* (1986), he declared, 'The religious division is the cause of the conflict': Catholicism and Protestantism are essentially oppositional in nature and if native and settler had shared the same religion, marriage would have eroded the ethnic boundaries (1987).

There is certainly evidence for this assertion. Church attendance figures are very high by international standards: about 90 per cent of Catholics claim to go to church at least once a week and 50–60 per cent of Protestants at least once a month. Churches also have a wide range of ancillary social functions (Whyte 1990:26–7). The Orange Order, open to Protestants of all denominations but closed to Catholics, and influential in Unionist politics particularly in the period of Unionist government, has often insisted that it is a purely or primarily religious organisation (see, *inter alia*, Orange Institution 1885, 1891 [proceedings of 1 June 1881], 1902, 1916, 1963; 'Veritas' 1813). The best indicator for voting behaviour in respect to nationalist and unionist parties is religious denomination (McAllister 1983:194); and Northern Ireland is remarkable both in the close correlation between religion and voting and in the stability of this pattern over time (Whyte 1990:72). Intermarriage across the Protestant–Catholic divide, discouraged from the first by all the churches, is still extremely low today; Rose (1971:329, 341) found that only 4 per cent married across the religious lines and a number of later studies support this low level (Buckley 1982:64; McFarlane and Graham 1979:194) although the incidence of intermarriage varies from place to place (Whyte 1990:41). This degree of endogamy arises partly from the particularly hostile attitude of the Roman Catholic Church to marriage with non-Catholics and partly from the limited chance to meet people of the 'opposing' religion, due in part to residential segregation where it exists but mainly to educational segregation. Since nearly all schools are either state-supported (with Protestant clergymen on the board of governors) or Catholic, the majority of people (over 95 per cent of Catholics and nearly all Protestants) receive their primary and the bulk of their secondary education at unidenominational schools or schools with a very small percentage of 'the other sort' (Whyte 1990:43).

Yet this picture of religious influence and two-fold division in Northern Ireland needs qualifying. The influence of the churches is unevenly distributed, probably at its lowest among working-class Belfast Protestants; the leaders of the Roman Catholic, Presbyterian, Episcopalian and Methodist Churches meet regularly; the churches are involved in a high proportion of the peace and reconciliation projects; there are around fifty different and in some cases mutually hostile Protestant denominations so Protestants do not form a monolithic group; and the churches can be divided into fundamentalist and liberal, with different attitudes to Roman Catholicism (Whyte 1990:27–30). Furthermore Bell (1986:13) states that religious observance among Protestants is in decline, particularly in the 17–30 age group.

The Orange Order's claim to be purely religious is not accepted by most academic observers (for example, Roberts 1971:278) or borne out by its history (see, for example, Boyle 1962; Gibbon 1972; Patterson 1980a), and is belied in two ways. Firstly its assertion that it stands for civil as well as religious liberties in itself contradicts its claim, even though it is argued that the two are inextricable in Protestantism. More important, however, are its interventions in politics both as an organisation (see, for example, the monthly newspaper the *Orange Standard*) and through individual members' involvement. A survey of Orange literature, including that of the Independent Orange Order, also reveals a political mission behind its protestations of political innocence (see 'An Orangeman' 1799; Crawford 1904; Cupples 1799:8–9; Dewar 1958:7, 22; Long 1972; 1978:2–12; Niven 1899:25; Orange Institution 1813, 1885, 1891; Rogers 1881; Smyth 1972).

It would probably be more apposite, in the light of Horowitz's study (1977:9) of the relationship of culture to ethnic movements, to see the origins of the Orange Order in the need to maintain or restructure boundaries, and since 'boundaries must be underpinned by a suitable mythological apparatus', a cultural movement is a necessary precursor of political action. Its strength is another consideration: only about a third of Protestant men are members; its strength is unevenly distributed, appearing to be greatest in rural border areas (Whyte 1990:31–2); and some Protestants are very hostile towards it (Patterson 1982:26).

As for the influence of religion on voting, although it is true that Protestants are particularly cohesive in their voting behaviour (Whyte

1990:76), and they support in overwhelming numbers parties which favour the link with Britain, doctrinal differences in themselves have little impact on political attitudes (Lijphart 1975:87; McAllister 1982:342). There is one exception, the case of the fundamentalist Protestantism from which Todd (1987:3) sees loyalism deriving its power. The best example of this is the kernel of Paisley's Free Presbyterian Church at the centre of the loyalist DUP. Even here the picture is complicated. A survey of Belfast Protestants by Boal and Livingstone (Whyte 1990:30) published in 1986 indicates that fundamentalists are a minority, albeit a large one, in Northern Ireland and that the UUP draws support from both fundamentalists and liberals whereas the DUP is more likely to be favoured by fundamentalists. On the other hand, much of the DUP's voting strength comes from the urban working class with no formal religious affiliations; and moderate unionists such as Todd's Ulster British tend to dislike this brand of sectarian politics, seeing their unionism as a product of their adherence to the progressive, liberal, tolerant and democratic 'British' ideals (Todd 1987:13).

Wright (1973:233) defines the majority of loyalists as anti-Catholic and especially anti-Irish rather than positively Protestant. Other observers too see the conflict as politico-religious. Rose (1971:300–1, 397–407), finding religion and nationality the most important indicators of political attitudes, puts forward the basic thesis that the reason the conflict is so intractable is because it is about religion and nationality which, unlike material benefits, are non-bargainable. Easthope (1976:450) offers a different perspective in understanding the conflict as a religious war in the sense that 'the "churches" in conflict are Loyalism and Republicanism, each with their own rituals, symbols and traditions'.

Despite the unusually prominent role of religion in Northern Ireland, actual doctrinal differences are hardly ever seen as fundamental to the conflict (Brewer 1992:357). Bruce himself adds to religious conflict 'differences in language, ethnic identity and economic circumstances' as basic divisions which meant that 'the formulation of political interests would deepen and reinforce the religious divisions' (1986:247–8). He also supposes that, although the Northern Ireland conflict is religious as far as the ideology of evangelical Protestants is concerned, secular unionists are driven to vote for parties like the DUP because modern secular Britain can no longer be relied on to maintain the constitutional link (1986:137). A joint publication, *No Surrender!* (Wallis, Bruce and Taylor 1986) makes it quite clear that the authors follow Durkheim in seeing religion as a sign, a symbol of something else. For Durkheim, religion was a symbol of society, and its rituals functioned to maintain social solidarity; in worshipping a totem or a god, people were in a sense worshipping the ideal of society. Society was seen in very positive terms as a defence against the anarchy of individual desires. For Wallis *et al.*, on the other hand, religion is a sign of identity in a situation of inter-group conflict.

Bruce qualified his earlier assertion thus:

for Protestants, the Northern Ireland conflict is a religious conflict ... the only strong ideology which can provide a basis for unionism is evangelical Protestantism. Thus, at least for one side of the battle, the Northern Ireland conflict is, to a far greater extent than most of us with our liberal Christianity or our atheism have been prepared to recognise, a religious conflict. (Bruce 1987)

The use of religion for political purposes does not, however, make it a religious conflict in the sense of a conflict caused by religion or informed by purely religious values. It is open to question whether there has ever been such a conflict. Religion can be seen as intimately linked to power. It is very clear from the history of the early Christian church, for example, that power-struggles among true believers were endemic almost from the start, with fragmentation along the fault-lines of ethnicity, wealth, status, gender and so on. This is only one example. Another is the split in Islam between Sunni and Shia, which in its origins was social, political and factional, anything but doctrinal.

Similarly in the case of Northern Ireland, religion is frequently viewed in academic writings as intrinsically political rather than spiritual. For example, Namier (Wallerstein 1974:207) dismissed religion as 'a sixteenth century word for nationalism'. Lichtheim (1971:34) treats it as a legitimating ideology for imperial expansion, pioneered in Ireland under Cromwell, whose policies led to Catholicism becoming a major element of Irish identity (Smith 1986:245). Cahill (1970:236) sees it partly as a disguise for economic motives in the anti-popery campaigns with which Irish Protestants greeted the 1829 Catholic Emancipation Act and O'Connell's 1834 civil rights programme. Similarly, Anderson (1988:138) holds that, although unionist ideology from 1886 onwards was often expressed in religious terms, the opposition to home rule was essentially secular, and Savage (1960:196) points to the use that the Ulster Loyalist Anti-Repeal Union made of religion, as propaganda to be used whenever speakers in Great Britain considered it effective. Finally, the political significance of the religious divide has been seen as situational; comparison with societies similarly divided in religious terms, such as the Netherlands, Belgium and Switzerland, suggests that religion is not an independent variable, and that causal factors for conflict on the Northern Ireland scale must be sought elsewhere (Brady 1978:97–8; Smith 1981:51; Whyte 1990:72).

History

Undoubtedly politico-religious factors were important in the relationship between England and Ireland. In the twelfth century, the first Norman incursions into Ireland were authorised by the Pope. This was Adrian IV, the only Englishman ever to attain the Holy See – surely not a coincidence. At the time Roman Catholicism was the religion in western Europe, but Irish Catholicism retained certain practices which were sufficiently different from English/Norman Catholic ones to allow them to be castigated as essentially non-Catholic, and even pagan (Canny 1973). It takes only a small degree of difference for a group inferior in power to be stigmatised. The magnification of differences and the focus on these differences to the exclusion of similarities are normal features of derogatory discrimination in many kinds of inter-group relations. So even when the would-be conquerors and their intended victims were of the same religion, religious differences were used to legitimate aggression.

At the time of the more successful conquest of Ireland by the English Elizabeth I in the sixteenth century, England had left the Roman Catholic Church whereas Ireland was still Catholic. This is not to say, however, that England had become 'Protestant' through doctrinal disagreements. From the time of the Plantagenets, England had refused to obey the Papal will where there was a conflict of interest with English national and territorial aspirations. Its great distance from Rome and its strong defensive position as an island guarded by unpredictable weather facilitated these tendencies in English monarchs to disobey the Pope when this best suited their interests. The best-known example is Henry II's defiance, culminating in the assassination of Thomas à Becket. The official split with the Roman Catholic Church, as is well known, came finally with Henry VIII, most notorious for his six marriages, only three (or perhaps four, since the marriage with Anne of Cleves was not consummated) of which were legal under Church law. The subsequent seizure of monastic lands and church properties was undoubtedly more than a happy unsought bonus for the royal treasury: several years before Henry sought his divorce, all monasteries with fewer than seven inmates had been suppressed and their revenues expropriated to provide revenue for him to pursue his foreign policy. Henry remained Catholic in all but one respect: he proclaimed that he, not the Pope, was head of the Church in England; otherwise he tried to live up to the title of 'Defender of the Faith' bestowed on him by Pope Leo X for his former reply to Luther defending all Catholic doctrines. It was only after Henry's death and the accession of Edward VI that the drift to Lutheran Protestantism began. Even so, despite additions such as the Thirty-Nine Articles and Book of Common Prayer under Elizabeth, today's Anglican and Catholic services are almost identical.

The original break with the Catholic Church, then, was inherently political, not doctrinal; it was only under Elizabeth I that English Protestantism and English nationalism merged. Even then, in the face of the Spanish Armada – whose stated purpose was to restore the Catholic faith in England but whose real object was to put a stop to English piracy and trouble-making in the Spanish Netherlands – Protestants and Catholics alike were enrolled for defence of the realm.

What is also relevant to understanding the new incursions into Ireland is that England was moving recognisably towards capitalism. Capitalism and Protestantism, according to Weber (1930), have an elective affinity; but Weber was talking about Calvinism, and this was detested by English rulers until the time of Cromwell. Indeed, the origins of capitalism can be traced much further back, at least to the twelfth century (Macfarlane 1978). So England's move towards capitalist values and practices owed nothing to Calvinism; but the sixteenth-century conquest of Ireland can be seen as driven partially by the flowering of capitalism with its insistence on the private ownership of property (Crotty 1986).

At the same time, English foreign policy increasingly came into conflict with the Catholic nations of Europe, and her back doorstep was Catholic Ireland, which could be expected to put out the welcome mat for enemies of England. So in the European context, this new attempt at controlling Ireland made political sense. Religion was a factor, but it was a political factor. And one way, perhaps, in which Ireland could be more successfully controlled, was through what is called 'plantation' – which means the establishment of colonies of settlers, in the Irish case in Munster, the southernmost part of Ireland, and Ulster.

The more popular accounts of Ulster history and mythology give the impression that all the planted settlers were Scottish Presbyterians, that is, Calvinists, Dissenters – true Protestants in that they challenged many of the doctrines and practices of the Catholic Church (and also the Anglican Church) as well as its temporal authority. This is by no means accurate. The 'undertakers', who were granted lands to which they were to recruit settlers, were members of the Anglican establishment. Under Elizabeth, plantation was an English venture, and the attempt was made to attract English settlers. These, however, could not be recruited in sufficient numbers for such a distant and unknown region, whereas Scots, particularly from Galloway, were much more accustomed to travelling over to Ulster. The two regions, a mere nineteen miles apart at the narrowest, had exchanged populations over thousands of years, long before Christianity, or capitalism, or nation-states. In more recent times, too, Scottish Presbyterians had migrated to Ulster and were living peacefully among the 'native' Irish. Dissenters, however, were frowned upon, particularly by James VI of Scotland and I of England, who continued Elizabeth's Irish policies, and they formed no part of the official Plantation. Furthermore, like Catholics, they became subject to various legal disabilities, less severe than those of Catholics but strong enough to drive many Presbyterians onward from Ulster to America in search of religious liberty and freedom to perform civic duties. So certainly the official purpose was not to populate Ulster with Scottish Presbyterians, and the counties where today Presbyterians are most numerous, Antrim and Down in Northern Ireland, did not form part of the Plantation but were settled autonomously by individuals and families both before, during and after the Plantation. These, contrary to the myth of Ulster as a 'desert' made to bloom by Anglo-Scots husbandry (*Portadown News*, editorial, 10 October 1969), were attracted by Ulster's fertility and the prospect of relative prosperity (Bardon 1992; Robinson 1982).

The six Plantation counties which comprised the official English garrison, Derry, Donegal, Tyrone, Armagh, Fermanagh and Cavan, even today count a predominance of Church of Ireland (that is, Anglican) members among their Protestant populations, for the official settlers were English, and later and more successfully, Scottish episcopalians. According to Lecky (1916), the 1641 rising by the Catholic Irish was aimed at the official settlers and largely spared Presbyterians, notwithstanding the fact that doctrinally Presbyterianism stands opposed to Catholicism far more firmly than Anglicanism. And as every Irish republican knows, the 1798 attempt to oust the British from Ireland was not only supported by some Presbyterians but was also dominated by the Presbyterian United Irishmen. It was only in the nineteenth century that Presbyterians, Anglicans and smaller sects came together to form 'the Protestant people' in response to the growth of Irish nationalism and the threat that the relatively privileged Irish Protestants would become a powerless minority in a semi-independent Ireland. Doctrinal differences among Protestants continued to matter even when politically they were more-or-less unified, and even in the early twentieth century, 'sectarianism' referred to disputes between the Church of Ireland and the Irish Presbyterian Church.

Although a significant feature of the Catholic majority in Ireland is precisely that it is Catholic, and various 'No Popery' campaigns addressed the fears of many Protestants who had a horror of being 'ruled by' the Pope, this needs to be set in context. Irish Catholics were not merely members of a different Christian sect, they were also a colonised people, a conquered people, a people who had been inferiorised from the twelfth century onwards. They had been subject to more disabilities than Irish Dissenters and they had been unrepresented in the short-lived Irish Parliament which was abolished by the 1800 Act of Union. In short, they had experienced different and inferior treatment from Protestants and had been powerless, so they had much to avenge. But their only strength had been numerical and until the successive extensions of the male franchise throughout the nineteenth century, culminating in the 1884 Third Reform Act, this strength was of little use, except to British Army recruiting officers. The superior firepower of the British Army made it more profitable for Irishmen to join it than to fight it, as many had found to their cost over the centuries, and the Irish of all sects, along with the Scots, formed a disproportionate number of fighting men in the imperial armies, putting Irish Catholics in the curious position of being both imperialists and 'imperialised'. The dangers of training Irish Catholics in British Army techniques may, however, partly explain the fall in this proportion as the nineteenth century progressed (Kiernan 1982). In any case, Catholics became an electoral majority in Ireland and an increasingly worrying situation for Protestants became a critical one.

This is not to say that religious differences are of no consequence at all. Of course they are, and some individuals hold the opposing religion in sincere abhorrence. But if there had been no religious differences between the Irish and the English who expropriated their lands and subsequently settlers under English protection, some other cultural marker to distinguish between coloniser and colonised would undoubtedly have been sought and found, such as language, history, lifestyle and so on, just as myths had to be invented to mark out assimilated Jewish Germans from 'real' Germans. The Irish from the sixteenth century onward, however, were kind enough to retain their Catholic faith, thus obviating the necessity for too much strenuous myth-making.

One result of the doctrinal difference is that much of the discourse is formed by biblical language, by ideas about the 'Church of Rome' and its alleged effect on its followers, and so on. For example, there was a reference to 'the SDLP hierarchy', in a newspaper which purports to see the SDLP as a respectable constitutional party but wishes to remind its readers that it is a Catholic Party whose members defer to the more-frequently mentioned 'Roman Catholic hierarchy' (*Belfast Telegraph*, editorial, 24 November 1994). Lying behind this reminder, however, is the widespread feeling that the SDLP has more credibility with the British and Irish governments than do the unionist parties – in other words, the real issues are power and influence, not doctrine.

The colonial background

With a few exceptions, British imperial theorists have paid little attention to Ireland, which is curious considering that it was Britain's oldest and longest-held colony; and the few who do largely ignore the large settler minority in the North and the effects of colonisation on the Catholic Irish. Similarly, in British accounts of settler–metropolis relations the Irish Protestant resistance to home rule is rarely mentioned. Both Marxists and republicans have focused, though for different reasons, on imperialism as the cause of Northern Ireland's ills; but they have tended to minimise the role of settlers, or to believe that once Protestants recover from their 'false consciousness' of having different interests from Catholics, a settlement will be possible. Protestants themselves have ceased to proclaim their pride in their settler origins (Jackson 1989), which is not surprising since the fate of most settlers in the twentieth century has been dispossession. More regrettably, few writers on Northern Ireland have accepted that the settler colonial origins of the six counties still play an important part in the explanation of the current stalemate (for useful expositions of some who do hold this view see Clayton 1996, Lustick 1985, MacDonald 1986, Moore 1972, O'Dowd 1990, Weitzer 1990).

Yet Ireland's history has been colonial since the reign of Elizabeth I of England and the Plantation consisted in the brutal seizure for Protestant settlement of large tracts of land, and the removal of Irish inhabitants. This was justified in terms familiar in similar actions in East and Southern Africa: the 'natives' were pagan, culturally inferior and in need of 'civilising'. Since they continued to outnumber the settlers, Ireland was a mixed colony and there was always a danger of 'native trouble'; but the closeness of Ireland to England facilitated rapid retribution, which enabled the settlers to flourish. The Treaty of Limerick which ended the conflict brought about by the replacement of James II of England by William of Orange asserted Ireland's colonial status and severely restricted Catholics' civil rights (Wallerstein 1980). The 1798 rising led to a change of status. The Protestant parliament was abolished and Ireland was brought under direct metropolitan control through integration into the realm of the United Kingdom. This was soon followed by Catholic emancipation and successive extensions of the franchise, until the 1884 Reform Act resulted in Irish nationalists sitting in the British House of Commons.

All reforms which attempted to give Catholics equality of status and treatment were met with virulent opposition from the Irish aristocracy and the Orange Order, particularly in Ulster (Gailey 1987). This opposition seemed doomed to failure, however, by the time of the 1912 Home Rule Bill, when the Liberal, Labour and Irish Nationalist parties together had a majority in the House of Commons. Only illegal resistance could defeat the measure and this Irish Unionists determined to do by whatever means necessary. Led by Carson, they formed the illegal Ulster Volunteer Force, smuggled in arms and formed a provisional government. They were supported by all the major Protestant Churches and huge numbers of Ulster Protestants signed a Solemn Oath and Covenant against Home Rule for Ireland. The Bill became law in 1914 but the intervention of the 1914–18 war, the Easter Rising of 1916 and British government timidity and ambivalence resulted in six counties of Ulster being excluded from the eventual Free State of Ireland.

Unionists had been debating since at least 1912 how much of the settlement could be 'saved' for Protestants. The border was finally settled so as to leave a remnant where Protestants outnumbered Catholics by two to one, though they held a clear majority in only three counties and Derry was a Catholic city. The British government declined to continue ruling any part of Ireland directly, and separate parliaments were set up in Belfast and Dublin, though legally the Northern Ireland Parliament was subordinate to Westminster (where Northern Ireland voters were also represented). Northern Protestants now effectively had their own settler state; their illegal armed forces were allowed to become a 'special constabulary' and draconian security legislation was enacted, which remained in place when the IRA threat ended in 1922; thousands of Catholics had been expelled from their homes and jobs; and the 1922 Conservative government established the convention that Northern Ireland's domestic affairs could not be discussed at Westminster, although Britain paid for Northern Ireland's 'security' forces and allowed the Stormont government the use of British troops as requested (Farrell 1983).

The Free State, later Republic, of Ireland was economically and militarily weak but it posed a threat in providing an 'ideological homeland' for the North's disaffected Catholics. The granting of residence permits for southerners to do war work in Northern Ireland raised the spectre of Protestants being outnumbered and ultimately voted out of the United Kingdom and the advent of a Labour government in 1945 increased such fears, leading to a campaign for dominion status.

The 1949 Ireland Act allayed these fears for the time being; but another Labour government, in 1969, ended the policy of non-interference when television showed the world the violence committed against the Northern Ireland Civil Rights Association by Protestants and the police, and by 1972 the 'settler state' was no more. Westminster had now taken over decision making in security policy and suspended the Northern parliament. Since then successive British governments have been trying, with varying degrees of commitment but without lasting success, to create an internal settlement through institutions in which Protestants would share power with 'moderate' Catholics, that is, those willing to accept a six-county solution, at least for the time being. All such attempts have foundered on the resistance of Protestants, from non-cooperation to violence, most notably when the British have officially involved the Irish government. Westminster rule has been in place since 1972, a situation which few openly favour and which has not yet permanently ended the violent conflict. It is too early to predict the long-term effects of the 1998 agreement and referendum.

Northern Ireland as a settler society

Those who have argued against the settler thesis (for example, Aughey 1989, 1990; Buchanan 1988; McCartney 1985a; Walker 1990) make a number of points: the Plantation was a long time ago, Ireland ceased to be a colony in 1800, Northern Ireland has a majority of Protestants, it has been an integral part of the United Kingdom at least since 1972 and for all these (and other) reasons there is no reason for Protestants and Catholics to continue to be divided, they should forget the past and look to a peaceful friendly future together. History, then, 'begins' whenever it is convenient for the particular theorist.

If only it were that simple ... The settler mentality has proved extremely durable, for Northern Ireland retains the key elements of a settler society even though the settler state has been replaced by what many Protestants themselves feel is 'colonial rule'. Protestants and Catholics are still seen as distinct groups and their political interests opposed. Non-sectarian political parties attract overall a small minority of votes. Many Protestants still see Catholics as a threat and the majority of Catholics vote for parties aspiring to an all-Ireland state. The security apparatus is still seen by many Protestants as more important than 'talking to the enemy'. There is still an economic gap which disfavours Catholics. There are undoubtedly important elements of a common culture, but this is normal in settler societies.

Each settler colonial situation has its unique features. Not least among these is that 'settlers' and 'natives' in Northern Ireland are indistinguishable in appearance (see McVeigh, this volume). Nevertheless the similarities are more remarkable than the differences. For example, both twentieth-century Northern Protestants and White settlers in Rhodesia have claimed that the 'natives' had no history worthy of the name before the settlement; 'native' protests and insurrections were proof not of genuine grievances but of the need to maintain control over them; the 'natives' had certain immutable characteristics which made them unfit to rule themselves and certainly precluded them from wielding power over settlers.

Other basic features of settler societies, theorised notably by Hartz (1964), Fanon (1965, 1967) and Memmi (1990), have been observed by a wide range of writers. All of these have been documented for the settler societies of Rhodesia, Kenya, South Africa, Algeria and Israel and some telling comparisons have been made between Northern Ireland and each of these countries (see, for example, Crotty 1986; Guelke 1988; Lustick 1985; MacDonald 1986; O'Dowd 1990; Schutz and Scott 1975; Weitzer 1990). These include the 'fixity' of the basic ideology, which arises from the need to defend interests; the fear and hatred of change; and the intransigence of fixed positions. The peculiarity of class relations in Northern Ireland is normal in settler societies, where typically a range of classes emerges among settlers themselves. Instead of class conflict, intra-class solidarity is the norm and this is reinforced by frequent appeals to unity. Socialist parties make little headway in the face of the overriding determination to retain settler power. Those who advocate friendship or equality for the powerless group are labelled 'traitors'. 'Democracy' is proclaimed as a settler value and the settler society is indeed more egalitarian than metropolitan society; but this democracy is partial and attempts to exclude the 'natives'. In the case of Northern Ireland, the very boundaries were chosen to ensure a permanent Protestant majority; minority rights were not guaranteed and there was no possibility of alternation in office.

A less well-known feature of settler societies, with parallels in Northern Ireland, is that settler attitudes towards their territory range from a fanatical and if necessary murderous resolve to retain it to an equally fierce resolve to work towards ending settler power by whatever means, including terrorism, is thought necessary (Fanon 1965). The presence of a minority of both moderates, ready to accommodate the 'natives' and share at least some resources, and dissidents, ready to join the 'natives' in their campaign for an end to settler domination, is well attested and certainly applies to Northern Ireland. To label people 'settlers' is to describe their structural situation, not to stigmatise members of the group.

Ethnicity as an explanation of the Northern Ireland problem

What explanations in terms of both ethnic and settler colonial divisions have in common is that they conceptualise religion as a sign of identity in a situation of inter-group conflict. Weber's definition of ethnic groups as 'those human groups that entertain a subjective belief in their common descent because of similarities of physical type or customs or both or because of memories of colonisation and migration' seems peculiarly apt (Sinnott and Davis 1981:398). It is in the roots of that inter-group conflict that disagreement arises.

In the literature on Northern Ireland 'ethnicity' is a common term used to describe Protestant–Catholic difference. To speak simply of ethnic groups implies nothing about inequalities in power, but this danger is avoided by placing ethnicity within the context of a plural society, where groups attempt to retain their separateness and where one or more groups are subordinate to the most powerful group. One of the most important, albeit flawed, works on Northern Ireland as a plural society is Wright's *Northern Ireland: A Comparative Analysis* (1987). Wright's personal concerns included the ending of the violence and support for the Anglo-Irish Agreement, so he underplays Ireland's colonial history in an attempt to delegitimise violence. Hence he argues that Northern Ireland is an 'ethnic frontier' rather than a settle-ment colony, on the grounds that it is close to the metropolis – even though he describes it in terms which apply equally to settlement colonies, admits that it betrays the ideological features of a settlement colony such as Algeria and cites Fanon on 'native'-settler force rela-tionships in support of his explanation of the violence. In a later paper (1990) he makes the basis of his objection clearer: taking 1921 as his starting-point, he states without satisfactory explanation that 'their numbers are part of the reason why they are less like settlers than were the colons of Algeria', and 'leaving aside all moral questions' he stresses that the large number of unionists means that 'to impose upon the settler-descendants the choice between being Algerian/Irish or emigrating to France/Britain would involve a qualitatively higher level of coercion by the metropolitan government in the Northern Ireland case than in Algeria' (p. 4). The moral issue is also sidelined in his 1987 work, where, admitting that it is not 'necessarily out of place' to apply through 'rationalistic understanding' concepts such as '"colo-nialism", "racism", "fascism", "self-determination of nations"', nevertheless to do so is to 'place a moral barrier between themselves and whatever people they find guilty of the "problem"' and fall prey to 'the romantic illusion that divides the world into guilty and inno-cent parties' (*ibid.* 1987:xii-xiii). In other words, he implies that both reason and ethics should be excluded from social science. This cultural relativism has its strengths, in its empathic approach and attempt to avoid ethnocentrism; but there is always a danger, exemplified by the 'ethnic' explanation, of marginalising the disadvantage suffered by rel-atively powerless groups in favour of an ultimately doomed attempt at 'value-neutrality'.

Racism and 'race'

There is a tendency in the literature on Northern Ireland to consign racial stereotyping of Catholics to pre-partition days. Symptomatic of this is Rex's attempt (1986) to reverse his earlier definition of race rela-tions. This had seemed to include Protestant–Catholic relations in Northern Ireland 'which is a somewhat abnormal usage ... it seemed misleading to suggest that a situation of cultural and religious conflict, albeit with political overtones, like that in Northern Ireland, should be called a race relations situation' (pp. 20, 36). Despite acknowledging the alleged genetic basis of both racist and ethnocentric attitudes (p.21) he first distinguishes between racial and ethnic conflict in such a way that Northern Ireland is excluded (pp.22, 36), then returns to his 1970 definition which includes it, on the grounds that the classification of groups is at least partly subjective and that ethnic conflict is similar to race conflict. He then evades the Northern Ireland issue by limiting his study to colonial societies and those with immigrant minorities in the metropolitan countries (p.37).

There are problems in using either 'ethnicity' or 'race'. Not only does 'racism' seem inappropriate in a White European context, but using the term 'race' implicitly supports the dangerous (as well as unscientific) notion of genetic and therefore immutable differences between groups of people. 'Ethnicity' and 'ethnocentrism' are more appropriate in focusing on culture and the imagined community but they also can be used to conceal the historical origins of the divisions as well as still-existing inequalities.

Which term is used is not, however, the main issue. Mason (1970) is among those who see commonalities in all situations of dominance and inequality, colour merely adding 'a special sharpness'. What is important is that Catholics are seen by an important section of unionists as belonging to a group which is both distinct and inferior, and that the real and potential danger posed by this group has been met with attempts at political exclusion and wide-ranging security legislation.

All the same, despite its problems, the term 'racism' seems more appropriate than 'ethnocentrism'. 'Racism' can exist separately from notions of race; and only the term 'racism' adequately implies the viciousness of the stereotype of the inferior group and the peculiar mixture of contempt, hatred and fear that characterises the feelings of members of the dominant (but insecure) group towards the inferior (but threatening) group. Furthermore, the Catholic Irish as a whole have been described and stigmatised as a 'race'. Given the shift from biological to cultural justifications, Fanon's term 'cultural racism' (1967: 32–3) seems the most appropriate. (See McVeigh, this volume.)

Perhaps the most telling evidence for the continued existence of the settler mentality, however, comes from an examination of statements about Catholics by Protestants in local newspapers over the course of this century (Clayton 1995, 1996). Moderates and dissidents on the whole avoid stereotyping Catholics, focusing instead on what Protestants and respectable Catholics have in common and seeing nationalist violence as an aberration by a small minority.

The more obdurate, however, display many features of settler racism and attitudes towards the 'natives'. Settler racism has the added dimension of fear that the settlers will be dispossessed – a fear that is perfectly rational. Many Protestants see Catholics as the Other, the eternal enemy, always a threat. Not only do Catholics have no right to regain their lands, they have no right to complain. Their 'woes' are imaginary, invented by agitators and swallowed by people who cannot think for themselves. As a group Catholics are considered both inferior and dangerous. They have been accused of being lazy, dirty, devious, treacherous, violent, over-fecund, irrational, emotional, inferior in education and skills, ungrateful, easily manipulated, superstitious, priest-dominated and in thrall to manipulative leaders. By contrast, Protestants portray themselves as hard-working and competent, independent in deed and thought, peaceful and law-abiding, but manly and resolute. All of these stereotypes mirror those found in other settler colonies, and constitute the 'mythical portraits' of the colonised and the coloniser described by Memmi (1990).

Details of the discourse change over time. Overt references to 'race' diminish and after the establishment of the Irish state most of the derogatory remarks refer to the 'southern Irish', until the late 1960s, with the exception of a new stereotype, that of 'dirty' Catholics 'breeding' too many children, which emerged when Protestant birth-rates noticeably fell faster than Catholic. The accusation of 'poverty' as a mark of inferiority began to lapse when Protestant poverty could no longer be overlooked. Although Protestant self-reliance continued to be asserted as a basic character trait, Northern Ireland's dependency on Britain has stifled most claims that the territory is or could be self-sufficient or independent. Nevertheless, implicit in Protestant attitudes is the assumption that Catholics will never change. The continuity of the 'mythical portrait' of Catholics allied with the consistent determination on the part of most Protestants to resist not merely rule by Catholics but even the sharing of any degree of real power with them suggests a form of racism little distinguishable from settler racism.

Conclusion

Northern Ireland is not an example of religious conflict, although doctrinal differences play an important role in defining the main opposing political aspirations. It is perfectly reasonable to analyse it as a plural society, with one dominant and one subordinate ethnic group. It is wholly inadequate to subtract it from its historical and global context. The parallels with settler societies illuminate the picture, although it is not claimed here that Northern Ireland's history as a settler colony explains the whole situation. No explanation which ignores this fact, however, can be complete.

CHAPTER 3

Irish nationalism and the conflict in Northern Ireland

Joseph Ruane and Jennifer Todd

The role of Irish nationalism in the conflict in Northern Ireland is a matter of dispute. The most influential view today is that the conflict is essentially a nationalist one (McGarry and O'Leary 1995: ch. 9; O'Leary 1997), but there are still important arguments that the roots of conflict lie elsewhere – in religious division, cultural opposition, economic competition (Hickey 1984; Fulton 1991; Smith and Chambers 1991). If the conflict is essentially nationalist, further questions arise. Is Irish nationalism the primary source of the conflict (Hewitt 1991; Compton 1991; O'Brien 1994) or is it but one of the two competing nationalisms which generate conflict (McGarry and O'Leary 1995; Kearney 1988; Pringle 1985)? And what generates Irish nationalism? Some view it as a response to British domination (Ryan 1994); for others it is an ideological cover for Catholic supremacism and anti-Protestantism (O'Brien 1994). Allied to these contrasting views are different proposals for resolving the conflict: combating Irish nationalism, finding a balance between the two conflicting nationalisms or transcending both.

In this chapter we question the explanatory primacy often attributed to Irish (and also British) nationalism in the conflict. We do this not in order to deny the role of nationalism in the conflict: it is an important aspect and cause of conflict. But it is a variable whose intensity and importance is itself a product of changing historical conditions. Our intent here is to do justice to the complexity of those conditions and to situate Irish nationalism among the multiple determinants of conflict. To this end, we look at the role of Irish nationalism in four key periods – the late nineteenth and early twentieth centuries, the Stormont years, the crisis years of 1968–72, and from 1972 to the present. In our conclusion we look again at proposals for resolving the conflict and criticise the argument that the solution to the conflict lies in the emergence of post-nationalism.[1]

Irish nationalism and conflict in the late nineteenth and early twentieth centuries

The late nineteenth century saw Ireland divide into two rival political camps – nationalist and unionist – each pursuing a political project diametrically opposed to that of the other. Civil war was avoided only by partition. The development of Irish nationalism played an important role in this conflict. The union had been passed in 1800 with the tacit support of Catholics. The conflict arose when Irish nationalists sought to overturn it. In this respect, Irish nationalism is the proactive force in the conflict and unionism a reaction. But it raises the question: whence Irish nationalism and why did Irish, and especially Ulster, unionism resist it with such determination?

Explanations tend to be of two kinds. The first emphasises religious differences and sees the emergence of nationalism and the conflict between nationalism and unionism as simply a further twist in the continuing struggle between Catholic and Protestant in Ireland: Catholics became overwhelmingly nationalist because independence would give them unchallenged power in Ireland; Protestants opposed it for the same reason (O'Brien 1994). The second stresses the economic and cultural impact of union on Ireland: economic and demographic decline outside of east Ulster and the erosion of Ireland's cultural and linguistic distinctiveness. Nationalism was a reaction to this, just as unionism was strongest in that part of Ireland – east Ulster – whose economic well-being depended on access to British and imperial markets (Pringle 1985).

We see both factors as important and as part of a longer historical process (Ruane and Todd 1996: ch. 2). Ireland has been shaped historically by two sets of forces – its geographical contiguity and peripheral relationship to a larger and more powerful neighbour, Great Britain, and the specific mode of its political integration into the British state in the sixteenth and seventeenth centuries. The integration of Ireland, in contrast to that of Scotland and Wales, left a highly conflictual legacy. Largely for religious reasons, the process of integration provoked a crisis in the relationship of the Catholic Old English and Gaelic Irish elites to the crown. They rebelled, were defeated militarily, dispossessed and their lands allocated to Protestant English and Scottish settlers. This was accompanied, particularly in Ulster, by a colonising process at the lower levels designed to secure the position of the new elites. The result was two distinct communities in Ireland divided by religion, ethnic origin, settler–native status, cultural stereotype and (later) national identity and allegiance.

This conflictual mode of integration attached Ireland to the crown but in a distinctive and ultimately fragile way. It rested on the loyalty of Protestant settlers who had been given control over the country's resources and political institutions, but who remained a vulnerable minority dependent on the support of the British state. The Catholic majority was not actively rebellious, or even disloyal, but it was anti-

Protestant and anti-English. Their hostility was a source of concern to the British government but there was little room for manoeuvre – any attempt to buttress the new political order by addressing Catholic grievances risked alienating Protestants and destabilising the order it attempted to secure.

The relationships laid down during that period might have endured but for the structural transformations unleashed by modernisation from the late eighteenth century onwards. From the mid-eighteenth century the growth in the numbers of Catholics and the strengthening of their middle class increased their capacity to extract concessions from the British government over the heads of Protestants. Democratisation in the nineteenth century gave them political power in proportion to their numbers; by the end of the century they dominated electoral politics. By then land and local government reform had substantially eroded the position of the Protestant elite. Protestants were by no means a spent force, however. A Protestant urban bourgeoisie remained in control of the increasingly important industrial and financial sectors; Protestants were greatly over-represented in the professions, in the government administration and at the higher levels of the army and police (Bowen 1983: 15–16). They also had the sympathy and support of powerful sections of the British establishment.

Despite their advance, Catholics continued to feel aggrieved. They were acutely conscious of their inferior social and cultural status and their subordination to Protestants in important sectors of the economy, administrative system and public culture. They had learned to exploit the electoral power their numbers gave them but they were a minority in a parliament which mistrusted them and which felt a traditional loyalty to the Protestant community. In such circumstances, nationalism had an immediate appeal to Catholics. Its cultural message offered them a positive self-image as the historic Irish nation and a moral justification for the political struggle in which they were engaged; its political message promised real political power (Boyce 1982:212–17). Protestant rejection of nationalism and attachment to the union were the reverse side of the coin – resistance to a version of Irish history and a political programme which favoured Catholics at their expense.

Nationalism also had other roots – in the unequal relationship between Ireland and Britain and, more specifically, the effect of the union on Ireland. Geography alone – the unequal size of the two islands and the proximity of the South of England to the European mainland – dictated that the relationship would be unequal in some degree. But the way in which Ireland had been integrated into the British state ensured that inequality would be deep and pervasive: it made Ireland subordinate to the metropolitan parliament and ensured the subservience of its ruling minority to metropolitan interests. Whatever its intent, the Act of Union of 1800 deepened that inequality and gave it new institutional and cultural form. It concentrated political power in London and exposed the Irish economy to the full force of British competitive pressures. The Irish economy developed in a strikingly uneven way. The north-east industrialised; elsewhere there was de-industrialisation and de-population and devastating famine at mid-century. In the post-famine period there was a steady erosion of Irish cultural distinctiveness, including the language, making Ireland appear to many to be more and more a cheap and second-rate version of England.

Attitudes to these developments divided sharply, in part along geographical but primarily along religious lines. The Protestants of the north-east had benefited economically from access to British capital, skills and markets and saw no reason why the rest of the country could not do the same. Catholics saw the industrial success of the north-east as an aberration and of minor importance – the rest of the country was suffering and the economy as a whole had been damaged. Cultural factors were equally important. Catholic attitudes to English culture had long been marked by ambivalence. English cultural influence was now intensifying at a time when England was becoming an industrial, urban and secular society, imperial in style and sentiment, with a popular mass culture. Irish Catholics reacted with alarm. In contrast, Protestants had traditional cultural ties to Britain and Ulster Protestants in particular could identify positively with cultural patterns that were also emerging in the urban–industrial setting of the north-east.

At this point the British-mediated communal conflict and the conflicting interests in the union began to fuse in a process of ideological escalation. Catholics embraced a nationalist understanding of themselves as the ancient and oppressed (Gaelic) Irish nation whose economic and cultural decline was not simply an individual or local tragedy, but a national calamity. Protestants responded by identifying more closely with Britain and the empire and conceiving their role in Ireland as a civilising and modernising one. The more Catholics identified with the Gaelic tradition and pledged their loyalty to Ireland alone, the more Protestants identified with Britishness and Britain; the more Catholics sought national salvation in independence, the more Protestants sought it within the union; the more unionist Protestants became, the more Catholics saw them as the agents of British rule and the enemies of Ireland; the more nationalist Catholics became, the more Protestants feared for their future on the island.

There is a sense in which nationalism was the proactive force in this process of escalation and unionism a reaction. But to say this is to say very little. Nineteenth-century nationalism and unionism emerged as part of a conflict that was already two centuries old. They aggravated that conflict but were not its primary cause.

Nationalism and conflict from partition to the 1960s

Partition did not bring the conflicts of the pre-partition period to an end. They persisted in the mutual antagonism of the Catholic and Protestant communities in Northern Ireland, in the hostile relationship between the government of Northern Ireland and the Irish Free State/Republic of Ireland, in the antagonistic relationship between the Irish and British governments. What was the role of Irish nationalism in these conflicts?

It certainly played a role. Nationalists on both sides of the border refused to accept the legitimacy of partition or the state of Northern Ireland and all nationalist parties aspired to Irish reunification. For a brief period before the start of the civil war in the South, Michael Collins aided the IRA in its attacks on the Northern state. When in power DeValera frequently raised the matter of partition with the British government and his constitution of 1937 affirmed the Irish national territory to be the island of Ireland. Irish neutrality during World War ll was justified by reference to partition and the post-war period saw the Inter-Party government of 1948–51 launch an international anti-partition campaign. The IRA remained in existence throughout this period, carrying out a short-lived bombing campaign in England in 1939–40 and from 1957 to 1962 an armed attack on the Northern state.

Nationalist claims, attitudes and policies had the effect in turn of aggravating unionist fears, strengthening loyalism and providing justification for the policies the Stormont government adopted against the Catholic minority (Kennedy 1988). They also provided unionists with a defence to counter intervention by the British government in support of the minority. The illtreatment of the minority engendered in turn further Catholic grievances which attached them all the more firmly to nationalism. Nationalism was, therefore, an important factor in the conflict of this period. But how important?

One issue concerns the measures which the Unionist government put in place against the Catholic minority and the extent to which these were due to its nationalism. The nationalist threat was real but there were many ways they could have dealt with it. Of these the least useful were the policies that were followed – marginalisation and exclusion – since they simply increased the threat. Some effort might have been made to win the allegiance, or at least the toleration, of the minority for the Northern state. The failure even to attempt this (Whyte 1983), the evident satisfaction which many unionists took in disadvantaging Catholics and the scant respect they paid to their sensibilities, suggest that the motivation went much deeper than simply countering nationalism.

Similar considerations apply to unionist attitudes to the South. The extent of the actual, as opposed to the rhetorical, threat from the South during those years does not explain the depth of unionist hostility to that state, the contempt with which unionists viewed its efforts at state- and nation-building, or the satisfaction with which they received evidence of Catholic Church dominance in such episodes as the Mother-and-Child controversy. Again, something deeper seems to have been at work. Different considerations apply in explaining British policies but with the same conclusion. Nationalist irredentism may have played some role in discouraging the British government from curbing unionist excesses, but British policy was determined by other considerations – not least indifference to what happened in either part of Ireland once its security interests had been taken care of.

To explain the conflicts of this period one needs, therefore, to go beyond Irish nationalism and unionist reactions to it. One needs indeed to go to the same sets of relationships which produced the conflicts of the preceding period – the British-mediated communal conflict and the unequal relationship between Britain and Ireland. So much has been written on the changes effected by partition that it is necessary to point to the continuities.

Partition had deep and lasting consequences for the political economy of the island. But it had relatively little effect on its communal structuring or the British role in this (Ruane and Todd 1996: 290–2). Catholics and Protestants continued to oppose each other and constructed their differences in much the same way as before – by reference to religion, ethnicity, settler–native status, cultural stereotypes of modernity and backwardness and national identity and allegiance. The most significant shift was the fracturing of the island-wide Protestant community as Southern Protestants came to accept a uniquely Irish national identity and allegiance. The island-wide Catholic community was weakened and Northern and Southern Catholics developed as distinct communities. But though tensions emerged, each remained committed to the idea of an island-wide (predominantly Catholic) Irish nation.

Similarly, while partition brought the historic alliance between Irish Protestants and the British state to an end, the alliance was renewed with Northern Irish Protestants. Indeed partition gave Northern Protestants a firmer base in state power and more assured British support than Protestants throughout the island had enjoyed since the eighteenth century. It also reversed in Northern Ireland the improvement in status which all Catholics had experienced in the decades before partition. Northern Catholics bore the burden of this, but their grievances were felt by Catholics throughout the island. Moreover despite their demographic strength and the support of the British state, Northern Protestants continued to feel vulnerable and, like their forebears, placed their trust in British support and maintaining a firm grip on the levers of power.

There was also substantial continuity in British–Irish relationships. The settlement of 1921 went some way to reducing British dominance over Ireland. The Irish Free State was granted self-government and over time secured total independence. But the new state remained within the British orbit and both the economy and culture were profoundly marked by the legacy of British rule. The British refusal to accord total independence to the 26 counties from the outset had led to a destructive civil war which almost bankrupted the new state, sapped national morale and sowed divisions which lasted for two generations. Northern Ireland was granted a devolved government, but Britain was the ultimate source of authority and a powerful influence at all levels. But as in the past, once British security concerns were met, Ireland was low in British priorities.

The conflicts of the post-partition period were articulated to an important extent in nationalist and unionist terms. But the terms in which a conflict is expressed should not be confused with its causes. Catholic anger focused on partition, but as a point of condensation of multiple grievances against both Protestants and the British government and as the point of departure for addressing these. The unionist response was articulated around the need to defend the union, but the union as the safeguard against the multiple threats directed against their community. In other words, for both communities the forces pushing them towards conflict had deeper historical and motivational roots and more complex determinations than is implied by the nationalist terms in which they were expressed.

Finally, it is worth pointing out some of the changes at the end of this period which led – temporarily – to a less intense nationalism. From the late 1960s onwards the Republic of Ireland was beginning to strike a more independent path. The two governments had resolved many of their differences and the expression of anti-British sentiment became less frequent. In the North, the creation of a welfare state and improvements in infrastructure, educational opportunities and social services softened the blow of partition for many Northern Catholics and presented the British state in a new light. The advent of Terence O'Neill led to accommodating gestures towards Catholics and to an exchange of visits between the two prime ministers in 1965. The Nationalist Party responded by accepting the role of official opposition in Stormont. The nationalist commitment to unity remained but as an aspiration to be pursued peacefully and pragmatically.

Nationalism and the crisis of 1968–72

The easing of relationships during the first part of the 1960s proved short-lived. By August 1969 the Northern state was in crisis, precipitated by the civil rights movement. The first serious public disturbances took place at the civil rights march in Derry in October 1968. As disturbances continued the British government pressured the Stormont government to introduce reforms. The prospect of reform divided the Unionist Party and the prime minister, Terence O'Neill, was forced out. Loyalists intensified their criticisms of government policies and Protestant paramilitaries regrouped. Each civil rights demonstration met a loyalist response and rioting became a feature of the sectarian interfaces in Belfast. The crisis came to a head in August 1969, beginning in Derry and spreading to Belfast and to other parts of the North. As the situation deteriorated the Stormont government appealed to London for British troops to restore order. The British government sent the troops but also intensified its pressure on the Stormont government to reform.

By this time, however, the political system had been destabilised. Sectarian rioting and clashes between rioters and police became endemic. The IRA split and the Provisionals emerged as defenders of

Catholic areas against loyalist attack; in autumn 1970 they went on the offensive bombing public targets and attacking the security forces. Local loyalist defence associations were formed to protect Protestant areas. The reform process got underway but the situation continued to worsen. Internment was introduced in August 1971, directed solely at Catholics, and further polarised political opinion. The shooting dead of 13 unarmed Catholics at an anti-internment march in Derry in January 1972 was followed three days later by the burning of the British Embassy in Dublin. By the end of March the British government had abandoned hope of reforming the Stormont government and instituted direct rule from London.

What role did nationalism play in this process of destabilisation? Some have seen it as the primary cause for which the civil rights movement was simply a cover (Hewitt 1991). But its role was more complex than this allows. It operated at a number of levels. First, as we saw above, nationalism helped reproduce the conditions of conflict. It exacerbated the communal division, intensified the Catholic sense of grievance and underpinned ideologically its refusal to accord legitimacy to the state. It convinced Northern Protestants that their state was in danger from within and without and encouraged them to put in place the discriminatory measures that would later discredit them. It made them fearful of attack and prone to overreact to any threat to their rule. It provided the cement to bind Northern and Southern Catholics together in a single overarching community despite partition and sustained the claims of the Republic to jurisdiction over Northern Ireland.

Nationalism also played a role in the civil rights movement. The movement was no nationalist front but there was a considerable nationalist presence within it (see Purdie 1990: 150ff.). Alongside ecumenically minded Protestants animated by a sense of social justice, Catholics content within the United Kingdom and socialists pursuing a radical social agenda, were nationalists who accepted the present constitutional framework only because they saw no alternative and republicans happy to have an opportunity to challenge a state they detested. This nationalist presence within the movement was important in securing the support of the wider Catholic community and of Southern nationalists.

Finally, nationalism played a critical role in turning the conflicts of 1968–9 into a crisis of the state itself. The modernising constitutional nationalism of the newly formed Social Democratic and Labour Party (SDLP) contributed to the defeat of Stormont by refusing to accept the limited reforms on offer. The traditional, militant nationalism of Provisional republicanism did so by creating an insoluble security problem.

To understand the precise role of nationalism in this regard, however, it is necessary to look at the structural roots of the crisis of 1968–72. The settlement of 1921 was not founded on political consensus; it was determined by the balance of power that then obtained between Catholic nationalists, Protestant unionists and the British state. On both sides of the border the settlement was imposed by force and it left a legacy of bitterness and contested legitimacy. The Southern state gradually acquired legitimacy. The Northern state did not, and because it rested on power it was vulnerable to any shift in the balance of power.

In the decades that followed such a shift took place in the Catholic favour (Ruane and Todd 1996: 125–7, 139–46). Northern Catholics emerged as a political community in their own right with an enhanced political capacity; independent Ireland developed from the divided, impoverished entity it was in 1922 into an independent sovereign state with an expanding economy. Over the same period Northern Protestants suffered the erosion of their traditional industrial base and became increasingly dependent on the British exchequer. The United Kingdom too was in decline – no longer the world power of the beginning of the century, its empire gone, its position in Europe unsure, its economy crisis-prone.

By the 1960s the change in the balance of power was considerable, although its extent was not yet apparent. The civil rights movement set in motion the series of events that would reveal it. The events of August 1969 tested the state's coercive apparatus and found it wanting. Once the British government was forced to intervene, the state as a whole came into question. But it did not fall easily. For three years the British and Stormont governments made a determined effort to buttress it by a combination of reform and harsh security measures. The failure of that attempt was a measure of the erosion of the British and unionist position and the new strength – political and military – of the Catholic community. That strength was political in the broadest sense – a combination of leadership, organisation, determination, refusal to compromise and willingness to risk (and to inflict) injury and death. Here nationalism was important in that it provided ideological support for this political struggle. As we have seen, its two forms – constitutional and militant republicanism – were politically critical in moving from the civic unrest of 1968 to the fall of Stormont in 1972.

In short, the role of nationalism at this time has to be seen in context. Nationalism helped initiate the crisis and then gave it direction, but it was not its ultimate source. The roots of the crisis of 1968–72 and the destabilisation of the Northern state lie ultimately at the structural level and in the realm of power rather than ideology. The shift in the power balance between Northern Protestants, Northern and Southern Catholics and the British state in the decades after partition made some form of crisis inevitable. An earlier stage in that balance of power produced the partition settlement of 1921; a subsequent shift produced the crisis of 1968–72.

Nationalism and conflict since 1972

The abolition of Stormont brought to an end the Unionist monopoly of political power in Northern Ireland. But it did not bring peace or a new political settlement. In the resulting power vacuum, violence became endemic, claiming more than 3000 lives in the decades that followed.

All the old lines of fracture opened up to become zones of conflict – between Protestants and Catholics in Northern Ireland, between Northern Protestants and the South, between Northern Catholics and the British government, between Northern Protestants and the British government, between the British and Irish governments. Other minor lines of fracture also opened up – between Northern Catholics and the South, between constitutional nationalists and republicans on the island as a whole, between loyalists and unionists.

Efforts to end the violence by more effective security measures and by new constitutional and institutional structures had limited success. The current attempt, the 'peace process', is the most promising to date. So far it has delivered conditional IRA and loyalist cease fires, a mechanism for the 'decommissioning' of arms in the event of a settlement and the beginning of multi-stranded political talks. But there are major differences in the aspirations of two sides and the Democratic Unionist Party, with a third of the Protestant vote, is boycotting the talks. Agreement is far from certain. Even if it is reached, it is unclear how long a settlement will last.

How much has Irish nationalism contributed to this continuing conflict and to the failure of successive political initiatives? For some commentators it is its primary cause. They point out that Protestants are the majority community in Northern Ireland and wish to remain within the union; the conflict continues because nationalists, particularly republicans, refuse to accept this (O'Brien 1994; Compton 1991). The SDLP insists on strong cross-border links and a role for the Irish government in Northern Ireland's affairs. Republicans have waged a violent campaign for Irish unity until very recently and still refuse to decommission their weapons. For others, the conflict is produced, not by Irish nationalism alone, but by the combination of Irish and British nationalism – the co-existence of two communities each with its own national symbols, allegiances and aspirations, one committed to Britishness and the union, the other to Irishness and Irish unity (McGarry and O'Leary 1995).

There is no doubt that nationalism contributes to conflict. The primary political goal of Sinn Féin as a political party, and of the IRA as a military organisation, is the achievement of Irish unity. Both organisations justify their actions in terms of the 'right' of the Irish people to 'self-determination' (Adams 1986) and their supporters are strongly committed to Irish unity. The SDLP is more nuanced in its language; it articulates its demands much more in the language of the two traditions on the island, the need to establish equality between them and to reach agreement about how the island is to be governed. There is little reference to Irish unity in the territorial sense, and its supporters are also more lukewarm about it (see Sinn Féin/SDLP 1988) On the other hand, most would like to see a united Ireland at some time in the future; in the meantime they insist on a tangible expression of the Irish identity of the nationalist community in the North. This means 'parity of esteem' within Northern Ireland and a role for the government of the Republic in Northern Ireland's affairs. For unionists and loyalists both sets of demands are anathema and they articulate their opposition in the language of British nationalism – the British identity of the Protestant people of Northern Ireland and the sovereign rights of the British government over Northern Ireland.

At this point the evidence appears overwhelmingly to support the view that the conflict is a nationalist one. However, as in the past, it is important not to take the terms in which the conflict is expressed for its causes. There is, for example, evidence that national identity and aspirations are less important to either community than the nationalist interpretation implies. Empirical research raises some doubts. Surveys have shown that Catholics are as concerned about economic matters as about constitutional matters (Smith and Chambers 1991: ch. 3). They also confirm that Catholic aspirations to Irish unity are uneven, strong among a minority, otherwise lukewarm (Ruane and Todd 1996: ch. 3). Other evidence suggests that the appeal of Irish unity is based as much on the belief that Northern Ireland is irreformable as on nationalist principle (Breen 1996: 44–5; O'Connor 1993: 74ff). Indeed it is striking that in recent polls only half of Catholics are willing to describe themselves as 'nationalist' (Curtice and Gallagher 1990: 193; Breen 1996:37–8).

Similar doubts arise on the Protestant side. There is no doubt about the commitment to the union: over 90 per cent of Protestants wish to preserve it. But they do not all wish to do so as an expression of a British national identity and allegiance. In fact Protestant identities vary considerably, as do their motives for wanting the union. If some have a British national identity and loyalty to the crown, others have a more cerebral allegiance to British liberal values and constitutional procedures, while still others have a more external and strategic sense of dependence on the British link – as defence of the Protestant interest, as a guard against Catholic and nationalist dominance, as a means to sustain present living standards (Ruane and Todd 1996: 54–60). Motives are of course mixed, but to see them all as evidence of British nationalism is dubious.

These data suggest that nationalism is not sufficiently strong in Northern Ireland to explain the depth of conflict there. The communities are polarised on political and constitutional issues, but this polarisation is not simply a function of national identity. In fact, there is considerable ambiguity within each community and overlap between them on issues of identity. The causes of political polarisation are multi-dimensional. The overlapping yet distinct dimensions of cultural difference – religion, ethnicity, settler–native status, stereotypical notions of modernity and backwardness, national identity and allegiance – are compounded by structures of power and inequality. Within each community, views on political and constitutional issues tend to converge, and to conflict with those of the other community. The causes of this political polarisation include, but are not reducible to, nationalist or even ethno-national opposition.

The nationalist interpretation unduly prioritises the national (or ethno-national) dimensions in its explanation of conflict. This leads to inaccuracies in interpretation. First, the nationalist interpretation does not do justice to the complexity of individual motivation or individuals' mode of relation to their community (Ruane and Todd, 1996, ch. 3). It is precisely the overlapping yet distinct dimensions of cultural difference that form the substance of communal division and permit a radical diversity of motivations within each community to coexist with a common identification with it. Each individual in the community can find something to identify with in their own community and to fear in the other, even if he or she strongly distinguishes him/herself from stereotypical notions of Protestant/British/settler or Catholic/Irish/native.

The second problem with the nationalist interpretation is that by emphasising identities and aspirations, it obscures the role of structural factors in the persistence of the conflict. In particular it distracts attention from those factors which have led to a high degree of volatility and uncertainty in the current situation. One of the reasons cultural difference matters so much in Northern Ireland is because it is inscribed in relations of power and inequality. We have seen that the political settlement of 1921 rested on a particular set of power relationships, and that a change in those produced the crisis of 1968–72. The balance of power has not remained constant since then. Catholic numbers are growing, their position in the economy and in local government is strengthening, their cultural symbols and traditions are intruding ever more into the public domain. The traditional underwriter and guarantor of the Protestant position – the British state – has adopted a more neutral stance; the new forces on the scene – the government of the Republic, Irish Americans, the government of the United States – explicitly or implicitly support the Catholic community.

This unstable power balance makes the precise form of political settlement all the more important for each community. The political institutions put in place could swing the power balance with lasting consequences. An advantageous settlement for Catholics would provide them with the basis for further advance; a disadvantageous one could lock them into their current position for many years to come. An advantageous one for Protestants could conceivably allow them to recover lost ground; a disadvantageous one would further erode their position. The difficulty is that neither side can be sure exactly how far it is capable of pushing forward its interests now, or of the consequences of particular constitutional or institutional provisions for those interests.[2] The difficulty of reaching a lasting and agreed settlement is only in part because of the conflicting national aims. It is also a function of the uncertainty of the situation and the difficulties each side has in assessing its interests in this unstable context.

Finally, the nationalist interpretation neglects the multiple meanings which each community brings to the constitutional question. For example, strongly nationalist Catholics may value the achievement of a united Ireland or a role for the Irish government in Northern Ireland's affairs as a symbol of their national identity and as the fulfilment of a deeply felt nationalist aspiration. But for less nationalist Catholics the same constitutional ends may be sought for more instrumental reasons

– for greater access to employment, an end to harassment by the security forces or simply a way of discomforting the other community.

Similarly while Protestant opposition to Catholic constitutional demands are frequently expressed in (British) nationalist terms – as a defence of their British identity or of British sovereignty – such references do not exhaust the possible motivational bases of Protestant resistance. For some, the diminution of a sense of Britishness may appear a real loss to their sense of national identity and belonging; for others the religious threat posed by constitutional change may weigh much more heavily; others may be fearful that a settler–native dynamic is at work which would lead to the ultimate destruction of their community; still others see it as a threat to their haven of cultural modernity on the island; others may resist simply because they refuse to yield to republicans who have killed members of their community. In other words, for both Catholics and Protestants, one cannot assume an equivalence between constitutional aspiration and national identity.

Our intention here has not been to deny the role of nationalism in the conflict, but to situate it among the multiple determinants of the conflict. More divides the communities than simply national identity, and alongside cultural differences are powerful structural forces which push the communities towards conflict. The most sophisticated nationalist interpretations recognise the existence of these factors but relegate them to a secondary position in explanation (McGarry and O'Leary 1995: 355–63). But this robs the explanation of the capacity to grasp and explain the complex character of politics in Northern Ireland: the multiplicity of diverse motivations and meanings that, in a context of inequality and changing power relations, together generate a stark communal polarisation.

One question remains. We explained the rise of nationalism in the nineteenth century in terms of the British-mediated communal conflict and Ireland's disadvantageous relationship to Britain. Why does it persist today? The answer to this question differs for the two parts of Ireland. Southern nationalism is now much less intense than its Northern counterpart. The last three decades have seen an enormous improvement in Protestant–Catholic relations, due in part to ecumemism, in part to the adoption by Protestants of an exclusively Irish identity. Communal conflict has intensified in the North but Southern Catholics distinguish Southern from Northern Protestants and are at one remove from the conflict in the North. Similarly there is less ground now for a nationalism that springs from the British–Irish relationship since the Republic has had control over its destiny for more than 70 years. The past is not completely over, however. Northern Ireland and partition remain unfinished business; there is residual anger about the more distant past and considerable sensitivity to British slights to Irish amour-propre.

In Northern Ireland the continuities with the past are more obvious. First, Northern Ireland is still firmly within the British orbit. The economic role of the British state is no longer the main factor in generating nationalist grievances, not least because it has been essential to maintaining living standards there for the past 25 years. It is now the political and cultural dependence associated with British rule, and, most important of all, the character of British security policy, that gives nationalists a sense of living under foreign occupation. Second, the communal struggle, always more intense than in the South, continues. Nationalism remains the main ideology in which the multiplicity of communal interests are expressed and a vehicle for communal assertion against Protestant resistance. Finally, the British state remains central in defining the arena for communal struggle and providing or redistributing the communal resources used in the struggle (Ruane and Todd 1996: chs 5–8). The state's role in the communal struggle – most particularly in funding and arming a predominantly Protestant police, prison and security service – has reinforced Irish nationalist perceptions of it as malign.

Conclusion: Post-nationalism and the end of conflict

We have argued against a nationalist interpretation of the conflict, whether it is seen as a product of Irish nationalism or of both British and Irish nationalism. There is a nationalist aspect to the conflict – a conflict of national identity and allegiance – but it is one factor in a complex set of determinations whose basic structure was in place long before nationalism emerged on the scene.

Two conclusions follow. First, as long as a conflict of national identity and allegiance exists, some balance between the two nationalisms is necessary and urgent. Important work has already been done in sketching the possible forms of such a balance (O'Leary *et al.* 1993; McGarry and O'Leary 1995: ch. 9). But to focus solely on this aspect of conflict and settlement is to miss those aspects of conflict which will tend to destabilise any hard-won balance of nationalisms. The multiple and incommensurable meanings of constitutional status for nationalists and unionists make contestable the very concept of a 'fair and egalitarian' balance. The changing balance of power threatens the stability of any such settlement. In short, a balancing of nationalisms is a necessary and urgent task, but it cannot of itself lead to a lasting peace.

Second, and in view of the difficulty of balancing nationalisms, it may be suggested that the solution to the conflict lies in the emergence of some form of postnationalism. On our view, this would reduce the intensity of the conflict, but it would not resolve it. We have seen that the communities divide on much more than national identity and allegiance – there is also religion, ethnicity, attributions of settler and native status and stereotypes of modernity and backwardness. A move away from rigid notions of national sovereignty would widen the scope for constitutional innovation, but it would not in itself diminish the struggle for power between the communities. Indeed it could intensify it by opening up new indeterminacies about the future and new arenas in which to struggle.

Nationalism could, therefore, fade away in a postnationalist age while leaving two culturally distinct communities still in differential relations to the British state and still confronting each other. Each could still perceive its interests as in conflict with those of the other and could feel compelled to struggle in defence of those interests, remaining conscious of the relevance of power to the outcome and of the changing balance of power. In these circumstances, each would still seek to harness the power of the British state to protect itself or to advance its interests. It is in the complex structural and cultural conditions which produce that struggle, rather than in Irish or British nationalism as such, that the sources of the conflict lie. It is in altering those conditions that the best, indeed the only, hope of resolving the conflict can be found.

Notes

1. Definitions of nationalism vary widely. For us nationalism has two interrelated dimensions. First, it is an ideology of and for the nation conceived as an (imagined) national community; as such it centres on a sense of national community – a national identity. Second, it is a set of cultural and political practices intended to bring the nation into being and/or advance its interests; as such it centres on political allegiance to and alliances within the national community. In this chapter we take these broad attributes of national identity and allegiance as the essential features of nationalism.
2. For example, recent attention has centred on whether cross-border bodies would have a 'dynamic' for growth – nationalists seek this, unionists oppose it. But the precise functioning and long-term consequences of such bodies cannot now be predicted.

CHAPTER 4

'New Unionism', British nationalism and the prospects for a negotiated settlement in Northern Ireland

Liam O'Dowd

When David Trimble, an academic lawyer, became leader of the Ulster Unionist Party in September 1995, the cover of the party journal, *Ulster Review* (1995–6) celebrated his election by proclaiming the arrival of a 'new unionism': 'pro-active, inclusive, open, pluralist, dynamic, progressive, outward, articulate, intelligent, coherent, professional, confident'. While contributors to the same issue argued that much work remained to be done in modernising the party, they now felt that some of its leaders were capable of absorbing the ideas of a new group of academics, journalists and other professionals who, since the early 1980s, had sought to renovate the intellectual case for the Union.

The main purpose of this chapter is to interrogate critically the main themes of the 'new unionism' in order to ascertain whether it inhibits or enhances the prospects for a negotiated political settlement of the Northern Ireland conflict. Any such settlement crucially depends on the willingness of unionists to negotiate constructively, and reach an accommodation, with Irish nationalists. In the absence of any prospect of, or progress towards, a negotiated settlement, no political dynamic exists to counter the deepening sectarian chasm between the two sides of the communal divide in Northern Ireland. The failure to grasp the opportunity of the cease fires and to advance the 'peace process' is the latest and perhaps most telling symptom of the crisis of politics in Northern Ireland.

The chapter begins by specifying the nature and origins of the 'new unionism'. This is followed by five sections examining a number of interrelated and sometimes overlapping themes in 'new unionist' discourse:

1 its concern to make unionism comprehensible to a wider audience within, and beyond, Northern Ireland, i.e. to improve its public relations image;
2 its attempt to redefine and clarify a positive content for unionism;
3 its relationship to a revitalised British nationalism;

4 its attitude to nationalists in Northern Ireland and to Irish nationalism generally;

5 its specific orientations to a negotiated settlement in Northern Ireland.

The chapter concludes by assessing the potential of the 'new unionism'
to engage constructively with Irish nationalists in a negotiated resolution to the conflict in Northern Ireland.

Locus and origins

The initial locus of the 'new unionism' may be traced to the 'equal citizenship' campaign of the 1980s including a series of publications
demanding that British political parties organise in Northern Ireland
(see Coulter 1994: 14). It has been developed further by writers such as
Arthur Aughey, Paul Bew, Brian Barton, P. J. Roche, Graham Gudgin,
Dennis Kennedy, Robert McCartney, Richard English, Esmond Birnie,
Graham Walker, John Wilson Foster and Norman Porter.[1] Their arguments vary and their output ranges from polemical pamphlets to
journalistic commentary to more sustained academic analysis. What
they all share, however, is an advocacy of the Union of Great Britain
and Northern Ireland and a stated determination to clarify and communicate to others an intellectually defensible case for the Union.
Their motivations are twofold: firstly, effectively to combat what they
see as the dominance of nationalist analyses and propaganda and, secondly, to advance a positive case for unionism in its own right both at
home and abroad.

More recently, 'new unionist' thinking has become more politically
focused in the pamphlets of the Cadogan Group (1992, 1994, 1995a,
1995b, 1996),[2] the publications of the Ulster Young Unionist Council,
and a number of collections, notably Foster 1995b; Roche and Barton
1991; Barton and Roche (eds) 1994 and English and Walker 1996. What
has emerged is an informal or loosely articulated intellectual grouping
servicing the broad unionist movement and committed to shaping
strategy and ideology. The group's influence has been most marked
among the Young Unionists, and with politicians such as David
Trimble and Robert McCartney. 'New unionists' have found allies
within the revitalised British nationalist movement in Britain, most
notably in the right wing of the Tory Party and among the editors and
leading journalists of some conservative newspapers. A small number
of Southern Irish writers (who are frequent contributors to English
papers) such as Conor Cruise O'Brien, Eoghan Harris and Ruth
Dudley Edwards have also become converts to the unionist position.

In its broadest definition, the 'new unionism' exhibits a number of
diverse strains. Its proponents proclaim a secular and 'anti-populist'
orientation, distinguishing themselves from the Protestant unionism of
Ian Paisley and the loyalism of the Protestant paramilitaries. Strongly
opposed to the IRA and Sinn Féin, they also consistently condemn
Irish nationalism in general as narrow, insular and sectarian. Within

Northern Ireland, according to Coulter (1994: 14–15), these unionist intellectuals represent 'political impulses that are modern, secular and progressive' within the 'complex and variegated ideology' of unionism as a whole.

On the surface, it might be expected that the emergence of an articulate, self-confident, intellectual cadre committed to modernising traditional unionism, and to rational argument and debate on the merits of the Union, would enhance the prospects of constructive dialogue and negotiation with opposing political positions. As O'Neill (1994: 375) observes, for most of its history 'the Union with Britain has been defended not with reasons but with power'.

Whereas Irish nationalism has relied on its political intellectuals to 'invent the nation' and map its historic trajectory, Ulster unionism has relied more on its power-brokers, armed adherents and populist clergy and its capacities for popular mobilisation (O'Dowd 1991b). Since the Home Rule agitations of the 1880s, Ulster unionists have steadfastly refused to negotiate the constitutional status of Ireland or Northern Ireland with Irish nationalists. The boundaries of Northern Ireland (as part of the UK) were set not through a democratic plebiscite or by unionist–nationalist negotiation but rather by the balance of coercion existing in Ireland between 1912 and 1921. The irony was that in the setting up of Northern Ireland unionists appropriated for themselves something which they denied to Northern nationalists, namely the right to belong to a state of their own choosing. (Their justification, of course, was that Irish nationalists, given the chance, would likewise deny them by incorporating them into a united Ireland.) Thereafter, the justifications for a unionist/British Northern Ireland were based on the initial capacity to coerce, on the 'democratic majoritarian' status thus gained, and on the resigned acquiescence, apathy and disorganisation of the large nationalist minority in Northern Ireland. For unionists, the power to coerce co-existed easily with the self-evident superiority of their cause. But the capacity to coerce remained infinitely more important in unionist politics than the capacity to persuade intellectually or assimilate the Northern Ireland minority. By the 1980s, however, some unionists were coming to question the effectiveness of some of the old practices and rationales.

The conflict of the last 30 years has challenged key elements of the 1920 settlement. The IRA campaign has sustained a prolonged challenge to the state's monopoly of force. The Catholic community has become much more organised and unwilling to accept passively their continued exclusion from political power. Between 1971 and 1991, the Catholic population increased from roughly 36 per cent to around 43 per cent of the Northern Ireland population with signs that there is a long-term tendency to a broad parity in the size of the two communities. Finally, under Direct Rule, from the unionist perspective the British government has shown a less than wholehearted commitment to the Union. For example, McCartney (1995: 67) saw the Anglo-Irish Agreement as preparing the way for a long-term strategic British withdrawal from Northern Ireland.

In the last 25 years, economic and political change has altered the structural conditions within which unionism operates. Massive economic restructuring and the costs of the conflict have created a state-dependent economy relying heavily on British subventions (O'Dowd 1995). Administrative reform and fair employment legislation have either abolished or undermined some of the key agencies and practices through which unionist domination was maintained under Stormont. While not all changes have been in the same direction, (e.g. the build-up of the Protestant-dominated security forces) most changes have occurred, not because of, but in spite of, unionists.

Unionist politicians have opposed all the major concessions to nationalists, sought to reverse the thrust of change, and maximise what was non-negotiable. Unwilling to negotiate directly with republicans and nationalists on the central issue of the conflict, the constitutional status of Northern Ireland, unionists had change imposed upon them and complained about the lack of democratic consent for these changes in Northern Ireland (see Foster 1995a).

The emergence of the 'new unionism' is a response to these altered circumstances and to the emphasis placed by both governments on nationalist–unionist negotiation and agreement. 'The seemingly terminal decline of party-based unionism' (Holmes 1996: 4), meant in practice that, from the mid-1970s, unionists reconstituted themselves in two main (oppositional) parties within a much widened political arena which included the British government and political parties, the nationalist and republican parties in the North, the Irish government and more recently the US administration.

As well as providing the political impetus for the 'new unionism', Direct Rule strengthened its socio-economic basis by encouraging growth of an intelligentsia, supported directly and indirectly by high levels of state expenditure. The unionist elements of this intelligentsia (both Northern Irish and British) have come to recognise the material and cultural advantages of a Direct Rule administration. In this they have shared the benefits of British subvention with the rest of the Northern Ireland middle class, including its nationalist section. Relatively untouched by the 'troubles' (compared to the Catholic and Protestant working classes), they have become even more deeply wedded to a British Ulster (Todd 1987; Coulter 1994).

Like many middle-class Protestants, the 'new unionists' have been drawn more closely into the mainstream of British socio-economic and cultural life and their career paths, be they academic, administrative or journalistic, have crossed both Great Britain and Northern Ireland. They read British newspapers, listen to British radio stations and watch British television daily, thereby partaking of a British 'imagined community'. Far from being discouraged by the ambiguity of successive British governments on the Union (and, in part, because of it), they have come to assert their Britishness with increasing clarity and force. This has involved demanding 'equal citizenship' with people in the rest of the United Kingdom. They have sought to distance themselves from traditional loyalism as a failed and inappropriate strategy in the altered political landscape. Given the importance of unionist unity, however, they differ among themselves on the degree to which populist unionism is integral and crucial to the unionist cause.

The ebb and flow of the conflict and the evolution of British policy in Northern Ireland have shifted the parameters of unionism. According to Aughey (1995a) unionists have been 'alarmed into reflection' by events in the manner of their ancestors between 1880 and 1920 and conservatives after the French revolution. The events include abolition of Stormont, the institution of Direct Rule, the growing influence of the Irish government in the Anglo-Irish management of the conflict – evidenced most notably in the Anglo-Irish Agreement (AIA), the Downing Street Declaration and, more recently, periodic British talks with Sinn Féin – the Hume–Adams peace process, and the framework documents aimed at guiding the current 'peace process'.

Despite the continued capacity of unionist politicians to mobilise their electoral bloc and the continued 'potency of the good cry of "no surrender" or "not an inch" or "this we will maintain" ' (Aughey 1995a: 10), unionists see themselves as having suffered a series of defeats and reverses over the last 25 years. Furthermore, from the early 1970s, it became clear from opinion polls that the majority of the British electorate wanted to be rid of Northern Ireland with only a minority adopting a straightforward unionist position (McGarry and O'Leary 1995:152). Summarising consistent opinion poll evidence in Britain, Cochrane (1994: 386) argues that support for political detachment *vis-à-vis* Northern Ireland among the British policy-making elite reflects an electorate at large characterised by 'emotional detachment' (1994: 388). Hayes and McAllister (1996: 79–80) summarise British opinion poll evidence by pointing to a persistent majority which favours any solution other than the constitutional status quo.

To the 'new unionists', the mixture of indifference and hostility in Britain contrasted with the growing mobilisation of the Irish government behind Hume, Adams and Irish-America in what they termed a 'pan-nationalist front'. (See Dixon 1995 who argues that unionists are far more isolated than nationalists in terms of external support.)

In these unpropitious circumstances, Arthur Aughey has posed the options for unionists in terms of a stark dichotomy: (1) 'gently managing decline' and 'negotiating intelligently the long-term conditions of lifting the siege. This means accommodation with a new Nationalist Ireland and the end of Unionism'; (2) change in order to preserve the constitutional status quo. This means engaging in an 'intellectual war' 'now that the shooting war is over' (Aughey 1996: 12). Clearly, Aughey and most other proponents of the 'new unionism' favour the second option. In advancing a more aggressive and articulate unionism, they seek to challenge an undercurrent of defeatism and fatalism in unionism in the wake of sustained political pressure which they see as aimed at incorporating unionists into the rest of Ireland 'without the permission of articulate demur, or the dignity of an intellectual existence' (Foster 1996: 92).

Selling Unionism and Improving the Public Image of Unionism

'New unionists' believe that for much of the last 25 years, the case for the Union has been allowed to go by default, by an inability to communicate the merits of unionism to a wider audience in a rational and coherent manner. Against this background, they have sought to address two constituencies simultaneously. The first is primarily local Protestants but at times these are incorporated in a term used with growing frequency: the 'greater number' of people within Northern Ireland. This is a deliberately elastic term which, depending on the circumstances, can be variously defined as consisting of an electoral majority within Northern Ireland, Protestant unionists or all pro-union people which includes some Catholics with a utilitarian interest in the status quo. The second constituency is external and mainly British. It includes the government, right-wing conservatives and beyond these a broad spectrum of those who defend the integrity of the British state, the monarchy and the existing 'constitution'. In wider international terms, it appeals to the interests of existing states, to the need to recognise existing national boundaries against the claims of terrorists and secessionist groups. The main external opportunity for the new unionism, however, is that presented by the revitalisation of a British nationalism devoted to defending the integrity of the UK and its sovereignty against the threat of the EU and secessionist tendencies.

A recent academic collection on unionism begins with the familiar complaint that Ulster unionism is 'commonly portrayed as irrational, backward and deviant'. The author traces this to the perceived refusal of unionists to reach an accommodation with Irish nationalism, to fully embrace 'a genuine sense of Britishness' or to develop 'their own distinctive Ulster nationality' (McBride 1996: 1). The need to reverse the negative public image of the unionist case is a primary rationale of the intellectuals discussed here.

One powerful, if indirect, indicator of the failure of Ulster unionism to communicate to the outside world, is the large number of published works which have sought to interpret the 'puzzle' of Ulster unionism to a wider public (O'Dowd 1991a). By comparison, the roster of contemporary social research on nationalism is surprisingly empty. It is as if nationalism and republicanism does not need explaining, whereas Ulster unionism seems anomalous and paradoxical. One study of Ulster loyalists succinctly summarises the problem of comprehensibility:

> They (the loyalists) are loyal to Britain, yet ready to disobey her; they reject clerical tyranny, yet oppose secularism; they proclaim an ideology of freedom and equality, except for Catholics; they revere law and authority, then break the law. And they refuse to do the rational obvious thing.
>
> (Nelson 1984: 37)

Fully aware of the implications of such an image, John Wilson Foster (1994: 37) observed in a critique of the Downing Street Declaration:

> The stern task facing those who believe that they are British, and wish to remain so, is to display to England (sic) and the world, the benign, rational, positive, engaging face of unionism.

Foster's 'call to arms' is mirrored in the writing of many others (see e.g., McCartney 1985; Clifford 1988; Oliver 1978).

Following McCartney (1985), Foster (1994) argues that the prime responsibility is 'on those best equipped to perform the task – academics and professionals' who believe in the union, who have prospered and been educated under it, and 'who now slumber over their subsidies and grants and salaries without saying a public word in its defence'.

Here there is a strong sense that the defence of the union had been left to the 'wrong people', e.g. to the ghettos (McCartney 1985), to a 'Protestant working class that rightly feels betrayed' (Foster 1996: 92) or to Paisley's brand of archaic fundamentalism (Burnside 1995). In a spirited defence of Ulster Protestant culture, Foster (1996) decries the 'political incorrectness' of unionism and the anti-unionist orthodoxy in the academy and in British and Irish government circles. He traces this to the 'almost systematic humiliation and isolation of Ulster unionists over two decades and their abandonment by intellectuals' (1996: 92). The 'anti-unionist consensus' discerned by Foster is to Aughey (1995b: 7–11) the 'last respectable form of bigotry, anti-Unionist bigotry'.

The Ulster Young Unionist Council pamphlet, *Selling Unionism: Home and Away* (Augheny et al. 1995) expresses a sense of urgency about communicating the unionist case to a variety of audiences, not only in Northern Ireland (Aughey), but in the rest of the UK (Burnside), the USA (Donaldson), Republic of Ireland (Harris) and the EU (Adams).

Aughey (1995b: 14) calls on unionists to reject fatalism and defeatism. He concludes that contemporary unionism lacks 'a concept', 'a sense of itself as an active political idea larger than the day to day struggle in Northern Ireland' and he contrasts this with Unionism's great strength historically 'its sense of being part of something wider and larger than the narrow ground of Irish nationalism'. Burnside stresses the need for unionists to target their audiences in the UK and to combat the successful resources and techniques of John Hume and the 'pan nationalist front'. Burnside lists British audiences sympathetic to the unionist case: new right think-tanks and lobby groups; key newspapers such as *The Times, Sunday Times, Sunday Telegraph* and *The Sun*; the Friends of the Union founded in 1985 by Ian Gow, Lord Cranbourne, Sir John Biggs Davidson, and 'friends in the Labour Party who believe in the Union'. Burnside's concern is with positive image building and networking, and he stresses the need not to appear anti-Catholic.

Donaldson (1995) argues the unionists should seek to mobilise those of Ulster–Scots heritage in the USA building on the work of the Ulster Society in Northern Ireland. Gavin Adams's (1995) main concern is to counter nationalists' attempt to use the EU to further the cause of Irish unity. He suggests that the EU be used to acknowledge and strengthen the 'national rights of the greater number of people in Ulster' (1995: 50).

By far the most remarkable contribution to *Selling Unionism* comes from Eoghan Harris, a Southern Irish columnist with the Irish edition of the *Sunday Times*. Harris has used his various roles as a controversialist, journalist and television current affairs producer to publicise his metamorphosis from Marxist-inspired republicanism into a leading propagandist of consumerist capitalism and of anti (Irish) nationalism. He begins by bluntly stating that Catholics have certain cultural advantages over Protestants when it comes to communication. They 'tell a good story' and thus have rhetorical advantages over Protestants who are more prone to preach, make a case, pay attention to the 'text'. For Catholics unlike Protestants, the 'truth is in the tone, not in the words'. Harris (1995: 46) concludes that the 'siege mentality plus the evangelical and preaching tradition produce a public, polemical sound that is not suitable for television or radio'.

Harris provides a mini-handbook for unionists incorporating twelve rules for winning the 'propaganda war' on the media. But he does point to a deeper problem, i.e. that unionists lack a theory of change, 'of political struggle as a process of political change'. They 'seem to want to stop things short, and settle down. But life never settles down ... The same cognitive flaws that allow unionists to see politics as a product rather than a process, prevent them doing well on the mass media' (1995: 29). Hence, according to Harris (1995: 30) (1) unionists don't understand the dynamics of change; (2) they 'don't believe the basic rule that freedom is the recognition of necessity, that you can only win ground by giving ground'; (3) 'unionists are reactive and serial thinkers when they need to be proactive and dialectical thinkers'.

It is doubtful if Harris's polemic will persuade many unionists to 'pack in their flawed theory of politics' and to recognise the superiority of Catholic techniques of communication in a consumerist age. He does, however, point to some key weaknesses of unionism which recur as 'new unionists' attempt to clarify the positive substance of their case.

The positive content of the 'new unionism'

Unionist intellectuals have long acknowledged that unionists have been better at specifying what they are not, rather than what they are. In other words, they have tended to define themselves negatively in terms of others, especially Irish Catholics and nationalists. Historically, unionists have put the blame for this negativity on others: the aggressive politics of Irish nationalism, the IRA and the Catholic Church; the inconstancy of successive British governments, and outsiders' misunderstanding of what Ulster unionism really is.

Despite their wish to elaborate the 'positive' aspects of the union-ism, the writers discussed here devote much space to attacking nationalism and nationalists' perception of unionism (see Aughey 1990, Coulter 1994; Foster (ed.) 1995; Cadogan Group pamphlets). They attempt, however, to make a case for the Union which goes beyond the imperative to reject its political opponents. This case asserts that unionism is based on a claim to citizenship of the UK which is a multi-ethnic, multi-national, multi-faith state. For Aughey and McCartney in particular, UK politics is about citizenship, rights and interests, whereas the politics of Irish nationalism is about identity.

Thus, having rejected reductionist and essentialist interpretations which explain unionism in terms of religious beliefs, conditional loy-alty and a politics of identity crisis, Arthur Aughey then proceeds to advance a reductionist and essentialist argument of his own:

> The idea of the Union is a very pure political doctrine in the sense that it is concerned, almost exclusively, with issues of right and citizenship. (1990: 198).

Of course, Aughey, McCartney, Foster and others recognise that union-ism has its fair share of adherents who advocate exclusivistic forms of identity – religious fundamentalists, bigots and supremacists – but they deny that these contaminate the purity of the 'idea of the union' based on 'universal liberal principles'. Ironically, this imperviousness to empirical reality is reminiscent of Catholic vocationalists of the 1920s to 1950s who never allowed the empirical realities of Irish society of the time to impinge on their arguments for a social order based on Catholic social principles. While negative empirical manifestations of unionism might be overlooked, if not excused, this latitude is not extended to Irish nationalism where its objectionable manifestations (e.g. the IRA, its economic and cultural backwardness and the policies of the Irish state) are taken to be indicative of its very essence (Coulter 1994).

The key argument here is that the core of unionism is a 'liberal, secu-lar political conscience' (Coulter 1994: 17). This 'conscience' stipulates that the idea of the modern state is superior to the idea of the nation. And, in Aughey's words, 'the identity of unionism has little to do with the idea of the nation and everything to do with the idea of the state' (Aughey 1990: 194). As a fellow-member of the Cadogan Group states, unionism attempts to 'elaborate a positive liberal philosophy based on British citizenship which is secular, progressive and inclusive' (Roche 1995: 129). Unlike Roche, Aughey believes there is no such thing as a British nation, only British citizens (and the British state).

This allows Aughey, Foster and others to suggest that a whole range of cultural identities (Ulster, British, even Irish) are compatible with citizenship of the British state. Aughey (1996:39) is also able to argue that symbols of the Irish state should be separated from sym-bols of Irish nationality which could then be shared by unionists and nationalists in Northern Ireland. Thus, unionism cannot be portrayed as another form of exclusivist ethnicity or ethno-nationalism like Irish nationalism. Nor, unlike cultural nationalism, is it a 'totalising way of life' but a political identity with 'room for any manner of cultural expressions' (Aughey 1995b: 15). Unionism, in this view is qualitatively different, and cannot be understood in terms of nationalist concepts of 'culture' or 'self-determination'.

Allegiance to the UK state, therefore, is of a different order from allegiance to the Irish nation-state. The former is multi-national and multi-ethnic and must be understood in terms of citizenship and not substantive identity.

> 'It expresses the democratic ideal of different nations, different religions, different colours, and all equal citizens under one government. It is to this notion that intelligent unionism, which embraces both Protestants and Catholics, owes allegiance. (Aughey 1990: 195)

Two questionable dichotomies are posited here: a universalistic politics of citizenship versus a particularistic identity politics and intelligent unionism which practices the former versus unintelligent unionism (and nationalism) which adheres to the latter. Thus, 'new unionists', proclaim themselves as the carriers of a privileged and superior political idea within the British Isles as a whole, just as the UK state is the carrier of superior universalistic and inclusive notions of citizenship in the face of narrow, exclusivistic nationalisms and ethnicities.

Trimble (1996a) reasserted the principle of unionist and British superiority to the UUP annual conference in response to criticism from a party member:

> It is only unionism that can be genuinely multinational and multi-cultural. It believes that the whole is greater than that of the parts. This is a better vision than anything sectarian Irish nationalism has to offer.[3]

The dichotomy between a politics of citizenship and a politics of identity conveniently ignores the fact that the former is also about *identifying* those who 'belong' and those who do not, i.e. those who are included or deemed to have rights, and those who are excluded who have lesser or no rights. The 'new unionists' ignore the ways in which citizenship is intimately bound up with state formation and sovereignty while following different trajectories in the national states of Europe. The UK follows only one of several possible models of citizenship (see, e.g., Brubaker 1990; Baldwin-Edwards and Schain 1994). For the 'new unionists' as for other unionists full citizenship rights are contingent on accepting the legitimacy of the boundaries of the UK state. Nationalists who are unwilling to accept these boundaries make themselves responsible for turning themselves into 'second class citizens'. It is this 'loyalty test', for example, which has allowed unionists either to ignore, deny or justify discrimination against the minority in Northern Ireland (see Doyle 1994). The liberal unionist version of this is that Catholics are entitled to full civil and religious liberties as individuals but not as nationalists.

Unionists root the merits of citizenship in a universalisation of a particular view of the British experience. For the 'new unionists' the superiority of British citizenship is true by definition because of their essentialist view of the Union and because the UK obviously includes many cultural groups. In advancing a profoundly ahistorical and idealistic understanding of the UK state the 'new unionists' ignore the extent to which the British empire and state sought to create and institutionalise a 'British world' based on an elaborate hierarchical system of national, ethnic and racial groups (see Ruane and Todd 1996: 211–12).

The attempts of 'new unionists' to universalise their identity seem curious at a time when the particularities and distinctiveness of the British path to statehood and citizenship are becoming more clearly visible in both historical and comparative terms (McGarry and O'Leary 1995: 130–7). Moreover, the role of war, popular Protestantism, ethnicisation and empire in the evolution of British citizenship are, if anything, harder to obscure in Northern Ireland than in the rest of the UK.

'New unionism' and the embrace of British nationalism

One of the few self-reflective explorations of the 'new unionism' has effectively undermined the distinction by 'liberal unionists' between 'citizenship' and 'identity' (Porter 1996). Porter ignores a much more far-reaching problem, however, i.e., the failure of the 'new unionism' to recognise itself as a form of nationalism, the very ideology which it claims totally to reject.

For unionists in Northern Ireland, a largely unacknowledged British nationalism is the bridge which links the cultural (or Protestant unionism) of Paisley and the Orange Order to the 'liberal unionism' of McCartney, Aughey and elements within the UUP. It is nationalism which overrides abstract dichotomies of citizenship and identity. Porter (1996), while avoiding any discussion of British nationalism, highlights what unites both cultural and liberal unionism – the conviction of both that the Union is an end in itself, 'or better, as the end to which all other ends are subservient' (1996: 169). This commitment to 'the Union, the whole Union and nothing but the Union' (1996: 213) is the basis of unionist political unity in Northern Ireland, whatever its myriad internal divisions and disagreements. It is based on identifying the survival of unionists, or more specifically, the Protestant community with its membership of the British state.

The identification with the British state, the 'Crown in Parliament', and the constitution links unionism with a wider British nationalism. It is the latter that makes Ulster unionism part of a 'wider concept', raising it above the 'day to day struggle in Northern Ireland' (Aughey 1995a: 14). Of course, it would be anathema to 'new unionists' to see themselves as nationalists. Such self-recognition would undermine their self-proclaimed qualitative difference from, and superiority to, Irish nationalists. As carriers of British (and therefore 'universal') liberal political values, they assert that they do not speak the same political language as their opponents and as a result this conveniently means that they can have no genuine political dialogue, negotiations or compromise with them *qua* nationalists. After all, unionists speak the language of universal rights and citizenship while nationalists are mired in the insular language of identity and self-determination.

It follows, therefore, that 'new unionists' with 'liberal' views must refuse to see the conflict as a fundamental struggle between two political nationalisms, British and Irish, the outcome of failures of nation and state building (McGarry and O'Leary 1995: 248–353). This implies a form of equivalence and therefore grounds for compromise which they could not entertain. Trimble's (1996b) assertion (along with his fellow unionist leaders, Paisley and McCartney), that there can be no compromise between unionism and (Irish) nationalism is elevated by the 'new unionist' intellectuals to the status of a principle of political philosophy.

These 'new unionists' are not alone in failing wilfully, or otherwise, to acknowledge their British nationalism. In this, they subscribe to a more general blindness to state nationalism in liberal–democratic states and to the process by which the latter seek to generate their own forms of 'imagined community' and 'national interest'. Official 'nation-building' in established states is an ongoing process forged in wars, conflicts and competition with other states. It seldom, if ever, succeeds in fully identifying state and nation and may have to confront alternative formulations of state nationalism within the state as well as external threats.

In the 'new unionist' lexicon, nationalism is equated with secessionism, ethnic particularism, the 'sentimental and romantic invention of nations', and the violence which has attended the break-up of the large multi-cultural state-empires. Like many liberals, socialists and moderate conservatives in large and relatively stable national states, the 'new unionists' see nationalism as a problem identified with separatists, guerrillas and fascists. They ignore their own 'banal (if not benign) nationalism' associated with the flag, the anthem and the designation of 'Others'. As Billig (1995: 6–7) has pointed out this banal or taken-for-granted state nationalism can mobilise mass support behind wars as in the Gulf and the Falklands. It can support huge armament industries, arbitrary interventions to support all manner of tyrannical regimes, and the flouting of the rule of law to suppress internal enemies – all in the national interest.

Here the 'new unionists' *qua* British nationalists fall prey to many of the fallacies identified by Benedict Anderson (1992). They 'forget' the centuries of wars and violence which went into the creation of stable, 'integrated' states such as the UK (much of it perpetrated outside the territorial borders of Great Britain): that only big countries are modern and progressive because of the relationship between capitalism, markets and state size; and that there is some inscrutable connection between large states, capitalism and peace. Even more fundamentally, perhaps, they ignore the possibility that the very durability, stability and democracy of the English/British state may have been rooted in some ways in its capacity to externalise violence to the empire and to its own periphery – a violence in which unionists themselves are embroiled. Claims that the 'culture of violence sustained by nationalism means that it is devoid of what is required for moral esteem' (Roche and Birnie 1996: 15) are worth putting in the context of British state violence over the last two centuries – far more Irish people, both Protestant and Catholic, died fighting for the British state, than died for Irish independence.

There are of course many types of state and secessionist nationalisms (for one typology, see Hall 1993). What they all share in common is their attempts to improve the fit between state and nation, or in other words, to fuse institutional power and collective identity. Of course, the assertion that the United Kingdom is based purely on principles of citizenship and not on substantive identities has added to one of the strengths of British nationalism, its 'taken-for-granted' and unacknowledged nature. When the 'new unionists' acknowledge British nationalism, it is in order to dismiss it in terms of its marginal importance (*vis-à-vis* citizenship) (Aughey 1994a: 148) or in terms of a denial that the UK has a 'fully developed sense of nationalism' or the 'same form of aggressive nationalism as has existed elsewhere in Europe' (Trimble 1996b: 31).

Of course, denying the ethno-national content of Britishness, and universalising British liberalism, may be seen as a form of ideological management of decline from state-empire to middle-ranking national state and EU member. It may be understood as a response to what Taylor (1991) terms 'post-hegemonic trauma'. In Northern Ireland it may be a means of counteracting what Anderson terms the 'deflated superiority complex' of some unionists.

British nationalism is akin to the 'banal nationalisms' of other states. But it also has another more unique dimension, a peculiarly powerful state myth which sacralises the very longevity (or archaism) of state institutions – an unwritten constitution centred on the 'Crown in Parliament' and a monarchy which 'binds the state together' (Nairn 1988). Ironically, for all the 'new unionists' emphasis on citizenship, to be British means being 'subjects' rather than 'citizens'. It involves a state myth rather than a 'myth of the sovereign people'.

British nationalism celebrates the continuity and unique intrinsic merits of the ancient Anglo-British constitution married to an imagined British community. As Colley (1992) has shown, this myth was originally forged in a common Protestantism, in foreign wars, in reaction to the rise of modern nationalisms elsewhere and, above all in the imperial experience of the 'nations' of the British Isles. In the course of British state formation and imperial expansion, both 'Europe' and the Irish came to be defined as British 'others', a process resisted, but never fully overcome, by Ulster Protestants.

In the course of the twentieth century, the demise of popular Protestantism and the gradual demise of empire distanced Ulster Protestants further from British identity, even if the monarchy remained as a major focus of common identification (Loughlin 1995: 226). But British nationalism retained its interwoven strong and weak

variants throughout the twentieth century with Ulster unionists identifying mainly with the former (see Loughlin 1995; Hennessey 1993,
1996). The strong variant, most prominent between the mid-nineteenth
century and the end of the Second World War, emphasises monarchy,
war memories, official militarism and Protestantism. The milder variant stressed British forms of parliamentary democracy, stability,
justice, law and order and welfarism. The latter often saw itself as anti-
nationalist and therefore given to moderation, compromise, democracy.

The current re-opening of the 'British national question' threatens
the complex identities of Ulster unionists while simultaneously allowing the 'new unionists' to push their concerns with maintaining the
integrity of the state and exclusivistic British sovereignty into the
mainstream of political debate. The question at issue is whether the
British state can survive intact the decline of empire and political
Protestantism, the relative decline of its military and economic power
and the demystification of the royal family. The prospects for, and
likely consequences of, proposed constitutional reform *vis-à-vis* the
survival of the UK remain unclear (McBride 1996: 14; Gillespie, P.
1996), as are the implications for unionism.

In this debate, the 'new unionists' sacralisation of the 'Union' provides them with a precarious niche and an audience on the right wing
of British politics which has variously included the National Front,
Powellites, right-wing Tories, Eurosceptics and the overwhelmingly
conservative national press (Greenslade 1996). More recently, the
Ulster Unionist Party has allied itself with James Goldsmith's
Eurosceptic Party in the EU parliament. Unionists find common
ground, therefore, with British nationalists who wish to maintain the
integrity and sovereignty of the UK in the face of internal and external
threats such as the EU, Scottish devolution or separatism (see, e.g. Bew
1996), and the activities of the IRA and Irish nationalists who wish to
dilute British sovereignty in Northern Ireland (Bevins 1996).

In the 1990s, British nationalists have often adopted the unionist
cause as a litmus test of the government's commitment to defending
the state, sometimes equating appeasement of nationalists and the IRA
to servility to the EU (see Bevins 1996; Alcock 1995–6). For example,
Daily Telegraph editor, Charles Moore (1995: 5), complains that the
British administrative class refuses to accept that Northern Ireland
should be unambiguously British, while persisting in perpetuating and
institutionalising 'uncertainty about its constitutional status'. He
argues that by 'refusing to decide the issue of Britishness they throw it
open to ever more dispute'. Moore (1995: 5) favours full integration of
Northern Ireland into the UK and sees it as a 'cautionary lesson against
devolution'. Remarkably, an editorial in the *Daily Telegraph* (13 July
1996) used the occasion the Orange Order's 'victory' at Drumcree to
call for the scrapping of the Anglo-Irish Agreement and the reassertion
of the British government's 'exclusive prerogatives in the loyal
province'. All this is scarcely an encouragement to negotiation in
Northern Ireland.

Yet, although British nationalists may be moved to utilise the Northern Irish issue to serve their purposes in Britain, more often a familiar ambiguity recurs which sees Northern Ireland as a semi-detached part of the state. Thatcher, the prototypical British nationalist of the 1980s, signed the Anglo-Irish Agreement. Ambiguity towards Northern Ireland was neatly encapsulated by Michael Forsyth's celebration of British nationalism in the face of devolutionary and separatist pressures at the Tory Party conference in 1996. Proclaiming the integrity of the UK, he stated:

> God has smiled on this island. No aggressive neighbour disputes our boundaries: the sea is our timeless frontier. Although our liberty has been threatened twice this century, the fortitude of our peoples – Scots, English, Welsh and Ulstermen – secured for us our way of life. (cited in Millar 1996).

The inclusion of 'Ulstermen' (sic) as an apparent afterthought indicates an extraordinary 'mainland' amnesia that since the early twentieth century Ulster unionists have been 'the only community in the state committed to defend – through membership of the legal military and illegal paramilitary organisations' the present borders of the UK (Richard Rose cited in Loughlin 1995: 226). It also points to what Taylor (1991) has termed 'the territorial enigma' of Anglo-British, especially English nationalism which places a low priority on the defence of precise territorial boundaries. In Northern Ireland, British nationalism can never be taken for granted – it is always contested and often assertive and aggressive. To moderate nationalists in Britain, unionism is replete with un-British-like qualities, and an unwelcome reminder of some of the elements that contributed to building the British state – Protestantism, ethnic dominance, settler mentality and violence. Its intimate, antagonistic, if relentless, reciprocal relationship with Irish nationalism further distances it from 'mainland Britain'.

Attitudes towards Irish nationalists: parity of esteem?

Attitudes to Irish nationalists, therefore, are a more important constitutive part of unionist identity than they are of national identity in Britain. The debate over so-called 'parity of esteem' provides some important insights into 'new unionists' attitudes to nationalists.

The launching of the term 'parity of esteem' in Northern Ireland political debate has been traced to two speeches by Mayhew, Northern Ireland Secretary of State, in December 1992 and April 1993 (English 1995: 135). In the first, he suggested that the aspiration to a united Ireland is no less legitimate than unionists' attachment to the UK. In the second, he suggested that any settlement must accord parity of esteem to both traditions. Parity of esteem proved a useful rhetorical reference point for nationalists but was rejected by unionists who wished to deny the possible implication that the British government was a 'neutral arbiter' between two opposing, but equally legitimate arguments.

One of the consistent themes running through the 'new unionism' is the sustained attack on 'parity of political esteem'. This stance is shared by all strands in unionist politics. The Cadogan Group (1996: 22–3) support the position of the DUP in the 1991 talks as that which underpinned the whole unionist stance on the issue. This denied the SDLP's claim that both traditions had equal legitimacy, holding that only states and peoples, rather than 'traditions', had the right of self-determination. According to the DUP the 'people' of Northern Ireland rather than Northern Ireland nationalists had the right of self-determination. Thus existing states defined 'peoples', thereby obliterating the political claims of Northern Ireland nationalists.

Richard English (1994, 1995, 1996) has been to the forefront in developing academic arguments against 'parity of esteem'. Unlike others such as Aughey, Kennedy, even McCartney, he sees little virtue in applying British cultural pluralism to Northern Ireland because 'the situation – politically, culturally, demographically – is so appalling' (1994: 101). He rejects even parity of cultural esteem in that it leads to parity of political esteem which is 'fundamentally incoherent' in that it accords equal legitimacy to those who would maintain and those who would dismember the state (1994: 98). English argues that the British government's ambiguity raises loyalist anxieties and republican illusions (a familiar unionist refrain). On balance, he seems to be arguing that there is no 'solution'. But he strongly asserts the superior intellectual logic and practical feasibility of the unionist position (1995: 135–8) and advocates diminishing loyalists fears and republican hopes that the status quo can be changed.

As befits one of the leading academic critics of Irish literature, John Wilson Foster has rather more respect for cultural nationalism (see Foster 1995a and b, 1996) than most of the 'new unionists'. Moreover, unlike Aughey and other unionist political scientists and activists, he defines unionism as a cultural rather than a merely political position (1995a: 59). He states 'I am a unionist because unionism is my culture' and that the Union 'has been forged through 350 years of history and culture'. For Foster, in a cultural sense, 'big is beautiful' and unionism is a far bigger and more encompassing cultural field than republicanism or nationalism (1995a: 62). He traces his conviction of the superiority of unionism to republicanism to his own study of Irish literary culture between the 1880s and the 1922. Green (1995: 24) is also enamoured with the larger 'British and English-speaking worlds' (although he is less keen on Europeanness). Unlike Foster he is positively disdainful of what he deems to be 'Irish cultural separatism'. Like any nationalism, the 'new unionism' frequently embraces divergent and contradictory views.

Most of the 'new unionists', however, are more concerned with politics than with culture and make a clear distinction between the two. Their main preoccupation is that, whatever about culture, parity of *political* esteem is impossible. This is because the aspiration for Irish unity, and the political project which advances it, are intellectually, morally and practically inferior to unionism. It follows that nationalism is incompatible with unionism and that no compromise is possible between the two. Thus, the aspiration for, and objective of, Irish unity is 'illogical' or 'intellectually threadbare' (Kennedy 1995: 29) or 'entirely without validity because it is self-refuting – its assertion proves that there is no single nation in Ireland' (Roche and Birnie 1996: 15, see also English 1995: 138).

In the 'new unionism', essentialist arguments and the elaboration of 'political principles' take precedence over empirical analysis. Nevertheless, economists such as Gudgin (1995) and Birnie and Roche (1995) have sought to provide an empirical rationale for the Union which seek to demonstrate the economic superiority of the Union to a 'united Ireland'. They are highly suspicious of 'politically-motivated' attempts to bring about an all-Ireland economy in the context of the European Union. Nevertheless, their own accounts of the Northern Ireland economy are typically static and geared to the highly *political* objective of minimising the prospects for cross-border economic co-operation in order to defend the *political* status quo (see Munck and Hamilton in this volume).

Just as other unionists insist on analytical distinctions between politics and culture, the economists distinguish between 'economics' and politics, only to fuse the two in the way they interpret the data and reach conclusions. For example, in studies of the unemployment differential between Catholics and Protestants, Gudgin has continued to adopt a zero-sum approach which is reminiscent of the type of sectarian headcounts central to traditional unionism – in other words, the more jobs Catholics gain, the fewer there will be for Protestants. He follows Compton's (1991: 75) view that higher Catholic unemployment and structural disadvantage 'lies not in discrimination but primarily in the structure, attitudes and aptitudes of the Catholic population'. Gudgin is sceptical of fair employment policy, arguing that 'even under conditions of completely fair employment' 'higher birth-rates together with an *insufficiently rapid* rate of migration' will tend to ensure that Catholics have higher unemployment rates than Protestants (Gudgin 1996: 21). Thus, it would appear that, despite the convergence of Catholic and Protestant birth-rates and the continued propensity of Catholics to migrate at a faster rate than Protestants (acknowledged by Gudgin), defective Catholic behaviour patterns explain their disadvantage.

The hardline attacks on 'parity of esteem' are softened at various points by advocacy of limited forms of North–South economic co-operation (Cadogan Group 1995, 1996). 'Culture' is stressed as having potential to link nationalists and unionists. Indeed, Reynolds (1995: 28) observes that 'culture is the only arena in which parity of esteem can exist'. While English has little time for cultural pluralism, Aughey supports the existence of multiple cultural identities within the UK and Kennedy (1995: 35) sees 'non-political Irishness' as something which can be shared by all. Of course, this highly 'apolitical' notion of the culture of civil society is tenuous given the extent to which the state penetrates civil society in Northern Ireland.

At one end of the 'new unionist' spectrum Foster (1996: 86) adopts a maximalist view of culture arguing that it is been used by state-funded groups such as Cultural Traditions 'to "hibernicise" unionist Ulster to a degree consistent with unification'. Clearly 'parity of cultural esteem' is not appropriate here. At the other end of the spectrum are minimalist views such as Roche's view of Irishness based on 'recreational and cultural conviviality' (see also Haslett 1995: 127). It will appear as no great concession to nationalists that they are allowed to follow cultural pursuits such as Irish dancing, the Irish language, Gaelic games and their own forms of religious worship.

Norman Porter (1996: 167) in his penetrating book of unionist self-criticism acknowledges that 'liberal unionism (exemplified by Aughey and McCartney) is as closed to political movement in Northern Ireland, on terms other than its own, as is cultural unionism' (as practised by Paisley and the Orange Order, for example). 'It too subscribes to a notion of unionism that can admit of no compromise.' Even Porter, however, is wary of 'parity of esteem' and substitutes for it the term 'due recognition', although he fails to state who decides what is 'due'.

The 'new unionists', in common with unionist politicians generally, continue to attack the concept of 'parity of esteem' just as they use the notion of equal citizenship to deny parity of treatment to undeserving nationalists. To accede to 'parity of esteem' would undermine unionists' claim to determine the status to be accorded to the political and cultural practices of nationalists. It is as if a key constitutive element in unionist identity is its sense of superiority to Irish nationalism in its political and cultural forms. This view brooks no sense of 'parity', no compromise, and precious little negotiation. It is the intellectual equivalent of Orange marches which seek to demonstrate dominance rather than encourage consensus or common purpose.

Negotiations: the illusory search for permanence

Much has changed in Northern Ireland over the last three decades, economically, politically and culturally. Yet, unionist politicians continue to use the 'language of finality and permanence that they have employed since 1920' (Aughey 1994b: 54). The 'new unionists' are no exception. They categorically reject the language of the 'peace *process*'. Kennedy (1995: 36) suggests that 'what is needed now is not a political process but a stable settlement'. Aughey (1995c: 48–9) too rejects the language of 'process', 'transition' and 'dynamism', complaining that 'the British government does not speak clearly enough for unionists in the language of status and durability' (1995c: 52).

Unionists believe in the 'solid rock' of the Union but even this has been undermined. Aughey (1995c: 48) credits John Hume with developing a more sophisticated form of nationalism which has replaced 'the traditional outright rejection of the Union by a strategic redefinition of its purpose'. Thus the Union is being used against unionists – the 'constitutional guarantee' is redefined as a political process aimed at producing a framework 'substantially Irish and residually British'. Aughey (1995c: 49) contrasts 'a steady state Union where UK membership has permanent worth and value' with 'a dynamic Union which sees it as provisional, of diminishing significance and ultimately worthless'. The policies of the two governments, the constitutional nationalists and pressure from the IRA are all seen as conspiring in the same direction – to use the Union to complete the unfinished project of Irish nationalism.

Against this background, the 'new unionists' continue to demand an end to uncertainty, ambiguity and evasiveness in the policies of the British and Irish governments in favour of policies which finally accept the legitimacy of Northern Ireland as an integral part of the UK. Gudgin (1995: 105) echoes a pervasive unionist theme when he complains of the way in which nationalists seek to build on past gains to generate a dynamic for Irish unity. He argues that both governments should work towards 'a genuine settlement which would decide the long-term and permanent status of Northern Ireland'. More explicitly, the Cadogan Group (1995: 46) asserts '(I)f a genuine and lasting settlement is to be reached, the objective of Irish unity must be shelved'. Inevitably, this means that political nationalism must be the loser in a permanent solution where there are reinforced guarantees of minority rights and 'new cross-border institutional links' (Kennedy 1995: 34).

The implication here is that the 'permanent solution' will not be attained by negotiations or agreement with nationalists and republicans. Rather it is to be achieved by a recognition of unionists' national rights and the suppression of any opposing national rights. The suppression would be legitimate because it would be coercion based on the wishes of a Northern Ireland majority.

A 'final' solution is then presumably to be based on making permanent the current verdict of the 'democratic' majority in Northern Ireland and by convincing the British government to live up to its responsibilities. This proposed strategy removes from the ambit of negotiations the central issue at the heart of the unionist–nationalist conflict over the last 30 years (and the preceding 50). The British constitution is sacred – to be guarded, not traded, least of all with 'hereditary enemies'. As O'Neill (1994: 375) observes, such a view 'incredibly presupposes that the real source of conflict, whether NI should be British or not, is not an issue at all'.

But there is an irony in the unionists' illusory quest for permanence – in pursuing it they achieve a certain paradoxical form of permanence – the permanence of impermanence and insecurity. It is not in their power to compel nationalists to shelve their aspirations or to force the British government to see Northern Ireland as fully part of the British homeland. In rejecting serious negotiations over what constitutes a 'democratic majority', and 'democratic consent', unionists are forced to

rely primarily on their power to resist change than on rational discourse with their opponents. In adopting this stance, 'new' and 'old'
unionists confirm what unionism has offered historically to Ulster
Protestants, an identity rooted in permanent beleaguerment. It is a
bleak vision of history – in Oliver MacDonagh's (1983: 14) words, 'one
of endless repetition of repelled assaults, without hope of absolute
finality or of fundamental change in their relationship to their surrounding and surrounded neighbours'.

Conclusion

'New unionism' is not a single homogeneous entity. It contains many
ideological strands woven together in often contradictory ways as is
common in other nationalisms. Certain continuities and internal con-
vergences are apparent, however. Clearly, there is much that is not new
in the 'new unionism', even if its political and economic context has
altered substantially over the last three decades. Its proponents continue to operate with highly exclusivistic and traditional notions of
national sovereignty which seems somewhat archaic in the context of
globalisation and European integration (see Anderson in this volume).
Most significantly, however, their understanding of a democratic settlement seems to be that it should be unionists or the 'greater number'
within Northern Ireland who should determine the terms of any agreement, not the electorate of Ireland nor of Britain and Ireland, nor even
of the United Kingdom itself to which unionists profess their allegiance.

The linked themes explored in this chapter confirm that the 'new
unionists' see themselves as agents of a superior political idea in
Ireland – an idea of the British state and citizenship – which they claim
to be integral to their own survival as a distinct community. This idea,
and consequently their identity, is non-negotiable – a stance which
bodes ill for a negotiated settlement in Northern Ireland. Much of the
commentary analysed above implies that the 'new unionists' see themselves as *in loco parentis*, teaching Irish nationalists the merits of
citizenship in the UK (e.g. Aughey and McCartney), economic lessons
(Birnie and Roche) and even the advantages of harmless expressions of
Irish culture suitably detached from power and the state. The tone of
the argument is sometimes patronising and marked by a kind of insecure supremacism which is antithetical to genuine dialogue. Although
secular in content, the form of some of the commentary recalls Ulster's
long tradition of theological disputation about abstract, almost meta-
physical, ideas and principles.

'New unionists' consistently demand from Irish nationalists that
which they reject for themselves: the separation of culture from politics
and the shelving of their national rights and aspirations. They demand
that dialogue and negotiated settlements be secondary to rights of the
'democratic majority' in Northern Ireland to assert its will and ultimately to democratically coerce those who refuse to accept it. Yet it is

precisely the status of this 'democratic majority' which is at the heart of the Northern Ireland conflict. They assert that unionist consent be a pre-condition of negotiations rather than accepting that the nature of unionist and nationalist consent is something to be worked out in negotiations. In these negotiations, unionists must contemplate forms of Irish unity, just as nationalists must contemplate forms of union with Britain.

The 'new unionist's' claim to be anti-nationalistic obscures their own linking of politics and culture in a form of British nationalism which is undergoing a revival in Britain. Refusal to acknowledge this nationalism is a means of denying any equivalence between unionism and nationalism in Ireland. While British nationalism certainly differs from its Irish counterpart in many respects, it is nationalism none the less. It is scarcely a persuasive negotiating strategy to assert that the 'new unionists' unacknowledged nationalism is better than the Irish version, more humane, more tolerant, more advanced and more civilised. Of course, the promulgation of British nationalism promises allies in Britain who assert that the integrity of the British state and its sovereignty are sacred and non-negotiable. Even here, however, there is insecurity, in that British nationalists in the rest of the UK are not fully convinced that Northern Ireland is part of the British homeland.

'The new unionism' may be interpreted as a means of coming to terms with the crisis of unionism in the wake of the upheavals of the last 25 years and as a means of communicating the unionist case more effectively, especially in Britain. Whatever its successes and limitations in these respects, it shows little signs as yet of being a means towards a constructive, negotiated settlement of the Northern Ireland conflict. Of course, new or traditional unionism is not the only barrier to genuine negotiations. The critique of the 'new unionists' advanced here does not imply that they are the sole obstacle to successful negotiations. The British and Irish governments as well as nationalists and republicans also have major responsibilities to create the conditions for constructive dialogue. Without unionists, however, that dialogue will count for little. The 'new unionists' may be more secular, articulate and middle-class than the Orange Order, the loyalist paramilitaries or Paisley's supporters, but, so far, they show few signs of being more constructive in their approach to political dialogue and agreement.

Acknowledgement

I would like to thank James Anderson and Joe Ruane for their comments on this chapter.

Notes

1. Some of these writers have no party affiliations and claim to be 'pro-union' rather than unionist. Their common project, however, is to mount an intellectual defence of the Union. This has been increasingly influential in the Ulster Unionist Party. They distinguish themselves from the thinking of loyalist paramilitaries who have a different tactical approach to negotiations. It is unclear, however, if loyalist paramilitaries have a substantially different analysis of the 'Union' from the writers considered here, although they have occasionally mooted a form of Ulster independence. The latter has been supported by attempts to create a separate Ulster nationalism and 'myth of origin' (see Adamson 1974) which should be distinguished from 'new unionism' as a form of British nationalism. The 'new unionist' writers also adopt a largely secular and 'rational' stance generally distinguishing themselves from the politics and ideology of the Orange Order and Paisley's Democratic Unionist Party.
2. Membership of the Cadogan Group includes Arthur Aughey and Paul Bew (political scientists), Graham Gudgin and P. J. Roche (economists), Dennis Kennedy (journalist) and Arthur Green (retired civil servant).
3. Trimble was here responding to a book by a party member (Porter 1996) that urged the replacement of both cultural and liberal unionism by a 'civic unionism'.

Postscript

The above chapter was written in early 1997. This postscript is being added just after the conclusion of the recent Northern Ireland Agreement and prior to the referendum on the Agreement in both parts of Ireland on 22 May. After May 1997, a whole series of factors combined to bring pressure to bear for a negotiated accommodation – the renewal of the IRA cease fire, the election of the Labour government in the UK, the successful devolution referenda in Scotland and Wales, and close co-operation between the Irish, British and US governments in pressing for a settlement. The development of the 'peace process' to date provides an interesting retrospect on the 'new unionist' ideology discussed above.

Two main strategies were adopted by unionists from the outset. The first, followed by Ian Paisley and Robert MacCartney (one of the progenitors of the 'new unionism'), sought to undermine the talks from without by boycotting them. The second, largely identified with the Ulster Unionist Party (UUP) led by David Trimble, involved participation in the talks with a view to narrowing their scope. The UUP tried with considerable success to limit the areas on which they had to negotiate with the SDLP while refusing throughout the process to negotiate directly with Sinn Féin or to participate in the media discussions with them.

The relative success of the UUP strategy is reflected in the content of the Agreement. Control over taxation and policing remains firmly under UK government control. North–South bodies have a limited remit and will be accountable to a unionist-controlled Assembly. The UUP have also insisted that Sinn Féin will not be eligible for executive seats in the Northern Ireland administration prior to 'decommissioning' of weapons. Finally, the Irish government has agreed to hold a referendum to abolish its constitutional claim to Northern Ireland.

The strategy of the unionists *vis-á-vis* the talks reflects many of the themes of the 'new unionism' discussed above. They have held consistently to the view that British claims to sovereignty over Northern Ireland are non-negotiable. The Agreement specifies that nationalists will share limited power with unionists although it leaves open the question of whether republicans will be included. At least, this commits the UUP to some working compromises with the SDLP in some areas of regional administration. The Agreement incorporates an 'equality agenda', promises on early release of prisoners and a proposed commission on police reform. While the Anglo-Irish Agreement has been set aside, it has been subsumed into a new intergovernmental British–Irish conference dealing with matters not devolved to the new Assembly.

Many of these elements are unpalatable to unionists and unionist critics can draw on 'new unionist' ideology in suggesting that the Agreement uses the 'Union' against unionists by making Northern Ireland more 'Irish' than 'British'. Arguably, the Agreement is most heavily influenced by the political ideology of the SDLP, led by John Hume, although the SDLP may not be its political beneficiaries. Pro-Agreement unionists are arguing that it is 'permanent', rather than 'transitional', i.e. that it consolidates Northern Ireland's place within the UK. Sinn Féin support for the Agreement, on the other hand, is predicated on it being transitional to a united Ireland. Both governments, the SDLP, and the smaller parties including the two Loyalist parties, emphasise its objective in building cross-communal co-operation in the short to medium term.

The ideology of the 'new unionism' analysed above may be used either to oppose or support the Agreement. Certainly, a detailed interrogation provides little evidence that unionists have prepared themselves to accept a genuine compromise settlement with nationalists. In this sense, the 'new unionism' provides as much ammunition to Paisley and McCartney as it does to Trimble and other pro-Agreement unionists.

The 'new unionist' attempt to advance a 'positive' case for the Union made unionists in general susceptible to the intense pressures for an accommodation. While they have sought with some success to limit the scale of the accommodation, it has become clear that the slogans of 'not an inch' and 'no surrender' were not sustainable in the context of the 'peace process'. It remains to be seen if any new structures arising from the Agreement will be able to undermine gradually unionists' tradition of 'insecure supremacism' and their illusory search for 'permanence'. Alternatively, it is possible that the Agreement will be used successfully to exclude Republicans by insisting that they acknowledge military defeat by handing in their weapons. In this, and in other areas impinging on state sovereignty, unionists can call on support from other British nationalists in the UK.

The dense networks of relationships and institutions envisaged in the Agreement do constrain, however, unionists' capacity to determine the way in which the new political structures will work. Much depends also on the role played by the SDLP, Sinn Féin and the British and Irish governments.

It will take a long time before the full implications of the Agreement for unionism become clear. Recalling Aughey's (1995b: 12) stark dichotomising of the options facing unionism, does it mean an accommodation with a new nationalist Ireland and the ultimate 'end of Unionism' (especially the 'siege mentality' on which it rests)? Or, does it reflect change to underpin the constitutional *status quo* and the incorporation of Northern Ireland into a new United Kingdom, which is quasi-federal, multi-national, multi-cultural and European? The latter option is obviously favoured by many 'new unionist' intellectuals. Perhaps the dichotomy is false, however. Both options would seem to mean also a closer incorporation of unionists into a new Ireland, a challenge which most unionist ideologists have not yet begun to contemplate seriously.

CHAPTER 5

Walking backwards into the sunset: British policy and the insecurity of Northern Ireland

Mike Tomlinson

The whole drift of British policy through the present prolonged period of unrest has been to tilt the internal balance in Ireland in favour of the Irish nationalist position.

Clifford Smyth (cited in Pollak, 1993: 187)

I cherish Northern Ireland as part of the United Kingdom and it will remain so for as long as this reflects the democratic wish of a greater number of its people.

Prime Minister John Major, 1995

Introduction

The central purpose of this chapter is to examine the character of contemporary British policy towards Northern Ireland. This is not quite as simple as it may sound, as the above quotes are designed to illustrate. All the parties to the conflict over the past, present and future governance of Northern Ireland – including the British themselves – have sharply differing views on what British policy is, let alone what they would like it to be. This is not just a problem of perception, coloured by political preferences. It is because, as this chapter illustrates, British policy is, of its very nature, profoundly ambiguous about the key questions at issue. The chapter begins by discussing the nature and scope of British policy and then goes on to characterise two of its principal facets, firstly, the deployment of military and police power, and secondly, the approach to the constitutional issue.

A plausible case could be made that, certainly at particular moments of crisis, Britain appears to have *no* policy on Northern Ireland or at least seems paralysed as to what to do. In this view, British 'policy' is more accurately described as cautious crisis management than being informed by a strong sense of aims and objectives. There are times when Northern Ireland Office ministers behave more like absentee landlords than representatives of government with real political authority. Arguably, the contemporary period has strong parallels in this respect with the last great crisis in British/Irish relations whose resolution – partition – many assumed had successfully expelled Irish affairs from British politics for good.

Commenting on the war of independence (1918–21), Lee argues that the British government muddled through and 'lacked any clear-cut political design'. This was not due to the shortage of time or political talent devoted to the issues, but to a lack of thought and decision making:

> the prevailing impression left by British policy in Ireland ... is one of decision makers out of their depth ... The cabinet could not make up its mind on either a war policy or a peace policy. (Lee 1989: 43)

On the other hand, a quick dive into the Northern Ireland Office's internet site soon reveals pages and pages of policies on anything from training to constitutional matters. Far from being absent, policy is all-pervasive and encompassing, and mission statements stretch from the Social Security Agency to the prisons. Much energy has been devoted to convincing international audiences of the beneficial nature of British policies (Miller 1994), as well as to harnessing the support of the Irish and US governments to a particular approach to constitutional and other policy questions. The Anglo-Irish Agreement (1985), the Downing Street Declaration (or 'Joint Declaration for Peace' – 15 December 1993), the Frameworks Documents published in February 1995, and the work of the Mitchell Commission, all testify to this.

This chapter is written from the standpoint that the conflict in Northern Ireland cannot properly be understood without scrutinising the nature of British policies and the central part these play in shaping the conflict. In other words, it follows the analysis of O'Dowd *et al.* (1980) that not only is Britain an integral part of the problem of Northern Ireland, but also that British policy has effects on both class and communal divisions. To those who are relatively unfamiliar with the Northern Ireland conflict, and to many who know it well, this approach will be seen as contrary to the conventional wisdom. Certainly the British government's self-image is that it 'holds the fort', managing the communal tensions as it relates to the internal forces in a well-intentioned and even-handed way. The plausible watch-words of policy are consent, parity of esteem, dialogue, fair employment, developing community relations, and balance. It is not up to Britain what happens in or to Northern Ireland: Britain's political role is simply to convince the parties that the future of Northern Ireland 'is firmly in the hands of the people of Northern Ireland' (Ancram 1995).

This view informs some academic accounts, such as Cunningham's exhaustive description of British policy in the 1970s and 1980s. Britain is portrayed, very largely, as making the 'best of a bad job' ever since it graciously decided to grant home rule to 26 of Ireland's 32 counties (1991: 2). The effective partitioning of Ireland under the Government of Ireland Act of 1920 and the 1921 Treaty, according to this logic, neither flew in the face of the 1918 general election results in which Sinn Féin won a landslide victory, nor denied the right to national self-determination. It was instead a measured – even democratic – reaction to internal Irish political forces. Likewise in the period of direct rule from 1972, the argument runs, British policy has not so much done the pushing as been the pushed:

> Events within Northern Ireland have frequently undermined, and forced reappraisals of, policy. This helps to explain tactical shifts within the same area of policy and changing emphases between different policies over the last twenty years.   (Cunningham, 1991: 252)

The conclusion is that British policy is largely reactive in nature, shaped principally by the overriding goal of conflict management and the twist and turns of political forces within Northern Ireland. But it is not problematic in its own right.

What is British policy?

The first complication in approaching the analysis of British policy, therefore, is that there are serious disagreements over the status of Britain in relation to the conflict itself. On the one hand there is the view that British policy is neutral to the competing claims of unionism and nationalism: in the absence of agreement it is a stabilising and modernising force for good. In some versions, this involves demonstrating that British and unionist concerns are more divergent and 'autonomous' (Bew *et al.* 1995) than key 'nationalist' texts suggest (Farrell 1976; 1983). Britain only becomes a major impediment to progress when it gets drawn into pandering to Irish nationalist aspirations and fails to provide necessary reassurances to unionists that the constitutional status of Northern Ireland will not change (Bew 1995; McGarry and O'Leary 1995: 147). Similarly, the Irish government could become more neutral and less predatory if it supported a referendum to drop Articles 2 and 3 from the Irish constitution.[1] If, on the other hand, the analysis concludes that 'policy patterns of the British state tend to intensify communal conflict in Northern Ireland' (Ruane and Todd, 1996: 229), the clear implication is that changing, reducing or removing the British role altogether provides a better basis for overcoming the conflict than defending the current status quo. It does *not* imply a naive belief that British withdrawal from the North of Ireland provides a simple and painless cure to the conflict, or an easy route to greater equality throughout Ireland as a whole.

The analysis of British policy is surrounded by other complications. Firstly, the literature on Northern Ireland varies enormously in what it regards as the *scope* of 'British policy'. Leaving aside for the moment those 'big boys' books'[2] which tend to champion military solutions, the policy debate is typically couched in terms of constitutional questions, including attempts to construct workable political institutions. In a sense, this 'political science' view of the problem of British policy is both correct and inevitable (O'Leary and McGarry 1993). But, as Gaffikin and Morrissey (1990) point out, it has an obvious drawback in that other types of policies are either not considered or get improperly downgraded in terms of their importance in everyday life and material well-being. Hence, one important strand of policy analysis is to take Northern Ireland as a 'case study' of British social and economic policies (Evason 1985; Ditch 1983; Harris 1991), where the impact of communal divisions and political conflict on the policy area in question are seen as minimal.

There are also particular areas of policy explicitly addressing Catholic/Protestant inequalities, which at times have functioned as a surrogate for *the* political question. These areas, including education, housing, community relations, community development and employment, are mainly discussed in terms of their contribution to social justice and conflict resolution (Smith and Chambers 1991; Birrell and Murie 1980; Cormack and Osborne 1991). They are also assessed for their capacity to achieve change within the confines of Northern Ireland as an entity. In other words, they are often seen as a test of the 'reformability' of Northern Ireland and a measure of just how well-intentioned and 'neutral' Britain really is (O'Dowd *et al.* 1980). Most notably, the politics of employment/unemployment inequalities between Catholics and Protestants intensified in the 1980s and 1990s. Such inequalities, their degree, cause and meaning, became the focus for an increasingly well-organised and powerful Irish-American lobby (Sheehan 1995). Within Ireland, academic debate became publicly hostile and privately litigious, fuelled in part by the considerable research resources put into the strategic investigations of the Fair Employment Commission (and its predecessor) and the government's formal review of the 1989 Act (Gudgin and Breen 1996; Gillespie, N. 1996; Sheehan and Tomlinson 1996; McLaughlin and Quirk 1996a).[3]

One of the criticisms of policy analysis in the economic and social fields, however, is the tendency to ignore the structure of British/Irish relations as a relevant framework. The most obvious (if somewhat instrumental) expression of the debate on this issue concerns the extent to which economic and social policies are deliberately co-ordinated around strategic political and counter-insurgency objectives. But this question is not the fanciful product of conspiracy theory. Not only is policy-making and resource distribution highly centralised in Northern Ireland, it is also co-ordinated within overarching frameworks of conflict management. Referring specifically to economic policy and welfare state provision, Evelegh gives one of the better-known military versions of what is required: 'In a counter-terrorist campaign, the battle runs across every level and every activity of society. Thus the conflict must be seen by Government in terms of co-ordinating the whole social system' (1978: 52; see also Wilkinson 1986). Evelegh's book was published just at the time when Labour Secretary of State, Roy Mason, was arguing vigorously in cabinet meetings for millions of pounds of public expenditure (eventually totalling £78m) to be invested in the De Lorean car plant, intended for West

Belfast. Although a consultant's report advised against the project as being too high-risk and experimental, the cabinet minutes record Mason's thinking as being firmly focused on wider strategic concerns:

'It is of the utmost political, social and psychological importance that the project should go ahead. This would be a hammer blow to the IRA.'[4]

In the 1980s, it became increasingly obvious that if community development and training resources had to go into working-class areas, government policy was to channel them through the most conservative elements within those communities, namely through the Church and the rapidly growing SDLP-voting Catholic middle class. Above all, it was essential to prevent resources getting into the hands of the increasingly well organised Sinn Féin, a policy formalised by Douglas Hurd in 1985 and which became known as 'political vetting' (Rolston and Tomlinson, 1988: 119–31).

It is important, then, not to underestimate the contribution of social and economic policies to the dynamics of political conflict. Such policies and their application have 'vital material, symbolic and strategic meanings' (Ruane and Todd, 1996: 175) and cannot simply be separated from wider political identifications and aspirations. Nor should this argument be confused with the idea that the achievement of greater material equality between Catholics and Protestants in Northern Ireland will necessarily make the British constitution and policy any less British – from either the nationalist, republican, loyalist or unionist viewpoints. Lastly, social and economic policies may be brought to bear on micro-political objectives as well as contributing to the government's often-stated number one policy objective: the defeat of terrorism.

The second main problem in the analysis of British policy is one of recognition. How do we know a policy when we see one? Levin's discussion of 'policy' is critical of many academics for failing to capture those features which are most relevant to the politicians and civil servants who make and implement policies. The intentions, language, commitments and statements (including legislation) of the policy-makers should be the starting point for identifying what policy is, he argues (Levin 1997: 24). Action is another matter: measures taken to implement policy may well produce outcomes which differ from stated objectives. While this approach – including the distinction between policy and action – is usefully grounded amongst the 'key players', it only becomes workable in relatively transparent political systems, or applicable to past situations once crucial papers, memoirs or other records become available. Nor does it give much credence to alternative constructions of what policy is, held by those on the receiving end of policy.

The clearest statement of the intentions of British policy are to be found in the annual Command Papers on expenditure plans and priorities. While the Northern Ireland programme does not cover the costs of the military presence[5] or the considerable resources devoted to

Northern Ireland affairs by the Security Service (see Tomlinson 1995a: 10), it still provides a useful guide to government spending rationales in other areas, including the RUC and prisons. For many years, the top spending priority has been 'Law and Order', whether this has been rhetorically justified in terms of defeating terrorism or dealing with public order. In effect, this budget line has had a blank cheque for the duration of the current conflict. Spending on the RUC, prisons and the Northern Ireland Court Service, around three-quarters of which may be regarded as conflict-related, increased in real terms by 45 per cent in the eight years from 1984 to 1992 alone (Tomlinson 1994; KPMG 1995). This was at a time when the prison population was falling (Tomlinson 1995b) and the threat from republican groups, certainly within Northern Ireland itself if not in Britain, was declining.[6]

The second public expenditure priority, 'economic growth', cannot be pinned down so easily. But as Bradley observes, 'most Northern public expenditure is oriented towards health, social welfare, education, etc., rather than towards policy domains that bear more directly on industrial development' (1996: 84). The third priority – and relative newcomer on the scene – is the much criticised TSN: 'targeting social need'. Introduced in 1991, TSN exists more on paper than in terms of measurable changes in expenditure programmes and priorities. In fact, one study (McLaughlin and Quirk 1996b) found little evidence that TSN had influenced departmental spending and decision making. Most departments were reluctant to monitor their expenditures in terms of Catholic/Protestant or social class impacts. This was confirmed in another study which found that the Department of Agriculture for Northern Ireland seemed to have ignored the policy altogether: 'it hands out money to rich farmers, while cutting subsidies to poorer ones and it entirely ignores the impact of its programmes on the Protestant and Catholic communities' (McGill 1996: 57). The inescapable conclusion was that, far from being an expenditure priority, TSN was 'a principle awaiting definition, operationalisation and implementation' (McLaughlin and Quirk 1996b: 183).

The integrated nature of the Northern Ireland Office's mission is not in any doubt. In the 1996 plan, for example, the government sought to achieve its aims through 'a co-ordinated and coherent approach to all aspects of Government policy which recognises that the fundamental political, security, and economic and social problems of Northern Ireland are closely inter-related' (Treasury 1996: 17). But as with other stated intentions, such policies may not have obviously measurable effects. On the other hand, there are many examples where certain outcomes are only too evident and yet the existence of coherence and 'policy' is vigorously contested and denied. Nowhere is this clearer than in the 'law and order' field. As Asmal comments in the context of 'shoot-to-kill-policy', discussed more fully below,

> Policies can be formally adopted and documented, or they can be inferred
> from a pattern of practice, even though the existence of a policy is officially
> denied.   (National Council for Civil Liberties 1993: 24)

Indeed, as Cohen (1993) argues, a 'spiral of denial' is very common throughout the world as governments and state agents firstly deny the human rights abuse, secondly re-construct the event as something else (e.g. self-defence) and thirdly, go on to say that what happened was entirely justified in terms of 'national security' or the 'defeat of terrorism'. Denial, therefore, is an *expected feature* of policy in the 'law and order' field (see also McLaughlin 1996).

Enforcing British rule

State killings

The intensity of the struggle over the future of Northern Ireland, and dissatisfaction with past and present, is most evident in the willingness of republican and loyalist groups to challenge the state's monopoly of the legitimate use of violence. Responses to republican and loyalist violence have provided some of the most important and contentious policy debates of the contemporary period. It is particularly difficult to assess 'counter-terrorist' policies with regard to Northern Ireland because they are notoriously inaccessible, often deliberately so. In fact secrecy, in the interests of 'national' security, is one of the core characteristics of great swathes of British policy in Northern Ireland. At one level, policy principles are simply stated: democracy versus violence; the rule of law versus criminal conspiracy. In Wilkinson's words,

> One of the largely unsung achievements of the British Army and the Royal Ulster Constabulary has been to prevent an escalation to civil war with all its attendant death and destruction. The corollary is that the security forces have succeeded in 'buying time' for the politicians to find a stable political framework acceptable to the overwhelming majority of both the Protestant and Catholic communities. (1996: 12)

The reality has never been quite that simple. Leaving aside the point that no stable political framework has been constructed in 25 years of direct rule from Westminster, Wilkinson's analysis assumes that there is a widespread consensus on counter-terrorist measures and that the latter have little or no impact on politics within Ireland or further afield.

The 'shoot-to-kill' controversy is a good example of how British policy may increase political antagonisms and polarisation. The first accusations that there was a 'policy' for state forces to kill people in certain circumstances arose following 'Bloody Sunday', the day (30 January 1972) when the British Army opened fire on an anti-internment march in Derry, killing 13 people outright (a fourteenth man died shortly afterwards) and wounding another 13. It was one of the defining moments of the Northern Ireland conflict (Newsinger 1995). All street demonstrations had been banned with the introduction of internment without trial the previous August, and less than two months after Bloody Sunday the unionist government, which had ruled continuously since partition, was stood down. James Callaghan,

Labour Home Secretary at the time the decision was taken to deploy troops in August 1969, recalls that he had asked his officials as early as the winter of 1968 to draw up contingency plans for a British takeover of the Stormont government (Callaghan 1973). In so doing, they had referred to section 75 of the Government of Ireland Act 1920 which claims British jurisdiction over Ireland in the following terms: 'Notwithstanding the establishment of the Parliaments of Southern and Northern Ireland . . . the supreme authority of the Parliament of the United Kingdom shall remain unaffected and undiminished over all persons, matters and things in Ireland and every part thereof.' On this basis the judgement was that no special legislation was required to institute direct rule from Westminster.

For some months, the army had been looking for an opportunity 'to give the Bogside a bloody nose' (McCann 1992) and to challenge the area's 'no-go' status. The plans for controlling the demonstration that day were certainly sensitive enough for Prime Minister Heath to know about them (Winter 1997: 15). Once the killings had taken place, an inquiry was unavoidable. It was already a public scandal that some internees had been tortured by means of five special in-depth interrogation techniques practised on colonial subjects elsewhere (McGuffin 1974; Compton Report 1971). While Lord Chief Justice Widgery's inquiry into Bloody Sunday (Widgery Report 1972) was widely regarded as a whitewash at the time, it was not apparent until a quarter of a century later just how anxious the government had been to legitimise the army's role. Many of the relevant tribunal documents deposited in the Public Records Office are 'closed' for 75 years. In 1995, however, human rights activist Jane Winter did discover the minutes of a meeting between Heath, Widgery, 'truth economist' Robert Armstrong and Lord Chancellor Hailsham,[7] held in Downing Street just two days after the killings. The meeting was clearly more concerned with narrowing the scope of the inquiry, the safety of soldier witnesses, where the inquiry should be held and where Widgery should stay, than with establishing the truth. At one point Heath is recorded as saying to Widgery 'It had to be remembered that we were in Northern Ireland fighting not only a military war but a propaganda war' (Mullan 1997; Statewatch 1995a). Not only did the Widgery tribunal ignore the testimony of more than 700 eyewitnesses, it rewrote some of the testimony it *did* accept such as that given by BBC correspondent David Capper (*Irish Times* 19 March 1997). One of the soldiers who witnessed the shootings had his own eyewitness account for the tribunal torn up and was ordered to sign a prepared statement. This soldier also revealed that in a briefing prior to being sent to Derry, a senior officer had told his unit: 'Let's teach these buggers a lesson – we want some kills tomorrow.' On the day itself, soldiers had made widespread use of 'dum dum' bullets (which are banned under the Geneva Convention) (*Sunday Business Post* 16 March 1997). In retrospect it is clear that the Widgery Report was determined to ignore the role of a group of soldiers who were firing from high up on the old city walls and who may have been responsible for up to six of the killings.

In addition, 'the army had snipers operating in the attic of derelict buildings just outside the old City Walls' (Mullan 1997: 61).

By the 1980s, much of the British Army's experience in counter-insurgency techniques had been passed on to the Royal Ulster Constabulary (RUC) as Northern Ireland-based forces were brought to the fore and the idea of 'police-primacy' was promoted. Under the latter, the British Army supposedly supports the RUC, and the Chief Constable is the upholder of the rule of law. In the early 1980s, following six killings by the RUC (see below), accusations grew that covert forces – the RUC's E4A unit, the army's 14th Intelligence Co. and the SAS – were operating a shoot-to-kill policy, with top RUC sources apparently confirming this to the *Irish Times* in December 1982 (Jennings 1988). Whatever the political explanation for the policy – the electoral success of Sinn Féin after the deaths in 1981 of ten republican prisoners on hunger strike being the foremost – the legitimacy of the killings was strongly disputed. Police primacy may be the theory, but in practice the army was responsible for over 300 of the 357 killings carried out by the police and army between 1969 and 1993 (Sutton 1994). Similarly, the SAS has killed considerably more people than the RUC's covert units (Tomlinson 1995c: 445).

The courts became a particular focus for establishing the intentional nature of the killings, but with very limited success. During the 1970s, nearly a dozen soldiers from British regiments (i.e. excluding the Ulster Defence Regiment, for which see below) had been prosecuted for murder but all of them had been found not guilty. The courts were generally accepting the notion that when soldiers kill, they do so in self-defence; and it was not difficult for soldiers to convince the courts that they had acted in good faith in this respect. In one case (in 1977), described by Jennings as 'one of the most overt indications of the judiciary's sympathy for the security forces' (1988: 112) Justice Gibson argued that 'shooting [by the security forces] may be justified as a method of arrest'. In 1984, a British Army soldier (Private Thain) was found guilty of murder for the first time by a Northern Ireland court.[8] An incidence of 'joyriding' in 1990 in West Belfast led to a second murder conviction (of paratrooper Lee Clegg) after members of the Third Battalion of the Parachute Regiment opened fire on a stolen car, killing two of the occupants. The 'good faith' of the soldiers was challenged in this case by a policeman who witnessed the soldiers fabricating an injury to make it appear that the car had struck one of them (the policeman was on foot patrol, escorted by an eighteen-strong army guard). A few months after the killings, the leader of the Labour opposition at the time, Neil Kinnock, visited Northern Ireland and was photographed in the Paratroopers' Officers' Mess laced with Christmas decorations. Embarrassingly for Kinnock, the photocall revealed an additional decoration: a large cut-out of the joyriders' car, complete with bullet holes and a caption, parodying car TV commercials at the time and celebrating the shootings. It read, 'Vauxhall Astra. Built by robots. Driven by joyriders. Stopped by A COY III'. Above the Astra was the loyalist version of the Ulster provincial flag.[9]

A further twist to these convictions was that in both cases, the soldiers were released from prison very soon after receiving their mandatory life sentences – they spent little more than two years in prison. Both re-joined the army. Secretary of State Mayhew's release of Lee Clegg (the second of the cases mentioned above) came after the rejection of a legal appeal by the House of Lords which was followed by a chauvinistic 'release Clegg' campaign by elements of the British military establishment, ably assisted by the British popular press. Clegg continued to contest his conviction and in February 1998 the Northern Ireland Appeal Court ruled his conviction unsafe and ordered a re-trial. A campaign by the Scots Guards Release Group has been less successful, however, failing to secure the release of Guards Fisher and Wright given life sentences for a murder which took place in North Belfast in 1992.

The two most publicised shoot-to-kill episodes were the RUC killings in 1982 which led to the Stalker Inquiry, and the SAS operation in Gibraltar in 1988. In November and December 1982, six people were killed in three different covert operations in the Armagh area. At one level, this episode illustrates the capacity of the RUC to resist investigation, but at another it reveals the power of the executive (in the form of the Secretary of State for Northern Ireland and other members of the Cabinet) to prevent unwelcome information emerging in court hearings. In the much-criticised practice of the 'police investigating the police', Stalker, as Deputy Chief Constable of Manchester, was appointed to investigate the Armagh killings in 1984. Initially, the Secretary of State had resisted calls for an inquiry and this had prompted an international group of lawyers to set up their own investigation. This unofficial inquiry concluded that,

> an administrative practice has been allowed to develop in Northern Ireland, by which killings in violation of the European Convention and the International Covenant are at least tolerated, if not actually encouraged. Undercover units of the British Army and the RUC are trained to shoot to kill even where killing is not legally justifiable and where alternative tactics could and should be used. (Asmal 1985: 134)

The government's inquiry did not proceed smoothly. Two years after his appointment, Stalker was removed from the inquiry just three days before he was due to submit his final conclusions, on the grounds that he had links with criminals and had misused a police car (Stalker 1988; Statewatch 1995b). Stalker had been obstructed in a number of ways, including the refusal of the RUC Chief Constable and MI5 to release a tape recording of one of the incidents. Nevertheless, from the government's point of view, the inquiry (completed by Sampson) was a success in that it found no evidence of a shoot-to-kill *policy*. It did conclude, however, that eight police officers had conspired to pervert the course of justice and that prosecutions should follow. The Attorney General at the time, Sir Patrick Mayhew (later Secretary of State), thought otherwise, concluding that the 'national security' would be better served if the officers concerned were kept out of court. Three policemen had already been through the courts in 1984 on murder charges pertaining to the first three killings but had been acquitted in another celebrated judgement of Justice Gibson, in which he praised the officers for their 'courage and determination in bringing the three deceased [unarmed] men to justice; in this case, to the final court of justice.'

While these cases and inquiries proceeded, the inquest into the deaths was postponed on several occasions. The inquest itself became the focus of legal battles over the release of information and the appearance and questioning of witnesses, and over the years the issuing of 'public interest immunity certificates' became routine.[10] The inquest into the killings of all six men was eventually abandoned in 1995 by the fifth coroner to preside over the case, following his unsuccessful attempt to have documents and tapes gathered in the course of the Stalker/Sampson inquiry presented in court.

The Gibraltar killings of three IRA members carried out by the SAS put the shoot-to-kill issue into the European Court of Human Rights. For the first time in its history, the court made a ruling on the 'right to life' which in effect drew the line as to the circumstances in which it is legitimate for a state to take life in the wider interest of protecting the public from unlawful and life-threatening violence. The British government lost the case mainly on the grounds that the deployment of the SAS 'automatically involved shooting to kill' by definition and training. In Defence Minister Portillo's memorable jingoistic statement to the Conservative Party's annual conference, shortly after the court's ruling,

Around the world three letters send a chill down the spine of the enemy: SAS. They spell out a clear message: Don't mess with Britain.

The court's decision unexpectedly overturned a previous Commission judgement by a narrow 10–9 majority. The ruling argued that the decision to deploy the SAS inevitably meant using operatives who 'lacked the degree of caution in the use of firearms to be expected from law enforcement personnel in a democratic society, even when dealing with terrorist subjects'. The claimed 'arrest operation' should have been much more carefully controlled by the authorities (European Court of Human Rights 1995).

There has been little corroboration of the ECHR's view, or of a shoot-to-kill *policy*, from the spate of biographies of undercover soldiers and police officers published recently (for example, Bruce 1995: Rennie 1996; Holland and Phoenix 1996). But occasionally, the official denial of shoot-to-kill is punctuated by journalistic claims to the contrary. According to one former intelligence officer, special operations against suspect IRA members were co-ordinated by the Joint Communications Unit Northern Ireland, comprising MI5, the SAS and senior army officers:

> There was certainly a shoot-to-kill policy, but it was a strictly sectarian one. Soldiers would not kill Loyalist terrorists because we saw them as being on the same side as us ... The decision would be made by Pat 1 [codename of the MI5 controller for Northern Ireland] to seek final permission from the Government ... But nothing was ever given in writing for security reasons.
>
> (McCashin 1997: 2)

It is clear that not all killings by state forces can be regarded as the outcome of an intentional shoot-to-kill policy. The killings of 'joyriders', for example, or plastic bullet victims (whether in the vicinity of riots or not), do not have the degree of forethought and planning that goes into an undercover operation or SAS ambush. But even in the former cases, there is evidence of an official culture of secrecy, tolerance, support and (if needs be) leniency for the perpetrators.

Intelligence and collusion

There have been many other controversies over 'security policies' in Northern Ireland, involving police powers and practices, aspects of prison regimes and the work of intelligence agencies. The most important strand running through all of them is the argument over the political purposes and effects of counter-terrorist policies and 'public order' policing. Although the idea that the police and army are 'neutral', are 'caught in the middle', and have no allegiance other than to the law is repeated *ad nauseam*, the doctrine enjoys limited credibility. And on occasions, the doctrine has been exposed as empty rhetoric, relying as it does on a proper 'separation of powers'. The expansion and normalisation of 'emergency powers' (Hillyard 1987) has so distorted the meaning of the 'rule of law' that human rights lobbyists have been driven increasingly towards international provisions in their attempts to restrain the actions of state forces (National Council for Civil Liberties 1993; Amnesty International 1994). Indeed, part of the problem has been that particular branches of the security apparatus have been seen to operate as 'a law unto themselves'.[11]

The work of the Security Service (MI5), RUC Special Branch and military intelligence units has been the main focus in this respect, as counter-terrorist strategies have become increasingly dominated by routine surveillance, electronic sources and informers. One implication of the ECHR's Gibraltar ruling – however much this was disparaged at the time by the British press and government ministers – is that the authorities have to think very hard about the circumstances in which the SAS is now deployed. All these factors may herald a 'post-shoot-to-kill' strategy in which the 'golden thread of intelligence' is used to intercept bombings and shootings at the planning stage (Weeks 1997). The Lloyd Report certainly adopts this perspective:

> As for *catching* terrorists, I am thinking not only of catching them red-handed after the terrorist incident has occurred, but also, and even more important, of catching them *before* the incident occurs.
>
> (Lloyd Report 1996: xi, emphasis in original)

The extent and significance of intelligence-gathering activities are rarely glimpsed. For instance, although the number of warrants issued for telephone taps each year is published for Scotland and England and Wales, no such figures are available for Northern Ireland, presumably because the bugging of phones is too extensive to admit to without political embarrassment. Occasionally, however, sources are compromised in some way, or wish to 'escape' from their handlers.

Probably the most well-known case is that of Brian Nelson, a member of the loyalist Ulster Defence Association with responsibility for collecting information on possible targets (for other examples, see Bloch and Fitzgerald 1983). After a brief period in the Black Watch regiment of the British Army, Nelson joined the UDA in 1972. Two years later he was given a seven-year prison sentence for the kidnap and torture of a partially sighted Catholic. On release from prison he was recruited by military intelligence in the mid-1970s at a time when there was intense rivalry between the RUC, the British Army and MI5 (Urban 1992; Tomlinson 1993: 92–5). In 1985 he left Northern Ireland after being sickened by the apparent pleasure of one UDA operative who would return from a killing in a state of frenzied excitement (Statewatch 1992: 4). MI5 persuaded him to return to Northern Ireland in 1987 by giving him a £2,000 lump sum and a wage of £200 per week. The Army's Force Research Unit (FRU) (part of the 14th Intelligence Company) reportedly helped Nelson to reorganise and streamline his intelligence files and even helped out by taking photographs of intended targets and premises. In at least 92 cases, the unit had detailed knowledge of who the UDA was going to shoot, including who would actually carry out the killing, when and where. Recently revealed minutes of the FRU/Nelson meetings show how the Army put their well-placed agent to use. The aim was to provide the UDA with profiles of IRA suspects so that the loyalist 'kill all Catholics' policy would be replaced by the targeting of 'known republicans'. One document, dated 3 May 1988, records that under FRU/Nelson influence, 'targeting has developed, and is now more professional'. On 4 August that year it was noted that Nelson's 'appointment enables him to make sure that sectarian killings are not carried out, but that proper targeting of Provisional IRA members takes place prior to any shooting'. (*Sunday Telegraph* 29 March 1998). At least 16 people on Nelson's target list, a list which must have been known to Nelson's handlers, were killed, including a solicitor regarded by RUC interrogators as 'working for the IRA and [who] would meet his end like every other Fenian bastard' (Amnesty International 1994). Nelson was sent to South Africa by the UDA in 1984 to investigate an arms deal.[12] In January 1988 a shipment of 500 grenades, 200 rifles and some rocket launchers arrived and was divided up between three loyalist groups. While the RUC intercepted the UDA's share, the question remains why Nelson's handlers allowed even part of the shipment to get through. As BBC journalist John Ware put it, the South African deal was 'one of the least publicized and biggest intelligence scandals in two decades of Northern Ireland's dirty war' (*Spotlight*, BBC Northern Ireland,

February 1993). It also equipped loyalists to increase their annual rate of killings by ten times between 1985 and 1991.

The reason anything at all is known about the involvement of military intelligence with the UDA at this time is because Nelson was eventually put on trial and given a ten-year prison sentence after pleading guilty to conspiracy to murder and some possession charges.[13] Nelson was arrested during the course of yet another inquiry into the activities of the RUC and army. This was the Stevens inquiry which was established to investigate the leaking of hundreds of intelligence files to loyalist groups in the autumn of 1989. As soon as the Stevens inquiry began, FRU moved to cover its tracks. Nelson was warned that should he ever be questioned by the Stevens team, he was not to reveal his work for the Army. FRU told Nelson to hand over the entire collection of 'P-cards' (summary information on targets for the convenience of UDA assassination squads) in order to conceal Nelson's true role and status. This might have worked but Nelson's fingerprints (which the RUC had from the conviction mentioned earlier) were found on some of the UDA leaked documents collected by Stevens. The inquiry team therefore planned to arrest Nelson at dawn on 11 January. But Nelson must have been tipped off because he fled to England the evening before. That same night at around 11.00 p.m., the Stevens team returned to their offices, located within a secure RUC complex at Carrickfergus. Mysteriously, they found smoke billowing out of their offices. One of the team smashed the glass on the fire alarm, but there was no response. None of the alarms in the building were working. She also tried to telephone for the fire brigade but, astonishingly, none of the telephones were working. By the time the fire engines arrived, many of the vital statements and documents collected by the Stevens team had been destroyed. Stevens reportedly regarded the RUC investigation into the fire, which found 'nothing sinister', as 'a travesty and a disgrace', though this conflict was never made public (*Sunday Telegraph*, 29 March 1998). When Nelson was eventually arrested, he told Stevens that he was an Army agent. The inquiry turned to the Army and requested evidence of Nelson/FRU contact, as well as the suitcase of 'P-cards' which Nelson had given to his handlers. There followed a long and bitter dispute as the Army refused to hand over any documents. Finally, the inquiry team threatened to arrest a number of senior Army officers for the obstruction of justice, at which point, FRU capitulated. FRU may have been given another name after the Nelson episode. Journalist Jim Cusack has claimed that 'senior loyalist sources' have told him that the British Army is once again operating in clandestine fashion with elements associated with the LVF (*Irish Times*, 30 March 1998).

What this episode reveals, then, was a set of relationships between different levels of the security apparatus and loyalist groups. For many years, allegations have been made of 'collusion' between state forces and loyalist groups and, once again, this has led to arguments as to whether this amounts to a 'policy', or is a reflection of the odd rotten apple and things going wrong in the wake of attempts to protect sources (for a rejection of the policy idea, see Bruce 1992). At the Nelson trial, for example, an unnamed colonel 'J' claimed that Nelson played a courageous, life-saving, counter-terrorist role and had provided in excess of 700 reports concerning the targeting of over 200 individuals. Nelson's defence lawyer was less sanguine, however, arguing that Nelson was a victim of an intelligence system which turned a blind eye to criminal activity when it suited and washed its hands of brave heroes when the full extent of intelligence penetration of paramilitary organisations became known. Losing a well-placed source like Nelson, the army argued, meant that it could no longer keep the lid on loyalist killings. Certainly, in the early 1990s (with the new South African arms), killings by loyalist groups doubled compared with the numbers in the late 1980s, but equally, loyalist killings during the 'Nelson era' of the late 1980s were averaging *six times* the killings recorded for 1985. At very least, it has to be recognised that the use of informers or 'agents' provides state forces with choices as to whether they encourage, modify or scuttle such operations. At worst, special units are operating a policy of 'assassination by proxy'.

Practical assistance to loyalist groups has been more basic than in the examples above. Members of the Ulster Defence Regiment (UDR), one source claims, were implicated in more than half the killings carried out by loyalists in the 1980s (Sinn Féin n.d.). The UDR was formed in 1970 on the recommendation of the Hunt Report and it replaced the notorious special auxiliary constabulary, an exclusively Protestant organisation, which had existed since partition. While formally constituted as a regiment of the British Army, the UDR – like the special constabulary – recruited from within Northern Ireland only: indeed, 60 per cent of the 2,440 recruits to the new regiment in March 1970 were ex-Specials. The UDR lasted until 1992 when it was merged into the Royal Irish Regiment (RIR). The UDR's reputation never escaped its origins. Speaking at the launch of the RIR, Lt General Sir John Wilsey admitted that the UDR had a serious image problem: 'now the UDR has not sought to be sectarian, one-sided or filled its ranks with Protestants, but that's the way it turned out' (Statewatch 1991). Between 1985 and 1989, UDR members were twice as likely to commit a crime as the general public. The UDR crime rate was ten times that of the RUC and about four times the British Army rate. By the early 1990s, around 120 members/ex-members[14] of the regiment were serving prison sentences for serious crimes, and 17 had been convicted of murder, including three of the 'UDR Four' whose convictions were later quashed. Three of the four men arrested for the murders of the two Catholic and Protestant friends in Poyntzpass (March 1998) were ex-members of the UDR or RIR. As Ryder (1991: 181–2) states,

> The true extent of subversion and criminal indiscipline within the UDR is a carefully protected official secret ... Ever since the formation of the UDR and the emergence of the first concerns about Loyalist infiltration, the army, the Ministry of Defence and the government itself have gone to considerable lengths to shield the Regiment from embarrassment.

One of the political objectives of 'collusion' has been to influence public opinion and government south of the border. During the Nelson revelations, it emerged that military intelligence had devised 'Operation Snowball', a plan for the UDA to bomb commercial premises in Dublin and elsewhere in the Irish Republic (Statewatch 1992). The particular 'cause' at the time was extradition, the British view being that the Irish authorities were failing to deliver republican suspects. Generating hate for loyalists in the South would stimulate political demands for the extradition of loyalists to Dublin which could then be reciprocated by sending republicans to Belfast.

Another example in which British intelligence agencies appear to have used the threat of loyalist actions across the border to put pressure on the Irish government was in the weeks before the signing of the Downing Street Declaration of December 1993. On 24 November 1993, British customs officers displayed to the press a consignment of 500 grenades, 320 Kalashnikov rifles and two tonnes of Semtex taken from a container ship docked at Teesport, Cleveland. The ship had arrived the previous evening from Gdynia, Poland, having stopped at Tilbury on the way. They were seemingly acting on information from MI6 that the ship was carrying arms bound for the Ulster Volunteer Force in Belfast. The 'find' was initially put across as a big success story both for British intelligence and international co-operation. MI5, MI6 and the Polish security service, UOP, had worked together to track and intercept the weaponry. The Brian Nelson affair showed that British intelligence at best had bungled and at worst had actively co-operated in the re-arming of loyalist groups in the late 1980s. The Teesport operation seemed to show that the intelligence agencies could now be effective, even against loyalists. Oddly, the find was made on the same day that the British government published the Intelligence Services Bill designed to put MI6 and GCHQ on a legal footing for the first time.

The Polish shipment lent substance to warnings over the previous two years from the RUC Chief Constable that loyalists were preparing a major bombing campaign south of the border. Loyalists had indeed issued a statement that they were 'preparing for war'. The prospect of loyalist groups acquiring significant quantities of plastic explosives sent a strong signal to people in the South regarding loyalist opinion. The shipment, if real, also suggested that loyalists were now getting substantial financial backing from middle-class sources – the Nelson weapons deal was a fraction of the cost of this one.

There were other political ramifications. The Polish ship docked at Teesport just days before *The Observer* revealed that the British government had been engaged in secret exchanges with Sinn Féin's Martin McGuinness since 1990, and at a time when there were clear difficulties between the Irish and British governments over the wording of the Joint Declaration, finally published just three weeks later. As one 'security source' stated, 'the Irish know what to expect if the loyalist paramilitaries get their hands on proper explosives. It must have concentrated their minds wonderfully.' (Statewatch, 1994 Jan/Feb).

The customs seizure was greeted with considerable scepticism, however. No arrests accompanied the weapons find, either at the Polish or British end of the operation. Even the London *Evening Standard* was sceptical: 'on the face of it, all that has happened is that Polish government weaponry has been shipped across the Baltic to attend a photocall in Britain'. The evidence began to suggest that Polish and British intelligence had conspired, albeit with different immediate interests, to organise the whole operation.

Irish Press reporter Emily O'Reilly was told weeks later by the Polish authorities that MI5 organised the shipment and its 'discovery' in order to influence the Northern peace process by raising fears in the South of a massive loyalist backlash. A Polish embassy official told her 'the intention was to generate public concern' and 'to make political and public opinion sensitive to the loyalist threat' (*Irish Press* 28 January 1994).

A final example of attempts to influence public opinion in the South through some sort of collusion with loyalists, concerns the worst day of attrocities in the history of the post-1968 conflict. On 17 May 1974, 33 people were killed by bombs in Dublin and Monaghan. The loyalist group involved included members of the UDR and, according to a 1993 *First Tuesday* TV documentary, it was assisted by MI6. The programme argued that the official reluctance to prosecute those involved was based on the fear that they would expose the full nature of British intelligence backing for the operation (Yorkshire TV 6 July 1993; see also Bowyer Bell 1996).

The idea of exerting pressure through 'bombs in Dublin', whether or not seen as the mirror image of the IRA's 'England campaign' from the late 1980s onwards, became common currency amongst arch-unionists and conservatives in the 1990s. During the summer of 1993, a crucial period for the Hume/Adams 'peace initiative', Democratic Unionist MP Peter Robinson openly advocated the bombing of West Belfast and Dublin as an act of 'self-defence'. Shortly afterwards, Norman Tebbit (former chair of the Conservative Party and a close ally of Margaret Thatcher) appeared on Sky TV and stated that the only thing that would force Dublin to give up the constitutional claim on the North was 'when bombs begin to blow in Dublin in the way that they have been in Belfast and London' (Statewatch 1993a).

Partial policing

More generally, the whole stance of the policing effort is to characterise the threat posed by republican and loyalist groups differently and to skew resources accordingly towards the 'principal enemy' of republicanism and the IRA. This policy is openly acknowledged. At the same time as loyalists were cranking up their rate of killing, coming close to that of republican groups (in 1993 loyalists exceeded the republican kill rate), the Secretary of State referred to the IRA as offering 'the main, if not the only threat in Northern Ireland' (Brooke 1992: 2). The Chief Constable agreed with him: 'the principal resources of the RUC are and will continue to be deployed against the Provisional IRA . . . Almost all loyalist activity is reactive to that threat' (BBC Radio Ulster, 20 October 1991). Paul Wilkinson's assessment of 'the current and future threat to the UK from international and domestic terrorism', carried out as part of Lord Lloyd's review of counter-terrorist measures, is likewise instructive of the mentalities shared by the top echelons of the military, judiciary, police and intelligence services.[15] When outlining the 'historical context', Wilkinson appears to identify a very substantial threat when he refers in general to 'Protestant Unionists' – *note*, he is not talking about unofficial loyalist armed groups – as being 'so adamantly opposed to the unification of the island of Ireland under the Catholic-dominated Republic that they are prepared to wage full-scale civil war, if necessary, to prevent it' (Wilkinson 1996: 10). This rather dramatic political assessment, however, dissolves into nothing by the time 'current threats' are discussed. While the IRA, animal rights groups, Scottish and Welsh nationalism, and a range of Arab and other international groups are all included, loyalism is completely ignored. Wilkinson's assessment for the Lloyd Report also has nothing to say about neo-fascist groups.

The observation that 'nationalists still consider the RUC to be inherently anti-nationalist' (Pollak 1993: 61) or that policing is always partial, is typically explained in terms of the fight against terrorism. Impartial and 'ordinary' policing is impossible while the main task of the RUC is to counter republican terrorism: in other words, the perpetrators of violence are the ones responsible for the one-sided nature of policing. The issue runs deeper than this simple 'cause and effect' formula suggests, however, as graphically illustrated by events surrounding the Orange Order march at Drumcree in July 1996. The failure, after four days of confrontation, to uphold a simple decision of the Chief Constable to re-route the march away from a Catholic area, effectively exposed the RUC, the British Army and British government as submitting to the authority of the Orange Order. They demonstrated neither the willingness nor the capacity to tackle the 80,000-strong organisation.

The order had mobilised throughout Northern Ireland during the four-day stand-off, and unionist leaders widely defined the police decision as yet one more milestone along the road of British rejection. They saw the issue in the same terms as described by Orangeman Melvin McKendry in February 1994, 'When will the majority of people living in Northern Ireland realise that while they wish to be British, that the Queen, the Government, and the entire opposition in Parliament don't want them as part of Britain' (Clayton 1996: 187). It was time, once again, to draw 'a line in the sand': in Paisley's words, 'we are here to save Ulster. We are going to win.' In similar tones, the Orange Order's Grand Master, the Rev. Martin Smyth MP, declared, 'There comes a time when if we are breaking the law then we have to suffer the penalty' (Statewatch 1996).

The police allowed thousands of Orange Order supporters to assemble at Drumcree. Elsewhere, roads were blocked, thousands of people were threatened, access to and from Belfast International Airport was closed off, Catholics were burnt out of their houses, businesses were forced to close, and public and private transport was disrupted. The Portadown unit of the UVF shot dead a Catholic taxi driver, an action which contributed to the subsequent shutting down of the unit. In the words of the North Report, Drumcree 'brought Northern Ireland close to anarchy' (North Report 1997). The police response to the protests was widely criticised (Committee on the Administration of Justice 1996). There were many reports of officers standing by while intimidation took place, or of officers claiming they were under orders not to confront protestors and of off-duty officers joining the Orange roadblocks. Other reports suggested that officers were going sick and failing to report for duty, and there was evidence of a virtual mutiny in support of the Orange Order in some areas. Parliamentary questions requesting information on the numbers of RUC officers in the Orange Order and the numbers failing to report for duty during the 1996 Drumcree confrontation have drawn evasive answers, but the government has admitted that the average number of days off per RUC officer rose from 3.15 days in the April to June quarter to 3.61 in the July to September quarter. These figures suggest that almost 1,600 officers, or 12 per cent of the force, were not available for duty during the Drumcree crisis.[16]

The Drumcree standoff, according to Gordon Lucy, demonstrated to rank and file Orangemen 'what they had always intuitively known. The Orange Order was "a sleeping giant" which could accomplish great things when roused from its slumber' (Lucy 1996: 59). RUC officers are permitted to be members of the order (and the Masonic Order) but actual numbers are unknown (a figure of 2,000 has been suggested). At least two members of the Police Authority are in one or other of the Loyal Orders and it appears that 13 per cent of all RUC members killed during the past 28 years of conflict were in the Orange Order. Some officers have been disciplined for disobeying police standing orders which forbid activities which might bring the force into disrepute – they had participated in an Orange Order parade. So while membership itself is not contrary to regulations, some public manifestations of membership are! (Pat Finucane Centre 1997).

The RUC's partiality in dealing with the Orange Order actions during the four day Drumcree stand-off was confirmed by subsequent events. The apparent relish with which the RUC cleared the Garvaghy road of nationalist protestors once the Chief Constable had reversed the re-routing decision, the 26-hour curfew of a nationalist area in Belfast, and the indiscriminate use of plastic bullets in the days following, particularly in Derry (Pat Finucane Centre 1996), produced an outburst of anger from all shades of nationalist opinion. In an unprecedented attack on the British government's handling of the whole situation, Taoiseach John Bruton when interviewed by the BBC said,

A state cannot afford to yield to force; a state cannot afford to be inconsistent; a state – a democratic state – cannot afford to be partial in the way it applies the law and I'm afraid we have seen all three basic canons of democracy breached in this instance.   (BBC News 12 July 1996)

Has British Policy Changed?

So long as there are British troops in Ireland so long will the Orangemen hold out. While they can look to Britain they will not turn towards the South.   Michael Collins, 1921 (1995: 80)

While the above statement was made three-quarters of a century ago, it expresses the key relationship and power behind the constitutional position of Northern Ireland today. Between partition and the collapse of the Stormont government in 1972, the position of Northern Ireland within the United Kingdom was rarely questioned in government circles. If anything, the possibility of a united Ireland receded as the 'free state' moved further away from Britain by declaring a 'republic', and Northern Ireland drew closer to Britain through agreement to finance the welfare state. There had been a critical moment during World War II when the British sought to involve the 26-county Eire in the war effort in exchange for Irish unity, but de Valera's assertion of neutrality and Irish sovereignty meant that the offer was neither tempting nor trusted. Most of the details of the British offer (made in 1940) concerned the war itself – the use of ports, internment of German and Italian aliens, and the supply of military equipment. The British also wanted to see the immediate establishment of a joint north–south Defence Council. In addition, the British government would make a declaration accepting the principle of a united Ireland. It would also give whatever assistance was necessary to a joint committee of the Northern and Southern governments 'to work out the constitutional and other practical details of the Union of Ireland' (Fisk, 1983: 201).

The post-war Labour government's 1949 Ireland Act placed the question of change firmly in the hands of the Stormont regime. There would be no alteration to the status of Northern Ireland 'without the consent of the parliament of Northern Ireland'. Theoretically, there could be an end to partition but, legally, that was now up to the unionists to decide. The next moment for reviewing Northern Ireland's status came with the decision to commit British troops in 1969. While there was some discussion within the British cabinet of pulling out of Northern Ireland altogether (Benn 1989), there was a more immediate and pressing concern. If the troops went in and it became necessary to suspend the government of Northern Ireland, then there was little value to the 1949 Act's guarantee. The August 1969 Downing Street Declaration not only reminded people of the Ireland Act's provisions, but also added the reassurance that 'Northern Ireland should not cease to be a part of the United Kingdom without the consent of the people of Northern Ireland'. The Northern Ireland Constitution Act (1973), which followed the suspension of Stormont, repeated this formula. It included, however, provisions for establishing a power-sharing executive, a devolved assembly and the possibility of an 'Irish dimension'. When the details were thrashed out in the Sunningdale Agreement, the latter took the form of a Council of Ireland which was to have both an executive and a 'parliamentary' tier drawn from the North and South. The agreement was destroyed by the Ulster Workers Council strike in 1974.

The focus on political system-building and relations with the South was then set aside in favour of internal conflict management. The most important development, as already indicated, was the building up of the RUC and other indigenous forces, coupled with a strongly argued policy of 'criminalisation' – the denial of any political content to the IRA's campaign. While, for the British, this period of 'hands on' direct rule represented a marked change from the years of 'absenteeism', it also seemed to be a retreat from the idea that a political settlement required an 'Irish dimension', even if the latter had always been circumscribed by the 'unionist veto'. The 1985 Anglo-Irish Agreement, regarded as a disaster by unionists, re-established a Southern interest in the North in the form of an international agreement (formally lodged with the United Nations) and a permanent secretariat based not far from Stormont Castle. It repeated previous guarantees to 'the majority of the people of Northern Ireland', and sought to set up a devolved government. But it also formalised a basis for regular discussions between the Irish and British governments over a range of policy issues.

No doubt uppermost in Prime Minister Thatcher's mind at the time (she had just survived the IRA's Brighton bombing of the Conservative Party's 1984 annual conference) was the promise of better cross-border co-operation on counter-terrorist matters. The signing of the agreement signalled a growth in security expenditures and an extensive militarisation of the North/South border, as well as an increase in joint security operations (for details, see Tomlinson 1993: 95–98). The agreement also contained two articles covering social and economic affairs.

Progress on internal political arrangements between what were increasingly referred to as the 'constitutional parties' remained elusive. Such rhetoric, and the later coining of the label 'Sinn Féin/IRA', was of course designed to keep republicans, and their growing electoral strength, out of any political process. In many respects, as we have seen, the conflict was worsening in the late 1980s and early 90s as loyalists stepped up their campaign and as the IRA turned its attention to England, threatening the viability of London as the financial capital of Europe (Tomlinson 1995a: 5). During this period, however, representatives of the British government were engaged in secret talks with republicans with a view to securing an IRA cease fire in exchange for a seat at the negotiating table to work out an 'agreed Ireland'. While even in the darkest of days there have always been 'lines of communication' between republicans and the British (Beresford 1987), as well as the better-known instances of 'negotiated cease fires' during the 1970s, the early 1990s 'contacts', as the British preferred to call them, were different, argue Miller and McLaughlin (1996: 422–3). The talks suggested a change of British policy insofar as a 'settlement' was now considered impossible without the involvement of republicans who up to then had been thoroughly criminalised. In a similar vein, Ryan (1994: 161) argues that,

> overnight, the criminal status attached to Irish Republicanism has been dropped and the government has officially declared its indifference towards the future shape and constitution of the British state.

Subsequent events indicate that any changes which may be detected in British policy are still shrouded in a pre-partition view that it is legitimate to thwart Irish self-determination on the basis of unionist (and British) coercion. This notion is at the core of successive re-statements of 'self-determination' for the majority of Northern Ireland when coupled with the extraordinary investment in Protestant-dominated 'security forces' since the mid-1970s.

'Sticky patches' or sticking plasters?

John Major has now adopted an entirely unionist agenda in an attempt to buy unionist votes in Westminster.
> Gerry Adams, 24 January 1996

The peace process has hit a sticky patch at present.
> Prime Minister John Major, 22 January 1997

There is a major contradiction at the centre of the joint declaration of 1993 and it is repeated in *A New Framework for Agreement*. Simply stated, the British government has agreed to the principle of self-determination 'for the people of Ireland alone' (British and Irish Governments 1993: 26), and yet this right will not be recognised if a majority in the North object. In essence, this is no different from previous statements guaranteeing Northern Ireland's status on the basis of what the 6-county majority want, except that the Framework Documents provide a much more elaborate discussion on the possibilities of cross-border co-operation than has hitherto been placed in the public domain. The 'consent' of the unionist majority which is being invoked here has a certain superficial appeal, but no justification in international or humanitarian law is given for why 'Northern Ireland' should be the determining unit of analysis.[17] Furthermore, any changes – including presumably a decision by 'the people of Ireland alone' to unify the country – would be subject to a triple lock of 'safeguards'. As far as the British are concerned they have to be agreed by the political parties in the North, by a majority in the North and finally by the Westminster parliament.

Aside from this problem, there are major weaknesses in the Framework Documents regarding the British view of 'possible arrangements' for the government of the North, which bear directly on the question of sovereignty. These limitations are replicated in the restricted agenda developed by the parties to the talks which commenced in the summer of 1996 and from which Sinn Féin was excluded on the grounds that the IRA had decided to end its cease fire (in February 1996). 'Policing', 'defence' and taxation remain British concerns.

These ambiguities in British policy at the constitutional level are repeated in political practice and in the whole range of policy areas and especially policing. The case can certainly be made that British policy appears to be to secure an agreement over the government of Northern Ireland with the involvement of Sinn Féin – a real settlement is impossible without this. Yet this is hard to believe when the unionist parties, with the exception of the loyalist groups, do not want it and the Major government appeared to be content with the IRA cease fire as an end in itself. Driven by short-term political interests and heavily influenced by 'friends of the union' (such as Lord Cranborne) within the Northern Ireland cabinet committee itself, British policy wavers between an accommodation with Irish nationalism and a desire for victory over republicanism, heavily coloured by personal experience of IRA actions. Just as in the past, the various political and economic interests involved cannot decide between war and peace.

There have been many inquests over the IRA's decision to end its cease fire in February 1996. In terms of British policy, attention needs to be given to the 'mixed messages' which pervade British political practice. At a time when many assumed the loyalist cease fire had already broken down in all but name, loyalists were invited to Downing Street so that the Prime Minister could entreat them not to go back to war 'officially'. Republicans, on the other hand were kept at bay throughout the cease-fire period on the grounds that they had to prove they were at peace by handing in some weaponry. The same problem pervades the distinction or lack of it between Sinn Féin and the IRA. Legally, there is a clear distinction between the IRA as a proscribed organisation under the Northern Ireland (Emergency Provisions) and the Prevention of Terrorism Acts, and Sinn Féin, a political party that participates in elections and whose elected representatives play an active role in the day-to-day affairs of district councils (even if they often have to withstand orchestrated personal abuse – shouts, spitting, whistling – in the council chambers), and who regularly mingle with civil servants. But the 1990s coupling of the two as 'Sinn Féin/IRA' ideologically excludes Sinn Féin the political party from 'constitutional politics' and is a direct denial of political citizenship for its supporters.

Similarly, official policy is that 'parity of esteem and treatment' should prevail in the government's dealings with 'both traditions in Ireland'. As has been shown, this appears to be an impossible objective, particularly in the law and order field. If this was a serious aim, the very constitution of the power of the state – police and military forces – would be at the heart of the political process. Instead, these questions are kept at a distance. Just as Secretary of State Mayhew continued to assert throughout the IRA's cease fire that there was nothing wrong with the RUC, so too his Security Minister slapped down arguments about amnesty and early release by saying 'there are no political prisoners'.

On occasions, minor changes are quite pathetically represented as 'responsive measures' in the construction of peace. Yet none of the forty 'security initiatives' which the British government claims to have made in response to the cease fire up to November 1995 (Northern Ireland Information Service 1995), including 'berets worn instead of helmets', resulted from political talks or were the product of explicit agreement. In this sense the peace process 'owned' nothing of substance and remained at the level of word games and 'gestures' of uncertain status. Equally, it was open to the government to both claim to foreign audiences that prisoners were being released under the Northern Ireland (Remission of Sentences) Act, while denying that the new rules were connected to the 'peace process': they simply brought Northern Ireland in line with the rest of the UK.

Even when more serious initiatives are taken, such as the review of anti-terrorist legislation jointly commissioned by the British Home Secretary and Secretary of State for Northern Ireland (Lloyd Report 1996), the result seems to be to strengthen the hand of those who favour a 'security' rather than 'political' response to the Northern Ireland conflict. This review was designed to examine the need for anti-terrorist laws, assuming a lasting peace in Ireland but taking account of other threats to the UK. Nevertheless, its central recommendation is that the UK requires permanent legislation, incorporating two recommendations at the top of the RUC's shopping list. The first of these is the legalisation of the use of telephone taps as evidence in court and the second is the introduction of the Italian-style 'pentiti' law of 1980 which allowed substantial reductions in sentences to those supplying evidence against their former comrades. A further recommendation is that courts should be obliged under the law to give tougher sentences in the case of 'terrorist offences', potentially a significant departure from the policy of 'criminalisation' or treating political offenders as ordinary criminals. Such recommendations are almost certain to find their way into the existing 'emergency' legislation (Tomlinson 1997).

In conclusion, British policy at every turn is characterised by ambiguity and contradiction. It is both contingent and consistent. It promises change with one hand and denies the possiblity of progress with the other. Britain plays honest broker but remains the power in the land. Nevertheless, it is possible to detect a gradual, if uneasy, shift in British policy towards an accommodation with Irish nationalism and away from the goal of defeating militant republicanism. As yet, however, British governments have failed to bring their power to bear in such a way as to sever support for unionism or to challenge the latter's ultimate power base within Northern Ireland's security forces.

Postscript

I believe in the United Kingdom. I value the Union ... none of us in this hall today, even the youngest, is likely to see Northern Ireland as anything but a part of the United Kingdom ... Unionists have nothing to fear from a new Labour government ... The government will not be persuaders for [Irish] unity.

Prime Minister Tony Blair, Belfast, 16 May 1997

The union has undoubtedly been weakened ...

Martin McGuinness, Sinn Féin Ard Fheis, 18 April 1998

Immediately following the election of a Labour government in May 1997, most political attention was focused on 'Drumcree 3' and the prospect of another stand-off between the Orange Order and the RUC. The British government, in consultation with President Clinton and Taoiseach John Bruton, was, however, anxious to reinvigorate a talks process from which Sinn Féin, in the absence of an IRA cease fire, was expressly excluded under the Northern Ireland (Entry to Negotiations, etc.) Act 1996. Although the talks had made very little progress *without* Sinn Féin (and the SDLP and Alliance Party were no longer participating in the parallel Forum) the formal position of both Conservative and Labour governments was that they preferred all parties to be involved in talks, notwithstanding the position of Paisley's Democratic Unionist Party *never* to sit at the table with Sinn Féin. By May 1997, Sinn Féin had demonstrated its growing electoral strength in both the Westminster and local council elections and the IRA campaign, until the shooting of two policemen in Lurgan, had been wound down to such an extent that a *de facto* cease fire appeared to be in place; but Sinn Féin remained barred from the talks. On the other hand, loyalist groups were engaging in murder and military actions (mainly under the breakaway label of the Loyalist Volunteer Force) while the loyalist political parties remained at the talks table.

The original sticking point for the Major government had been 'Washington 3', the condition that the IRA should demonstrate that the 1994 cease fire was 'permanent' by surrendering at least some armaments. Only then would Sinn Féin be permitted to engage in 'exploratory talks' with government. Blair dropped this condition. Sinn Féin would be allowed into the talks within six weeks of a renewed IRA cease fire and decommissioning of arms would be considered in parallel with talks, as recommended by the Mitchell Report (1996). In a letter to Sinn Féin MP Martin McGuinness sent early in July, the Northern Ireland Office addressed other points concerning 'confidence building' measures (*Irish News* 18 July 1997).

The IRA duly declared another cease fire and Sinn Féin leaders commented favourably on the 'new attitude' of the Labour government. At very least, British policy appears in the short term to have undergone a style change and has clearly lowered the hurdles for Sinn Féin's entry to negotiations. The new style is both a reflection of New Labour's consensus-building, pragmatic one-nationism – forged in Britain from nearly two decades of radical Conservative rule – and of the prevailing mentalities of the Northern Ireland Office. The former was summed up by Blair's view that a solution can be found 'if there were good will on all sides, and a little give and take, understanding and reason' (*Hansard* 9 July 97, col. 930). As Lee points out, however, such comments are largely irrelevant in the context of Northern Ireland, an entity established on the basis of conflict politics, not consensus politics. Britain can never be part of the solution, he states, while presiding in Olympean detachment above the impossible, irrational, unreasonable, conflicting Irish factions … [but] The main reason Britain *has* to be a major part of the solution is because Britain is a major part of the problem' (Lee 1997: 16).

Remarkably, the talks produced an agreed document on 10 April 1998, even though throughout the negotiations, the Ulster Unionist Party delegation refused to talk to Sinn Féin. Regarding constitutional issues, the shape of the Belfast Agreement is very much in keeping with the Framework Documents discussed earlier. The British and Irish governments have agreed to change their constitutional laws to incorporate the 'principle of consent'. A new 108-seat Assembly will be set up in the North with legislative powers over 'non-devloved' matters. This will operate on a system of parallel or sufficient consent which means that moderate unionists and nationalists will have to co-operate to get anything done. The 'government' of Northern Ireland, aside from the important powers retained by the Northern Ireland Office, will be represented by a First Minister (unionist), a Deputy First Minister (nationalist) and an Executive Committee of 12 ministers who will be chosen by individual parties according to party strength in the Assembly (the d'Hont system). The First Minister and Deputy (and any relevant ministers) will participate in a North/South Ministerial Council along with the Taoiseach and relevant ministers from the South. The council has a time limit to produce a programme of cross-border and 'all-island' work. The assembly and the North/South Council stand or fall together: under the Agreement, one cannot work without the other. In addition to these Ireland-based bodies, there is to be a British–Irish Council, involving representatives from Scotland, Wales, the Isle of Man, the Channel Islands, Northern Ireland and the British and Irish governments. The two governments have also set up a permanent 'British–Irish Intergovernmental Conference' (replacing the arrangements under the Anglo-Irish Agreement) to continue discussions of security and other 'non-devolved' issues.

The Agreement includes a number of matters already signalled by the British and Irish governments for action, including the incorporation of an expanded European Convention on Human Rights into Northern Ireland law via a Bill of Rights. The Irish government will ratify the Council of Europe Framework Convention on National Minorities, implement enhanced employment equality and equal status legislation, and establish a Human Rights Commission. A similar body will be set up in the North and the two Commissions may establish a joint committee. The Agreement anticipates that the British will establish a unitary Equality Commission for the North to replace the Equal Opportunities Commission, the Fair Employment Agency, the recently set up Commission for Racial Equality (NI) and the Disability Council. The Agreement contains several clauses on economic development and the targeting of social need, and there are eight specific points concerning the promotion of the Irish language.

In terms of this chapter, some of the most interesting parts of the Agreement concern the military, the RUC and prisons. Under 'security' the British undertake to 'make progress towards the objective of as early a return as possible to normal security arrangements in Northern Ireland, consistent with the level of threat and with a published overall strategy'. No firm undertaking is given as to when the 'published overall strategy' will appear, but when it does, it will cover 'the removal of security installations; the removal of emergency powers' and a reduction in troop numbers and deployment 'to levels compatible with a normal peaceful society'.

Apart from statements of aspiration and intent, what the document actually proposes on policing is the setting up of an 'independent Commission' which will be 'broadly representative with expert and international representation among its membership and will be asked to consult widely and to report no later than Summer 1999'.

The Maze Prison could be closed within two years because the Agreement commits the Irish and British governments to 'an accelerated programme for the release of prisoners, including transferred prisoners, convicted of scheduled offences ... or similar offences'. The British scheme involves increasing remission for fixed-term prisoners by 15 per cent (to 65 per cent). The text continues 'In addition, the intention would be that should the circumstances allow it, any qualifying prisoners who remained in custody two years after the commencement of the scheme would be released at that point.'

In summary, the Multi-Party Agreement consists of two principal streams. Firstly, there is the range of 'non-devolved' matters – arguably the most important aspects of sovereignty, such as taxation, the NI budget, rights issues and law, order and security – which the British government retains control of and always intended to modernise as political and other conditions prevailed. This first stream will continue to proceed with or without the backing of popular consent, and will continue to involve regular co-operation and consultation with the Irish government through the now permanent British–Irish Intergovernmental Conference. The second stream involves a network of institutions and policies, including the new Assembly, the North/South Ministerial Council and the British–Irish Council. The Agreement interlocks these institutions and policies in an attempt to bind together moderate nationalist and unionist political forces. It also makes participation in the Executive, the reform of policing and prisoner releases, all conditional upon continuing cease fires, and decommissioning, though unionists are concerned that this is ambiguous in the wording of the Agreement.

What is unclear at the time of writing is whether the document represents agreement and consensus, or merely a pause in the argument. There is much in the Agreement which is open to interpretation and contest, and the British approach to a whole range of policy issues will be central to the way unionists or nationalists progress under the new institutional arrangements. The real and immediate challenge for British policy remains the dismantling of a security apparatus in which past governments have invested vast material and ideological resources.

Notes

1. Article 2 of the Irish constitution states that 'The national territory consists of the whole island of Ireland, its islands and territorial seas'. In similar fashion to the Basic Law of the Federal Republic of Germany prior to German re-unification, Article 3 makes it clear that 'pending the reintegration of the national territory', laws passed by the Dáil (the Irish parliament) apply to the 26 counties only.
2. This is an adaption of the title of Mark Urban's (1992) book on the covert war against the IRA. 'Big boys' is a term used by the British Army's Special Air Service regiment but it is used here to denote the broad genre of memoirs and biographies of anyone who has been engaged in special anti-IRA operations (e.g. Rennie 1996; Holland and Phoenix 1996; Bruce 1995).
3. During the passage of the 1989 Fair Employment Act, the government gave an undertaking to review progress within five years.
4. Normally covered by the 'thirty year rule', the cabinet papers were ordered to be produced in a US court as part of the legal action surrounding the role of Arthur Andersen auditors in the De Lorean collapse. Thatcher apparently thought the 'gull-wing' sports car produced by De Lorean was 'rather dashing'. In February 1981, a cabinet minute similarly noted, 'we cannot settle this on commercial grounds alone. The De Lorean venture has become something of a symbol for HMG's commitment to Northern Ireland' (*Daily Telegraph*, 17 August 1996).
5. The costs of the British Army's presence in Northern Ireland is borne on the Ministry of Defence budget.
6. The IRA was responsible for 93 killings in 1979 and 39 in 1986; after a rise to 70 in the following two years, numbers once more declined to 40 in 1992.
7. *Irish Times* journalist Conor O'Clery recalls that when he asked Hailsham in the mid-1970s 'what effect it had on British government policy when Irish-American politicians like Ted Kennedy called for reforms in Northern Ireland, he angrily slapped his hand on the table and retorted, "Those Roman Catholic bastards! How dare they interfere!"' (O'Clery 1997: 39).
8. Two other soldiers were given life sentences in England in 1981 for two notorious 'pitchfork murders' committed in 1972 in County Fermanagh. The irony of these convictions is that they only came about as a result of the intensive police operation to identify the 'Yorkshire Ripper'.
9. The traditional Ulster provincial flag shows a red hand placed on a shield in the centre of a red cross on yellow background. The loyalist version of the flag replaces the shield with a six pointed star with a crown on top, all on a white background.

10. The principle of 'public interest immunity', or what used to be known as 'Crown privilege', has existed in British law since the nineteenth century. It provides for the non-disclosure in court of documents and key witness identities when these would compromise 'national security'. In practice public interest immunity is usually asserted by the Secretary of State for Northern Ireland (or other ministers) signing a certificate claiming public interest (see Statewatch 1993b).

11. Two former intelligence operatives have provided ample evidence of 'dirty tricks' which were not only out of view of government, but in some cases were directed at ministers and against the (Labour) government itself. See Holroyd with Burridge (1989) and Foot (1990).

12. At the time, the apartheid South African regime was interested in acquiring blueprints of missile technology produce by the East Belfast company Shorts.

13. Nelson's trial might have revealed much more about collusion between loyalists and official forces had the prosecution not dropped 15 charges, including two of murder.

14. Ryder (1991: 182) points out that 'With a regularity that implies that it is standard practice, the UDR connections of accused soldiers have been suppressed in the courts ... When [UDR] soldiers get into trouble they are frequently forced out of the Regiment at the earliest opportunity.'

15. See Appendix A of the Lloyd Report (1996) which lists those who attended a special 'inquiry seminar' in June 1996. The list includes RUC Chief Constable Ronnie Flanagan, Director General of MI5 Stephen Lander, General Sir Michael Rose, the Legal Adviser to the Foreign Office Sir Franklin Berman and Douglas Bain, Director of the Northern Ireland Office's Terrorist Finance Unit.

16. This calculation is based on the assumption that all of the extra 'days off' reported in the July–September quarter occurred during the five-day period of the Drumcree standoff.

17. There is the argument that, because the 1985 Anglo-Irish Agreement defines self-determination in terms of Northern Ireland only and is lodged as a bilateral agreement with the United Nations, then this constitutes the international legal position.

Part Two

Spaces, Structures and Struggles

CHAPTER 6

Rethinking national problems in a transnational context

James Anderson

Intensified globalisation and European integration have already stimu-
lated some 'rethinking' of the conflict between Irish nationalists and
unionists. It is, however, typically one-sided and sometimes grossly
exaggerated thinking, particularly in its popular and potentially most
influential forms. A federal 'Europe of the Regions' or a 'European
super-state' – whether propagated as a 'post-nationalist' ideal by liberal advocates, or as a 'Europhobic' warning about the threat to
'national sovereignty' – are ideologies which misinterpret contemporary trends. The very processes of transnational integration can
reinvigorate traditional national allegiances, whether to an Irish or a
British state. On the other hand, while notions of 'postnationalism' are
wishful thinking, conservative attempts to insist that nothing has
changed, or that sovereignty defined in traditional territorial terms
remains sacroscant, are perhaps even more misleading. The spatial
organisation of politics is indeed being changed by globalisation, particularly in the European Union (EU), and especially since the
establishment of the Single European Market (SEM).

Fresh thinking is certainly needed. Reality is changing, and the
stalemated national conflict is not solvable within the traditional
nationalistic terms of reference which are shared by Irish nationalists
and by unionists both in Ireland and Britain. Irish unionists, apparently believing their own propaganda about 'British betrayal' and
inexorable 'nationalist advance', may feel that their cause is lost in the
long run, but they find that rethinking their basic position is literally
'unthinkable'. Nationalists have shown more creativity, though that is
not saying much in the circumstances. There is indeed more onus on
them to come up with fresh ideas and strategies – it is mainly they who
want to change an unsatisfactory and still unionist status quo – though
they also need to resist wishful thinking.

Contrary to apocalyptic notions about 'the death of the nation
state', conflicts of national sovereignty and nationalism are not about
to disappear. Their underlying assumptions are, however, becoming

increasingly problematical. Exclusive forms of state sovereignty and politics based on 'national' territory are in some respects being transcended. Thus, the prospects for a significant recasting of exclusive territorialities in Ireland through North–South institutions seem better than in the 1920s, or even the 1970s, which saw the failure of previous attempts to 'bridge' the border with a 'Council of Ireland'. Such 'bridging' would puncture the pretensions of exclusive sovereignty which are at the nub of the conflict. Taking 'national sovereignty' and 'nation state' as unproblematical was always deficient for imagining a solution and it is now becoming even more so. There are disagreements over what 'sovereignty' means, even whether it is still relevant, at the end of the twentieth century, and there is a growing awareness that if the national conflict is to be settled a rethinking of territorial sovereignty is essential. This would be 'emancipatory' in the sense defined by Ruane and Todd (1996), to the extent that it 'dismantles' the ideological and material structures which reproduce the conflict.

Drawing on earlier research (eg., Anderson 1994, 1996; Anderson and Goodman 1995, 1996), this chapter discusses how the conflict and North–South relations might be rethought in a more transnational context. Based on critiques of nationalism and international relations theory, it outlines how national problems might begin to be solved by rethinking them theoretically (Section 1), empirically (Section 2) and politically (Section 3).

As Northern Ireland amply testifies, the nationalist theory of 'sovereign independence' and 'national self-determination' generally promises more than it can ever deliver. The 'realist' and 'liberal' theories of international relations which tend to inform party politics and government policies are also deeply flawed (Section 1). Empirically, the trends towards transnationalism have to be kept in perspective, but they are opening up new possibilities for a settlement based on North–South institutions and 'parity of esteem' for Northern nationalists, as first envisaged in the joint 'Framework Document' published by the British and Irish governments back in February 1995 (British and Irish Governments 1995). Such institutions are also necessitated by the quite separate economic dynamic of the Single Market which points to the creation of a single, unified 'all-Ireland' economy (Section 2).

However, though the time may be ripe, actually establishing adequate institutions, and achieving a settlement based on them, will require fundamental changes from the sorry saga of nationalistic posturing by party politicians and political mismanagement by the two governments. Both governments have pandered to the mistaken notion that a solution can be achieved without impinging on traditional sovereignty. Both also seem to think that a settlement can be reached by an electoral majority within the territorial framework of Northern Ireland, operating through the normal party political channels of representative democracy. Against this, there are strong grounds for believing that much more imaginative and proactive strategies by the two governments and others are required. Mainstream party politics reflects entrenched sectarianism and suffers from decades of 'one party' unionist rule followed by more than two decades of colonial-style 'direct rule' from London; and – the really crucial point – the conflict is not amenable to 'normal' democratic resolution precisely because what is at issue is Northern Ireland as the territorial framework for democracy. Both the framework and the forms of democratic decision-making need to be rethought, to include a wider electorate and participatory democracy as well as the normal representative variety. Bringing the necessary political pressure to bear will require political mobilisation around a variety of *non*-national issues which have generally been 'crowded out' by the all-consuming nationalisms. Perhaps paradoxically, non-nationalist mobilisation is just what is needed to defuse the national conflict and give substance to the idea of 'emancipation' (Section 3).

1 Rethinking theoretically

Theories of nationalism and international relations are important not only for observers trying to understand the conflict but also for the participants. Remembering J. M. Keynes's quip about anti-theoretical 'practical' people actually being under the spell of some long-dead theorist, we can note that the doctrine of absolute territorial sovereignty beloved by unionists, including the fundamentalist Protestant Ian Paisley, was invented, ironically enough, by a sixteenth-century Frenchman who wanted to solve the problem of religious civil wars in favour of Catholic monarchy.

Nationalism's flawed ideal

The modern territorial state incorporating this sovereignty doctrine was a pre-condition of nationalist theory and practice. State territorialisation involved formal sovereignty over everything, secular and spiritual, being 'bundled' together into territorial 'parcels' called 'states', and later 'nation states'. The transmutation of royal sovereignty into 'national sovereignty' and 'national self-determination' was central in the development of popular democracy. Nationalism links historically and culturally defined territorial communities, called 'nations', to political statehood, either as a reality or as an aspiration. Nations and states are specifically *territorial* entities – they explicitly claim, and are based on, particular geographical territories, as distinct from merely occupying geographical space which is true of all social activity (Anderson 1986: 117). The nationalist ideal is that the two entities should coincide geographically in *nation states*: the nation's territory and the state's territory should be one and the same, each nation having its own state, and each state expressing the 'general will' of a single, culturally unified nation.

The ideal of each nation freely exercising its right to self-determination in its own sovereign, independent nation state has a powerful democratic appeal, and especially where that right is denied by imperialistic neighbours or colonial powers. But nationalist theory promises to deceive. In practice, nations and states often fail to coincide, frequently leaving sizeable 'national minorities' on the 'wrong side' of state borders. The happy spatial coincidence of cultural community and political sovereignty is rarely achieved in reality. Attempts to make reality fit the ideal have often had unhappy, indeed tragic, consequences, with nationalism implicated in some of the twentieth century's worst atrocities such as so-called 'ethnic cleansing'. Furthermore, even where the ideal of geographical coincidence is approximated, democracy is often sadly lacking. Nationalism is 'two-faced' in several respects: forward-looking but also backward-looking to an often mythical or invented past; and divisive at the same time as it is unifying. It brings together different groups and classes in a political–cultural community defined as 'the people' or 'nation', but it simultaneously separates out different 'peoples', thus fuelling conflicts between nations and between states, or at the very least impeding transnational co-operation. And the limited unity it offers around 'the national interest' often serves the interests of dominant social groups and classes, rather than 'the whole nation'.

Far from approximating nationalism's flawed ideal, Northern Ireland is the result of a succession of failures in nation-building and in state-building, both from a British nationalist and an Irish nationalist viewpoint, though this formal symmetry masks great inequalities. British nationalism was state-sponsored and its development was, according to its leading historian Linda Colley, 'heavily dependent . . . on a broadly Protestant culture, a massive overseas empire,' and recurrent war with France (Colley 1992, 6). But Ireland, more Catholic than Protestant,

> was never able or willing to play a satisfactory part in this Britishness . . . cut off from Great Britain by the sea . . . it was cut off still more effectively by the prejudices of the English, Welsh and Scots, and by the self-image of the bulk of the Irish themselves, both Protestants and Catholics.
>
> (Colley 1992, 8 and 322–3)

Irish nationalism, by contrast, originated as an 'anti-state' movement inspired by the republican ideals of the French Revolution, and it is in principle anti-sectarian (even if some of its adherents have not always lived up to this in practice). 'The Society of United Irishmen' – committed to 'breaking the connection with England, the never-failing source of all our troubles', and to the explicitly anti-sectarian objective of replacing 'Catholic, Protestant and Dissenter with the common name of Irishman' (sic) – was mainly initiated by Belfast 'Dissenters' or Presbyterians and established in 1791. But it was defeated militarily and politically by the British state and by Ireland's ruling class of Anglican landlords who had sponsored the explicitly sectarian Orange Order, instituted in 1795, for just this purpose. Ever since then, Irish unionism has relied on anti-Catholicism for popular mobilisation. Its failure to retain control of the whole of Ireland resulted in partition and a Protestant-dominated Northern Ireland in 1921. But by the same token, this caused Irish nationalism to fail in its objective of gaining control of the whole island. Preserving Northern Ireland's built-in Protestant majority has been unionism's 'territorial imperative', and one which has been sharpened by the recent increase in the size of the Catholic minority from about 35 per cent in 1971 to around 42 per cent in 1991 (see Anderson and Shuttleworth 1994). While Northern Irish unionism is increasingly distanced from an over-arching British identity – declining in Britain with the weakening of its formative influences such as the empire and Protestanism (Colley 1992, 8) – the Northern unionists do get support, as we shall see, from an influential right-wing Tory rump of British nationalists.

National conflicts such as Northern Ireland's are essentially about national sovereignty defined in traditional territorial terms, and the failure or impossibility of achieving nationalism's ideal. Where people with conflicting national allegiances are intermingled in the same territory, their conflicts are likely to lead to problems of political deadlock, or violence, or both. Hence the attractions of redefining sovereignty, but also the dangers of vesting inflated hopes in transnationalism.

Approaches to transnationalism

Here the three most important theoretical perspectives are conservative 'realism', liberal 'functionalism', and Marxist-influenced or 'neo-Marxist' approaches (see Brown 1992). 'Realism', the dominant theory of international relations, shared by right-wing Tories and unionists, rests on a traditional reading of state sovereignty as absolute. It sees civil society as primarily 'state-contained' society, and relations between societies as subordinate to, and dependent on, political relations between states.

In many respects the liberal 'functionalist' perspective on international relations developed as a 'mirror-image' opposition to the dominant 'realism'. States are created by civil society, to further the needs of society, rather than the other way around; transnational integration is primarily a matter for civil society, and is facilitated by avoiding the contentious 'high politics' of state sovereignty. Some 'functionalists' suggest that globalisation and increased international interdependency are making the nation state and nationalism redundant, an argument echoed in recent years by some Irish nationalists, most notably John Hume, leader of the North's Social Democratic and Labour Party (SDLP) (Kearney 1988). Societal pressures are shifting governance away from states towards 'world regions' such as the EU, and states are becoming just one of many sites of political life. Hence 'functionalists', unlike the 'realists', emphasise globalisation and avoid the 'territorial trap' of assuming that 'state' and 'civil society' are necessarily co-terminous (Agnew 1994). But they tend to exaggerate political change and see it as occurring because of relatively smooth, almost harmonious changes in civil society, implying that the obstacles to smooth transnational integration are simply anachronistic state structures.

These very sketchy depictions of 'realism' and 'functionalism' must be qualified by explicit recognition of their 'neo' versions. With the rise of multinational corporations and transnational organisations like the EU, 'realists' had to come to terms with the fact that states were not the only important international actors; but they did so by arguing that states remained the most important actors, and that states were actually strengthened rather than undermined by a supporting web of transnational institutions. Hence, for 'neo-realists' the EU is first and foremost an inter-governmental organisation, primarily serving state interests. Similarly, 'neo-functionalists' propagating transnationalism came to acknowledge, not only that states cannot easily be side-stepped, but also that they can be crucial as positive agents of international integration. This should start with the 'low politics' of economic co-operation, but the process will call for the further development of transnational political structures, as in the EU.

These 'realist' and 'functionalist' perspectives are criticised from a Marxist-influenced or neo-Marxist standpoint on international relations which emphasises that civil societies and states are all interconnected sites of conflict and struggle, an approach more attuned to the contradictory nature of international developments. As Rosenberg (1994) has demonstrated, 'realism's' fixation with state sovereignty, and its sharp 'inside/outside' dichotomy between 'internal' and 'external' affairs, is based on the specifically capitalist separation of supposedly 'non-political' economics from the 'political' realm of states and sovereignty. In class-divided societies, subordinate social classes and other groupings resist exploitation or oppression, and to do so they have to challenge existing political arrangements and present their own alternative agendas for social organisation and state action. They may resist or seek to change the nature of integration in the EU, for example, while seeing that it opens up new needs and new possibilities for class solidarity and for a broader democratisation through transnational 'movement politics'. In principle, and sometimes in practice, such developments question the separations of 'national' and 'foreign', and of 'politics' from supposedly 'non-political' economics; they challenge the legitimacy of the states' system and highlight its authoritarian character in maintaining the capitalist order (Gill and Law 1989; Hirsch 1995). Thus, in this perspective there is no possibility of the smooth transition from nation states to transnationalism envisaged by 'functionalists'; but nor is the state preeminent as in 'realism'. Instead, political change is seen as emanating from struggles between dominant and subordinate groups and classes. Their conflicts, which have generally been contained within states, will increasingly spill-over and inter-mingle as different groups increasingly make common cause across state borders.

The different perspectives lead to different visions of North–South integration. When unionists and Tories oppose cross-border institutions as infringing British sovereignty and being merely an unstable transition to full Irish sovereignty over the North, they argue on 'realist' grounds. In the 'realist' perspective inter-state integration must lead to the dominance of one or other state, one nationalism at the expense of the other, as reflected in the 'zero-sum' terms of unionist political rhetoric. Either Northern Ireland is absorbed into a Dublin-run all-Ireland republic as traditionally nationalists have hoped and unionists have feared; or, alternatively, as unionists have unconvincingly speculated, the Irish Republic is re-absorbed into the British-dominated ambit from which it tried to escape in 1921.

On the other hand, when nationalists see EU integration and its erosion of state sovereignty as leading to Ireland's re-unification they reflect 'functionalist' influences. The 'apolitical' notion that North–South integration is mainly an economic matter which can be left to civil society, without any need for border-straddling state institutions, was a central element of the mainly Southern and ineffectual 'technocratic anti-partitionism' (Lyne 1990) which developed from the 1950s. Its professed hope that joint membership of the 'European community' would solve the national problem has a 'post-nationalist' equivalent in the hope that regional identities in the EU might replace nationalist ones (Kearney 1997).

In failing seriously to address the need for North–South institutions, there has in fact been collusion between 'realists' and 'functionalists'. The former wish to separate 'politics' from 'economics' in the hope of preserving political sovereignty as sacrosant, while the latter think that integration would be facilitated if the contentious 'high politics' of sovereignty could be avoided or down-played.

But sovereignty, far from being sacrosant, has already been substantially altered by EU integration; and far from being avoidable, it remains the nub of the conflict in Ireland. This is implicitly recognised by the two governments in their essentially 'neo-functionalist' proposals for North–South institutions, but critics taking a 'Marxist' or similar oppositional perspective would go much further. They would argue for the actual implementation of these proposals and for their extension – partly on the grounds that direct state management and encouragement is essential for North–South integration because the economics of civil society are closely entwined with the state in both parts of the island. Beyond that, they would also see the need for political movements to challenge class domination and social oppression North and South on a mutually supportive, if not immediately all-Ireland, basis. Integration could stimulate new popular pressures for a democratisation in Ireland as a whole, creating more political room for economic, social and cultural issues which, especially in the North, are often distorted or sidelined by the all-consuming antinomies of the national conflict. Despite their potential for democracy and *non*-dependent development (Munck 1993), cross-border politics tend to be stifled by the national conflict. Emancipation from its stalemated confines will only be achieved through struggles on an island-wide basis which include class, gender, environmental and other *non*-national issues.

The stalemate is directly related to nationalistic 'realist' perspectives and the peculiarly archaic British conception of sovereignty as a territorial absolute and the exclusive and indivisible preserve of the 'Crown in Parliament' – in reality the Westminster government of the day. This encourages the 'zero-sum' approach which precludes any solution in Ireland short of the all-out but unattainable victories both 'sides' have traditionally sought. In fact the supposed 'zero-sum game' is really a *negative*-sum game' in which the majority on *all* sides lose. The unionist assertion of exclusively British territoriality has been a pyrrhic victory, the financial costs of which are mainly borne by the increasingly alienated taxpayers of Britain. In theory the unionists have a 'winner takes all' form of sovereignty, but most of the supposed 'winners' are actually losers, with working-class Protestants as well as Catholics bearing the brunt of the conflict. Hence the necessity of rethinking sovereignty and territoriality. If the non-coinciding reality of nations and states falls tragically short of nationalism's ideal, and changing reality to fit the ideal is either impossible or not worth the cost, clearly it is the ideal which should be changed.

2 Rethinking empirically

Contemporary transnationalisation provides the empirical basis for changing the ideal, contrary to the 'realist' perspective, as Susan Strange admonished a 'realist' in a memorable article title, 'Wake up Krasner! The world has changed!' But there is also a danger of exaggerating the change – we must avoid the trap of simply 'mirror-imaging realism'. Sovereignty in the EU is being redefined, and the chances of a settlement based on North–South institutions which would 'bridge' exclusive sovereignties are being increased. However, the changes are limited and uneven. They do not offer any automatic solutions, and their impact on Ireland depends on how people in Ireland and the wider 'powers that be' respond.

Globalisation and 'Europeanisation'

The nation state ideal, always deficient as a guide to political action, has become even more so with the increased transnationalisation of the last two decades. The search for alternatives is at once more pressing and more plausible. But the North and South of Ireland coming together harmoniously as two regions of a 'postnational' federal EU super-state is only the bogeyman of 'realists' and the pipedream of 'functionalists'. Glib notions of a 'borderless world', an 'end of territorial sovereignty', or a European identity replacing national ones, are actively misleading. Rumours about 'the death of the nation state' are greatly exaggerated (Anderson 1995). The EU is not about to transform itself into a federal state, 'postnational' or otherwise. The contradictory processes of globalisation can actively stimulate nationalism at the same time as calling for transnationalism. John Hume repeats that what is important are 'people not territory', but unionists, not surprisingly, are suspicious of a 'postnational' regionalism which, rather than delivering Northern Ireland as a separate autonomous region of the EU, seems to be interpreted as promising the traditional nationalist demand of Irish unity. The choice of 'people' rather than 'territory' could be spurious for the two are not unconnected. Hume may believe that 'The day of the nation-state is dead and gone'. 'But I haven't had mine yet' retorts Bernadette McAliskey, the prominent socialist republican (O'Connor 1993: 371).

On the other hand, as argued in more detail elsewhere (e.g. Anderson 1996), globalisation is shifting the ground under established political concepts and arrangements. Federalisation to a 'Europe of the Regions' misinterprets contemporary transnationalisation, but John Hume's exaggerated political rhetoric is tapping into an emerging EU reality. Non-territorial or functionally-defined political communities are growing in importance (see McGrew 1995), and, of all world regions, the EU has the most developed forms of transnationalism, especially since the advent of the Single Market (SEM) in the late 1980s. European integration is strengthening sub-state regionalism and it is encouraging a more 'fine-grained' region-to-region integration across state borders, including the Irish border, as distinct from simply state-to-state co-operation (Anderson and Goodman 1995).

However, a number of qualifications are necessary in assessing the possible implications for Ireland. Firstly, the 'unbundling' of state sovereignty is limited: it affects different state activities very unevenly and is most marked in the sphere of economic development. While state territoriality is becoming less important in some fields (e.g. financial markets), for many aspects of social, cultural and indeed political life, the state is still the main spatial 'container'. Secondly, although a new political form, the EU itself is still territorial, and in many respects traditional conceptions of sovereignty remain dominant, whether exercised by the member states or by the EU as a whole. Thirdly, the EU's 'democratic deficits' are at least partly due to the diffuseness of its 'shared' or 'overlapping sovereignty' and the relative powerlessness of its central parliament (see Kuper 1996; Goodman 1997).

Thus, the foreseeable political reality is likely to be a complex mixture of conventional and new or hybrid forms at different spatial scales, with territorial and non-territorial types of community and authority co-existing and interacting. Territorial sovereignty and states will remain important, but increasingly the political stage has to be shared with other new, or newly important, 'international actors'. The case against exclusive territorialities has been substantially strengthened and with it the need for innovative politics beyond the confines of existing states.

North and South in the EU

For Ireland, the main implications of European integration could be improved possibilities of escaping 'zero- and negative-sum games'; or the potential losses and gains foregone from failing to do so. In particular, the SEM has introduced an important new economic dynamic into North–South relations which, in combination with 'parity of esteem' for Northern nationalists, could conceivably facilitate a political settlement.

But, again, some qualifications are in order. For instance, the UK's and the Irish Republic's joint membership of the European 'Common Market' did not 'dissolve' the national conflict or the Irish border, as the 'technocratic anti-partitionists' had hoped. Indeed, it initially led to greater divergence between North and South as the two states reacted very differently to European integration; and it could quite conceivably do so again, if for instance London and Dublin respond differently to monetary union. Hopes of 'European' salvation were in fact grossly inflated, if not an excuse for a lack of pro-active policies (Anderson 1994).

However, despite the unrealistic hopes and indeed the party political 'sectarianisation' of EU issues for local consumption in the North, the present hopes (and fears) vested in 'Europe' are not entirely fanciful. In some important respects it is a new situation. The EU with its SEM is now much more integrative than previously. The unionist adherence to the traditional British conception of absolute sovereignty is even more out of line with the current reality of a substantial 'sharing' or 'pooling' of sovereignty across the EU.

Furthermore, although not always admitted, constitutional developments in Northern Ireland already impinge on a strict definition of 'absolute and indivisible' Westminster sovereignty. A majority in Northern Ireland could now hypothetically take the region out of the UK if it so wished, a right not granted to any other part of the state (e.g. Scotland – where there could conceivably be a majority in favour of actually exercising that right). 'Westminster orthodoxy' is also breached when Irish nationalists and unionists appeal to external authorities for support, whether it is to the Irish Republic, the EU or the USA. The 1985 Anglo-Irish Agreement gave another state, the Irish Republic, a limited consultative role in the affairs of Northern Ireland. Furthermore, full British–Irish sovereignty in the sense of joint London–Dublin authority over Northern Ireland (O'Leary *et al.* 1993) was considered as a policy option by the British Labour Party; and some such extension of the AIA remains a possible option if the unionists try to sabotage direct North–South (i.e. *Belfast*–Dublin) institutional arrangements.

However, the SEM now constitutes the most important new dynamic behind North–South integration. The threat of Ireland's further peripheralisation due to stiffer competition from the stronger continental economies in the SEM has led to widespread calls for greater political and economic co-operation between North and South. On both sides of industry, in both parts of Ireland, minds have been concentrated wonderfully on the need for economic co-operation, a pooling of resources and policy co-ordination across the island.

The peripheralisation threat, likely to increase as the EU expands eastwards, is especially serious for the weaker Northern economy, chronically dependent for about one third of its GDP on the massive subvention from Britain's taxpayers. This helps explain why Northern business people of unionist background, who in the past might have shown little interest in the South or looked down on it as 'backward', are now among the most enthusiastic supporters of the call for a 'single island economy'. In 1992, the year the SEM was officially completed, Dr George Quigley, a leading banker and then head of the Northern Ireland branch of the Institute of Directors, proposed that 'Ireland, North and South, should become one integrated "island economy" in the context of the Single European Market' (Quigley 1992). The unified economy should be supported by a special EC fund for projects agreed by the British and Irish governments together with the EC Commission; and this would ensure a direct route to Brussels for a Northern Ireland administration if powers were devolved from London.

Business leaders North and South clearly see economic integration as a desireable end in itself, rather than a means to an end; and to distance themselves from the nationalist objective of a politically united Ireland, they not surprisingly adopt a 'non-political' posture. Nevertheless, and equally unsurprising, they have been attacked by unionist political leaders, with a further fracturing of the traditionally close links between the main unionist party and Northern business interests. For clearly the integration of the Northern and Southern economies does have profound *political* implications, despite its 'economic' motivation and the 'non-political' posture business people feel compelled to adopt. It necessitates some measure of political integration. Contrary to 'functionalist' notions, private business interests cannot achieve economic integration on their own, partly because of the importance of the public sector, and besides integration is too important to be left to them. Integrating the economies requires North–South institutions, not only to give the process coherence, but also to provide democratic accountability in North–South policy-making (Anderson 1994). There are now growing numbers of North–South community, voluntary, trade union and other campaigning networks, some of which are calling for more popular control of integration. And there are other dynamics behind North–South integration apart from the economic and nationalist ones – the women, or environmentalists, or gay rights campaigners, who increasingly find cross-border co-operation useful, are not motivated by the SEM or nationalism.

Although basically an economic dynamic, the SEM is probably the most important new element in the deadlocked political conflict. This is especially so because the economic imperatives of the SEM coincide with the quite separate political objective of achieving 'parity of esteem' in the North. Both require political institutions linking North and South, and together they provide the basis for the settlement envisaged by the two governments.

3 Rethinking politically

Empirical circumstances are now much more favourable for a settlement based on border-straddling institutions than in the early 1920s when 'Council of Ireland' proposals were still-born, or in 1973–4 when the similar 'Sunningdale' scheme was stopped by the so-called Ulster workers' 'strike'. The EU itself now comprises a variety of well-established border-straddling political forms. Contrary to unionist rhetoric, North–South institutions need be neither transitional nor unstable, just as 'shared sovereignty' in the EU should not be seen as transitional to a single 'Euro-state'. But in order to capitalise on contemporary circumstances, the British and Irish governments need much more open, imaginative and pro-active policies, in order to counter delay in building a genuine settlement. The territorial context and forms of democracy need to be substantially extended. There needs to be more emphasis on *non*-nationalist politics, though not as a separate 'stage' or alternative to dealing with national problems.

The governments' North–South institutions

The joint 'Framework Document' saw 'parity of esteem' for Northern nationalists as requiring a significant 'Irish dimension' in the politics of Northern Ireland to combine with the existing 'British dimension'. It recognises that Northern nationalists need practical recognition of their identity in the form of institutional linkages with the South. Following 'neo-functionalist' theory, representatives drawn from the Dáil and from a Belfast assembly would be mainly concerned with the 'low politics' of economic development and apparently non-contentious issues such as island-wide tourism. They would have various executive and harmonising functions in economic and other social fields, to be initially decided by the two governments. There would be mechanisms to secure against possible boycott by politicians; and there would be possibilities for a subsequent expansion of functions as agreed by the North's own representatives and those from the Dáil. The 'Framework Document' also proposed an island-wide 'Parliamentary Forum' where unionists and nationalists could 'acknowledge their respective identities'; and an island-wide civil rights 'Charter' to protect the rights of nationalists and unionists, Protestants and Catholics, North and South.

It has been clear for some considerable time that this type of hybrid institutional arrangement, if properly explained and 'sold' by both governments, would very probably be accepted by a clear majority of the Northern Ireland electorate, as well as by the electorates of the South and Britain. But most public discourse, as if mesmerised by the 'nation state' ideal, poses just two options, an exclusively British Northern Ireland, and its 'mirror-image' of exclusive Irish sovereignty, both of them totally unacceptable to a big majority of one or other national community. Yet even prior to any 'proper explanation' by government, it has seemed clear that the only generally acceptable settlement would involve a power-sharing assembly in Belfast in combination with some cross-border institutional arrangements, whether inter-governmental as in the Anglo-Irish Agreement, or based on North–South institutions which would be significantly more democratic.

In recognition of this, 'Democratic Dialogue' proposed a referendum or preferendum on *three* options. As Robin Wilson suggests, 'a shared, pluralist Northern Ireland, linked to both the UK and the Republic' would have a good chance of getting most support even in a first-choice referendum – a majority of Catholics plus a sizeable minority of Protestants would clearly defeat the other two main options of 'Irish unity' and 'fuller integration into the UK' (Wilson 1996, 63).

The 'integrationist' option is vigorously canvassed by so-called 'new unionists' such as Robert McCartney and Conor Cruise O'Brien in the 'UK Unionist' party. But, following the long-established pattern where supposedly liberal or 'non-sectarian' unionisms depend on the sectarian mobilisation of 'the lower orders' – a pattern going back to the birth of the Orange Order in 1795 – the 'UK Unionists' rely on the support of the decidedly 'old' unionism of the Rev. Ian Paisley's Party. In the bigger Ulster Unionist Party, talk of a 'new' unionism shorn of its links with the Orange Order has come to nothing. In reality, integrationist unionism, far from being 'liberal', is a very 'hardline' reassertion, indeed exacerbation, of the 'winner-takes-all' non-solution of Northern Ireland's exclusive and sectarian 'Britishness' (see O'Dowd, this volume).

A settlement based on North–South institutions would not satisfy the goal of 'Irish unity' either, but then nationalists, including Sein Féin strategists, have clearly lowered their sights from a unitary Irish state. Percival (1996: 59–62) argues that they 'now see national self-determination as a process rather than as a prescribed outcome or solution'; and interviews with nationalist and republican leaders had already confirmed that they do not see the traditional goal of a 'united Ireland' as an immediate or realistic objective, and none of the loyalist leaders interviewed seemed worried that it might be (Anderson and Goodman 1996).

Delaying tactics and government mismanagement

So why, instead of moves to implement the 'Framework Document' solution, was there a breakdown in the cease fire a year after the document was published? The full story of unionist intransigence and delaying tactics, the malign influence of British nationalists in Britain, government collusion and opportunism, and 'militarism versus politics' in paramilitary circles, has yet to be told and is obviously beyond the scope of this chapter. Suffice to note several factors which need to be avoided or confronted, before suggesting some positive policy innovations.

A significant number of Unionist leaders, finding a 'rethink' of their basic positions literally 'unthinkable', have so far seen their best negotiating tactic being to delay negotiating. Disputes over Orange marches at Drumcree and elsewhere have served as a diversion from, and surrogate for, political negotiation while reasserting and hardening sectarian divisions. In the political vacuum sectarianism has flourished as rarely before, but rather than strengthening unionism's position it further damages it, proving – if further proof were needed – that Northern Ireland on its own is unreformable.

Unionists have resisted any institutional expression of Northern nationalist identity, and the separate economic imperative for North–South institutions. For party leader David Trimble, who insists that his nationality is 'a zero-sum issue', such institutions would diminish his 'Britishness' and make Northern Ireland a 'condominium' ruled over by London and Dublin. This, however, is a misrepresentation. North–South institutions do *not* mean London–Dublin rule. On the contrary, they would centrally involve the representatives of the North itself, who currently under 'Direct Rule' have no executive powers even within Northern Ireland. Representatives from both North and South would *gain* a role in the common concerns of people in both parts of Ireland. Rather than being a 'one-way street', North–South institutions would express *reciprocal* linkages.

What is proposed is not a 'London–Dublin condominium', but continuing unionist intransigence could perversely lead to just that. If there is continuing refusal to 'compromise' on exclusive sovereignty, the two governments will have no other viable option but to move towards joint authority over the North, effectively by-passing Northern politicians. It might be argued that in the hybrid North–South settlement, it is really only unionism which has to 'compromise', apparently losing the *actuality* of exclusive British sovereignty whereas Irish nationalism only has to give up an *aspiration* to its ideal. But the 'actuality' has been that unionists have no effective executive power, while the Southern government had an *un*reciprocated role in Northern affairs. It is only the perversity of a 'zero-sum' fixation on absolute sovereignty which can see a gain in power and reciprocity as a 'compromise' or 'loss'. Contrary to the unionist argument that North–South institutions would be an inherently 'unstable half-way house' to a unitary Irish state, an increase in their scope would be dependent on the agreement of a Belfast assembly. There would actually be greater stability in a settlement based on international treaty between the two states (and perhaps involving the EU) than in a continuing conflict where unionists depend on British sovereignty, not least because 'British sovereignty' means whatever a Westminster government of the day decides it should mean.

Unionist power, however, is only 'negative', and the main responsibility for the delay in taking positive action rests mainly with the 'sovereign power', the British government, and to a lesser extent with its junior partner, the government of the Irish Republic. Firstly, their tactic of trying to 'reassure' unionists that cross-border institutions would not affect sovereignty is implausible and counter-productive. It simply confirms unionist suspicions that both governments are not to be trusted, and it loses the opportunity to explain that the whole point of such institutions is precisely to overcome some of the problems of sovereignty as currently interpreted. If the institutions did not affect sovereignty, it could only be because they were completely ineffective.

As we have already seen, less substantial changes have already breached the absolutist conception of Westminster sovereignty.

Secondly, the joint 'Framework Document', far from being 'properly sold', was played down by British spokespeople as unionists objected to it. Both governments, whether by (British) design or (Irish) ineptitude, allowed it to be virtually forgotten almost as soon as it was published in February 1995, their agenda dominated by fruitless semantics about whether the cease fire was 'permanent', and by public posturing about the unattainable objective of prior 'decommissioning' by the paramilitaries. The failure to actually engage the paramilitaries' representatives in meaningful negotiations was further compounded in January 1996 when John Major summarily rejected Senator Mitchell's proposals that 'decommissioning' should proceed in parallel with substantive negotiations. The ending of the IRA cease fire followed almost immediately. It was only when the IRA blew up London's Canary Wharf in early February killing two people that the British government, just as quickly – moving with uncharacteristic speed, and contradicting its own 'mantra' about 'never giving in to terrorism' – acceded to demands that a date be set for inclusive all-party negotiations, and on the basis suggested by Mitchell.

Major's failures can be partly, but only partly, explained by his reliance on unionist votes in Westminster. The British authorities have been able to hide behind the unionists' intransigence, letting them take the blame for failure, but more attention should be given to British nationalism in Britain and to the ideological importance of the Union for many mainstream British politicans, Labour as well as Tory. By abdicating the usual responsibilities of a parliamentary opposition, the Labour Party must share responsibility for Major's appalling record, although it has made some amends in government. We can also speculate that some groups, in Britain as well as Ireland, did not want an end to war, or at least not just yet. There are people in the security apparatus with an immediate vested interest in the Irish conflict continuing. Just as Irish republicanism has its 'hardline militarists', there are no doubt some in the British 'establishment' who wanted the IRA to resume full-scale war, believing that 'softened' by cease fire it could now be decisively beaten. Influential members of Major's Northern Ireland Committee included Michael Howard (who, after the cease fire, hardened rather than relaxed the prison conditions for some republican prisoners), Michael Portillo (in charge of military forces), and Viscount Cranbourne (alleged 'leaker' of the 'Framework Document' to *The Times*, and grandson of Lord Salisbury a key opponent of Irish 'Home Rule' in the late nineteenth century). British commentators have not been slow in pointing to supposedly 'irrational' nationalist elements in Ireland, but the same phenomena exist in Britain's nationalism. The British authorities have been rightly accused of only *managing* the conflict rather than trying to *settle* it, but *mis*managing would be more accurate.

That may not apply with as much force to the new Labour government, but it is basically continuing the strategy devised by a

discredited Tory administration. Even if delaying tactics are confronted, there still need to be innovative extensions to the framework
and forms of democracy.

Extending democracy

Following 'neo-functionalism', it can be argued that a limited start
with the 'low politics' of economic co-operation will initiate a process
which will call for the further development of cross-border political
structures. Yet notwithstanding this possibilty, and the real advance
the government proposals would represent if implemented, they do
have serious deficiencies which, among other things, impede implementation. As Ruane and Todd (1996: 297–9, 316) indicate, it is difficult
to see them achieving radical change or doing much for socio-
economic inequalities in the North, because they are so bureaucrati-
cally over-complicated with 'checks and balances' for dealing with the
conflicting communities and their power imbalances. They are not in
themselves 'emancipatory' in that they emphasise rather than 'disman-
tle' the nationalistic terms of reference of the conflict.

But they do at least underline the fact that the 'realist' insistence on a
purely 'internal settlement' within Northern Ireland is a contradiction
in terms. It is the framework itself which is at issue. The conflict is not
susceptible to conventional democratic resolution precisely because it is
fundamentally about who should 'have a vote', and which state body
or bodies should organise the elections or referenda in the first place.
Mainstream unionist appeals to 'democracy' and 'majority wishes' in
Northern Ireland are disingenuous when the core problem is disagreement over Northern Ireland with its built-in unionist majority as the
only framework for democracy. But quite apart from historical arguments about Northern Ireland itself being an undemocratic
gerrymander, democracy, as distinct from the North's familiar unionist
majoritarianism, can only be enhanced by involving the electorates of
the South and Britain; by having publicly accountable North–South
bodies answerable both to the Dáil and to a Belfast assembly; and by
increasing participation in cross-border democratic movements.

One of the consequences of intensified globalisation is the realisation that actions within particular states increasingly have direct
impacts on supposedly 'sovereign' neighbours. Various transnational
mechanisms for 'cosmopolitan democracy' are therefore needed as
David Held (1995) has persuasively argued. Others, such as Richard
Falk (1995), put their faith in transnational movements 'from below'
which are 'animated by a vision of humane governance', rather than
simply extending the institutional networks of established power.

On grounds both of democratic principle and pragmatic politics, the
entire electorates of Ireland and Britain should be directly involved in
deciding a settlement, something precluded by nationalistic terms of
reference on both sides. Unionists object that Southerners, as citizens
of a 'foreign country', should not have any say in the 'internal affairs'
of Northern Ireland; and Irish nationalists would object to the elec-

torate in Britain deciding the Irish nation's future (not that Northern unionists would happily rely on a UK-wide majority decision). But such nationalistic reasoning blithely ignores the fact that all three electorates have a democratic right to be involved as all are affected in various ways by the conflict. Some of the biggest bombs and the worst episodes of mass slaughter have, respectively, been in Britain (e.g. London 1996) and the South (Dublin and Monaghan 1974, where 33 people were killed and over 300 injured in one day). More insidiously, the conflict has eroded the civil liberties of both electorates, as well as costing them 'hard cash'. The unsatisfactory status quo is only kept afloat by the massive subvention from Britain's taxpayers; and the per capita costs of the conflict are even higher for the much smaller population of the South. Yet the general population in Britain has never been properly informed about the conflict or directly involved in finding a solution. Westminster 'bi-partisanship' has effectively disenfranchised the British public; and it seems that the conflict only got serious attention in Britain when there was a bombing in Britain, a point not lost on the IRA. This makes not for rational, informed analysis, but for self-serving, often hysterical and sometimes racist, nonsense in the British mass media about Britain's impossible yet altruistic task of keeping the two 'Irish tribes' apart. In the circumstances, public boredom in Britain is hardly surprising.

Yet even on pragmatic grounds, the British public should be involved, as should the South's electorate. There can be little doubt that a settlement is more likely if the decision-making framework directly involved all three electorates. Confining the key decisions to the contested unit with its built-in unionist majority (or, even worse, to its atrophied political party system) is virtually guaranteed to produce stalemate as the past decades amply testify. The North's unionists constitute a less than 3 per cent minority of the over 55 million UK population, and an under 20 per cent minority of Ireland's population. They face a majority of the 97 per cent in Britain who are not committed to Northern Ireland remaining in the UK, and upwards of 80 per cent of Ireland's population who might be considered 'nationalist'. This clearly helps to explain unionists' chronic insecurity, but it does not excuse their sectarian responses, and their responses are self-defeating in that they invite opposition. It would be better for all concerned if their potential vulnerability on two fronts was explicitly recognised in appropriate human and civil rights guaranteed by both governments, rather than allowing them to continue as the aggressive 'tail' which has so far succeeded in 'wagging' the British and Irish 'dogs'.

Participatory democracy and non-nationalist politics

The governments' strategy is also overly confined to political parties (with their collusion, not surprisingly). It proceeds as if Northern Ireland was a 'normally functioning' representative democracy whereas the reality is 'Direct Rule', a party system effectively excluded from power and responsibility, a very high density of unelected 'quangos' even by British standards, a still heavily sectarianised state apparatus, and paramilitary organisation. Political parties are not the only, or in these circumstances necessarily the best, conduits of popular aspirations or willingness to reach agreement. On the contrary, relying on the parties in the first instance, and only involving the electorate to endorse (or reject) what they eventually agree, is pathetically flawed. All the precedents of 'talks about talks' suggest that if the process were to involve only the parties it will not get beyond 'the first instance'.

When wider public participation has been encouraged, it has rarely extended beyond genuinely felt but none the less pathetic one-off public demonstrations of support for 'peace' with moralistic condemnations of 'the men (sic) of violence'. Open to the criticism of being 'public relations' manipulations of the widespread yearning for peace, such demonstrations simplistically reduce the political problem to one of 'violence'. They also highlight the collective powerlessness of most people in the face of paramilitaries and governments at war, unintentionally raising the question of how should real public participation be encouraged?

One promising approach involves building on the existing North–South linkages of business, trade unions, cultural bodies, voluntary organisations and campaigning groups. The various cross-border networks and interests in civil society could be given their own North–South institution(s) with a direct input into shaping North –South policy. An 'Island Social Forum', perhaps modelled on the South's 'National Economic and Social Forum', has been floated (Anderson and Goodman 1996), followed by a somewhat similar suggestion for an 'Irish citizens assembly' modelled on the assembly campaigning for 'home rule' in Scotland (Percival 1996). The South's 'National Economic and Social Forum' draws up proposals on a wide range of social and economic issues, and includes representatives of women's organisations, environmental groups, the unemployed, young people, the elderly, the disabled, and other minority groups, as well as politicans, business people and trade unionists. An 'Island Social Forum' constructed on roughly similar lines could help in democratising North–South relations and reconciling unionists and nationalists. It could make informed submissions to the executive North–South institutions composed of politicans, supplementing their formal accountability with participatory democracy.

Rather than relying entirely on party politicans elected every four or five years, participatory democracy could involve a wide variety of organisations some of which are themselves vehicles for participatory democracy and open to continuous democratic pressures. Many people, and perhaps especially younger people, are alienated from conventional party politics but are nevertheless active in the 'small p politics' of civil society. By recognising their organisations as legitimate expressions of popular opinion, allowing them greater access to policy-making, and mobilising and harnessing their evident enthusiasm for closer North–South links, the two states and the EU could assist in building a much more democratic and robust integration process.

Furthermore, implementing some version of the 'Island Social Forum' could begin immediately rather than waiting for a formal settlement of the national conflict, or the setting up of executive bodies. Indeed, North–South participatory democracy, if instituted as part of the search for a settlement rather than awaiting the eventual outcome of party negotiations, would help to prevent party leaders or governments stalling or wrecking the construction of a settlement. It would be a 'confidence-building' measure – to use the jargon of the so-called 'peace process' – enabling the institutions of civil society to give the politicans some much-needed guidance and helping them to move away from entrenched positions. It would emphasise that there is much more to cross-border politics than the national question and sovereignty fixation. For example, various voluntary and women's networks point towards the emerging possibilities (though the Women's Forum constructed to represent women's interests on a cross-community basis in the 1996 election and 'peace talks', has 'spilled over' into formal representative democracy which is perhaps not playing to its own strengths).

A vibrant participatory democracy implies political mobilisation around a variety of *non*-national issues which have generally been 'crowded out' by the preoccupations of the conflicting nationalisms. But such mobilisation is just what is needed to defuse and settle the national conflict. Giving increased scope for other *non*-nationalist and *non*-unionist politics based primarily on social class, gender and other concerns which straddle the border and national divisions, would be 'emancipatory', not only 'dismantling the dynamics' of the Northern conflict (Ruane and Todd 1996), but actively replacing them with other structures and dynamics more broadly based in civil society.

However, the notion that class and other concerns could displace or replace the national issue should be rejected. This mistaken strategy was codified in Stalinism as the 'stages theory' and adopted by the 'Official IRA' in the 1960s and 70s: stage one, unite nationalist and unionist workers on a purely class basis, then at a later stage deal with the question of nation. The problem is that there is no 'pure' class basis, and the national question cannot be side-stepped or put off to a later date. Parties in Northern Ireland which attempted to do that, explicitly 'Official' Sinn Féin, implicitly the Northern Ireland Labour Party, either failed to get support or, in the case of the Labour Party, quickly lost their support base when the national issue came to dominate the political agenda in the late 1960s. But we should also reject the mirror-image 'stages theory' of 'nation first, class later', which has epitomised some of the practice if not the rhetoric of 'Provisional Sinn Féin'. Issues of class or gender cannot be put off to the 'promised land' of a united Ireland, and attempts to do so can be guaranteed to leave many workers and feminists unimpressed. But conversely, the national issue cannot be solved by simply concentrating on it to the exclusion of other major sources of identity and material interest. There will always be tensions between class and nation, and tactical questions and disagreements about the relative weighting each should be given in particular circumstances. Both, however, have to be fully taken into account. Whatever the leadership, it is mainly working-class people who do the fighting and suffering in national conflicts. Or, as the United Irish leader Henry Joy McCracken put it, 'the rich always betray the poor', though he himself was one of the exceptions which prove the rule.

Conclusions

North–South institutions offer a route out of the dead-end conflict over territorial sovereignty, an escape from a 'parity of poverty and dis-esteem' which is the reality for many Catholics and Protestants. The fixation with exclusive territoriality feeds 'zero-sum' thinking and 'negative-sum' practice. It misleads people into believing that there are just two options, an independant all-Ireland republic or a purely British Northern Ireland, when in reality these are no more than mutually unattainable 'bargaining positions'. North–South institutions, in contrast, would provide a practical alternative to these traditional goals of unionism and nationalism and their opposing versions of the nation state ideal. By 'bridging the border' they would puncture the pretentions of exclusive territoriality in line with the realities of the European Union and the Single Market. Enhanced by something like an 'Island Social Forum', they would help to meet the threat of economic peripheralisation in the Single Market, facilitate the cross-border links of social, community and campaigning groups, and democratise the growing connections between the two parts of the island.

Participatory democracy and a North–South framework would create much more scope for non- or anti-sectarian modes of political mobilisation based primarily on class, gender, and other concerns which straddle both the border and the sectarian divide. And this in turn would help to diffuse the deadlocked national conflict, transcending its 'zero- or negative-sum' terms. In a cumulative, mutually reinforcing process, it would further boost the so-called 'normal' politics of other identities and interests, though these will continue to be subverted or downgraded until the national conflict is solved. The 'vicious circle' of sectarianism could be replaced by a 'virtuous spiral'.

The Single Market implies a 'single island economy' which in turn requires some island-wide institutions of governance. Together with 'parity of esteem' in the North, this implies moving towards a more unified political culture and an 'all-Ireland society'. In time, a North–South framework in the context of the EU would help foster genuinely all-Ireland identities and a stronger European identity as well, for identities are moulded in part by the institutional setting. Paradoxically, this could also result in a more unified Northern Irish identity, instead of the competing and largely sectarianised identities separated over the sovereignty issue.

The EU and the SEM, are no longer 'outside developments', they are already 'internalised' in the North, the South and the interrelationships between them. The outmoded 'inside/outside' dichotomy of 'realism' gives rise to an outmoded debate about 'internal' versus 'external' solutions, as if you could have one without the other. A so-called 'internal' settlement within Northern Ireland would simply preserve intact the framework that is at issue, 'bottling-up' the sectarian conflict as in a pressure-cooker.

Rather than seeing North–South integration as a state-centred 'national takeover' in either direction, or as as the harmonious convergence of two civil societies into a unified island region of the EU, island-wide integration is better conceived as involving multi-dimensional conflicts within and between civil society and states, North and South. As we saw, 'functionalists' and 'realists' collude in the fallacy that transnational integration can simply be left to agencies in civil society leaving state sovereignty undisturbed; but because of the continuing importance of states the issue cannot be side-stepped in the hope of facilitating further integration. Walker (1993) is right to highlight the conceptual limitations of 'realism's' 'inside/outside' dichotomy, yet, after several centuries of the modern state, it has a material reality which cannot simply be wished away. Changes to sovereignty are unavoidable and indeed have already happened because of EU integration and the changing relationship between the British and Irish states. However, further substantial changes in the shape of North–South institutions are necessary, in order to achieve both the possibility of economic viability for the North and a political settlement to the national conflict. And even more necessary if there is a political settlement, because the economic subvention from Britain will inevitably decline.

Acknowledgement

The chapter draws on joint research with James Goodman, and also with Ian Shuttleworth, and both commented on earlier versions of these ideas, as did Douglas Hamilton and Liam O'Dowd. My thanks to them, but sole responsibility for the chapter rests with me.

CHAPTER 7

Politics, the economy and peace in Northern Ireland

Ronnie Munck and Douglas Hamilton

In recent years, the debate on economic policy in Northern Ireland has become increasingly politicised. Some professional economists have resisted this trend, clinging to the technocratic, apolitical spirit of the discipline. However, the political nature of economic debate is now out in the open. This is no bad thing because it is simply neither possible nor realistic to insulate economic debates and policies from their political context. In particular, the big taboo of speaking about the Northern economy as part of the wider Irish economy is now broken. When we wrote some years ago (Munck and Hamilton 1993, 1994) about the 'Irish economy' embracing North and South together, it was regarded as novel, if not odd. Now, even unionist economists recognise the growing reality of all-Ireland economics, even while they strive to maintain the status of Northern Ireland within the United Kingdom (UK). This means that we can now move beyond a sterile counterposition of unionist and nationalist economic visions and policies. Our own developmental perspective on the Northern economy, based squarely within the critical political economy tradition, is aimed at taking us beyond old entrenched positions. Paradoxically, the politicising of the economic debate helps us to move beyond the frozen political orthodoxies.

When Northern Ireland remained part of the UK in 1920–1, most of its earlier economic success had evaporated. The upswing of the long wave was over and the secular decline of the engineering, shipbuilding and textile sectors had already begun. The artificial respite provided by World War II could not mask the slow long-term decline of the North's traditional industrial base. In the later era of the multinational corporation, the North did not do nearly as well as the South in attracting foreign direct investment. Indeed, a series of well publicised and costly failures, such as the De Lorean project, seem to symbolise the failure of the region to pursue anything more than short-term palliative measures. From the 1970s to the present, the North has been debilitated by the 'troubles', a set of political–military battles which took a heavy toll on economic mobility, business confidence and the very possibility of a long-term vision. It is now clear that without the massive public investment attendant on the conflict, the North would be in even greater dire straits. As the peace process moves forward, albeit hesitantly, so the deeper underlying economic problems will become more transparent.

While Northern Ireland and the Republic of Ireland took distinct development paths after partition, in recent decades they have begun to suffer similar problems. As two small, open economies, in the era of globalisation and increasing internationalisation, they were bound to face the same dilemmas. The South had 'caught up' with the North in terms of industrial development by the late 1960s and has now forged ahead. Since both jurisdictions joined the European Economic Community (now EU) in 1973, they have also had to face the similar constraints of small, peripheral European regions. It is these objective constraints which have led to (unionist) business leaders shocking unionist political leaders with their pragmatic embrace of all-Ireland or, more coyly, 'all-island' remedies. The convergence of the two Irish economies did not lead, of course, to an irresistible course of Irish reunification. However, the cross-border element can only increase in importance, especially if the peace process 'takes'. It is the polemics around this element to which we give attention in the pages below. Our own alternative, however, seeks to take the debate beyond the binary opposites of nationalism and unionism, advancing the prospect of democratic development.

What we propose is three different scenarios for the Northern economy. These should be conceived of as alternative pathways to economic growth, but also, inevitably, an articulation of distinct political subject positions. Our three scenarios/pathways are:

1 More of the same – a continuation of the present status quo whereby Northern Ireland remains 'locked in an unrelieved downward economic spiral' as Hutton puts it (Hutton 1994: 1).
2 Economic integration – a gradual move towards Irish economic integration in a managed process and as part of a renewed peace process.
3 Democratic development for Ireland – involving a radical rethink of conventional economic analysis, a move towards real community economic development and a genuine democratic settlement in Ireland.

It is important to bear in mind that these three alternative perspectives contain diverse economic theory orientations as well as the crucial – we might almost say overbearing – spatial dimension which has the territory of Northern Ireland in a liminal (betwixt and between) status with regard to the Republic of Ireland and the UK.

More of the same

This scenario, of course, is that which has been pursued in the North since direct rule from London was introduced in 1972. It is an economic policy perspective that is informed by the notion that Belfast is quite simply 'a more chronic version of Liverpool' (Hutton 1994: 3) – and it is certainly that. As Hutton shows in a clear-sighted and influential analysis (Hutton 1995), British capitalism is characterised by a chronic short-termism, underinvestment, underinnovation, and lack of commitment and co-operation, all of which are particularly marked in the peripheral regions. While Hutton's progressive thinking may have something to offer Britain's economic prospects, it may not be sufficient to lift Northern Ireland out of its vicious circle of economic decline. While juridically part of the UK, the North of Ireland is a distinct economic region, with its very particular problems and competing perspectives and aspirations that have led to decades of political and military conflict. It is thus less than helpful when we find one of the main economics textbooks on the North (Harris, Jefferson and Spencer 1990) producing accounts of all the standard economic topics – from incomes to the financial services and the role of the firm – with little acknowledgement of the region's history, economic or political, and its part in Ireland and the wider world today.

Rowthorn and Wayne (1988: 95) captured Northern Ireland's specificity with the striking metaphor of a 'workhouse economy', where those who are not unemployed are mainly engaged in servicing and controlling each other. Perhaps exaggerated, certainly unflattering, this metaphor captures a certain 'feel' about the North of Ireland. There are, indeed, too few people who are employed in the production of tradeable goods and services. Most of those remaining in employment are either engaged in repression work, providing for social reproduction (health and education) or are selling goods and services. If Northern Ireland began life as a contributor to Britain's imperial coffers, it was by the 1990s being subsidised to the tune of as much as £4 billion per annum, by the itself ailing ex-imperial power (Anderson and Hamilton 1995). Like the workhouse of old, it is taxes levied on an external population which alone can finance the growing gap between imports and exports. What came together in the 1980s was a catastrophic combination of international factors, monetarist-orientated government policies and the long-term decline of a small, peripheral economy separated from its natural hinterland – the rest of Ireland.

What now seems clear is that Northern Ireland does seem to have serious problems as a viable and self-sustaining economic entity. Even after a halting economic recovery in the early 1980s, the Northern Ireland Economic Council argued that 'The underlying negative feature has been and is the weakness of its manufacturing sector as a whole ... [and] the virtually static levels of real public expenditure' (NIEC 1989: 15). A certain expansion of private services and a partial recovery in the clothing industry could not compensate for these underlying structural trends. Northern Ireland is essentially a peripheral regional economy, steadily deindustrialising and increasingly dependent on state expenditure. The negative view of the more candid economic planners is exemplified by Charles Carter who in 1995 was telling a major conference on Northern Ireland's economy that 'unemployment will probably remain high' and that 'the difficulties of being a peripheral position will remain, peace process notwithstanding' (NIEC 1995a: 89). The North's position within the EU is described as 'draughty' and the prospects for a new world of employment generating high-tech industries is considered 'not quite as rosy as they are pretended to be' (NIEC 1995a: 89).

There have, of course, been a number of initiatives proposed over the years to deal with this seemingly intractable economic situation. The net result of these, however, has been less than positive. Thus, research by the Northern Ireland Economic Research Centre found in 1986 that 'only 65 firms employing 16,000 people remain to show for all the effort of industrial attraction from 1945 to 1973' (Gudgin *et al.* 1989). Recent studies of productivity levels in the North compared with other areas (Hitchens, Birnie and Wagner 1990) also suggest that, despite a high level of industrial assistance, little improvement has been forthcoming. Overall, during the 1980s when over £1 billion was spent on industrial development, manufacturing employment actually declined by 42,000 in the North (NIEC 1990). Past failures of industrial policy in the North have only recently been recognised by the British government, although rarely admitted to. Confusion in this regard was manifest in the *'Competing in the 1990s'* (Department of Economic Development 1990) government initiative which argued that future assistance to industry would only be granted to firms that showed signs that they would improve their competitive position. However, at the same time a document was issued requesting interested bodies to submit views on how competitiveness should be defined. This was hardly a stable and confidence-building base on which to develop industrial policy.

The most recent and arguably most far-reaching proposal for the North's regeneration is contained in the Northern Ireland Growth Challenge (NIGC 1995) launched by the private sector, though funded in the main by the EU. This new approach is based on Porter's influential work on competitive advantage and the attributes which shape the environment in which national firms compete (Porter 1990). What is remarkable about the Growth Challenge is its implicit admission of the deep problems that the Northern economy faces. While trying to strike an upbeat tone, the Growth Challenge admits that 'there are today no true competitive sectors or clusters in Northern Ireland' (NIGC 1995: 6). The document is candid about the decline of the North's traditional industries, its peripherality, small size and 'an increasingly insular/conservative culture' in business circles. Also, as many critical observers have previously noted, the 'troubles' have been used as an excuse for the failings of the entrepreneurial class and had created a situation where 'judgement and critical analysis were, to some extent, withheld in Northern Ireland' (NIGC 1995: 10). The business leaders associated with the Growth Challenge propose what they see as a radical change in economic policy to set the North on a new trajectory of growth and prosperity. This is evaluated in a subsequent section, at this juncture we register just the critique of 'more of the same'.

Clearly, in the last couple of years, there has been a focus on the economic implications of the peace process, the so-called 'peace dividend'. Previous debates on the 'economics of the troubles' had not been conclusive. While Rowthorn and Wayne (1988: 94) argued that there was a net loss of 10,000 jobs due to the troubles between 1970 and 1985, Canning, Moore and Rhodes (1987: 211) argued that 'while the troubles have led to a loss of manufacturing jobs, their net effect on the regional economy has been positive, due to the induced expansion of public sector expenditure and employment'. In retrospect, it seems impossible to decide with any degree of certainty what the economic costs of political and military conflict have been and what aspects of economic decline can be attributed to the political deadlock. A similar problem arises with estimates of the peace dividend. Neither economy wide nor narrow public finance counterfactuals assuming a conflict-free scenario are particularly realistic. Certainly, the effects of peace and political stability will have positive implications for the economy. The Northern Ireland Economic Council, while stating that 'it is difficult to estimate with any degree of precision the likely overall increase in jobs because of the end of the Troubles' (NIEC 1995b: 22), nevertheless refer to a possible additional 1,400 jobs annually. There is also the unquantifiable improvement in confidence which should arise and the long-term viability of investment projects. Balance is required between this positive long-term scenario and the major transitional issues involved in moving from a heavily security based economy to one geared towards democratic development. It is interesting to note in this context that the Northern Ireland Economic Council now recognises the critical importance of an 'appropriate governance structure' for stable economic prospects (NIEC 1995a: 26).

Another recent debate which gets to the heart of the North's economic status, if the current situation continues, concerns the so-called subvention – the difference between public expenditure and the level of tax revenue raised in the region. For economists who take a unionist perspective, the subvention has become somewhat of a talisman, pointing towards 'the financial impossibility of unification' (Cadogan Group 1992: 23). This issue, a technical one, we address in the next section. What is interesting to point out here is that unionist economics seems simply to accept the peripheral and dependent position of Northern Ireland within the UK. As Bradley points out, 'The implicit Cadogan assumption that the North is never likely to return a better balance between regional expenditure and taxation would appear to be a vote of no confidence in the peace process and in the future of the Northern economy' (Bradley 1996: 84). It also seems like a case where political ~hes have superseded economic rationality. It certainly can only dis-
~ur attention from the real problems and prospects of the North if

we focus narrowly on the British subvention. This 'begging bowl' mentality, which unionists criticise in others, is hardly an acceptable response to the North's economic problems. In a somewhat intemperate *Economics Lesson for Irish Nationalists and Republicans*, Roche and Birnie go so far as to argue that the South could benefit from integration with Britain as well: 'In short, the economic case for reversing some parts of the 1921 decision for Southern Irish independence may be just as strong as that in favour of ending partition' (Roche and Birnie 1995: 42). In a sense, this piece of sophistry, given the convergence in living standards between the South of Ireland and Britain over the past few decades, sums up the poverty of the 'more of the same' scenario and must constitute a strong warning against making a political football out of the economy. This does not help us chart a way forward for the Northern economy to the benefit of all its people.

Economic integration

George Quigley, in addressing the Confederation of Irish Industry in 1992, made the seemingly innocuous, but far-reaching, statement that 'I find no difficulty with the proposition that Ireland is – or should be – an island economy' (quoted in Bradley 1996: 147). Since that time the concept of an all-island economy has taken off, in spite of the predictable political, and at times highly vitriolic, objections from (some) unionist politicians. Joint economic studies between Northern and Southern business organisations have been set up, and the cross-border schemes in the North-West and elsewhere have given impetus to this simple but radical notion. It is not without contradictions, however, as many of its original proponents studiously denied any political dimensions to the project. Clearly, if economic harmonisation between the two Irish economies is to proceed systematically then political co-operation will be necessary. Reluctance to take the requisite political steps towards North-South harmonisation is seen in the dynamic Growth Challenge proposal which notes strong all-Ireland level clusters in health technologies, software and food processing, yet only makes timid moves towards cross-border co-operation, seeing the South as just one possible partner in development.

For Hutton, 'Economic logic is beginning to offer an all-island future .... growth corridors, firm networks, industrial clusters and state-led initiatives must come if the North is to turn itself around' (Hutton 1994). It was following on from Quigley's original idea of an economic corridor linking Belfast and Dublin that the Northern and Southern business organisations commissioned a feasibility study on the concept (Coopers and Lybrand and Indecon 1994). The growth centre idea is not a new one in development economics, nor even in Northern Ireland (in the 1960s certain towns were designated as growth centres), but when it takes place cross-border its political implications for a divide in Northern Ireland were considerable. The critics of economic integration question whether the benefits would really be as significant as some of its proponents argue. Essentially, they question the notion that the partition of Ireland had any deleterious economic effects in the first place: 'The prophets of North–South integration vainly assume that the border acts as some massive distortion acting to prevent all-Ireland trading links' (Roche and Birnie 1995: 35). From this stance, it then follows that the new-found business enthusiasm for economic integration is just a case of narrow economic interest leading them, mistakenly, to get on the 'nationalist bandwagon'.

The New Ireland Forum in 1984 looked at some of the important issues of economic integration in some detail (New Ireland Forum 1984). The partition of Ireland was seen to have had considerable economic costs. These included: the disruption of trade; the duplication and lack of co-ordination across almost all aspects of government policy, in particular industrial development; the creation of economically marginal areas on the border; a Northern focus on British economic policy when inappropriate; and the adverse economic effects of the structural discrimination present in the Northern economy. Further to this list we would add: the decreased opportunity to develop agglomeration economies and industrial clusters; the reduced ability to build strong indigenous industries based on a large and more coherent home market; not to mention the costs that arise from not having a single Irish currency and an integrated financial system (Sheehan, Munck and Hamilton 1997). Taken together, all these factors represent the cumulative economic costs of the partition of a small and peripheral economy. The net social costs of economic deprivation and an underdeveloped and dependent industrial base have been a consistently high level of unemployment and the persistent drain of labour through emigration.

The European context is of particular importance in the discussion of economic integration in Ireland today. Increasing European integration – at both the political and economic level – is, arguably, the most powerful incentive for developing a united Irish economy. The creation of the Single European Market and the proposed Economic and Monetary Union presents serious challenges for peripheral economies, such as the two parts of Ireland (NESC 1989). The political/administrative/policy divisions between the two parts of Ireland have led to the pursuit of separate, sometimes conflicting, agendas at the European level. This has acted as a major obstacle to the development of an effective response in Ireland to the effects of European integration, particularly bearing in mind the Northern economy's high degree of state-dependence (O'Dowd 1995). The prospect of integration is, however, a two-edged sword, as Anderson notes, 'strengthening Irish competitiveness against external competitors, but increasing competition as well as cooperation between North and South, and producing losers as well as winners' (Anderson 1994: 61). Nevertheless, economic integration is now proceeding at a whole range of levels, it is widely accepted at grass-roots levels among unionists, and it will necessarily have political effects, if not the simple ones feared and hoped for by some.

If we move beyond the narrow economic benefits of economic integration, we can see the wider ramifications of a peace process. These issues are explored in a joint North/South book entitled *Border Crossings* (D'Arcy and Dickson 1995), which explores the wide range of opportunities for closer co-operation under the new political atmosphere since the 1994 cease fires. Bradley's wide-ranging contribution to this project concludes that 'an island political settlement would be likely to release major economic forces that would work towards the regeneration of private sector activity in the North and permit North–South synergies to emerge' (Bradley 1995: 50). Going beyond a static perspective allows us to conceptualise a move away from the current vicious circle which the North's economy is caught in to a virtuous circle characterised by innovation, creativity and synergy. Despite the views of business representative bodies that attempt to keep the economic aspects of greater economic co-operation and integration completely separate from the political, the two are bound to be intertwined. Thus, a failure of the current peace process will probably result in a return of the North to its previous path of separate development and an evaporation of the element of trust which is essential to a virtuous development process.

Unionist economists have pointed to the difficulties involved in achieving North–South economic harmonisation. Certainly, integration will not be easy and it is not a magic wand that can sweep away the problems of underdevelopment. Roche and Birnie argue that 'there will be no great cross-border trade bonanza, nor a boom within the Belfast–Dublin corridor to float the cross-border executive bodies on a tide of rising prosperity' (Roche and Birnie 1995: 36). This may well be the case but the fact remains that the North, if it is not integrated with the Southern economy, will lack the critical mass to launch, and more importantly, sustain a virtuous cycle of growth and development (Bradley 1996: 136). What the unionist economists come back to is the financial subvention from Britain which would supposedly make it financially impossible for Irish reunification to occur. Thus, the Cadogan Group states bluntly that 'a large part of the Northern Ireland economy depends directly or indirectly on the subvention' (Cadogan Group 1992: 28). Loss of the subvention would lead to a 30 per cent drop in Northern living standards according to this scenario. They conclude that: 'The financial impossibility of unification is well recognised within government in the Republic, and is a significant part of the ambiguity, not to say hypocrisy, of the territorial claim' (Cadogan Group 1992: 23). This quote highlights how economic arguments are increasingly being used to preserve the status quo and would seem to point up an unhealthy and unhelpful degree of economic determinism in unionist political debate.

To ask whether Dublin could 'afford' economic integration is an odd question but worth answering to counter the Cadogan Group's misleading presentation. The costings and economic logic are simply flawed and their arguments ignore the dynamic growth possibilities of the 'peace dividend' and the economic benefits, indeed economic imperative, of North–South integration. Any analysis which focuses only on the subvention is inevitably partial and tendentious. Furthermore, in the Cadogan Group's view there is no economic growth at all, their static analysis assumes no GDP growth, which is in contrast to the projections of the New Ireland Forum. In political terms, the Cadogan assumption that Irish unification means an automatic end to the subvention is questionable. The British government will presumably retain a commitment to unionists, if not to the Irish peace process which is already receiving considerable European and US financial support. Equally telling is 'the complacency of ignoring the corrosive economic, political and morale implications of a chronic dependency, and not least for unionism itself' (Anderson and Hamilton 1995). Spurious predictions about the subvention in defence of a failed status quo can only help to perpetuate the vicious circle of economic decline and political stagnation in the North of Ireland.

Ultimately, our view on the prospects of economic integration in Northern Ireland needs to be a balanced one. The forecasts on the number of jobs which might result from increased North–South trade range from 7,500 to 75,000 which means we cannot be too optimistic. Conversely, an eastern economic corridor, improved cross-border co-operation and, most crucially, a single industrial development agency, can only make sense. For O'Donnell and Teague 'the best way to view increased North–South economic integration is in terms of encouraging positive co-ordination across a range of economic policy functions and ideas' (O'Donnell and Teague 1993: 266). This approach would deal with the 'co-ordination deficits' across the two jurisdictions, and as a result, certain externalities would be captured. Even so, these authors do not see huge economic benefits resulting. It is at this stage that we need to register the inherent limitations of a purely economic stocktaking. If development is to be sustainable, it needs to be democratic and economic policy-making needs to consider the whole range of political implications of various options. A move towards economic integration between the North and South of Ireland can thus be seen as part of a move towards democratic development in all parts of the island.

Democratic development for Ireland

We would argue that the negative implications of 'more of the same' and the limited focus of economic integration can only be overcome by a developmentalist perspective for the whole of the island. A necessary element would be a political settlement in Ireland which went beyond cease fires (permanent or otherwise) to address the underlying conflict through a comprehensive democratic compromise. As McGarry and O'Leary put it: 'The Northern Ireland conflict has been waged paramilitarily and politically between two communities with different national identities not between two aggregates of individuals mainly interested in promoting their economic well-being' (McGarry and O'Leary 1995: 306). Indeed, David Trimble, leader of the Ulster Unionist Party, stated in 1996 that 'the economic arguments are largely irrelevant when national identity is at stake' (quoted in *Irish Times* editorial, 11 May 1996). It is this situation which explains why some unionist economists can argue so vehemently, but ultimately incoherently, against the economic benefits of increased integration between the Northern and Southern economies. There is now some sign that, in practice, the economic dimension is being addressed with realism in most quarters and not being used as a simple political football. It is into that debate that we seek to insert a developmentalist perspective to raise its level beyond simple economic sums and constitutional political categories.

Without entering the sometimes contrived debate on whether Ireland is a Third World country (Caherty *et al.* 1992), it is insightful, as Kirby (1997) has recently shown, to look at the Irish economic experience from the perspective of development theory. In particular, we must start from the premise that the Irish economy, North and South, has been profoundly marked by colonialism. As O'Dowd notes in one of the few approaches which takes the colonial context seriously, the net result is 'an incoherent, disarticulated regional manufacturing economy, with poor linkages between indigenous and multinational industry, which is sustained only by massive state involvement in the local economy' (O'Dowd 1995: 148). As we enter fully into the era of globalisation, with its effects of economic internationalisation and national political disarticulation, these tendencies will become stronger. The global restructuring now underway is having a whole range of effects on the Irish political economy, not least in seriously undermining the prospects of a simple nationalist developmental path. As O'Hearn points out, 'EU regulations leave Ireland no control over the central instruments used by East Asian states [to pursue development] including foreign exchange rates, import protection and export subsidies' (O'Hearn 1995: 122). From colonial exploitation to dependent development in the era of globalisation, Ireland has faced severe external constraints on social development.

There have, however, been some attempts at articulating a radical development strategy for Ireland. Most notably, Crotty (1986) has helped to place the Irish case in the context of the broader radical development debates. However, ultimately Crotty's solutions are eminently neo-classical insofar as he sees colonialism as having caused underdevelopment (or what he refers to as undevelopment) in Ireland primarily by manipulating market mechanisms. Thus, for Crotty the solution is 'to get prices right', which seems hardly adequate. Various nationalist remedies (for example, Sinn Féin 1994) are also inadequate. A policy of macroeconomic populism (involving simple redistribution of income) has been shown to be both economically and politically unviable (Dornbusch and Edwards 1991). It is simply no use producing hazy visions of an Éire Nua if no viable path for its attainment is outlined. A nationalist economics in the era of globalisation is not only impotent but would probably be reactionary insofar as it was ever implemented. Nor can outdated notions of national economic sovereignty equip us to deal with the complex issues that a small open economy like Ireland faces in the international and European arenas. More realistic, radical strategies have been emerging from the economic policy debates recently.

For some years now there has been a current of thinking in Irish economic development which has realistically addressed its problems and prospects. For example, O'Malley has extended his earlier work on Ireland as a 'late industrialiser' (O'Malley 1989) to consider the problems of restructuring in the 1990s in the context of the Single European Market (O'Malley 1992). It is Bradley's recent work, however, which has gone furthest in articulating a dynamic alternative to current economic policy North and South (Bradley 1996). Bradley sees a convergence between the Growth Challenge in the North and earlier Southern industrial development initiatives such as the Culliton Report which stressed the need to develop dynamic industrial clusters (Culliton 1992). As Bradley puts it, 'If ever there was a good case for the Northern and Southern private and public sectors to co-ordinate their initiatives this is it' (Bradley 1996: 142). Yet, the North is currently in the worst of all possible worlds being locked into British policy norms yet not being integrated into the supply side of the much larger British economy. For Bradley, the choices for the North are stark: either learn the lessons of the Emilia-Romagna (Third Italy) region, with its systematic clusters of small and medium-sized enterprises or sink into the Mezzogiorno pattern of southern Italy where 'fiscal integration and large-scale public transfers have led to the decline of the traded sector and to a state of semi-permanent dependency and underdevelopment' (Bradley 1996: 58).

It is now increasingly recognised that economic debate in Northern Ireland needs to address the question of governance insofar as 'the present governance arrangements in the province are deeply faulty' (Clulow and Teague 1993: 115). Economic governance refers to the whole range of economic policies implemented by the state, including fiscal, monetary and labour market policies. At present, there are constraints on what a regional economy such as Northern Ireland can attain in terms of economic governance due to European and global pressures. Yet, as Bradley points out, 'the fact remains that policy norms in the North are those designed with the wider UK in mind, and can be unsuitable for a peripheral region' (Bradley 1996: 74). Over and beyond this is the broader issue of political governance and the consent, or lack of it, of those governed. In this regard, the blindness of some economists is extraordinary such that discrimination is reduced to half a page in an appendix to a major economics textbook on Northern Ireland (see Harris, Jefferson and Spencer 1990). It is key issues such as the continuation of structural economic discrimination (see Smith and Chambers 1991) which make it essential that development pathways for Northern Ireland are considered other than the failed status quo.

From an international comparative perspective it is clear that Northern Ireland is not a case of sustainable democracy. A recent international study on the conditions for sustainable democracy found that the state has an essential role in promoting universal citizenship and in creating conditions for sustained economic growth (Przeworski 1995). Northern Ireland is very far from fulfilling the basic economic, political and social conditions under which democracy is likely to generate sustainable and politically desired objectives. While some may find it an exaggeration to call Northern Ireland 'a failed political entity', nothing has indicated a transition to self-sustained growth and sustainable democratic modes of governance. In this regard, it seems self-evident that a durable peace settlement will be a necessary, if not sufficient, condition for democratic development in the North of Ireland. In this context, we can expect to see a different type of 'peace dividend', as popular participation would increase in all spheres, including the economic. At the moment economic policy-making seems remote from most people's lives, something that is done by 'experts' and frequently to the detriment of ordinary people. The British government's half-hearted programme 'Targeting Social Need' is unlikely to change this. In contrast, the efforts made to prioritise social inclusion in the EU's Special Programme for Peace and Reconciliation, both in terms of policy process and beneficiaries, is heartening. Interestingly, a recent discussion document by Sinn Féin places the community at the heart of economic development (Sinn Féin 1997).

Finally, we would argue for the need for a comparative perspective on Northern Ireland which has for too long suffered from insular and compartmentalised treatment (see, for example, Kennedy 1994). Mjøset (1992) has sought to compare the relative failure of Irish development with more successful small European countries, with a view to establishing the conditions for a virtuous circle of development. Mjøset's focus is on the national variables in institutions which are conducive to innovation. A hopeful hypothesis is that because Ireland largely missed out on the opportunities of the Fordist era, it is now in a position to take advantage of the post-Fordist restructuring race. Whether Ireland will be able to 'hook on' to expansive innovations in the core areas of Europe is, of course, an open question. Yet, despite a major recent study by Dunford and Hudson (1996) for the Northern Ireland Economic Council, which takes a refreshing European comparative and methodologically broad approach, these are the type of questions which cannot be addressed fruitfully in Northern Ireland while it remains a depressed and dependent region of the UK. If current moves towards Irish economic integration prosper, then the whole of Ireland will at least be in a position to look for a more favourable insertion into the international division of labour. This would, necessarily, be accompanied by the development of more adequate governance structures and considerations of how democracy might become sustainable in Ireland.

By way of conclusion

If a recent debate in the *New Left Review* is anything to go by the Northern Ireland economy seems to be over-politicised in radical discourse. Hazelkorn and Patterson (1994) write about the 'new politics' in Ireland which, according to their critics, 'By eschewing any discussion of northern economic crisis and state sectarianism, ... avoid[s] the issue of the unacceptability of a unionist solution to many radicals' (Porter and O'Hearn 1995: 133). The more nationalist-inclined Porter and O'Hearn, furthermore, take the 'revisionists' up because 'they recount southern economic and political weaknesses at length without any comparative analysis of the moribund northern economy and polity' (Porter and O'Hearn 1995: 134). The danger here is that we would end up in a charade of trying to vie for the worst economy in the world competition. It would seem to us sensible, therefore, to approach the Irish economy from a developmentalist perspective, as noted in the introduction, rather than through the binary opposites of unionist and nationalist economics which, ultimately, mirror one another. A broad international comparative approach focused on development from a structured and historical point of view seems both more productive and ultimately more useful from a radical political perspective.

The dominant development debate today is that around the extent and the implications of globalisation. The early literature (e.g. Ohmae 1990) presented globalisation as a universal causal agent, the explanation for all transformations, and the definitive end to national development strategies. More recently, authors have placed globalisation in question (e.g. Hirst and Thompson 1996), arguing that it may not be quite as 'new' as portrayed or as convincing an alibi for not developing national transformation strategies. While management of a national economy is undoubtedly more difficult today, the death of the nation state is much exaggerated, as is the irreversibility of globalisation. What is true is that globalisation has signalled an unleashing of market forces at an international level and the very weakness of the market is now being increasingly called into question (Boyer and Drache 1996). The constraints of globalisation are undoubtedly real in the case of a nation such as Ireland. Blind allegiance to the dictates of the market and global competitiveness are not, however, the only possible responses. To our mind, previous attempts to develop an alternative economic strategy have been dismissed just a bit too quickly.

The increasingly favoured strategy for development in progressive circles is one involving promotion of the 'third sector' or social economy. This socially useful third sector would exist alongside the private and public sectors, be community-orientated and play a social integration role (see Lipietz 1992). In Ireland, none other than the Organisation for Economic Cooperation and Development (OECD) has promoted this model, seeing it as a flexible, decentralised and participative way of addressing issues of social exclusion (Sabel 1996). Support for this view of urban and rural area-based partnerships in Ireland comes from Sinn Féin in a recent policy discussion document (Sinn Féin 1997). Sinn Féin praises the social economy for being 'people-centred', facilitating cross-community co-operation in the North, and for stimulating an innovative approach to developing local enterprise. These debates seem to supersede the old dichotomies of public/private and plan/market. Whether it constitutes a holistic approach to development or a short-term, cosmetic palliative to the jobs crisis, however, remains to be seen.

Certainly, its range of supporters should indicate the need to clarify its dynamic and political implications.

A final thought takes us to the limits of an economic/economistic analysis from the point of view of political transformations. It is already accepted that economic research in Northern Ireland focuses on issues of economic performance rather than the fundamentals of development. We can go further, however, and question the whole logic of 'talking economics', as Morris does when she examines the attitudes of white Australian men to 'the economy' (Morris 1992) who seem in awe, transported by fundamentalist reason and speak the language of pure necessity. Unhampered by politics or the concerns of lesser races and genders, they venerate their economic gods and trust in the effectiveness of their 'interventions'. As Gibson-Graham notes, 'Despite their divergent positions on every issue, the right and left share a discourse of the economy that participates in defining what can and cannot be proposed' (Gibson-Graham 1996: 93). There is now an increasing literature in 'post-development' which takes us forward (and back) to broader issues. Taking off the shackles of an economistic perspective should allow our imaginations more room to develop. The economy should certainly not be the limit of our political imagination if democratic transformation is to occur.

Acknowledgements

The authors are grateful to James Anderson, John Bradley, Liam O'Dowd and Denis O'Hearn for constructive and critical comments on an earlier draft of this chapter.

CHAPTER 8

Feminism and nationalism in Ireland

Carol Coulter

Western feminism has a problem with nationalism. To be more precise, it has a problem with the nationalism of people who are, or who consider themselves, oppressed, and who struggle, in whole communities, against that oppression. For feminists, not only does nationalism project an ideology which supercedes gender and which appeals for national unity against an outside oppressor, thereby subsuming women's interests into those of the 'nation' as a whole, this ideology has clearly been internalised by large numbers of women, evidenced by their mobilisation through it. The fact is that nationalism has been more successful in consistently mobilising hundreds of thousands of women into political activity in countries outside the imperial metropolitan centres than any movement based on 'feminist' demands.

This is as true in the Northern Irish context as in any country more obviously identified with the 'Third World'. In the working-class ghettos of Northern Ireland, where arguably the most oppressed women are to be found, it has been issues like internment and prisoners' rights (in the Catholic areas), or the Anglo-Irish Agreement (in Protestant areas) which have brought tens of thousands of women on to the streets and into other forms of protest usually, though not always, with men. At a less visible level, issues of community, welfare and linguistic and cultural identity have spawned action groups often led by, and composed largely of, women. These have had far greater resonance, and far greater support, than groups concerned with what are usually seen as more fundamental 'women's issues', like control of fertility.

It must be added, of course, that there have been periods in the North when thousands of women, from both the Protestant and Catholic communities, have been mobilised in peace movements, which are seen by many feminists as more quintessentially 'feminist' than movements concerned with national identity. While significant, and genuinely reflective of women's concerns at the time, they have not had the continuity of the groupings emanating from the nationalist movement. Not that issues of domestic violence and fertility control have been absent – they have been an important part of public debate for some 20 years now and it is interesting that, rather than drawing women away from the nationalist movement, they have been forced on to the agenda of the nationalist movement by women activists inside it, where they have an uneasy coexistence with the day-to-day exigencies of 'the struggle'. However, one constant feature of the situation of political crisis in the North over the past 25 years has been the involvement of large numbers of women in organisations or groups linked either closely or loosely to the republican movement. This has been the framework within which they have chosen to express their own concerns and demands, rather than organisations with a specific, and non-nationalist, feminist agenda. A prime example of this has been Bernadette McAliskey, whose militancy and youthful political success, along with her consistent demands for a voice for women, might have made her, in another context, a feminist role model.

The response of feminists in Britain and in the South of Ireland to this situation, and of some in the North, has been ambiguous. The majority have been influenced by the dominant agenda of Western feminism, which has focused heavily on women's rights to fertility control and to freedom in personal relationships, along with equal rights at work and before the law, which I will call 'classical' feminism, for the purpose of the argument here. They put down their failure to convince the women in Northern Ireland who seem so ready to engage in political struggle on other demands to the domination of the 'false consciousness' of nationalism, which they regularly denounce, but to no obvious avail. Feminism and nationalism are incompatible, they argue, and the women who claim to be able to combine their feminist convictions with nationalist ones are, at best, deluded. This has serious implications for specific women involved in the political conflict in Northern Ireland. For example, for many months Róisin McAliskey, daughter of Bernadette, was in a high-security unit in Holloway prison awaiting an extradition hearing following a German warrant. The German authorities wanted to charge her in connection with the bombing of a British base in Germany. She was pregnant and suffering from very poor health, as well as severe stress due to her fear that her baby would be taken from her at birth. Under British law she was innocent until proven guilty, and the German authorities stated that they were not insisting she be kept in custody until the hearing. Yet the British Conservative government refused, not only to grant her bail, but to keep her in more humane conditions. When Labour came to power she was allowed to have her baby in a normal hospital, but remained technically in custody, without bail until she was eventually released on health and humanitarian grounds in March 1998.

Such treatment of a vulnerable, pregnant young woman was met with a deafening silence from British feminists. Those newspaper columnists who never miss an opportunity to castigate the authorities for their attitude to women in general and women prisoners in particular have said scarcely a word (with a few honourable exceptions). Róisin McAliskey's politics seemed to make her plight as a woman invisible.

This position is best represented in the North of Ireland by Edna Longley (although originally from the South, when writing on the question of nationalism and feminism she does so from a Northern perspective). In a succinct statement of her position, 'From Cathleen to Anorexia', one of the Lip series of pamphlets from the Irish feminist publishers, Attic Press, she argues that there is 'a seamless join between Catholicism and nationalism', (1994a: 163) and denounces those feminists who are also nationalists: 'A nationalist/republican feminist ... claims that her ideologies coincide. And in so doing she tries to hijack Irish feminism' (177).

Longley quotes extensively from Robin Morgan's book, *The Demon Lover*, which argues that all women who engage in 'terrorism' (and Morgan equates the women involved in the Palestinian fight for self-determination, for example, with groups like the German Baader-Meinhof group) are in thrall to a death cult and deny their essential feminine natures. '"Feminism" and "physical force" ', writes Longley, 'is self-evidently a contradiction in terms ... Surely the chill, the stone, the self-destructiveness at the heart of Irish nationalism shows up in its abuse of women and their gifts of life' (1994a: 183).

Clara Connolly also contends that the ideologies of feminism and nationalism are incompatible. In the special Irish issue of *Feminist Review*, published the year after the declaration of the IRA and loyalist cease fires, she writes: 'For many years, republican and Southern Irish feminists have been involved in a war of mutual recrimination.' (Connolly 1995: 117). However, new possibilities for debate had been opened up by the cease fires, she said, and her article, a commentary on a report of a conference organised by the republican women's organisation, Clár na mBan, was intended as a contribution to such a debate. She set her own stall out clearly:

> I write as an Irish feminist, reared in the South to become implacably hostile to the twin pillars of reaction as I experienced them in the 1960s – the Catholic Church and official nationalist ideology. (Connolly 1995: 119)

However, she adds, she has spent the past 20 years living in England, which may be equally important in explaining her current views. She quotes the introductory speech to the conference by Oonagh Marron, who warned the leadership of the republican movement, 'This time around our support will not be unconditional,' going on to comment, 'The only way to ensure that "this time around our support will not be unconditional is to step out of the frame" ' of the republican movement (1995: 121). She takes issue with the contribution of this author of that conference:

> Nationalism burns bright when fuelled by injustice and exclusion; otherwise it turns toxic. So I fail to understand its resonance for Southern Irish women, such as Carol Coulter, a republican journalist ... Neither Northern loyalism nor Southern feminism can be addressed by republicans because they are (or have been) structurally in conflict with Irish nationalism.
> (Connolly 1995: 121–2)

An autobiographical note here may answer her question. I was also brought up in the Southern Ireland of the 1960s, but with a different experience from Clara Connolly's, as I was brought up in a rural Protestant background. As such I did experience exclusion – from the identification of nationalism and Catholicism which was the official state ideology taught in school. My identity was unambiguously Irish, and the Catholic–nationalist identification seemed to me, even as a young child, to be contradicted by history, as so many of the icons of Irish nationalism were Protestant. I never believed that Irish nationalism and Catholicism were one. Therefore, when I grew up and went to university, participating in the radical, socialist and anti-clerical movements of the time like many of my contemporaries (including, no doubt, Clara Connolly), I too rejected the ideology of the ruling elite. But unlike some of them this was not because as a woman I needed to confront a personal oppression by the Catholic Church, identified with the nation, but because the state's nationalist rhetoric was false to what I understood to be the real heritage of Irish nationalism. This I understood as of a piece with the liberationist struggles of other third world countries, and as such of great relevance to women, the poor, and all those interested in challenging the patriarchal power elites of the world (see Coulter 1994 for a proper exposition). I should add, in the light of Clara Connolly's description above, that this did not lead me to the republican movement, with which I have never been in any way involved.

I thought then, and I think now, that many have been excluded from the dominant narrative of Irish nationalism, especially women, the poor and Irish language speakers, and they need to reclaim their own part in Irish history, which includes a more diverse and diversified movement, seeking emancipation on a wide range of fronts, than the narrow, bigoted and prim ideology created in the 1920s and 1930s by 'Official Ireland' (Coulter 1993). Presenting the women's movement in Ireland as always opposed, implicitly if not explicitly, to Irish nationalism is a misrepresentation of Irish history.

Clara Connolly is not alone in identifying Irish nationalism with the official ideology of the Irish state, created in the 1920s and 1930s, and disseminated through the education system. Negating its own historical roots, this equated nationalism with Catholicism, and the Irish nation with the overwhelmingly Catholic population of the Southern Irish state. This official ideology was repressive, stultifying and anti-intellectual, and was rightly rejected by the majority of Irish intellectuals, many of whom either emigrated or lived in a kind of internal exile during the 1940s, 1950s and early 1960s. But it was only the generation of Southern Irish youth, and especially a layer of its intellectuals who were formed in the 1960s and 1970s, who rejected, not only this official ideology, but nationalism *per se*, often in the name of a cosmopolitan Eurocentrism which later dovetailed nicely with the then need of the Irish elite to join the Common Market.

It was not only Irish feminists, therefore, who came to regard Irish nationalism as inimical to all progressive thinking. And when this hostility to the now-outdated ideology of the Irish state was confronted from 1969 on with the permanent semi-insurrection of the Catholic population of the North, accompanied by a military campaign which included some dreadful atrocities, all in the name of Irish unity, that hostility turned to incomprehending and implacable enmity. For over two decades the dominant discourse in the academe and media of the South has been anti-nationalist, a position partially modified only when the cease fires were declared three years ago. Irish feminists were therefore far from being a repressed minority or an isolated pressure group when they argued against nationalism in the name of feminism.

Part of this argument has been to regard nationalism and unionism, in the Irish context, as twins, mirror images of each other. Feminists, and those generally interested in social and political progress, should equally reject both, it was argued. Those women who chose to remain within the republican tradition, or were active within the republican movement, were denounced as traitors to one of the causes they claimed to espouse, as Clara Connolly acknowledges above. Women in the unionist tradition were rarely addressed at all. Firstly, few women closely associated with political unionism make any claims whatsoever to be feminists and secondly, people from a Southern Irish nationalist background have tended, wrongly in my view, to see the anti-Catholicism of Northern unionism as compatible with their own secularist opinions. In fact Northern unionism is linked far more closely with religious fundamentalism (of the Protestant variety) than is Irish nationalism to Catholic fundamentalism.

But nationalism and unionism are not twins, and their respective relationships with the movement for women's emancipation is one of the things which shows this. As has been pointed out by Indian writers like Ashis Nandy, British imperialism has always been a deeply patriarchal construct (Nandy 1983). Therefore Unionism, which has always sought to glorify and defend the most backward-looking aspects of imperialism (the very language of Unionism, where the state is described as 'the realm', is no longer heard in political discourse in Britain itself) has always been deeply inimical to all progress for women. This is shown by the fact that its founding father, Edward Carson, opposed women's suffrage, leaving the Protestant women who organised in favour of the vote for women at the beginning of this century with nowhere to go without breaking with Unionism (Ward 1983). This heritage lasts to this day, with no part for women except in the role of tea-makers in any of the major unionist parties. Indeed, even Rhonda Paisley, the outspoken daughter of the leader of the Democratic Unionist Party, has been critical of the role allocated to women in unionist politics. (Paisley 1992: 32–3). Women born into the unionist tradition find they cannot express themselves within it, and are driven to find a framework outside that political tradition.[1]

Irish nationalism, on the other hand, was quite compatible with the fight for women's suffrage, and many of the women active in public life in the South of Ireland at the beginning of this century worked both for female suffrage and for national independence, though not without some resistance from the more conservative men in the nationalist movement. It was to ensure their place in this movement that Maud Gonne founded Inghinidhe na hEireann (Cardozo 1978: 188). Women were involved in the movement against the Boer War and the visit of Queen Victoria in their tens of thousands (Macardle 1968: 234; Cardozo 1978: 189). While Redmond and the Irish Parliamentary Party voted against female suffrage in Westminster, Sinn Féin supported it. Jennie Wyse-Power, then vice-president of Sinn Féin, told a huge suffrage demonstration in Dublin, 'as an Irish nationalist I cannot see why there should be any antagonism between the Irish women's demands for citizenship and the demand for a native Parliament' (Curtis 1994: 221).

The 1916 Proclamation of the Republic is addressed to 'Irishmen and Irishwomen' (Ward 1983 and 1990; Curtis 1994). Kathleen Clarke has written that, according to her husband, Proclamation signatory Thomas Clarke, one of the seven signatories was opposed to this, but he did not reveal to her which one (Litton 1991).[2]

This openness to women's involvement in public life changed with the foundation of the state, but the fact that the nationalist tradition contained this element in its history has allowed feminists in the republican movement to claim to be part of a vibrant and militant tradition. While their relationship with the movement of which they are a part may be problematic, it is not the same as the relationship of Protestant feminists to the main unionist parties, who have no place for them. Indeed, the venom with which the Women's Coalition is attacked by the unionist parties in the Forum in Belfast is evidence of the profound misogyny which runs through them. The recently formed loyalist parties, the UDP and the PUP, seem to be more open to women's involvement, but this has been too recent a development to allow for a meaningful analysis of women's role within them.

The simplistic counterposition of feminism and Irish nationalism, as well as flying in the face of history, has allowed the definition of Irish nationalism invented by the Irish state and its ideologues in the Catholic Church (summarised by Longley as a political–territorial project 'seamlessly joined' to Catholicism) to go unchallenged internationally. It also hampers the development of feminist thinking, and especially its relevance to women who are not white, or citizens of the wealthy countries of the world. It means the very relevant experiences of women who have had to deal with the combined oppression of imperialism and patriarchy are not brought to bear on it.

One of the most obvious problems with the ideology of western feminism is its failure to extend its influence significantly beyond a small, privileged minority of women in the universities, the media and the professions of the developed world – although this guaranteed it an influence in those societies. Yet surely any inclusive definition of feminism must encompass those women who are everywhere struggling to better their lives and those of their children, be it in village communes, in community groups and organisations in big cities, or in the many parts of the world where there is conflict. It is an irony that, while providing a valuable critique of the dominant ideologies, rooted in patriarchy, of western society, the feminist movement – equally the product of that society – has generally failed to cast a similarly critical eye on its own roots and limitations. When Irish feminism criticises Irish nationalism, therefore, it does so within a context which has far wider historical and geographical boundaries.

Yet feminism was itself the product of very specific conditions in the development of western capitalism, and bears the imprint of its genesis. Its philosophical roots lie in the European Enlightenment, with its emphasis on the primacy of the individual and the necessity for men and women to realise their full potential as individuals in society. In modern society this has been extended to include the full sexual self-determination of the individual, which in some strands of feminism has become the dominant concern. As the society which produced the Enlightenment developed, so did its international influence, first directly through colonialism and later, and more insidiously, through imperialism. The spread of colonialism brought the spread of the ideas of European enlightenment into the colonies of the European powers, bearing an ambiguous message. While on the one hand they introduced ideas of national independence and self-determination to the educated elites of these societies, thereby paving the way for the end of their direct domination, on the other they denigrated the cultures of the countries and societies which colonialism dominated, portraying the cultures and peoples as inferior to a European norm sanctified by Christianity. Thus, the relationship of those who sought to liberate themselves from the colonial yoke to the liberating ideas of the European Enlightenment brought by the colonisers themselves was always conflictual.

Writers like Cesaire, Fanon, Said, Bhabha and others have described the conflicts experienced by those who sought to disentangle themselves and their people from colonialism. Inspired by the liberationist ideas of the European Enlightenment, they could find it turned against them as it became an instrument of oppression in the form of the cultural imperialism of the oppressor. This is particularly well-illustrated in Fanon's essay 'Algeria Unveiled', where he described the French campaign against the veil:

> Around the family life of the Algerian the occupier piled up a whole mass of judgements, appraisals, reasons, accumulated anecdotes and edifying examples, thus attempting to confirm the Algerian within a circle of guilt. Mutual aid societies and societies to promote solidarity with Algerian women sprang up in great number ... What is in fact the assertion of a distinct identity, concern with keeping intact a few shreds of national existence, is attributed to religious, magical, fanatical behaviour ... To the colonialist

offensive against the veil, the colonised opposes a cult of the veil. What was an undifferentiated element in a homogenous whole acquires a taboo character, and the attitude of a given Algerian woman with respect to the veil will be constantly related to her overall attitude with respect to the foreign occupation.   (Fanon 1989: 38,41,47)

Eventually large numbers of Algerian women abandoned the veil – but only in order to participate in the resistance and travel freely in the French part of the cities on missions for the resistance movement. When the French authorities responded by harassing women, the veil was readopted with a vengeance, in the form of the haik (coat), under which bombs and weapons could be concealed. The eventual realisation of what was happening drove the authorities to a renewed and even more vigorous campaign to 'Westernise' Algerian women, routinely publicly unveiling them to the cry 'Vive l'Algérie Française!'   (Fanon 1989: 62)

I have dwelt on Fanon's work at some length because it illustrates very well the complexity of the relationship of questions of national identity, gender and political activism in countries which have experienced national oppression – and the religious and cultural oppression which goes with it. He goes on to argue that the demands of this national struggle turned the traditional relationships within the Algerian family on their head, and allowed Algerian women to win status and a place in public life. It is now a truism to state that the content of formal national independence disappointed, and continues to disappoint, the majority of the populations in the countries which successfully achieved it, and Algeria provides a particularly horrifying example of what such disappointment can bring.

The promises made to women by nationalist movements, like those made to the poor, have remained unfulfilled, in Ireland as elsewhere in the world. Yet what must be confronted by feminists is the fact that in every country which was dominated by colonialism and imperialism nationalism has had a powerful appeal for women as well as men, and has mobilised them in their millions, and, as long as those countries remain disadvantaged politically and economically on the world stage, this will continue. The ideas of western feminism have only a limited relevance here. Referring to Muslims in the Middle East and the Maghreb, Kabbani attempted to explain this in her book *Letter to Christendom*: 'Unlike Westerners, Muslims are for the most part too poor and insecure to afford the luxury of individual feelings; instead, their reactions to events are strongly shaped by communal memories' (Kabbani 1989: 2). She makes an explicit comparison between the Arabs and the Irish in being reputedly 'too preoccupied by history'. But, she adds, only those who have no unsatisfied grievances or no threatened identity can afford to forget history (Kabbani 1989: 2).

The views of women in Muslim countries are interesting in this debate, not only for their inherent merits, but because Ireland, and the supposed place occupied by Catholicism in public life in the South, has been compared by some commentators to the place occupied by Islam in the Arab world. The Egyptian feminist Leila Ahmed has explored the tangled roots of the debate about feminism in Islamic countries, and points out how feminism and western cultural superiority have gone hand in hand there. Referring to the veiling of women, she writes: 'to Western Eyes ... (it was) the most visible marker of the difference and inferiority of Islamic societies – it became the symbol now of both the oppression of women ... and the backwardness of Islam'. (Ahmed 1992: 152). She continues:

> colonialism's use of feminism to promote the culture of the colonisers and undermine the native culture has ever since imparted to feminism in non-Western societies the taint of having served as an instrument of colonial domination, rendering it suspect in Arab eyes and vulnerable to the charge of being an ally of colonial interests. The taint has undoubtedly hindered the feminist struggle within Muslim societies.   (1992: 167)

This charge does not only apply to Muslim societies. The Eurocentrism of the dominant agenda within feminism has led to an ignoring of the traditions and real history of struggle of women in other countries and other cultures, a blindness to the reality of their struggle because it does not conform to what they view as the norm. This is doubly unfortunate, because women have, by and large, played a greater role in public political activity in the first part of this century in those countries which have sought to end the domination of a colonial power than they have in many western European countries. While the suffrage movement was very important in these countries, the number of women actively involved was relatively small. Yet in India, for example, the number of women involved in Gandhi's salt marches ran to millions. Of the 80,000 arrested during these marches, 17,000 were women (Jayawardena 1986: 100). When the male leaders of the civil disobedience campaign in the 1930s were imprisoned, the women took over the running of the campaign, exactly as the Ladies' Committee had taken on some of the work of the jailed Fenian leaders in Ireland in the 1860s, and as the Ladies' Land League took on the role of the Land League 20 years later. Jawaharlal Nehru later related his father's astonishment at his mother's behaviour, because he and his friends had 'in no way encouraged these aggressive activities of women all over the country' (Liddle and Joshi 1986: 34).

It was Nehru who most perceptively saw the dual content of women's involvement in the nationalist movement at this time:

> They were mostly middle class women, accustomed to a sheltered life, and suffering chiefly from the many repressions and customs produced by a society dominated to his own advantage by man. The call of freedom had always a double meaning for them, and the enthusiasm and energy with which they threw themselves into the struggle had no doubt their springs in the vague and hardly conscious, but nevertheless intense, desire to rid themselves of domestic slavery also.   (cited in Jayawardena 1986: 98–9)

Equally, in Egypt there were political demonstrations by women from the early years of the twentieth century, and women were killed in anti-government demonstrations. Again, they saw themselves as an integral part of a movement led by their menfolk: 'We, the women of Egypt, mothers, sisters and wives of those who have been the victims of British greed and exploitation ... deplore the brutal, barbarous actions that have fallen upon ... the Egyptian nation. Egypt has committed no crime except to express her desire for independence' read the petition organised by Huda Sharawi, wife of the founder of Wafd and herself the founder of the Egyptian Feminist Union (Jawayardena 1986: 53).

This unity of purpose between women and men in nationalist movements drew particular strength from two specific conditions within the shared experience of colonial domination – the place of religion on the one hand and the family on the other. The family is an ambiguous institution for many women in societies oppressed by colonialism and imperialism. For women in western Europe who sought a role in civic life at the end of the eighteenth century the biggest obstacle was society, based on the family, which sanctioned their subordination to men within the family by depriving them of access to education and the means for an independent life (Wollstonecraft 1992). The debate which took place about the role of women concentrated on whether or not they were fit to assume an equal role, or whether they were essentially suited to playing a subordinate role to men within the family, a microcosm of the hierarchical structure on which their society is built. This debate has continued for two hundred years.

However, the experience of women in countries dominated by colonialism was different. Their public and civic life was dominated by an outsider who forcibly occupied that space. Those excluded from it were excluded by reason of colour, language, religion or other mark of origin and distinctness from the occupier. The exclusion was two-fold: the occupier took over the administration (and often ownership) of the colony; he allowed the native access to it only to the extent to which he (and only he – even if the native people allowed a role for women, the European colonisers of the nineteenth century certainly did not) was prepared to adopt the language and ways of the occupier.

So public space became alien for all the native inhabitants. It was a space where they had to proclaim their own culture and language as inferior. To take a place in it they had to betray themselves in some essential way. Yet doing so was, for some, necessary for survival. The family, however, was different. In the family one could speak one's own language, practise one's own customs, express one's own opinions, be oneself. It was an inviolate space, the one place where the occupier could not enter – at least, not without doing violence to his own rhetoric on the sanctity of the family. Small wonder, therefore, that the family sometimes became the locus of resistance to the occupier.

Thus, the family could become the crucible of rebellion, the training ground for a generation of revolutionaries, as the history of Irish nationalism attests. From the days of the United Irishmen, in certain families, children were reared within an ideology of political rebellion. The families were organised around the need for solidarity with those victimised because of it, and where political agreement was more a prerequisite for marriage than the more conventional requirements of property and position (Coulter 1993). The negative side of this is, of course, the dynastic elements in the politics of countries with a colonial past, of which Ireland and the Indian sub-continent provide examples.

Given the need for solidarity within families with a tradition of rebellion, the distinction between male and female roles could become secondary. At any time the women, as much as the men, could be required to suffer privation, to withstand interrogation, to sustain the family alone. This inevitably affected the attitudes towards gender roles of both women and men. Therefore in the writings of women involved in the nationalist movement we find an assumption of equality with men – even if, by the beginning of the twentieth century, this was combined with the realisation that this assumption was not widely shared. Further, the patriarchal model of public life was the one imported by the coloniser, and women could postulate a new form of public life which differed in every respect, including in the centrality of a male hierarchy.

This is not to suggest that such attitudes pervaded the whole of the colonised society. It is also true that in a colonised society the father or husband, treated as inferior at work and in the public world, where the model of maleness was authoritarian and often brutal, decided that the only place he could play this prescribed role was within the family, thereby brutalising his wife and children. It is also true that the colonial system reproduced its own codes of gender relations, often in exaggerated form, within significant layers of the families of the colonised, especially in the middle class. Irish literature from the beginning of the century is rich in examples. The fact that, despite the aspirations of many women activists in these nationalist movements, gender relations did not fundamentally change with political independence, underscored the legitimacy of the family models grafted on by imperialism. The family is an oppressive institution for many women and children in all societies, and the recent history of Southern Ireland has brought to light the private hell which family life meant for tens of thousands of people in the new 'free' state.

In the North of Ireland the combination of economic deprivation and colonial experience has given the family a strong role in community and social life, and contributed to assumptions about a 'matriarchal' culture in Northern Irish society. While these assumptions have been trenchantly, and convincingly, criticised by Eithne McLaughlin (1993: 553–68), none the less the political situation has contributed to the emergence of community groups, especially in the nationalist areas, based around the activity of women in defence of their families.

This complex history means that a simplistic denunciation of the family as an inherently repressive institution for women does not find a deep resonance in societies which have experienced colonial domination. The very recent debate surrounding the introduction of divorce in the South of Ireland, which was narrowly accepted by the electorate in a referendum on 25 November 1995, revealed the attachment which those on both sides in the debate felt for an ideal of the family, rooted in the memory of the family as a centre of solidarity and mutual support against an alien outside world, and in a living memory of the extended family. Ironically, this may be one of the factors contributing to the growth of single parenthood in Ireland. A recent study of a group of single mothers in a very deprived part of Dublin found that the main determining factor in deciding girls to keep their babies was the support of their mothers (McCashin, 1996: 44). While the experience of the new state brought repression, it also brought emigration, of both single women and married men. The former offered a model of independence, while the latter, many of whom sent remittances home, allowed the main responsibility for the family to rest on the shoulders of the women they left behind, thereby altering the power relationships within the family, albeit often at an unarticulated level.

The relative attachment to 'family values' shown by Irish women, and Irish people in general, does not mean that Irish women have just been passive victims of their subordination. Behind the statistics of exclusion lie the considerable resilience and creativity shown by Irish women in the face of economic adversity and personal hardship over the past two generations, despite their virtual exclusion from public life. With great ingenuity they found ways to circumvent some of the control of the patriarchy, and to carve out space for themselves to act collectively. This included the use of apparently innocuous organisations like the Irish Countrywomen's Association and the Irish Housewives Association to challenge the power of the government and major interest groups like farmers on questions of central importance to women like the control of food prices. For many women such organisations provided the only outlet outside the home, a forum for discussion, a place to learn new skills and a centre for solidarity with other women. Significantly, as mere 'women's organisations' they were ignored by the Catholic Church, and were the only organisations in the Southern state in the 1940s and 1950s which were genuinely non-sectarian and pluralist, involving proportionately large numbers of Protestant women. The ICA was one of the first organisations to seek the legalisation of contraception.

In the North it has been around issues of family solidarity that women in the nationalist community, and, to a lesser extent, in the working-class loyalist community in Belfast, have become politically active. The question of the treatment of prisoners, overwhelmingly sons, brothers, husbands and fathers, has been central. Tens of thousands of women have been involved in both public protests about the conditions of prisoners, and in giving practical support to the prisoners and their families. They have also been the ones to carry the burden of family responsibility when the men are in jail, and this has often caused great tension within families when they have refused to return to a subordinate role when the men came out (Coulter 1990).

But women have also played a part in the military campaign itself. Many feminists have found this, in particular, incomprehensible. How can women, whose essential role is a nurturing and life-giving one, partake of a form of activity which involves killing other human beings?

This is an important question, but one which cannot be dealt with in isolation from the broader debates about what feminism means and about the nature of nationalism in situations of oppression for minority groups. Should feminists accept this essentialist definition of women as nurturing life-givers, which has served to justify keeping women out of professional and public life? Are women who engage in military combat any more to be condemned than those who live with men who are thus involved, or women, like Margaret Thatcher, who took death-dealing decisions affecting far greater numbers of people? Can the decisions women make about their political activity be disconnected from the context in which those decisions are made by everyone? I think the answer to these questions must be 'no'.

Religion also has a special potency in countries with a colonial past, where secularism has been an aspect of the ideology of the coloniser rather than an indigenous product. Religion sanctifies the moments of significance in human lives – birth, passage to adulthood, marriage, death. All of these moments are celebrated within the context of the family, marking, as they do, points in its evolution. Religion also provides rituals for the mundane routines of family and community life – the marking of the seasons, the preparation of food. Further, it serves as a bridge between the family and the broader community, especially when that community is denied expression as a civic entity in an independent nation. The religious community substitutes for a civic community, and provides individuals and families with the mechanisms for participating in the life of the community when that is denied by an alien political power. And, as Blacks in the southern states of the USA will remember, it can provide powerful allegories for the experience of suffering and the hope of emancipation when these cannot be expressed in an overtly political form. Therefore in these situations religious convictions and religious imagery often play an important part in resistance movements.

In most countries dominated by colonialism resistance has been led by a section of the native middle class which acquired the education of the occupier, including its rhetoric of enlightenment and democracy, which was then applied to the situation of their own emerging nations. Modern nationalism is, above all, a European creation, and the dawn of nationalism in western Europe in the eighteenth century is linked by Benedict Anderson with the dusk of religion (Anderson 1983: 19).

However, European ideologies always suffer a transformation when they are exported to the colonies. The secular nationalism which first attracted the young intellectuals of the colonies was quickly combined with a rediscovery of and a reassertion of pride in the native culture,

which was often homogenised and idealised in the proc
conservative aspects enhanced. This went with the discov
turally and as a political force, of the peasantry and, son
urban poor, who were used by the emerging new elite, whi
solidated a new state perpetuating the inequalities of the ol

This demanded the creation of an ideology to justify the
quo. The native culture, inherently uncentralised and further frag-
mented by years of foreign domination, is given an artificial
centralisation and cohesion to serve the conservative needs of the new
rulers (Gibbons 1996: 134–7). The diverse, chaotic and often subversive
aspects of the indigenous culture are purged in the name of a new
'national' culture, inculcated by the education system, and combined
with a new version of history to justify it all. Usually the religion of the
mass of the people is pressed into service to assist in this role. This
proves a potent instrument for social control, especially the oppression
of women. But the resilience of religion in countries with such a history is also linked to secularism, whose shallow roots are seen to lie in
the ideology of the oppressor.

The power of religion comes, not initially from coercion (though this
becomes important when state power and religious power are fused,
after the colonial power has been expelled), but from real popular roots
in people's consciousness, drawn from the experience of the place of
religion under colonialism. When public life is totally invaded by a foreign oppressor, or by an all-embracing totalitarian system, and the
individual cannot freely express her or himself as a civic being, one of
the few places where humanness can be expressed is in the private,
intimate area of family and emotional life. The rituals of religion provide a bond between the purely domestic and the broader community
which shared the experience of exclusion from civic life. Religion,
therefore, has always been an important part of national culture, especially for oppressed nations – or cultures, when the nation is being
formed from diverse elements. It has often been a badge of separateness from the occupier, offering a sense of moral superiority in the
midst of social inferiority and transcendental salvation when there was
no sign of a temporal one. It is not surprising, therefore, that in many
former colonies women seek to reinterpret, rather than reject, the religion they were brought up with.

In the South of Ireland growing prosperity and a rise in the general
standard of education, linked with the integration of the state into the
European community and the western capitalist economy in general,
has brought a secularisation of the society. Yet Catholicism remains
part of the identity of most people, and, even among people who do
not practise on a regular basis, provides rituals for moments of significance in the lives of individuals and families and is part of their sense
of identity. This is combined with general support for ethical values
associated with Christianity, like social solidarity. The fact that there
has never been widespread support for the politics of Thatcherism in
Ireland has often been explained by the general influence of the

Catholic Church. In the North of Ireland religion is a central part of communal identity, and secularism has made little headway as a result. Indeed, alone of all regions of Britain and Ireland, Northern Ireland sees religion as part of public and popular discourse, especially the language of evangelical Protestantism. It is not uncommon for Biblical precedents to be invoked by local councils in strongly Protestant areas in support of policy decisions. This clearly makes the task of feminists very difficult.

In dealing with the situation of women in Northern Ireland it is necessary to place it in the context that women in oppressed communities in general, and therefore those brought up in the nationalist community in Northern Ireland, have suffered the same exclusion and discrimination as men. They have suffered additionally because they are women, though it is arguable that a well educated, middle-class Catholic woman in Northern Ireland has a wider range of life-choices than a second-generation unemployed male from one of the Catholic ghettos (and, indeed, over the past 20 years, than an unemployed male youth from the Protestant ghettos). It is legitimate, therefore, for women to express their response to both the experiences of their community and of their sex in any specific set of circumstances. The same can be seen with the Travelling community. There is no doubt that Travelling women suffer particular oppression both in society as a whole and within their community. But they are reluctant to articulate the oppression they experience within their community in public, because they do not want to become associated with attacks from the oppressive settled community, which, at the end of the day, would only make their situation worse. Denunciations of the backwardness of Traveller men are deeply unhelpful to them. They must find their own forum to articulate their problems and, indeed, are doing so, with the help of women who respect their culture.

None the less, acknowledging the need of women to find ways of articulating their needs within their own culture and their own political traditions does not mean refusing to criticise the limitations of those cultures or political traditions. Nationalism, although it has been the authentic response of people, male and female, who have experienced national oppression, has signally failed to satisfy all the aspirations expressed by the mass of the people involved in struggles against that national oppression. Further, when a genuinely free expression of the need for national autonomy and self-determination is too long denied, and when the competing claims for self-determination of other ethnic groups within the same territory have historically been the subject of foreign manipulation, nationalism can degenerate into genocidal barbarism, as the recent histories of the former Yugoslavia and Rwanda illustrate.

Some of the feminists within the Irish republican movement have indeed been critical of their own political leadership. But that criticism has tended to concentrate on the leadership's reluctance to take on board, or give sufficient priority to, women's concerns. Claire Hackett, a republican activist, also wrote in the issue of *Feminist Review* devoted to Ireland. She was one of the main organisers of the Clár na mBan conference of which Clara Connolly wrote in the same issue. She admitted that there was some pressure from republican ranks against this conference, fearing that it would criticise the leadership and give the appearance of disunity (Hackett 1995: 113).

However, she also responded to many of the points made by Clara Connolly. She defended the attempt to fuse the feminist and nationalist agenda on the basis that self-determination is a feminist as well as a nationalist concept, and involves all the areas in which women are currently denied autonomy (Hackett 1995: 111). She warns against seeking the kind of homogenisation on the basis of putative women's interests while denying the real differences which exist between women from different religious, social and political backgrounds, arguing that this will inevitably lead to a lowest common denominator kind of politics. She defends the organising of specifically republican women's groups: 'There is still much to be done to make feminism truly inclusive. But I believe that we can only create the basis for strong alliances by acknowledging the different identities of women rather than striving for a common ground that may only be an illusion ... Clár na mBan believes strongly that a multiplicity of women's voices in Ireland need to be heard' (Hackett 1995: 113). In this she is right. Any attempt to impose a single voice on women in Ireland, North or South, Protestant or Catholic, will drive women away from expressing their needs, which will inevitably vary according to class, geography and urban or rural background.

But her criticism of the republican movement is made from too narrow a perspective. It is not just that the leadership, predominantly male, as she says, is reluctant to give priority to women's issues. The very nature of the republican movement, like all nationalist movements, requires a centralisation and homogenisation which is hostile to dissent. The exigencies of a military campaign demand a culture of secrecy and discipline which is anathema to genuinely free and open discussion. The Irish republican movement aspires to a united Ireland and, while it is notably short on constitutional specifics, presumably envisages a unitary, centralised state, similar to other western European states. Since dumping the federal Ireland programme of the old Ó Bráidaigh/O'Connell leadership it has had little to say about the decentralisation of power in a united Ireland. Thus, it can be assumed that the leadership of the republican movement sees the future in terms of conventional political theory and practice, with Sinn Féin assuming a role as one party among others in a national parliament, governments being formed on the basis of parliamentary majorities, a professional civil service administering the country, and, then as now, very little say for ordinary people in the decisions which affect their lives. In such a system, similar to what exists all over the western world at the moment, the illusion of democratically choosing leaders covers the reality of a largely self-perpetuating political class, not only overwhelmingly male, but overwhelmingly white and middle-class as well.

The women who break into this system are subsumed into it (although their influence is more evident in the Nordic countries, for reasons specific to that part of the world). It demands an acceptance of a set of rules and a method of work which effectively precludes the expression of the interests of those who possess no political or economic power, and a lifestyle which most women would find very alien. It is interesting that one of the brightest, most innovative and articulate politicians in Southern Ireland, the first woman cabinet minister since Constance Markiewicz, left politics in January 1997,.citing as her reason unacceptable pressure on her family. Among her many achievements Máire Geoghegan Quinn (daughter of a Fianna Fáil dynasty), as Minister for Justice successfully introduced legislation legalising homosexuality on conditions more liberal than those pertaining in Britain.

The trade unions, centres for the organisation of ordinary people at the beginning of the century, when they occupied themselves with issues like food and clothing co-operatives and health insurance as well as work-place based issues, have now become ossified and, again, male-dominated bureaucracies mainly concerned with negotiating with governments. Today the vacuum at the heart of public life in the South of Ireland is occupied, however patchily, by organisations based on local communities and their immediate concerns, be they drug-dealing in Dublin's inner city, the need for facilities for families in the new suburbs or the problem of rural decline in the West of Ireland. They are organised mainly by women, and join the growing number of women's groups based either on the needs of women locally or nationally, like Women's Aid. In the North too there has been an upsurge in the development of women's groups in both nationalist and loyalist areas, although some of the groups in the loyalist areas have been regarded as suspect in their communities because of the links they have forged with similar groups in the South, and the support they have enjoyed from the Irish President, Mary Robinson.

While we cannot say that such groups can provide an alternative to mainstream politics, they are indicative of the emergence of a different type of politics, one closer to people's immediate concerns, and more accessible to women and the poor. They challenge the monopoly on political discourse held by the political parties, and open the possibility of seeking a more popular, responsive and genuinely democratic way of exercising power. While in the North, Sinn Féin is benign towards such groups in the areas it dominates, it has not been led by them to question the very model of politics it espouses, a model which would entrust political activity to ordinary people on a daily basis. This would require an openness to diversity, a voluntary relinquishing of control, which it shows no willingness to adopt.

It is interesting that the Women's Coalition in the North, a group which draws much of its strength from such groups, has been the first women's organisation to make advances in the political system. In the elections to the Northern Ireland Forum, set up to debate issues outside the 'constitutional issue' putatively being discussed in the all-party talks at Stormont, the Women's Coalition won almost one per cent of the vote after only six weeks in existence, and a number of highly articulate women, with origins in both communities, came to the fore, most of them with a background in the voluntary and community sector. However, it is unlikely they took many votes from Sinn Féin, as it achieved its highest-ever vote in this election. The Women's Coalition have consistently argued for genuinely inclusive talks, which, in the Northern Ireland context, means against the exclusion of Sinn Féin.[3]

They are treated with undisguised hatred by the unionist parties which dominate the Forum (the SDLP and Sinn Féin are not participating in it). This hatred seems to be more directed at the fact that, as women, they have dared to enter the political sanctum up to now dominated by men than at the fact that they argue for the inclusion of Sinn Féin. Yet the very sterility of the Forum and the pointlessness of the debates it holds (it has no legislative function) make their efforts seem vain. It remains to be seen if they can find an ongoing way of speaking for the constituency they undoubtedly represent. They will face difficulties in defining their attitude to the ever-present 'constitutional question' without alienating some of their support. None the less, their success so far shows the resonance a community-based women's movement can have.

It is clear that in Northern Ireland, as elsewhere, denouncing nationalism is a futile exercise. If feminists are to have a lasting influence there, it is necessary to empathise with the experiences which lead women from oppressed nations and communities to support the nationalist movements which arise out of their history. It is necessary to understand their culture and the part it plays in the establishment of personal and community identity, which are essential to the well-being of every individual. It is necessary to adopt a critical approach to feminism itself, and see how it has been limited by its own origins in western Europe and the United States, and its projection of the experiences and interests of essentially middle-class, white women on to the rest of the world (see Coulter 1995).

None of this requires an uncritical approach to nationalism. But criticism which echoes the complacent anti-nationalism of those based in societies whose nationhood is well established, which implicitly or explicitly assumes a hierarchy of nations in the world, according legitimacy to those who have established their statehood and questioning that of those who have not, will not find much acceptance. However, criticism which empathises with the sense of dispossession and the aspirations of the oppressed, and which attempts to explore with them ways to realise all their aspirations, something nationalism has failed to do in practice, will open the way to a genuinely fruitful discussion between those drawing their inspiration from feminism, nationalism and, indeed, that now much-neglected philosophy, socialism.

Notes

1. For first-hand accounts of the tension between Northern Protestantism and political, sexual and cultural dissent see Hyndman 1996.
2. For a detailed examination of the process whereby women were excluded from political life, see Litton 1991.
3. I am grateful to Anna Eggert and Susie Campbell for their insights into the development of the Women's Coalition.

CHAPTER 9

Is sectarianism racism? Theorising the racism/sectarianism interface

Robbie McVeigh

In the 1990s, Black British organisations have been increasingly concerned to have religion included as a category of identity protected by the 1976 Race Relations Act (Modood *et al.* 1997). The Act already outlaws discrimination on the grounds of 'colour, race, nationality, or ethnic or national origins'. The campaign for the inclusion of religion promises to push discussion of the connection between religion and ethnicity centre-stage in contemporary debates about racism. The principal reason that religion is not included in existing legislation is that, when the first race relations legislation was passed in 1965, there were concerns that it should not be 'complicated' by the Northern Ireland situation. These concerns had two important consequences. First, the Northern Ireland government at Stormont requested that the Race Relations Act (1965) would not apply to Northern Ireland – since it might offer redress to Catholics who, at that time, were experiencing overt and direct discrimination by the Northern Ireland state (Farrell 1980). Second, Stormont requested that religion might be excluded from the legislation – since it would be embarrassing to have anti-religious discrimination legislation everywhere in the UK other than the place where it was needed most (Dickey 1972). As a result, religion – which had been included as a category in early drafts – was withdrawn from race relations legislation. People in Northern Ireland had to wait until 1997 to receive any legal protection from racist discrimination. Thus, trying to make sense of the interface between religion and ethnicity – and racism and sectarianism – is nothing new. Furthermore, it is clear that the evolution of the debate on the connection between racism and sectarianism has been structured as much by political imperatives as academic debate.

Despite the legal separation of racism and sectarianism, people continued to identify similarities. In 1972 the British sociologist and 'race expert' Robert Moore provided a ground-breaking analysis of the Northern Ireland conflict entitled 'Race relations in the Six Counties'. His conclusion to a comparative analysis of racism and sectarianism was unequivocal: 'the Northern Ireland conflict is truly race conflict' (1972: 37). Moore's only concern in terms of 'Race relations in the Six Counties' was the ethnic dimension to unionist/nationalist conflict. It is striking in retrospect to draw out some of the questions raised by his argument. In particular, there was no mention of minority ethnic groups in Northern Ireland, even though at the time there were long-standing Traveller and Jewish communities in the North, and the development of newer Chinese and South Asian communities was already under way. In short, his was an analysis of 'race relations' in the North without minority ethnic groups or 'People of Colour'. Moore's analysis, however, also raised another contrasting question. He was convinced of the appropriateness of locating sectarian conflict in Northern Ireland in terms of 'race relations' – for him sectarianism was about racism. Since then there has been a movement away from this analysis, towards an approach that – consciously or not – constructs sectarianism as different from racism. This interpretation has usually hinged on the argument that sectarianism is about religion rather than 'race' or ethnicity (Bruce 1986; Fulton 1991; Hickey 1986). This approach implies that the Northern Ireland conflict as one with a specificity, if not a peculiarity, which requires a different approach to those grounded in ethnicity or 'race relations'.

The connection between racism and sectarianism is further complicated by the issue of anti-Irish racism – particularly the question of whether it is appropriate to recognise the existence of anti-Irish racism in Ireland. The notion of anti-Irish racism has been developed to the point where its existence outside of Ireland is less and less contested (Curtis 1984b; Hickman 1995a and b; Hickman and Walter 1997; Knobel 1986). Anti-Irishness manifests itself in Ireland – in the forms of anti-Irish jokes and so on. It is a crucial element in the construction of loyalist identity in the Six Counties. Loyalist murals have increasingly adopted slogans such as 'KAI' (Kill All Irish) and 'Irish Out'. This kind of discourse is not simply directed at Southern Irish visitors to the North – it constructs all Catholics/nationalists as Irish and unwelcome. This, of course, draws on a much older establishment unionist tradition of anti-nationalist rhetoric which used variations on a theme of 'if you (i.e. northern nationalists) do not like it here, move to the south' (Farrell 1980). This kind of expression of anti-Irish racism in Ireland often seems indistinguishable from sectarianism. At present, however, there is no consensus on how to connect these very different experiences. For example, in Britain the Irish have, albeit sometimes uncomfortably, been part of a broader minority ethnic and anti-racist coalition. The Commission for Racial Equality in Britain now regards the Irish community as one of its key constituencies (CRE 1997). There is no evidence of this happening in Northern Ireland with the recently appointed Commission for Racial Equality (NI). Indeed, such moves would probably be resisted by minority ethnic groups in the North in order to avoid further sectarianisation of their interests – they do not want anti-racism to be seen as an 'nationalist' or a 'unionist' issue.

Figure 9.1   Cormac's view of racism and sectarianism.

Moore's analysis therefore provides a fascinating departure point for any theorisation of contemporary racism and sectarianism in Northern Ireland for two very different reasons. First, it completely ignored the minority ethnic experience which is now so central to the debate around 'race relations' in the Six Counties. Second, it raised directly the sectarianism/racism debate which has subsequently been marginalised. This chapter suggests that both these issues have to be central in any attempt to make sense of the dynamics of racism and sectarianism in Northern Ireland. Moreover, they are central to wider tensions involving Black and White people, and Irish and British people, in Britain and Ireland. This debate has immediate ramifications in terms of how people name and understand and theorise sectarianism; but it also raises wider questions about the theoretical and political efficacy of the very concept of racism – whether it can and should it involve White groups as well as People of Colour; whether it is rooted in colonialism or something else like skin colour; how it is connected with ethnicity and religion and so on. The importance of these questions illustrates the need for recentring both Irishness and British involvement in Ireland within sociological perspectives on Britain. Such questions are also testament to the continuing importance of colonialism as a structuring element in contemporary British and Irish society. In consequence, the racism/sectarianism debate should be right at the heart of contemporary sociological analysis of key issues like racism, ethnicity and religion.

Racism and sectarianism

There is no doubting the resemblance of aspects of racism in Britain and sectarianism in Northern Ireland. These similarities are manifest in many different ways at both an interpersonal and an institutional level. Different social phenomena in Britain and Northern Ireland assume a specifically racist or sectarian form in much the same way. This comparison holds for a whole gamut of racist and sectarian phenomena: from name-calling, through discrimination, to murder. These similarities suggest the possibility of a more complex commonality. Both racism and sectarianism involve social conflict and inequality across an ethnic interface. The commonality is reinforced by parallels in the response of successive British governments to racism and sectarianism as 'problems'. These responses have involved much analogous legislation: directed at 'incitement to hatred' and racist and sectarian discrimination; establishing 'community relations commissions' and so on (Dickey 1972; Rolston 1983).

Thus, there is a *prima facie* case to suggest a commonality between racism and sectarianism within the British state. Furthermore, there is a case for arguing that this commonality deserves attention because it would in turn throw new light on the nature of both racism and sectarianism. In spite of this, the similarities and differences between racism and sectarianism have received relatively little academic attention. In fact, despite its currency in popular and political discourse, there has been little detailed empirical research on sectarianism *per se*. What little research has been undertaken has tended to be unimaginative, focusing on religious head-counting. As a consequence, the conceptualisation of sectarianism has been poor and its use as an explanatory term remains problematic – sectarianism remains profoundly *undertheorized* (McVeigh 1992a, 1995a).

In contrast, there has been a huge amount of empirical and theoretical work on racism in Britain. This work provides a useful sounding board for the comparison of sectarianism and racism. Comparative work of this kind is conspicuous by its absence in analyses of conflict in Northern Ireland. As Richard Jenkins puts it:

> I suspect that the six counties are neither totally different from, nor completely the same as, either Britain or the Republic. However, the contours of those similarities and differences are largely unmapped. In order for them to be understood, it is vital that comparative research on a scale as yet unimagined be carried out. Five immediately obvious areas in which such research is necessary – and this is to name but a few – are law and order, social mobility, youth culture, sectarianism and racism (i.e. discrimination), and state equal opportunity initiatives (a comparison between, for example, the Fair Employment Agency and the Commission for Racial Equality might prove to be most instructive). (Jenkins 1984: 261–3)

Where analysis involving racism and sectarianism has been attempted, it has tended to be an assertion or a denial of the identity of racism and sectarianism rather than a comparison of the two. For example, Liam de Paor argued in 1970 that:

> In Northern Ireland Catholics are Blacks who happen to have white skins. This is not a truth. It is an oversimplification and too facile an analogy. But it is a better oversimplification than that which sees the struggle and conflict in Northern Ireland in terms of religion ... The Northern Ireland problem is a colonial problem, and the 'racial' distinction (and it is actually imagined as racial) between the colonists and the natives is expressed in terms of religion.   (de Paor 1970: xii)

As we have seen, Robert Moore agreed with this. He had no doubt that 'the Northern Ireland conflict is truly race conflict'. Moore's analysis did not provoke the debate it deserved. Sarah Nelson (1975) wrote a critical rejoinder to Moore's article. Since then the relationship of sectarianism to racism has been addressed by different authors in a fairly summary manner (Brewer 1991, 1992; Clayton 1996; McVeigh 1990, 1996). Nelson's argument has assumed the role of being a definitive rebuttal of the 'sectarianism equals racism' thesis: Jenkins described it as 'a convincing critique of this model of the Irish conflict' (1984: 262). In fact – as Nelson herself admits – she was 'more concerned about asking questions ... than answering them'. Her conceptualisation of both racism and sectarianism is limited: they are considered only as 'ideologies'. Moreover her conclusions are tentative: 'what can be said is that the prime objection made against Catholics does not concern their "racial difference" but rather their "disloyalty"' (1975: 168).

In fact, this seems little different from the notorious 'cricket test' which Norman Tebbit suggested should be applied to gauge the 'loyalty' of Black British people. If anything, the emphasis on loyalty makes sectarianism seem all the more similar to what Barker identifies as the 'new racism' in Britain. His suggestion is that the 'new racism' is based upon the notion of a 'way of life' under threat by 'outsiders' and contrasts this with the notions of biological superiority and inferiority which underpinned the 'old racism' (Barker 1981). This notion of racism captures neatly aspects of the traditional 'siege mentality' of unionist sectarianism. Certainly, whatever its merits, Nelson's intervention did not represent the *coup de grace* for Moore's thesis. The questions Moore raised in 1972 are equally pertinent to discussion of racism in the Six Counties – practically and theoretically – in the late 1990s.

Despite this, Nelson's critique effectively failed to encourage anyone else to continue to 'ask questions'. This is not simply a consequence of flaws in Nelson's argument. Rather, it is symptomatic of the way that the whole debate on the connection between racism and sectarianism has plodded along. Many authors have recognised that there is some vague similarity between the two. Indeed it is unusual for an analysis which touches on sectarianism not to have at least one racism-related entry in its bibliography. But the connection has rarely been explicitly addressed. The debate has been, as it were, carried on in footnotes. Jenkins qualified his recognition of the need for comparative work on racism and sectarianism by saying (in a footnote!):

> This remark should not be read as support for Moore's contention that the ethnic conflict in Northern Ireland is a 'race relations' situation, an idea which has, unfortunately, recently been resurrected.   (Jenkins 1984: 262)

Given the absence of supporting evidence, Jenkins's dismissal of the 'sectarianism equals racism' thesis is premature. Moore's assertion of the thesis, however, was equally premature. The *a priori* nature of interventions on both sides of the debate is itself indicative of the need for much further substantive research and political debate. The assertion of an identity between racism and sectarianism can neither be made – nor dismissed – with any conviction before the similarities and differences between racism and sectarianism receive more attention. The jury on the 'sectarianism equals racism' thesis should remain 'out' until much further comparative research is done. Moreover, this is as much a political as an academic decision. In other words if people name an experience or an oppression as 'racism', the chances are it will be analysed as such, providing that the experience is broadly connected to issues of ethnicity and inequality. If the decision that sectarianism is racism were to be taken by political actors in the Irish context and, if this analysis were to be defended and sustained over a period of time, it is likely that academic analysis would follow this lead. This is precisely what happened with the use of the notions of anti-Irish racism in Britain and anti-Traveller racism in Ireland (Curtis 1984b; McVeigh 1992b).

Are racism and sectarianism the same thing?

The 'is sectarianism racism?' question has been central to those who have compared racism and sectarianism. Much existing analysis has lent weight to Moore's assertion. My own empirical work in this area found striking similarities between the lived experience of racism and sectarianism (McVeigh 1990). While this aspect has been undertheorised in most academic literature, the experience and threat of racist and sectarian harassment and intimidation is what defines racism and sectarianism. Moreover, the centrality of violence means that policing becomes the key interface between the British state and racialised and sectarianised communities (McVeigh 1994; Solomos 1988). There are also broad similarities in the ways in which discrimination and otherness characterise racism and sectarianism as lived experience – to be Black or Catholic is to be discriminated against in a whole range of ways and disadvantaged across a whole range of indices. Each of these similarities suggests at least a significant overlap between racism and sectarianism (McVeigh 1990).

Against this, it is clear that the experiences of racism in Britain and sectarianism in Northern Ireland are not identical. There are key differences: levels of racist and sectarian violence; the political mobilisation of sectarianism and racism; the relevant strength of different ethnic blocs involved in the two situations and so on. Obviously then, there are many differences between racism in Britain and sectarianism in Northern Ireland. None of these differences, however, is necessarily fatal for Moore's thesis. Racism assumes different forms in different situations – sectarianism might be very different to anti-Black racism in Britain but a form of racism for all that – just as South African racism is undoubtedly racism despite being different in many ways to racism in Britain. The development of the specific concept of 'anti-Irish racism' makes this point very clearly. If anti-Irish racism exists, it is certainly very different from other racisms – in Britain and elsewhere. This makes anti-Irish racism particularly pertinent to the question of the relationship between racism and sectarianism.

Anti-Irish racism

Discussion of anti-Irish racism brings us right to the heart of the connectedness of the experience of Irish people and Black people in Britain. The issues of the *possibility* and the *specificity* of anti-Irish racism have been clearly articulated in the context of the Irish in Britain over the past ten years. This has involved a debate which has been politically heated at times. Some analyses have been eager to include Irish people in the analysis of racialised groups. One way of doing this was simply to identify the Irish as 'black'. Sivanandan – in the process of critiquing the concept of 'ethnicity' and wanting to include the Irish within anti-racist struggle – identifies the Irish as 'politically Black': 'Ethnicity was a tool to blunt the edge of black struggle, return "black" to its constituent parts of African Caribbean, Asian, African, Irish' (1983: 4). Others argue that, in the same way as Cox (1970) distinguished between racism and anti-Semitism, so a distinction must be made between racism (which is experienced by Black people) and the qualitatively different prejudice and discrimination experienced by Irish people. In this analysis, colour – albeit mediated by colonial and post-colonial relationships – becomes the definitive interface within racism. This argument becomes definitional because, if racism is something which can only happen to Black people, then obviously White Irish people in Britain or Ireland cannot experience racism. This analysis precludes the possibility of anti-Irish racism:

[D]iscussion on the white/black power dichotomy negated the existence of an anti-Irish racism. It was based on a premise which was given expression in the equation 'racism = power + prejudice'. Inserting the proposition that all white people have power over black people meant, by definition, that all white people were seen to be in control of power structures ... The end result is a position where the reductionist argument of white over black does not accommodate an anti-Irish racism. Conversely, ethnicity, although useful in distinguishing the Irish and other ethnic groups in terms of disadvantage and need, does shift power relations to the personal and away from the white power structures of the British ruling class.   (Connor 1987: 23)

This debate is by no means exhausted but it is clear that the notion of anti-Irish racism has achieved new levels of acceptability – or perhaps even 'respectability'. In 1997, the British Commission for Racial Equality (CRE) published *The Irish in Britain* which provides a comprehensive analysis of the extent of anti-Irish racism. The CRE now regards the Irish as 'Britain's largest ethnic minority group' (CRE 1997: 1). It takes substantial numbers of cases on behalf of Irish people (CRE 1997: 3–4). Some of these cases have involved Northern Irish Protestants whose own sense of identity was ethnically 'Protestant' and politically unionist – so, in Britain at least, anti-Irish racism involves discrimination against Irishness abstracted from religious, political and national identity (Hickman and Walter 1997: 11). Furthermore, Hickman's definitive analysis of anti-Irish racism clearly regards anti-Irish racism and anti-Catholicism in Britain as different, if constantly overlapping, discourses (1995a: 19–53). Thus, in the British context, sectarianism and anti-Irish racism are not the same thing.

This tends to suggest that sectarianism and anti-Irish racism are also discrete discourses in Northern Ireland. This is supported by the fact that no one has suggested that Catholics in the North of Ireland *cannot* be sectarian. If Catholics are sectarian, and, if sectarianism is really racism, then they are either exhibiting anti-Irish racism (which appears absurd) or some other specific form of racism which has never been named at all. This lends further support to the idea that sectarianism should continue to be theorised as different to anti-Irish racism.

This analysis provokes a further question: to what extent are both of these discourses different to anti-Black racism? A specific perspective on this is offered by the question of the experience of People of Colour in the North of Ireland. It has become increasingly obvious that different minority ethnic groups experience serious and systematic racism from the White, 'majority ethnic' community in Northern Ireland – both Protestant and Catholic (Committee on the Administration of Justice 1992; McVeigh 1998). So, how different is anti-Black racism in the North of Ireland from sectarianism and anti-Irish racism?

Racism and People of Colour in the Six Counties

Robert Moore was not alone in failing to address the experience of minority ethnic communities in the North of Ireland when he looked at the relationship between racism and sectarianism. Indeed, with the exception of occasional debates around the situation of Travellers, there was little attention to either long-standing or new minority ethnic groups at any level of academic analysis or social policy until the late 1970s. The development of a politicised Traveller support movement, however, which used 'racism' as a key tool to highlight anti-Traveller discrimination, meant that the term would begin to feature in debates around equality in the North (McVeigh 1992b). At the same time, the emergence of other minority ethnic community organisations made recognition of the existence of communities of colour in Northern Ireland unavoidable. This development ensured that the analysis of racism had to be widened to include the experience of groups other than Travellers.

The new focus on racism produced an alliance of interests demanding anti-racist legislation for Northern Ireland. The campaign for effective legislation was given definitive expression in a conference on Racism in Northern Ireland and a subsequent conference report (CAJ 1992). Out of the campaigns and alliances around legislation, came the development in 1994 of the Northern Ireland Council for Ethnic Minorities (NICEM). NICEM was the first body rooted in the different minority ethnic organisations to take a strategic cross-ethnic alliance. NICEM defines itself as, 'a voluntary sector, membership-based, umbrella organization representative of ethnic minority groups and their support organizations in Northern Ireland'.

This minority ethnic and anti-racist advocacy assumed forms which were quite consciously and deliberately disconnected from the issue of sectarianism and the debates around equality between Protestants and Catholics in Northern Ireland. Indeed, this was one of the key reasons for responsibility for anti-racism not being assumed by the Fair Employment Commission. Minority ethnic people did not want anti-racism to become 'sectarianised' – or to be seen to become – a 'Catholic' or 'nationalist' issue. For this reason, the alliances which developed between Black and Irish agendas in Britain have been largely missing in Northern Ireland – although it remains broadly true that in Northern Ireland nationalist political parties are more supportive of anti-racist measures than unionists. Certainly, no one on the ground in Northern Ireland was particularly keen to forge an identity between the equality struggles of People of Colour – which were constituted around racism – and the equality struggles of Catholics – which were constituted around sectarianism. In this sense, the relationship between racism and sectarianism in Northern Ireland was significantly different from the relationship between anti-Black racism and anti-Irish racism in Britain.

While minority ethnic groups in Northern Ireland have often been wary of addressing the same agendas as the Black British community, the campaign for legislation had the backing of all the main minority ethnic organisations. This campaign had three key demands: distinct legislation; a distinct Commission for Racial Equality for Northern Ireland; and the inclusion of Travellers as a named ethnic group protected by any legislation. The campaign for anti-racist legislation culminated in the passing of the Race Relations Order (Northern Ireland) which was implemented on 4 August 1997. The success of this campaign was remarkable since there was little institutional backing for the demand. Other than the British CRE, few influential organisations or political parties were pushing the demand for legislation – although it was equally significant that few were actively opposing it. (Unionists remained equivocal because of their general opposition to equality legislation rather than specific concerns about anti-racist legislation.) There were concerns in government about the implications of anti-racist legislation for Northern Ireland. These were, however, informed more by fears about 'read-across' into other areas of law than equivocation on the moral imperative to protect Northern Ireland citizens from racism. These concerns about read-across between anti-racist and anti-sectarian legislation return us once again directly to the racism/sectarianism interface.

In particular, government was alarmed by the prospect of new remedies for sectarian discrimination. The FEA and FEC are limited to political and religious discrimination in employment. The Race Relations Act 1976 (RRA), while more limited in powers and sanctions, has a wider reference – it covers housing and education specifically as well as other goods and services. These are areas where there is still institutionalised discrimination in Northern Ireland. For example, if Protestants and Catholics (or 'British' and 'Irish') are recognised as ethnic groups for the purposes of the 1997 Race Relations (Northern Ireland) Order, then housing policy is institutionally racist under the Order, since it clearly segregates on the basis of sectarian identity. Similarly, continuing sectarian inequalities in the funding of education would be instantly problematised. Thus, the arrival of anti-racist legislation in Northern Ireland threatens a deluge of litigation based on Protestant and Catholic 'ethnicity'. This prospect is now right at the heart of the 'is sectarianism racism?' debate. What appeared to be a somewhat arcane academic debate is reconstituted as a question with immediate and profound practical implications. In this context, it seems likely that minority ethnic groups in Northern Ireland will continue to hope that sectarianism is not seen as being the same thing a racism. Sectarianising the experience of minority ethnic communities would only further marginalise groups that are already socially excluded by the combined process of British and Irish racism. Despite this, however, the debate is not going to go away. At present, legislation already hints at the overlap between racism and sectarianism. The definitive Mandla *v*. Lee decision (Mandla *v*. Lee [1983] 2 A.C. 548) made two key points about the Race Relations Act (1976): first, ethnicity was the most important and embracing of all dimensions of the Act; second, religion was often a constituent part of ethnicity. On the other hand, the Fair Employment Act (1976) effectively recognises politics and ethnicity (or 'perceived religious identity') alongside formal religious identity (Bell 1996: 5–6). Thus, on both sides, the religion/ethnicity divide is increasingly blurred.

Ontological versus dialectical definitions

Since addressing the relationship of anti-Black racism, anti-Irish racism and sectarianism raises so many theoretical questions, it is useful to distinguish between different ways of defining social phenomena. Here I want to focus on what I will characterise as *ontological* and *dialectical* definitions. The ontological focuses on what something *is*; the dialectical focuses on the social relations involved. For example, the definition of ethnicity used in British law from the Mandla *v.* Lee decision is classically ontological. It goes methodically through the different bits of identity which constitute ethnicity – 'long shared history', 'cultural tradition', 'language', 'religion' and so on. In contrast, the definitive sociological definition of ethnicity developed by Barth (1969) is classically dialectical. For him, the key to understanding ethnicity is the fact that it is about constructing and maintaining an ethnic *boundary* between groups – it is about social relationships. Moreover, the 'cultural stuff' which constitutes a particular ethnicity is arbitrary. Most analyses of racism take this focus on social relationships a stage further. They tend to see racism as an *asymmetrical power relationship* – that is, something which occurs across an ethnic boundary in an unequal way (McVeigh 1995b: 17–21). The notion of *institutional racism* is central to this theorisation (Carmichael and Hamilton 1967). Thus, whatever their intent, Black people cannot be racist in the same way as White people since they do not have the power to be racist. Racialised minorities lack the access to social power – particularly access to state power – which is crucial to the reality of racism. From this perspective it is impossible to see racism as a thing in itself – it only makes sense to name something as racism in the context of asymmetries of power.

It bears emphasis that there are virtues in both the ontological and dialectical perspectives – it is not that one is 'right' and the other 'wrong'. It is clear, however, that when people try to define social phenomena they sometimes confuse these distinct ways of differentiating between dissimilar situations. It is also the case that the conclusions reached are sometimes contradictory – things that look the same when viewed ontologically are different when viewed dialectally and vice versa. For example, the ways in which people experience anti-Black racism, anti-Irish racism and sectarianism may be broadly similar – involving different forms of harassment and discrimination and disadvantage. This does not, however, necessarily make them the same thing. (Sexism also involves harassment, discrimination and disadvantage but no one has suggested that sexism and racism are the same thing.)

Attention to the ontological perspective throws some light on the racism/sectarianism interface. It is clear that racism is sometimes manifested in a specifically sectarian form and sectarianism is sometimes manifested in a specifically racist form. Thus, within racism against Black people, groups are often attacked in terms of being 'heathens' or 'Muslims' or with other religious labels. In Britain, in the aftermath of the Rushdie affair, Muslim was often used as an ethnic label to attack all

South Asian people – whatever their religious identity. This is why so many anti-racist organisations are now campaigning to have religion included as a category protected by the RRA. Equally, within anti-Semitism and anti-Irish racism, anti-Judaism and anti-Catholicism add a specifically religious dimension to each of these racisms. So, there is no doubting the centrality of religious identity within notions of 'race' and ethnicity. Conversely, within sectarianism, ethnic labels like 'Taig' or 'Orangie' are often substituted for the generic use of 'Protestant' and 'Catholic' (McVeigh 1995a: 637–9). Thus, from the ontological perspective, there is little substantive difference between racism and sectarianism. In this sense, according to the Mandla v. Lee definition, the sectarian categories 'Protestant' and 'Catholic' fit the description of ethnicities, and sectarianism can be regarded as a 'race relations' situation.

The differences between racism and sectarianism become clearer, however, from the dialectical perspective. Put simply, these differences are rooted in the fact that anti-Irish racism characterises relationships between British and Irish people, and anti-Black racism in Ireland characterises relationships between 'People of Colour' and 'White' people, while sectarianism characterises relationships between Catholic and Protestant Irish people. This means that, in the specific case of the Irish experience, there can be anti-Irish racism, anti-Black racism *and* sectarianism. These are all distinct social phenomena in Ireland. They also appear to have an integrity outside of Ireland. For example, sectarianism occurs in Glasgow between groups that are both technically British – it cannot be reduced to being simply an example of anti-Irish (or anti-British) racism (Gallagher 1987; Murray 1984). Sectarianism in Britain is often connected to Irishness – particularly historical Irish emigration and the contemporary relationship to Irish politics – but it is not reducible to anti-Irishness (Neal 1988; Phillips 1982; Waller 1981) Likewise, anti-Irish racism can attach to unionists in Ireland whose self-identity is very clearly British and Protestant. Again, it is not reducible to sectarianism. Whatever their self-identification, unionists become stripped of their Britishness for the purposes of anti-Irish racism – it is the means by which the British construct the Protestant/Unionist/Loyalist bloc in Ireland as other, alien, and *Irish*.

In summary then, whether sectarianism is racism depends, not unnaturally, on how we decide to define both concepts. If we choose to define racism and sectarianism ontologically with a focus on ethnicity, then sectarianism seems indistinguishable from racism. If, however, we define racism and sectarianism dialectically, then they appear to involve groups which are constituted in substantively different ways and the two phenomena maintain a discrete integrity. From this perspective, there are good reasons to suggest that racism and sectarianism are not the same thing. This is not, however, to endorse the notion that the Northern Ireland conflict is primarily about religion. This is a fundamentally misguided analysis which I want to characterise as the 'theological fallacy'.

The theological fallacy

The theological fallacy is the notion that sectarianism in Ireland in general, and the Northern Ireland conflict in particular, should be explained in terms of religion. It is often used to make the case for a distinction between racism and sectarianism. While many people imply or assume this position, Bruce asserts it with refreshing clarity:

> The Northern Ireland conflict is a religious conflict. Economic and social differences are also crucial, but it was the fact that the competing populations in Ireland adhered and still adhere to competing religious traditions which has given the conflict its enduring and intractable quality. (1986: 249)

When we look at Bruce's own counterfactual argument, however, the limits of this approach become palpable:

> One way to grasp the significance of religion in Ireland is to try and imagine recent Irish history and development if the Scots and English settlers had also been Roman Catholics. Differences of power, status, and wealth between settler and native would have remained, of course, but a common religious culture would have encouraged intermarriage and eroded the ethnic boundaries. (1986: 6)

This assertion simply does not stand up empirically. In every colonial situation where there was an identity between the religion of the settlers and natives, other signifiers – 'race' or colour or nationality – served to mark and reinforce the boundary between coloniser and colonised. Moreover, this happened in Ireland, too, before the Reformation when the infamous 'Statutes of Kilkenny' were used to prevent intermarriage (and other social intercourse) between Irish natives and English settlers who shared a common Catholicism. After the Reformation, of course, religion provided a convenient signifier of difference between settler and native in Irish colonial history. This, however, was a *consequence* rather than a *cause* of ethnic differentiation forged at the colonial nexus. If we want to make sense of the connectedness of 'race', ethnicity and religion in Ireland, we have to go beyond the simplistic assertion that sectarianism is different from racism because it is about religion.

This is not to argue that religion plays no part in sectarian division. If religious labels like 'Protestant' and 'Catholic' are used to characterise social division then, to some extent, that division is 'about' religion. Rather than forcing us to accept the theological fallacy, however, this should instead encourage us to unpack the many secular dimensions to religious identity. It should challenge us to find the profane within the sacred, the ideological within the theological. In other words, religion is not about – or certainly not *only* about – religion. As sociologists have long pointed out, its other-worldly focus can often disguise the dimensions of religious identity which are uncompromisingly this-worldly

(Wallis 1975). It is unusual to find any religious project with claims to spiritual power and authority which does not simultaneously make an attendant claim to temporal power and authority.

With regard to sectarianism then, the Northern Ireland conflict is not about religion except in so far as religion is about colonial history and ethnicity and racism. To paraphrase Moore 'the Northern Ireland conflict is truly not religious conflict'. Moreover, I mean this in the strong sense of the word 'religious'. The 'sociology of religion' very properly addresses the specific dynamics of social life attached to belief. This discipline includes the study of tensions within and between different manifestations of religious faith. The sociology of religion, however, *does not and should not include discussion of the vast majority of the causes and consequences of sectarianism in Ireland*. While religious ideas and faith inform aspects of sectarian belief and conflict, these are less important than other factors. For example, debates around papal infallibility and transubstantiation and whether Catholics are Christian *do* matter to many people in Northern Ireland (Working Party on Sectarianism 1993). Ultimately, however, sectarianism is rooted in colonial history and politics and ethnicity rather than theology or religious practice (Liechty 1993). Sectarian blocs are nominally religious – 'Protestant' and 'Catholic' – but the way that they are constituted approximates much more closely to ethnicity than it does to religious belief. Moreover, while it is entirely appropriate to study the religious dimensions to sectarianism, this is in principle no different to studying the religious dimensions to racism.

The comparative analysis of racism and sectarianism

While examination of the overlapping nature of anti-Black racism, anti-Irish racism and sectarianism may raise as many questions as it answers, it at least illustrates the virtue of such comparative analysis. Examining the resonance between racism and sectarianism through the use of comparative method generates a whole series of insights and problematics. This resonance 'works' at both the general level of theorising racism and sectarianism, as well as the more specific level of making sense of how these phenomena actually become manifest in the context of the British state. It is my contention that the insights and problematics generated by the comparison of racism and sectarianism are ultimately much more informative than the attempt to resolve the question of whether sectarianism is 'really' racism. We cannot examine any of these insights here in any depth. We can, however, signal some of the key sociological issues which might be illuminated by the comparison of racism and sectarianism.

With respect to sectarianism, the chief virtue of the comparison is clear. The undertheorisation of sectarianism means that there is very little theoretical analysis of sectarianism to draw on or critique or endorse. Borrowing from different perspectives on racism facilitates a theorisation of sectarianism that is absolutely essential if it is to be properly analysed. While the theorisation of racism may have less to learn from the analysis of sectarianism, the latter nevertheless offers useful insights to the relationship between religion, ethnicity and 'race'. The necessity of integrating religion into ethnicity and racism theory becomes obvious when the contemporary importance of 'fundamentalism' is considered – whether in the politics of the USA or Algeria or Israel. Analysing the interface between racism and religion is just as important as analysing the interface between sectarianism and religion.

In this sense, the importance of sectarianism in Ireland appears much more 'normal' than its unimportance would be. In many countries, religion is a key component in the constitution of ethnicity. So, theorising the nexus between religion, ethnicity and politics is a challenge for any sociologist interested in social division. With this in mind, useful comparative work might be done between Ireland and different situations in which sectarian identity divides – communalism in the Indian sub-continent is one obvious example. Comparative work between sectarianism in Northern Ireland and the way that 'communalism' is re-worked, and yet persists, within the British Asian community, might provoke further relevant analysis. There is a continuing significance to politicised religion and religiously-influenced politics in every social formation with a history as either coloniser or colonised. The complex articulation of religion, ethnicity and politics should be the focus of any sociology of colonial and post-colonial societies. The comparative analysis of racism and sectarianism could play a key role in unpacking this matrix.

The comparative perspective also suggests that both racism and sectarianism should be researched and theorised in a holistic way. Research which atomises racism or sectarianism – and, in the process, analyses discrete parts of either – inevitably loses sight of them as spatial and temporal totalities. For example, the origins of 'colonial' racism and sectarianism within the process of British imperialism continue to have important structuring effects on contemporary manifestations of the two phenomena. Contemporary African Caribbean disadvantage in Britain cannot be disconnected from the historical experience of slavery; contemporary Catholic disadvantage in Northern Ireland cannot be disconnected from the historical experience of the Penal Laws. Atomising racism and sectarianism ignores these kind of connections. Moreover, it fails to provide any sense of the relative importance of different experiences of racism and sectarianism. Thus, police racism or RUC sectarianism remains an interesting subject for sociological research – but then so does, say, racism or sectarianism in literature for children. Atomising research in this fashion suggests that racism in children's literature is as important as police racism – or, at least, it has no means of suggesting anything to the contrary. Without a holistic approach to understanding the way in which racism and sectarianism work, these atomistic 'bits' float around without being situated within the totalities of both phenomena. In a similar way, atomising racism and sectarianism leads to the neglect of the primacy of violence and the threat of violence in both experiences (McVeigh 1990; 1994). Both state and non-state violence assumes a central role within the broader experiences of racism and sectarianism (Greater London Council 1984). Yet, if we examine the sociological literature, we might assume that discrimination rather than violence is the defining aspect of both.

The comparison of racism and sectarianism also raises questions about the very nature of ethnicity and 'ethnic relations'. Ethnicity involves identities and conflicts which fall well outside the usual definitions of either racism or sectarianism. From Bosnia to Guyana or Rwanda, there are conflicts which are clearly about ethnicity in some way and yet do not fit easily inside existing paradigms for analysing either racism or sectarianism. In this sense, both racism and sectarianism are specific subsets of the broader category of ethnic conflict. Ethnicity is often regarded as a neutral descriptive term. As we have seen, the Mandla *v.* Lee decision tried to define the bits of identity (the things which Barth called 'cultural stuff') which in combination constitute ethnicity. It is clear, however, that the notion of ethnicity also needs to carry some possibility of evaluation. Moreover, this evaluation needs to be able to go beyond the multi-cultural platitude that ethnicity is about difference and that difference is good. We need to be able to say that there is something pathological about some ethnicities. It is perhaps useful to illustrate this with an historical example. Few people would argue now that there was not something 'wrong' with whiteness as it was constituted in South Africa before liberation – in terms of both politics and *ethnicity*. I would argue that both White ethnicity in Britain and Protestant ethnicity in Northern Ireland need to be problematised in a broadly similar way. Both ethnicities are clearly problematic for people who are racialised and sectarianised by them, but they may be equally problematic for their members since they sometimes appear dysfunctional even in terms of their reference group. For example, it is often unclear how racism or sectarianism benefits the young people who play a central role in the construction and reproduction of White and Protestant identity (Bell 1990). This suggests that there needs to be a distinction between ethnicity which accepts or at least 'tolerates' the legitimacy of its significant other and ethnicity which carries with it the project of dominating and/or destroying its significant other. In short, ethnicity theory cannot accept ethnicity as a neutral quality; it needs to be able to critique the aspects of ethnicities which are racist, xenophobic and genocidal. It should be able to make sense not only of asymmetries of power but also asymmetries of value. Once again, the comparative analysis of racism and sectarianism could provide new and challenging perspectives on this issue.

Finally, at the more specific level of social relations within the British state, the comparison of racism and sectarianism focuses attention on the qualitatively different levels of conflict linked to these phenomena.

Given their similarities, the tired question 'How is it that sectarianism leads to war in Northern Ireland?' is less interesting than its converse, 'How is it that racism does not lead to war in Britain?' In this sense, Northern Ireland might be a portent of the direction in which inner city Britain is heading. This resonance holds as much for 'negative' interventions by the state (state racism and sectarianism) as is does for 'positive' interventions (state anti-racism and anti-sectarianism). For example, racism and sectarianism are mediated by the state in broadly similar ways – the Fair Employment Commission and the Commission for Racial Equality are examples of this. The British state, however, is also at the cutting edge of racism and sectarianism. The whole criminal justice system – from policing, through sentencing to imprisonment – impacts in a profoundly negative way on the lives of Black people in Britain and Catholics in Northern Ireland. In this sense, there may be ever more resonance in the racism/sectarianism comparison within the British state. As the structural impediments to intensified state/community conflict in British inner cities are increasingly withdrawn, comparisons with Northern Ireland – especially those that do not ignore the crucial *differences* between racism and sectarianism – will remain particularly pertinent.

Conclusions

The comparative analysis of racism and sectarianism has much to offer in terms of unpacking the religion/'race'/ethnicity nexus. There is a 'resonance' between racism and sectarianism which means that their comparison offers unique insights into the nature of both. In particular, the comparison has specific application in terms of the British State and the key role which it plays in the reproduction of both racism and sectarianism. Whether or not sectarianism *is* racism depends on the definition of racism adopted. From the perspective of the British Race Relations Act (1976), sectarian identity is indistinguishable from ethnicity and sectarianism is a 'race relations' situation. From the perspective of sociological notions of ethnicity, sectarianism involves different ethnic groups to racism and there is a point in maintaining the integrity of sectarianism as an explanatory concept – particularly in the context of social conflict in Ireland. In terms of broad distinctions: sectarianism involves the relationship between Irish Protestants and Catholics; anti-Irish racism involves the relationship between British people and Irish people; and racism in Ireland involves relationships between majority and minority ethnic groups either constituted as 'White people' and 'People of Colour' or 'settled people' and Travellers. Whether or not sectarianism is seen as the same thing as racism, it should not be regarded as a 'religious' phenomenon. In so far as the terms can be disaggregated, 'sectarianism' is about ethnicity much more than it is about religion. In this sense, sectarianism is much the same as racism – religion plays a part, but only a part – in the construction of both.

Despite my insistence that the comparison of racism and sectarianism is more important and fruitful than the debate about their similitude, it seems unlikely that the debate is going to go away. As we have seen, the increasing overlap between anti-racist and anti-sectarian legislation in Britain and Northern Ireland threatens to force the issue. Furthermore, in the aftermath of conflict around loyalist marches in 1996 and 1997, placards in nationalist areas began to adopt phrases like 'No more Orange racism'. This development threatens to lend new immediacy to the racism/sectarianism debate. It bears emphasis that whether sectarianism in Northern Ireland is seen as racism is, ultimately, a political choice. It will not be decided by either academic research or legal judgement – no matter how finely executed. This choice will be made primarily by Catholics in Northern Ireland since it is their experience which is to be described by the competing labels of 'racism' and 'sectarianism'. It is to be hoped, however, that the choice will not be made in isolation. Crucially, it should involve the input of People of Colour in Ireland and Britain. This is more than an intellectual courtesy – these groups are likely to be affected directly and materially by the outcome of a debate which at times appears both disinterestedly academic and narrowly provincial.

Part Three

Culture, Conflict and Representation

CHAPTER 10

Don't mention the war: Culture in Northern Ireland

Ronan Bennett

In the North of Ireland it is possible to see *The Wind in the Willows* at the Lyric Players Theatre, *Oliver* at the Grand Opera House, *Romeo and Juliet* at the Arts Theatre, *A Room with a View* at the Queen's Film Theatre. You can see Ken Branagh's *Hamlet* at the Waterfront Hall, hear Handel's *Messiah* at the Ulster Hall, or watch the Duchess of Kent open Castleward, the North's cut-rate version of Glyndebourne. This is the culture of the affluent and educated citizenry; it is Belfast masquerading as Bristol or Leicester. Middle-class taste in the arts is what you would expect to find in any provincial centre. It is liberal, non-sectarian and draws heavily on metropolitan influences, those of London and, to a lesser extent, Dublin.

The 'Troubles' scarcely figure. Not in art, not in life. The neutral middle class can afford to be aloof. The North's well-to-do have managed to come through the conflict almost completely unscathed: they live in pleasant residential suburbs that see no rioting; they are not arrested or raided; they suffer no casualties. Lower than average house prices and rates mean they enjoy relatively large disposable incomes. It is said the proportion of BMW- and Mercedes-owners is higher in the North than anywhere else in Britain or Ireland. The greatest inconvenience they are likely to experience is to be caught up in traffic jams caused by army and police checkpoints or office chaos after bombs or bomb alerts. They do not get involved, and the art they prefer similarly does not take sides. Preferably, it does not deal with the conflict at all: it does not mention the war. In 1969, at the time of the pogroms against the working-class population of West Belfast, a famous graffito appeared: 'Malone fiddles while Falls burns' – a rebuke to the prosperous Catholics in the nearby Malone Road for their indifference to the tribulations of their poorer co-religionists. The graffito is gone now, but as a summary of the class segregation that exists in the cultural life of the North its message is timeless.

On the rare occasions the conflict penetrates the arts, its treatment tends to be apolitical, disengaged, sceptical. There is a striking paradox at work: most of the artists and writers who have explored the strongly held political loyalties underpinning the Troubles have attempted to do so by disavowing strong political views of their own. The mainstream artistic mediators of the conflict have tended to opt, like the largely middle-class audience they serve, for an apolitical vision. The work is marked by aloofness, by being above it all, by self-conscious distance from the two proletarian tribes fighting out their bloody, pointless, atavistic war.

Bill Rolston, of the University of Ulster, sociologist, says the pressure on artists and writers 'not to get involved with the politics of the place is pervasive.' 'At the art college, for example, students are taught that getting involved in local issues is not what art is about. They're taught that art is about the great themes. It's the kiss of death for an artist to discuss local issues, and the same is true of academic circles.'

The 'kiss of death' can be very real. Arts funding is always a tricky issue. In the North of Ireland it is fraught. Theatre companies, with their large outgoings and relatively small audiences are particularly vulnerable. Those who prosper tend to be those who, like the Lyric Players, avoid controversy. Robin Midgley, the English-born artistic director of the Lyric, dismisses critics who claim his programme is timid, anodyne, middle of the road, fearful of biting the hand that feeds it. 'It would be blinkered to pretend there's no problem [in the North]', Midgley says, 'but equally wrong to make a theatre reflect what is problematic. I'm here to celebrate the extraordinary strengths there are. It is amazing how much activity there is here, the positive qualities there are in the community, especially the artistic community. It is incredibly vibrant. It is absolutely not true that the Northern Ireland Arts Council favours non-political drama. They've done an amazing job. Look at our last season – no one would call that safe.' The season in question (1994, a momentous year that saw the first IRA ceasefire) was dominated by the hardy and uncontroversial perennials of regional theatre, including *She Stoops to Conquer*, *All My Sons* and *The Taming of the Shrew*. The only piece touching on the North was a revival of a 13-year-old play, *Hidden Curriculum*, by Graham Reid, the respected Belfast-born playwright. The play – a humanistic exploration of the impact of communal violence on the young – can hardly be said to be challenging contemporary conventions. The Lyric's subsequent presentations included *Lady Windermere's Fan* and *Joseph and the Amazing Technicolour Dreamcoat*. As Pam Brighton, artistic director of Dubbeljoint, a company whose productions, including *A Night in November* and *Binlids*, have attracted enormous criticism for their alleged bias, put it: 'It is not that there is no place for the classics, but to ignore the contemporary situation is indefensible.'

It is not just mainstream theatre that is uncomfortable with the political issues of the conflict: serious fiction has often been equally ill-at-ease. The reasons for this are complex, but at bottom it is because most fictional work adheres to a set of complacent conventions about the conflict: that it is an irrational and bloody slaughter without solution; that both sides, republican and loyalist, are as bad as each other;

that normal, sensitive people do not get involved, or if they do it is reluctantly or through intimidation, and as soon as they are in they want to get out; that the British presence may at times be heavy-handed and blundering but at bottom it is well-intentioned and indispensable.

One could argue that from an artistic point of view it is irrelevant whether these conventions are true or false. But the real point is that art, if it is to be worth anything, should be in tension with prevailing norms and given wisdom. It suffers from attachment to any conventions. In the case of writing on the North, the conventions have contributed to uniformity and predictability in plot, character, tone and theme. Most writers pride themselves on disliking with equal intensity both sides (Graham Reid sums up the popular attitude: 'My view is a plague on both your houses'), and in fighting shy of political involvement, even at the level of marching in support of, say, the 1981 IRA hunger strikers; or joining the unionist and loyalist protestors against the 1985 Anglo-Irish Agreement; or supporting the Hume–Adams initiative that led to the 1994 IRA cease fire. Writers, by and large, do not get involved. During the Civil Rights years of the late-1960s, writers remained for the most part quiet. They did not speak when drunken RUC men invaded the Bogside and beat to death a defenceless semi-invalid. They did not speak when Bogsiders rose up to defend their homes and their families. They did not speak when Stormont introduced internment without trial in 1971. They squeaked once or twice about Bloody Sunday in 1972, but lost their voice – their public voice as well as their artistic voice – when British soldiers killed children with plastic bullets throughout the 1970s, when the SAS shot dead unarmed republicans, when 'inhuman and degrading' interrogation techniques were used on 'terrorist' suspects, when the North's prisons became places of brutality, torture and death, when innocent Irishmen and women were framed and jailed in England. They did not speak as the pressures on the first IRA cease fire mounted. They stayed silent, they did not get involved. Not in life, not in art. The Belfast academic and critic Edna Longley has argued that it is not the role of writers to be the mouthpieces of their communities (1994b). Leaving aside whether reflecting in your work the traumatic impact of these and other events makes the writer a mouthpiece, the result has been that one particular experience of the Troubles – the working-class nationalist – has gone almost entirely unnoticed by the arts.

In fiction – and the same is true of most film and television drama – the Troubles are thus presented as an appalling human tragedy, devoid of political content. Like any bloody struggle anywhere (Vietnam, Algeria, South Africa, Angola, Peru, Bosnia), it becomes nothing more than a series of repulsive and meaningless massacres, destructive of communities and the human spirit in equal part. The late Alan Clarke's television film *Elephant* is the epitome of the conflict presented as mindless slaughter. Without dialogue, *Elephant* is a series of unexplained assassinations: unknown armed men cutting down nameless victims in scene after scene. Identity and motivation have no place; all that matters is that people are dying.

The recurrent metaphor in fiction about the North is that of the charnel house, the abattoir, in which the blood and the carcasses are laid out for inspection by the horrified reader. Deirdre Madden uses it in her novel *Hidden Symptoms* (1988). One of her characters looks down from a bus on a lorry 'carrying meat for the knacker's yard. For well over two miles he had looked down into the tipper, which was full of skinned limbs: long, bloody jawbones; jouned, whip-like tails ... He remembered television news reports, where the casual camera showed bits of human flesh hanging from barbed wire after a bombing. Firemen shovelled what was left of people into heavy plastic bags, and you could see all that remained: big burnt black lumps like charred logs.' Bernard MacLaverty's sensitively written *Cal* (1983), one of the best known novels of the Troubles, uses the same metaphor: Cal's reluctance to enter the abattoir in which his father works stands as a metaphor for his reluctance to get involved with the IRA. In *Proxopera* by Benedict Kiely (1988), the charnel house image is taken to its ultimate and horrifying extreme. Observing the beauty of the Irish countryside, Kiely's narrator says you wouldn't guess at the horrors lurking beneath; but then, after all, 'the birds, they say, sang around Dachau'.

Even to ask why or how the bodies came to be there is treated as evidence of lack of compassion or, worse, support for terrorism. One only has to look at the furious rows provoked in both the British and Irish media by Neil Jordan's films *The Crying Game* and *Michael Collins*. In the first, Jordan's crime was to show Stephen Rea's IRA man, Fergus, as a decent if confused human being. In the second, the objections were to Jordan's lack of historical accuracy – criticisms not typically levelled against historical drama. Though on any objective valuation, Jordan's work could hardly be said to amount to full-throated endorsement of Irish republicanism, the criticism was vicious and sustained. The film-maker was accused of everything from encouraging terrorism to being an exponent of 'fascist art'. Similar rows have surrounded Jim Sheridan's *In the Name of the Father*, about Gerry Conlon who, as one of the Guildford Four, was wrongfully imprisoned for fifteen years, and Terry George's *Some Mother's Son*, about the 1981 IRA hunger strike. To judge by the reaction of sections of the British and Irish media, one could have been forgiven for thinking that the IRA had added film-making to its bomb-making capacities, even though the movies in question all contained characterisations of IRA men and women as, variously, cynical, psychotic, brutal, cruel and manipulative. Nothing less than full and unequivocal affirmation of the standard conventions, it seems, will do.

Speculation on the political causes of the conflict is territory most writers and artists refuse to cross. The problem, Bill Rolston says, is that this approach 'affects quality – all generalizations reduce nuance. Stuff that tries to be literature falls into the same cliches you find in thrillers: the psychotic republican, the poor soldier as piggy-in-the-middle, the daughter of the republican who falls in love with the British soldier. There are half a dozen characters who keep coming up over and over.' There are now some 300 novels on the Troubles. 'I kept reading, looking for something different,' Rolston says. 'For the most part I didn't get it' (Rolston 1989).

Writers capable of great insight into the motivation of ordinary human beings seem to break down when it comes to exploring the psychological hinterland of those involved in the conflict. These men and women are invariably depicted as of low intelligence, often with a severe physical deformity, cowardly, bullying – especially towards their own comrades – and driven by bloodlust. If they have politics, they are the politics of the fanatic or simple-minded, and easy to ridicule. In *Proxopera* the IRA man Bertie tells his hostage: 'It's the cause ... We must get the Brits out of Ireland. They want our oil.' To which the hostage gets to deliver an effective put-down: 'Our hair-oil? I never knew we had oil.'

Coming up behind the older, liberal, more humanistic generation of Brian Moore, Ben Kiely and Bernard Mac Laverty are younger writers like Robert McLiam Wilson (1989). Part of the self-conscious postmodernist generation that finds any strongly held belief inherently ridiculous, Wilson broadcasts a tabloid version of the more nuanced arguments of the so-called 'revisionist' historians (Roy Foster and Paul Bew, among others). The revisionists argue that Irish nationalism is essentially reactionary, racist, irrelevant and founded on 'pieties' and 'myths'; in Wilson's more robust lexicon Republicanism becomes 'fascist', and Irish culture a joke. Wilson wrote in a recent Picador anthology (1993: 199–200) that in 1989:

Attracted by the idea of an Irishman who didn't like the Irish, the BBC asked me to make a film about Belfast, my home town. Sharpened some knives and packed my bags ... The Irish justify cliché as their art form. It's all they've got. In Belfast, cliché isn't cliché – it's the cutting edge.

But when Wilson turns to the Troubles, the post-modern voice breaks and takes on tones familiar from Brian Moore (e.g. 1990) and others: the conflict as meaningless slaughter.

And they shot a man in Derriaghy. Twice in the head when he answered his front door. I watched TV as his wife cried at the funeral. Hers was a strange noise, not human – surrendering to the impossible horror of what had happened, suiting I thought. The only just and measured response to the prevailing circumstances ... And they apologized. They had killed the wrong man and they apologized. I had forgotten they did that.   (1993: 202)

It is always important to register horror at unnecessary human suffering. But the real question is whether this reduction of the conflict's complexities – also seen in Wilson's most recent novel *Eureka Street* (1996) – to good versus evil good art? Or is it something else? The familiar portrayal of the enemy in a time of war? If so, it is not art, but propaganda.

The sentiments behind Wilson's passage are found everywhere – in Ciaran Carson's poetry, in Derek Mahon's, and in countless other works of film, fiction and drama. They are also frequently followed by a testament to the indestructibility and essential goodness of the human spirit. We are ever on the look-out for honour and decency amid the squalor (hence the popularity among writers and producers of television drama of the 'love across the divide' storyline). Wilson's homily runs:

> The city has a remnant of grandeur that no poverty or violence can finally dent ... We're still shouting and bombing and whining and dying. But it's all right, don't worry – because I know. I still know that something good is going to happen. (1993)

Leaving aside the question of whether this piety reflects any reality, or if it does how that 'something good' is going to happen, the point is that this is the tone of mainstream culture in the North. Inevitably, escapism lurks here. *The Island* of the Paul Brady song is a place to which the Tyrone-born singer dreams of finding refuge: there he can make love and be happy, away from the war.

> I know us plain folks don't know all the story
> I know that peace and love's just copping out
> I know that young men dying in the ditches
> Is just what being free is all about
> And that twisted wreckage down on main street
> Will bring us all together in the end
> As we go marching down the road to freedom

The Island drew a stinging response from Christy Moore, *The Other Side*. Moore ridiculed the Tyrone boy who dreamed of lying on an island making love while other Tyrone boys lay imprisoned in the H-Blocks. *The Other Side* is a reminder that there exists another art of the Troubles. It is out of the mainstream and consequently less well-known, but it is growing in confidence and becoming more insistent. It stems from another culture, the one affected most profoundly by the conflict – the culture of working-class nationalism. Since partition in 1921–2, the nationalist experience in the North has been shaped by exclusion: from power, from jobs, from the mainstream. Seen by the ruling Unionists as dangerous Fifth Columnists, the working-class Catholic population was consigned to over-crowded and impoverished ghettos like the Creggan in Derry and Ballymurphy in West Belfast. The last twenty-five years have seen slow, painful, uneven improvement. But even so, unemployment in nationalist areas is still the highest in the 'UK', and the community's reputation for subversion remains. These are the poorest and most deprived corners of the territory. They are also, of course, under what most local people consider the occupation of a foreign army. This is the perception the artistic expression coming from this culture reflects.

Ironically, it was when nationalist West Belfast's reputation was lowest that the community dug deepest to recover its pride and self-esteem. In March 1988 three IRA members were killed by the SAS in

Gibraltar. Their bodies were flown to Dublin, then brought by hearse along crowd-lined roads to Belfast. At the funeral, attended by thousands of nationalists from all over Ireland, Michael Stone, a loyalist gunman, lobbed hand grenades and opened fire on the mourners, who included Gerry Adams, Martin McGuinness, Danny Morrison and other leading republicans. The attack was captured on television, and Stone himself was filmed as he fled from Milltown Cemetery towards the M1 motorway, pursued by enraged local youths. Every now and then, Stone would turn, take aim and fire. He was eventually brought down by his pursuers, but not before killing three people and wounding several others.

At the time, the media praised the youngsters for their bravery. Then three days later, when one of Stone's victims was being buried, two British army corporals in civilian clothes raced their unmarked car at the funeral procession, flashing their headlights. One of the soldiers produced a pistol and fired a shot. The car was surrounded, the soldiers disarmed and dragged away. They met horrible, cruel deaths. Those who a few days beforehand had been praised for their heroism were now vilified. For weeks after the corporals' killings, media pundits and politicians pontificated on the people of West Belfast, pronouncing on their shortcomings: the word 'animals' featured prominently in the tabloids.

Such was the onslaught that local groups decided to use the arts to help rebuild the community's self-esteem. The first West Belfast Community Festival was held the same year, in 1988, to provide a platform for local talent and creativity, as well as bringing in writers, artists and performers from outside to entertain and debate. At the same time, community groups adapted buildings in the area to provide a home for the arts – the Culturlann (culture centre), Conway Mill, the Rodaí Mac Corlaí club. The festival, partly because of official suspicions about its political connotations, had to struggle for funding. But while shortage of funds remains an issue, the organisers have succeeded in securing the festival's future.

Few people in West Belfast see why the conflict should be kept out of the arts. Their culture is increasingly secular (the Catholic Church's influence in daily life has been on the wane for some time), outward-looking (foreign – including English – visitors are encouraged), and it blends traditional Gaelic and contemporary Irish influences in music, the visual arts, writing and dance with those of modern youth culture. A centre piece of the festival is the annual Dubbeljoint production. These have included productions of Gogol's *The Government Inspector*, whose setting was relocated from Tsarist Russia to pre-partition Ireland and reworked as a bitter critique of the Irish middle classes' dependency on all things British, as well as work by Terry Eagleton (a provocative presentation of James Connolly's execution) and Shane Connaughton (who co-wrote the Oscar-nominated script of *My Left Foot*). The company has also staged *A Night in November* by Marie Jones, the inspiration for which came from the World Cup qualifying match between the Republic of Ireland and Northern Ireland. The game took place in 1993 at Windsor Park, in the heart of Protestant Belfast, shortly after the Shankill fish shop bombing by the IRA and the loyalist reprisal at the Rising Sun bar in Greysteel. The sectarian atmosphere of the predominantly loyalist crowd was shocking and deeply disturbing. At the Republic's players came on to the field, sections of the Northern team's supporters chanted 'Greysteel, Greysteel'. Jones, herself a Protestant from East Belfast, used the events of that night as a springboard from which to launch her examination of sectarianism and Protestant identity.

Many of the most active playwrights and poets in nationalist areas like West Belfast have served time in Long Kesh and the H-Blocks. Brian Campbell, now editor of the Republican newspaper *An Phoblacht/Republican News*, was in prison from 1986 to 1993, and in 1993 was co-founder and first editor of *An Glór Gafa* (*The Captive Voice*), a republican prisoners' magazine. 'After the hunger strikes,' Campbell says:

> 'the prisoners had a lot of political discussions about the tactics and consequences of the protests, but there was a lot of creative writing going on, and in 1988 we established poetry workshops. *The Captive Voice* was aimed at giving an outlet to the creative energy in the jail. In the past, others had spoken on behalf of prisoners and we felt it was time to speak for ourselves. The magazine also tackled issues not addressed elsewhere: relationships between prisoners and their partners, for example. Then we had a piece by a gay prisoner who came out. This created a lot of discussion. The response was broadly supportive, but it was shocking for some people because a section of our supporters would have a traditional outlook on the issue of homosexuality. There were always a couple of articles in Irish. The most enthusiastic Irish speakers in the jail dated from the blanket protests, when conditions were at their worst. They had no teachers and they developed a dialect, their own words, as everyday means of expression. It wasn't absolutely perfect Irish, and it became known as Jailic.'

Some of the best of the prisoners' writing has been anthologised in *H-Block: A Selection of Poetry by Republican Prisoners* (South Yorkshire Press, 1991) and published in academic journals. Campbell has described prisoners' poetry as 'political and revolutionary'. It is also, as creative writing must always be, personal. This is Laurence McKeown, a former lifer, on one of the things he hates about prison, *Hard Lines*:

> Right angles and straight lines
> they're everywhere
> and I detest their rigidity.
> Walls, ceilings, floor, straight, sharp, cold, clinically-exact lines
> meeting in right angles
>
> Robotic minds, administrators, bureaucrats
> created this world of geometric precision.
> Did they think it beneath themselves
> to apply their architectural skills to the humble toilet-bowl?
> The one work of prison art and anarchy.

Derry has a completely different atmosphere to that of Belfast. Political killings, even before the IRA cease fires, were rare and the city's local council is run by nationalists who have gone out of their way not to alienate or exclude the Protestant population. As a result, the art coming out of the city seems much less politicised than in Belfast. More than anything else, Derry seems to have managed to keep sectarian tensions to a minimum. On the level of professional arts, the city was probably best known for Field Day, the now all but defunct theatre company established by Brian Friel, Stephen Rea, Seamus Deane, Seamus Heaney and others, whose plays premiered in the city. Field Day's august line-up and internationally acclaimed productions did not save the company and its project from regular and vociferous attacks – by Edna Longley (1996), among others – for its alleged promotion of a narrow and self-absorbed nationalist ethic. 'The cultural wing of the Provos,' as one critic put it.

Derry has a reputation as the North's music centre – the city gave birth to, among others, the Undertones – but until recently bands had no place to practice. During a Red Wedge tour in 1988, Billy Bragg came to Derry to do a gig for unemployed workers. This was the starting point for the founding of the Northwest Music Collective. The collective got a building in 1990 from the council and linked up with the remnants of Derry Film and Video. Now thanks to a combination of outside funding from a number of sources and self-help, they have set up the Nerve Centre – a multi-media base for film, music, video, animation and CD-ROM. A community festival, the Gasyard Féile, runs every summer.

In other parts of the North, sectarian feeling has helped define an altogether different culture, one whose foundations were laid during the plantation and were built on during the long years of the Protestant Ascendancy. The culture of the Protestant working class has always tended to the exclusive and inward-looking. It has become more so because the relative positions of the Protestant and Catholic communities have changed radically in the last quarter of a century. At the beginning of the civil rights marches, in 1967–9, Catholics experienced discrimination in housing and jobs, and total exclusion from political power, even in the areas, like Derry, where they formed the majority. By organising, they forced reform and drove the Protestant community, whose political representatives had resisted even the most moderate reform proposals, into retreat on just about every front: cultural, economic, territorial, psychological and political.

Stormont, the parliament of Protestant supremacy, was closed in 1972. The B-Specials, the official armed defenders of the Orange state, went the same way. Derry City Council has fallen to the nationalist SDLP and Sinn Féin. In Belfast, where nationalist and republican representation in the City Hall has been growing for the last two decades, a nationalist lord mayor was selected for the first time in 1997. Most alarming of all from the loyalist perspective have been the demographic trends revealed by the 1991 census. Over the previous twenty years there had been rapid growth in the overall proportion of

Catholics in the state, now thought to be at least 40 per cent throughout the six counties. In the western counties – Derry, Fermanagh and Tyrone – the proportion is still higher. Though demographers argue about whether the present trends will continue (if they do the two communities will be roughly equal within the next twenty years), the speculations and statistics are less important than Protestants' perceptions of the changing pattern: one of unbroken Catholic advance.

The loyalist retreat has had a devastating impact on working-class Protestant culture. It has isolated further an already closed, defensive and inward-looking community that has only ever been able to define itself through a double negative: not Irish, yet not quite British either. They feel comfortable only among their own kind, or – a poor second – when their numbers are greater than 'the other kind', and have opted increasingly for residential segregation. Writers and artists from the Protestant community, while acknowledging the centrality of place in their work, describe an atmosphere of suffocation. One – who did not want to be named – put it this way:

> It is an intolerable mental world to have to inhabit. Think about it. What a weird physical sense of restriction – to be trapped in a tiny corner of a small island and not feel that you are able to move about. Most Protestants in the North would not venture across the border. What a restriction. That sense of confinement is inevitably reflected emotionally, psychologically, culturally.

The muscular Protestant fundamentalism pinches. On the north Antrim coast there is the beautiful little town of Portballintrae. It is one of the most scenic spots in Ireland, the spirit cannot help but rise approaching it. But the town is arid. On Sundays, nothing moves. I remember in my youth playing football in the streets, on the outskirts of Belfast, and glancing up to a window, behind which was the face of my Presbyterian friend, thirteen years old, son of an RUC man, locked in. The Sabbath. There is a famous photograph taken during the dark days of Stormont. It shows a playground: the swings chained up, the roundabout locked. No wonder Eamon McCann felt able to say: 'Taigs have more fun.' Belfast's swings have since been unlocked but, in towns like Portballintrae, enjoyment, celebration, play is still the whore of all temptation. None of this is an encouragement to the cultural life. Nothing better captures the atmosphere of this barren, angry, schizophrenic world – the 'culture of twigs and bird-shit' – than *Desertmartin*, a poem by Tom Paulin, himself a northern Protestant:

> At noon, in the dead centre of a faith,
> Between Draperstown and Magherafelt,
> This bitter village shows the flag
> In a baked absolute September light.
> Here the Word has withered to a few
> Parched certainties, and the charred stubble
> Tightens like a black belt, a crop of Bibles.

It's a limed nest, this place. I see a plain
Presbyterian grace sour, then harden,
As a free strenuous spirit changes
To a servile defiance that whines and shrieks
For the bondage of the letter: it shouts
For the Big Man to lead his wee people
To a clean white prison, their scorched tomorrow.

Desertmartin, like Portballintrae, like Portavogie (a fishing village on
the Ards peninsula where the Plymouth Brethren joined with Ian
Paisley's Free Presbyterians to oppose the granting of the town's first
liquor licence) – these, in Paulin's words, 'are the places where the
spirit dies'. Poking fun at the cultural wasteland that results from a
theology of clamps and locks and chains, Thomas McLaughlin's witty
radio play, *Seaside*, has its female protagonist swimming the Irish Sea
to raise money for a 'Protestant heritage centre'. But in undertaking her
swim, she has time to reflect, and when it's all over she asks: What do
you put in a Protestant heritage centre?

The Protestant North has produced art, but rarely is it art that celebrates the world that spawned it. More often it is an angry reaction to
the prevalence of bigotry, claustrophobia and paranoia. One of
Belfast's best known playwrights made his name (and Kenneth
Branagh's) with the *Billy* plays, made for the BBC in the early 1980s
and featuring a young man in perpetual conflict with his family and
surroundings. Graham Reid's tone is driven, enraged and denuncia-
tory, the voice polemical. The Belfast novelist Glenn Patterson's tone is
equally scathing, and leavened with an iconoclastic wit. Hailing from a
similar background to Reid, Patterson – in *Fat Lad* (1992) – uses a goldfish swimming around a bowl as a metaphor for the psychological and
emotional limitations of society in the North; even when placed in a
bathtub the goldfish continues in its predefined circles, unable to break
out when presented with the opportunity.

The dark world of the loyalist paramilitaries has attracted little
attention from writers. However, Eoin McNamee, originally from
Kilkeel in County Down and now based south of the border, explored
loyalist terror in his last novel, *Resurrection Man* (1994), loosely based
on the activities of the real-life Shankill Butchers, the murder gang led
by the deranged and now happily dead Lennie Murphy. McNamee is
not interested in the ideology of the murder gangs or the political ends
they serve: his preoccupation is with the inner life, and his portrait of
the interior landscape of Ulster loyalism – prefiguring Thaddeus
O'Sullivan's 1996 film *Nothing Personal* – is unremittingly bleak psy-
chopathologies shaped by neurosis, inadequacy and sexual fear.

Unsurprisingly, most artists and writers who have emerged from
Ulster Protestantism have tended to move away – physically and men-
tally – from the world that bred them. Stephen Rea, now best known
for his Oscar-nominated performance in *The Crying Game*, worked for
years in Field Day with Brian Friel and Seamus Deane, and is intensely

conscious of his Irishness. Before moving to Dublin, he lived for many years in nationalist West Belfast. 'What's he doing over there?' a Protestant man was quoted as saying when photographs appeared of Rea opening the West Belfast Community Festival. 'He's one of ours.'

Was one of theirs. Rea comes from a Protestant background, but his mental world is Irish, the artistic inspiration he draws on is Irish. Similarly, Van Morrison, though his early lyrics have to do with the Protestant streets he roamed as a youngster, has reinvented himself as a Celt, and his temporary teaming-up with the traditional group the Chieftains helped give his music and reputation a startling second breath. The flautist James Galway is another musician from a Protestant background who found inspiration in the Ireland beyond the Protestant North. Not all have reoriented their vision in this way: Kenneth Branagh, originally from York Street in Belfast, has chosen to reinvent himself by looking east – in search of what looks to those he left behind like Englishness. But though his choice is less frequently encountered, what Branagh shares with Rea, Morrison and Galway and a host of other lesser known artists, is the realisation that to find artistic fulfilment he would have to look beyond the confines of the Protestant world. To remain is to be enclosed in a world where 'culture' is restricted to little more than flute bands, Orange marches and the chanting of sectarian slogans at football matches. When, year after year, Unionist and loyalist politicians at the disgrace of Drumcree maintained that their triumphalist parading through Catholic neighbourhoods was an intrinsic part of their culture and heritage, it was eloquent testimony to the paucity of the Ulster Protestant cultural world.

Community activists on the Shankill Road, Sandy Row and the Waterside in Derry are now trying to emulate their nationalist neighbours on the Falls and in the Bogside by organising their own festivals, but as long as the political outlook of loyalism is defined by sectarianism it is likely that Lambeg drums will continue to preside over its culture, as Seamus Heaney put it, 'like giant tumours'.

CHAPTER 11

Representing gender and national identity

Sarah Edge

Examination of the relationship between women and Irish nationalism has tended to come from within the disciplines of history or sociology and to pay little critical attention to how national identity is formed in popular culture, and how it relates to the popular cultural formation of gender/femininity (Fairweather *et al.* 1984; Ward 1983; Coulter, 1993).[1] On the other hand, the limited number of publications which analyse mass media representations of the 'troubles' pay little or no attention to the specifics of how women are represented (Rockett *et al.* 1988; Curtis 1984a; McLoone 1991; Rolston 1991a; Hill *et al.* 1994; Butler 1995; Miller 1994; Rolston and Miller 1996). This article aims to begin to address such an omission by attempting to determine how messages about femininity function in relation to the contested national identities of Britishness, and more particularly, Irishness within recent television and film productions.

I will consider media representations not as entertainment or reflections of real life in Northern Ireland, but as containing specific messages or ideologies about how the conflict in Northern Ireland is to be understood. I will attempt to examine how these recent representations can be seen to redefine a number of key terms in the post-cease fire context, particularly in relationship to the representation of Irish nationalism.

The popular cultural understanding of Irish nationalism, particularly for the British viewer, is predominantly based on how the media depicts the IRA and its political wing Sinn Féin. This is partly because the political conflict in Northern Ireland is primarily covered by news and current affairs broadcasting which focuses on 'news' stories and pays little attention to the more local or generalised issues that relate to the cultural and national differences between the people of Northern Ireland.

However, prior to the cease fires a number of popular mainstream films dealing with different aspects of the political conflict in Northern Ireland were released. In 1992 the Hollywood production, *Patriot*

Games, was closely followed by *The Crying Game* directed by Neil Jordan and *In the Name of the Father* directed by Jim Sheridan. The BBC screened Ronan Bennett's television drama, *Love Lies Bleeding*, in 1993. Furthermore, within Northern Ireland itself the NIO (Northern Ireland Office) commissioned the production of three new short television adverts to publicise the confidential phone line. My argument here is that all these recent productions communicate messages about masculinity, femininity and national identity, messages which have profound effects on our understanding of the relationship between women and nationalism in the context of Northern Ireland.

The Good Gunman and the Bad Woman: popular reconstructions

Let us start with *The Crying Game* (see Edge 1995) which opens with the kidnapping of a black British soldier, Jody (Forest Whitaker), by an IRA unit. The first section of the film deals with the developing relationship between Jody and one of his captors, Fergus (Stephen Rea), a relationship that is tested when Fergus is ordered to execute the soldier and he finds himself unable to do so. During a subsequent army ambush of the hostage site Jody is run over and killed by an army Saracen. The IRA unit splits up and Fergus flees to London to carry out Jody's last wish, that he find his girlfriend, a hairdresser, Dil. Fergus falls in love with her, only to find out that she is a transsexual man. The IRA track Fergus down in London and Jude (Miranda Richardson), the IRA woman, informs him that they want him to carry out the killing of a judge. When Fergus does not turn up Jude seeks him out to kill him, but she is shot by Dil. Fergus takes the blame for Jude's murder and is sent to prison. The film closes with Dil, dressed as a woman, visiting Fergus in prison.

Critics predominantly interpreted the portrayal of the IRA man, Fergus, as one that broke away from the tradition of representing the IRA man as a psychotic madman. Instead Fergus was perceived as kind, sympathetic, sensitive, a more humane IRA man, who has come to doubt his violent ways.[2] However, what is interesting about this film from a feminist perspective is that it acknowledges, through the inclusion of a female IRA character, Jude, that women are involved in the IRA. This, though, should not be interpreted as conceding a historical or contemporary involvement in nationalist struggles by women, or as investigating a possible relationship between gender identity and national identity. Rather, it can be seen as part of the attempt to build a new definition of both masculinity and the male terrorist. This film projects a 'new' portrayal of masculinity where the men are depicted as finding a 'new' place to meet which bridges their national, racial and sexual differences.

However, this new place is ultimately established as patriarchal since it excludes women (as symbolised by the killing of Jude). Indeed,

the character of Jude, the only principal woman in the film, is represented as even more psychotic, violent and sexually perverse than the
past tradition of representing the male IRA terrorist. This is because
Jude is included in the film to articulate one of the film's central concerns, that of new masculinity. However, her very inclusion then
creates its own problems for the film text, because of the placing
together of two currently incompatible sets of signifiers: dominant
femininity (Jude as woman – gentle, caring, etc.), and violent 'nationalist' struggle (Jude – the international terrorist). Moreover, the film's
recognition of women's involvement in national identity struggles creates a further set of problems because, as I have argued elsewhere,

> women who are involved in violence disrupt dominant ideologies of the
> feminine as passive and peace-loving. Similarly, women's involvement in
> the public world of politics, disrupts ideologies surrounding women's space
> in the private world of home and family. In nationalist/cultural identity
> struggles, women's demand for a national/cultural identity dislocates the
> place and right of patriarchal authority to define such an identity for her.
>
> (Edge 1995: 176)

Because of this incompatibility Jude must be represented as an aberration of the feminine; she is sexually perverse, hard and full of hate,
untrustworthy, duplicitous and manipulating, selfish and self-centred.
In the film she represents the threat of women's challenge to traditional and dominant femininity through her nationalism. Her very
role, in this film, is to articulate this threat and to be punished for it.

In the Name of the Father is a film based upon the conviction of three
Irish men and one English woman, later known as the Guildford Four.
The film's story is set around their battle to expose their wrongful convictions and their release some fifteen years later. This film is less
concerned with gender politics in terms of women and the characterisation of the female characters are rather limited. However, it does
articulate anxiety about old forms of masculinity, which, in common
with *The Crying Game* is also symbolised by the violence of the IRA.
This is represented by MacAndrews (Don Baker) the cruel and psychot-
ically violent IRA man, who is displaced in favour of a new, caring
masculinity in the father/son relationship between Gerry Conlon
(Daniel Day-Lewis) and his father Guiseppe (Pete Postlethwaite). In fact
Jim Sheridan has made it clear that he could only gain funding from
America by stressing this father/son relationship (Linehan, 1993: 12).

In the television drama *Love Lies Bleeding* (1993), Irish nationalist
politics are central to the narrative. It tells the story of Con Ellis, an
IRA man who is released after 12 years from the Maze for a 24-hour
home visit. Part of the drama is set around the negotiations which are
taking place for an IRA cease fire, based on pro- or anti-cease fire
factions. None the less, most of the narrative is actually a love story-
come-thriller, with an investigative plot line. Once Con has access to
the outside world, in Belfast, he sets out to find the loyalists who have
murdered his girlfriend of 12 years ago, Leyla. Leyla is both a mystery

to the audience (this is marked by the fact that she is only shown as a child in photographs or as a very young woman, on 8 mm film) and to Con who seems to know very little about her. Initially we, like Con, believe she was murdered by loyalist paramilitaries, but as the story line progresses and Con begins to put the clues together it becomes clear that Leyla was not killed by loyalists but rather by some faction of the IRA. Moreover as the drama develops we find out that far from loving Conn and being an innocent victim of loyalist paramilitary violence, Leyla was part of the anti-cease fire IRA faction which was planning to execute Con. Thus, the characterisation of Leyla as 'a woman' becomes problematic once she is identified as an IRA terrorist. We now see that Con's love for and trust of Leyla was misplaced, and based on deception. By the end of the drama, we see her, like Jude in *The Crying Game*, as sexually duplicitous, untrustworthy and a liar.

What all these productions have in common is a redefinition of the IRA man and his 'cause' and they would seem to be doing this through a re-conceptualisation of masculinity and violence, in an attempt to create a base on which 'new' male cultural identities can be forged. In the post cease fire context of Northern Ireland this could have worrying implications for women. For it would seem that the new foundations of a 'lasting peace' based on the need to recognise differences (national identities) between men are ultimately being formed by situating them in opposition to women. Thus, these films situate the nationalist struggle – Irish or British – in Northern Ireland as an exclusively male 'problem'.

Irish national identity and 'Irish' women

It is important at this juncture to shift away from film and television representations to a broader consideration of the relationship between feminism and nationalism. We should acknowledge that nationalism is and has been viewed dubiously by women. Traditionally, nationalism has problems with gender differences, or, indeed, the recognition of any form of difference, which cuts across a unified sense of national self. Nationalism is, itself, a difficult term usually perceived as an identity formed by an allegiance to a nation state or territory. In Northern Ireland this is usually understood as either an allegiance to the British or Irish state. However, such a negative perception of nationalist (the state) identity can be challenged. National identity, whilst making up only part of an overall identity and subjectivity, is clearly a very powerful element. This is particularly true of situations like Northern Ireland where one way that people are defined as different to one another is largely based on their 'so-called' national identity (although in Northern Ireland this is usually defined through the religious terms Catholic/Irish, Protestant/British).

Benedict Anderson's (1983) much cited proposition of the nation as an 'imagined community' is helpful in understanding what national identity means to women. He proposes that national identity is a cultural construct and not an essence (though that does not deny that it may 'feel like' an essence to the individual). Thus, in Northern Ireland one is not born Irish or British, it is rather a sense of identity and self which is acquired over time. It is created in and through the cultural representation, traditions, histories and social practices of the different communities in Northern Ireland. Rather than employing this to dismiss national identities as false or untrue, the central question which must be asked of any national identity is whom and what does it represent and how it sees/defines itself in relation to Others? Central to any definition of self has been the designation of what it is not – 'the Other' – national, class, gender, location. Furthermore, it is fundamental to acknowledge that the right to define whom and what this 'Other' is, is rarely based on equal relationships of power or access to representation. This is made clear by Chris Weedon when she states:

> The relative domination of various groups by other groups is partly secured through the practices and products of cultural institutions. Here we are thinking of examples such as language, the family, the education system, the media, the law and religious organisations. It is through these institutions that we learn what is right and wrong, good and bad, normal and abnormal, beautiful and ugly. It is through them that we come to accept that men are better leaders than women, that Black people are less intelligent than Whites ... that Moslems are fanatical and 'we' are rational ... that my clan is better than yours, that the English are cleverer than the Irish ...
> (Jordan and Weedon 1995: 4,5)

In ... Northern Ireland the dominant position of Britishness has for many years had the power to define the 'Other' of Irishness.[3] Irish nationalism challenges this by attempting to create an encompassing national identity of Irishness which importantly has the potential to challenge the dominant and disempowering representations of Irishness. In its more progressive form this could be described as an empowered sense of cultural identity which has no specific allegiances to the actual nation state of Ireland (which could shift the discussion away from questions of location and the 'border'). However, in the current political situation in Northern Ireland this more progressive form of identity is always politicised, because individuals cannot currently choose to celebrate Irishness through cultural forms, music, language, history, sport, etc., without facing intimidation, fear and discrimination.[4] Because of the need to create a unity in opposition to the more powerful and dominant identity of Britishness, in common with other nationalist struggles, Irish nationalism in Northern Ireland has had major difficulties in acknowledging differences that cut across this 'imagined' Irish identity, and gender is one such difference. This reticence to take on board the specific oppression of women by Irish nationalism has also been hampered by the complex role patriarchal Catholicism has played in the creation of an 'imagined' community of Irishness within Northern Ireland.[5] In Northern Ireland Irish/Catholic[6] women are situated as a double Other, both the Other to patriarchal male power and the Other to dominant British national identity. The double discrimination that Catholic/Irish women face in real terms has been revealed in a recent report on women's employment in Northern Ireland which concluded, 'Catholic women are consistently more likely to be unemployed than are Protestant women; this pattern remains regardless of age, martial status, area of residence, age and number of dependent children' (Davis *et al.* 1995: iv).

The paramilitary violence of loyalist organisations and the double positioning of Catholic/Irish women is also significant. For instance in 1993, Anne Marie Smyth was tortured, humiliated and finally murdered by a gang of loyalist men in East Belfast because she was a Catholic. In 1994, Margaret Wright was taken to a loyalist band hall, where she was tortured, humiliated and murdered because she had been mistaken for a Catholic (see Ferguson and McWilliams 1994). These women, like women throughout the world, suffered from male violence against them and were murdered by men. This is a recognised concern of feminism. However, they were murdered not just because they were women but also because they were Catholic/Irish. This is a concern of nationalism. Considered together they raise a set of complex questions which not only exposes the similarities between the oppression of women but, significantly, also the differences.

In Northern Ireland Irish/Catholic women have their experience shaped (how they are treated in the real world) and their subjectivity formed (how they perceive themselves) by their position as a double 'Other'. Their right and desire to contest both these discriminatory positions draws together nationalist and feminist identity politics into what is undoubtedly a difficult and often antagonistic relationship. This is because feminist politics are always in danger of being subsumed into an imagined community of 'Irishness' which (currently) tries to ignore differences between 'Irish' peoples. This is often cited as a reason why women should not be involved in nationalist politics. However, it is just as important to recognise that some forms of feminism also have problems in acknowledging the differences that exist between women. Thus, the dominant interpretation of feminism, like nationalism, also needs to be challenged. Feminism, as Anne Kaplan (1987) has identified, does not have a single meaning. She outlines a number of different feminist positions and cites them as bourgeois, Marxist and, the most popular and dominant understanding of feminism (and therefore the most relevant to this article), radical/separatist feminism. She defines radical feminism as based on 'the designation of women as different from men' which accompanies the desire, 'to establish separate female communities to forward women's specific needs and desires' (*ibid.*: 216). However, more recent theories, dispute these positions, and she terms these poststructuralist feminism. The latter position is based on the assumption that as feminists 'we need to analyse the language order through which we learn to be what our culture calls "women" as distinct from a group called "men" as we attempt to bring about change beneficial to women' (*ibid.*: 216). What separates this feminist position from the others is its philosophical definition; the first three feminist positions are 'essentialist' and the latter 'anti-essentialist'. As Kaplan proposes,

> essentialist feminism assumes a basic 'truth' about women that patriarchal society has kept hidden. It assumes that there is a particular group – 'women' – that can be separated from another group – 'men' – in terms of an essence that precedes or is outside of culture and that ultimately has to have biological origins.   (*ibid.*: 217)

In common with many essentialist nationalist positions, which maintain that you are born Irish or British, these earlier feminist positions maintain that women are born with the qualities that define femininity ('more humane, moral mode of being , which, once brought to light, could help change society in beneficial ways' (*ibid.*: 217). In opposition to this anti-essentialist feminism (poststructuralist) attempts to understand the process through which female subjectivity is constructed in patriarchal culture, and they do not find an 'essential' femininity behind the socially constructed subject. 'The "feminine" is not something outside of, or untouched by, patriarchy, but integral to it'. (*ibid.*: 217)

'Mother Ireland Get Off Our Backs'

Considerations of such an anti-essentialist concept of both femininity and Irishness have been a central area of debate for many sections of the feminist movement in Ireland. In the area of film production there have been a number of film-makers which have concerned themselves with the tensions that arise between republicanism/ nationalism/Catholicism and feminism. These include *Maeve* (Murphy and Davies 1981), *Anne Devlin* (Pat Murphy 1984), *Mother Ireland* (Anne Crilly, 1988), *Hush-a-bye Baby* (Margo Harkin 1989) and *The Visit* (Walsh 1992).

For these Irish women film-makers, the attempt to produce films which deal with the contradictions, contests and possible coalitions between feminist and nationalist identity politics has created a number of problems, particularly in relation to how these films have been received and interpreted. This is especially true within Northern Ireland itself and is, I believe, the consequence of essentialist conceptions of both feminism and nationalism. Some of these relate specifically to discussions and writing on these films and others to more general political debates. On the one hand, these productions are trapped by the now dominant rhetoric of an essentialising feminism (as outlined above) in which their acknowledgement of, and concern with, the differences between women means that they are often interpreted as being exclusive to their Protestant 'sisters'. For instance Kathleen Nutt writes about her feelings of exclusion from such films, after attending a talk on Irish Women and Cinema. She felt 'elated' that a recognisable tradition of Irish women's film-making has been emerging but 'disgruntled' because all the films were concerned with what she perceives to be a 'nationalist' content of the films. Ultimately, she argues, they only dealt with 'the problems women face in the wider nationalist community' (1993: 42). She argues further that to be more successful as feminist films, films made by Catholic/Irish women should 'start to respond to the problems of more than one group of women in our society' (ibid.: 43).

Alternatively, other interpretations of the 'nationalist' content of these films have been influenced by the widespread perception of Irish nationalism as indistinguishable from the Republican politics of Sinn Féin. Here, any attempt to speak from the minority perspective is delegitimised by connecting it to the actions and position of the IRA. It is my belief that these two interpretations have had quite disastrous effects on the development of both nationalist and feminist politics. They have, in many cases, silenced women film-makers in their attempt to investigate the complex and often contradictory relationship between Irish national identity politics and feminist identity politics.[7] Such interpretations have also been used to condemn films[8] which would otherwise be of central importance to both feminist reclamation histories and female oral histories, and to the development of an understanding of the complexity of such identity politics in real life. I am thinking here particularly of Anne Crilly's television documentary *Mother Ireland*.

Furthermore, such interpretations have been instrumental in shifting how these films are understood by their female audience, often working to dismiss the more complex ways that they investigate the confrontation between such identity politics. For instance, Pat Murphy's film, *Maeve*, has generally been received as a film which attacks the anti-feminist and oppressive politics of republicanism. In this film the character of Maeve and her feminist critique of the republican position represented by her boyfriend Liam, has predominantly been interpreted as the position women viewers of the film should identify with because Maeve is seen to represent the voice of feminism.

The two main pieces of writing on the film (Johnston 1981; Gibbons 1983) do address the more complex interaction between characters in the film. However, subsequent discussion has focused predominantly on the two key scenes, at Cavehill and in Milltown Cemetery, where Maeve's feminism confronts Liam's nationalism. Moreover, whilst Luke Gibbons's overall text is more complex he introduces Maeve as a film that

> deals with the return from exile of a young feminist, Maeve Sweeney, to her family and friends in Belfast. Maeve's exile is both physical and political, in that she feels alienated not only from the threatening British military presence on the streets, but also from the ideological climate of her own community which revolves around a traditional, male-dominated republicanism. (1983: 149)

Thus, Gibbons clearly sets up an opposition between Maeve as a feminist and Liam and the 'community' as nationalist/republican. This emphasis is unfortunate, as the film is organised to offer up Maeve's separatist, essentialising and alienated feminist politics as an equally problematic position for women in the audience to identify with. As Pat Murphy explains, the film provokes both identification with and criticism of the main character Maeve (cited in Johnston (1981: 69)).

National and gender identity is a central concern of the film which recalls – through flashbacks – Maeve's childhood and the formative moments in the organisation of her gender and national identity. This is done through her father's story-telling, experiences of sectarian discrimination and violence and her Catholic schooling. Although the struggle for national identity is predominantly represented by Liam's allegiance to the republican movement, the film also – through the use of flashbacks and memories – situates this nationalist struggle in the everyday events and the real-life experiences of growing up as a Catholic/Irish woman in Northern Ireland – for instance, the scene in which the young Maeve and her father are warned off trying to sell their cakes in the Protestant town (visually marked by the reflection of the Union Jack in the windscreen of their van), or the scene when Maeve is beaten up by the police during a civil rights demonstration.

However, this tendency to sustain tension in the film exclusively between Maeve (the discourse of feminism) and Liam (the discourse of republicanism/nationalism) elides the film's underlying complexities. The film actually offers up in a number of different feminist voices. The character Maeve quite clearly represents a certain type of 'radical' feminism. As an exile and outsider Maeve is represented as being unable to function any longer within her own community, or indeed in relation to the other female characters in the film. Maeve functions in the film to represent a particular feminist rhetoric which is based on a belief in the possibility of an autonomous feminist movement. Whilst Maeve's critique of republicanism is without doubt impressive, her theories function as just as that: theories which are difficult to identify with in real life.[9] She states of Liam, 'I didn't make the rules or build this structure. All I can do is withdraw from it.' This, unfortunately, is an impossible and in many ways undesirable position for women to take up in real life.

Furthermore, *Maeve* is not a film that outrightly rejects nationalist politics in favour of feminist politics, rather it offers up a number of different female characters who function in the narrative to critique different feminist positions and different nationalist positions. The film employs an experimental narrative structure particularly in relation to Maeve, whereas Roisin, her sister, is predominantly situated in the realist narrative of the film, and because of this she is portrayed as a more realistic and likeable character. It is far easier, for the audience, to identify with Roisin and her sense of fun, community and resistance than it is with the alienated and aloof Maeve. This difference between them – one as a representation of the ideals of (radical/separatist) feminism and the other the reality of living as a Catholic/Irish woman – is represented in a number of scenes. In one Roisin tells Maeve that she went to some of her (feminist) meetings but adds 'they were no help to me, they just ended up sounding like mammy does sometimes, about men being the enemy out to take advantage of you. I don't need to close my eyes. That's what I've been hearing since I was five.' Maeve's reply represents the gap between ideology and the real world, 'Well you must have heard wrong.' Maeve's feminism is a feminism which often works to ignore or elide the different experiences of women in real life.

Our dis-identification with Maeve and the feminist position she represents was an intentional aspect of the film. As Pat Murphy has stated, 'One of the themes in *Maeve* is the problem of developing a theory of feminist politics which is not applicable to Maeve's reality' (cited in Johnston 1981: 69). However, this message has very often been lost in subsequent discussions of the film. This is because, ultimately, the film is unable to counteract the dominant perception of nationalism and feminism as incompatible. It should be important to recognise that Pat Murphy's film is not rejecting nationalist politics in favour of feminist politics, she is rather using this film to investigate and delve into the possibilities of a more accommodating and progressive relationship between the two. As Pat Murphy herself states, 'The question is really one of the film's identification of progressive forces within feminism and republicanism' *ibid*.: 70).[10]

Margo Harkin's film *Hush-a-bye Baby*, was also given a more nuanced reception in academic writing, but, like *Maeve*, it has also been interpreted as a film that attacks 'male' nationalist/republican sexual politics. In one such discussion, McLoone situates the film as anti-republican/nationalist. This interpretation is based on how he believes Republicans in Derry received the film. 'I've heard objections from that quarter ... Indeed if you think about militant republican politics and the situation where a person goes out to kill, or be killed, the last thing they want is exploration – to stop and think about it' (1991: 133). No one would dispute that some sections of the republican/nationalist community had problems with the content of the film. However, once again McLoone's interpretation favours a less complex reading of the film which actually disrupts just such a monolithic reading of republicanism, nationalism and feminism. Harkin herself replied that:

> In fact the issues that are discussed in *Hush-a-bye Baby* are very much issues that are discussed in the republican movement, in feminist and socialist groupings in Ireland. People are not aware of what those debates are because they don't hear them so I just want to correct that ... In a sense that film was actually representing a debate which is not normally heard or is assumed not to take place within those particular groupings.   (*ibid*.: 134)

However, the production that has received most criticism is Anne Crilly's television documentary *Mother Ireland*. The first section reclaims women from past nationalist history. Thus it automatically calls into question, and makes strange, the dominant patriarchal historical discourse of Irish nationalism which has hidden and ignored such female involvement. Moreover, for its contemporary female audience, it makes such exclusions visible and reveals the continuing selectiveness of dominant male (republican/nationalist) history. As a reclamation text it also functions to challenge contemporary ideologies, where a history of nationalism (especially relating to the use of violence) that excludes women works to naturalise the contemporary perception of national identity as an exclusively male concern.

The latter section of *Mother Ireland* also deals with questions of representation. It asks different Irish women how they feel about the idealised representations of womanhood and motherhood which have been central to Irish nationalist 'imaginings'. In this sense it investigates the space between representation, ideology and the real-life experiences of being a woman within a predominantly patriarchal nationalist culture. The film offers up a number of different and often contradictory female viewpoints on this subject. Regardless of this, it has been described as one that 'ultimately attempts to recuperate the hidden history of Irish women for the nationalist struggle with little sense of the ironic and self-defeating bind which this entails' and that it 'ultimately endorses the view that there can be no women's liberation until there is national liberation' (McLoone 1990: 57). Such an interpretation fails to acknowledge that the documentary does not endorse one viewpoint in relation to nationalism, but rather represents a number of different female viewpoints on the subject. However, it is ultimately perceived as nationalist rather than feminist because all the women express the wish, in some form or other, to have an Irish identity. Moreover the double 'othering' of Catholic/Irish Women in Northern Ireland means that the battle to remove the inequalities that affect them bring together both national liberation and women's liberation.

McLoone sees women's interest in nationalist identity politics as 'self defeating', and ' at odds with the perspective of feminism internationally' (*ibid.*: 57). This position is based on the idea that femininity is women's primary identity, which unites women in international feminism. I would have to disagree. It is precisely the documentary's acknowledgement of difference that places it at the centre of contemporary international feminism. Here the belief in an all-encompassing primary identity has been shattered by the need to recognise 'differences' between women (class, race, sexuality and location, to name but four).[11] This interpretation of Irish nationalism as something inherently at odds with a feminist position was and still is used to dismiss women's involvement or interests in nationalist politics.

Carol Coulter addresses both the historical and the contemporary relationship between feminism and nationalism for Irish women. She also acknowledges the need for the republican movement to change stating that, 'There is undoubtedly a continued implicit contradiction between a nationalist movement dedicated to the creation of a state and the growth in influence of community-based groups which are more readily associated with women's politics' (1993: 54). However, like myself (although I would replace republicanism with a more general understanding of nationalism (see also Meaney 1993)), she believes that this must equally be a debate that moves away from the dominant perception which 'presents republicanism as an essentially patriarchal ideology, and suggests that feminist consciousness among women will lead them to reject it, despite considerable evidence to the contrary'. She, too, believes that this position 'ignores the living links between women (as well as men) and their communities and culture and asks them to deny their culture in order to express themselves as women' (Coulter 1993: 54).

In Edna Longley's essay, 'From Cathleen to Anorexia: The Breakdown of Ireland' (in 1994a), these two ways of interpreting nationalism and feminism come to a head. Longley's understanding of the nationalist dispute in Northern Ireland is based on the dominant perception of 'an intensely local territorial struggle'. Missing from her article is any acknowledgement of the very real discrimination faced by Catholic/Irish people in Northern Ireland. Strangely, whilst she believes that feminism and unionist (Britishness) politics can co-exist, this is not the case with Irish nationalism and feminism. She goes on to attack women who call themselves nationalist/republican feminist, 'A Nationalist Republican feminist, less readily regarded as a contradiction in terms, claims that her ideologies coincide. And in doing so she tries to hijack Irish Feminism' (1994a: 187).

This quote illustrates a number of my points. Firstly, the perception that if you are a nationalist feminist you must also be a republican. Secondly, the tendency to ignore the tremendous struggles, tensions and conflicts between nationalist politics and feminist identity politics (which these feminist films attempt to deal with). Thirdly, the assumption that there is only one true feminist position to hold in Ireland and that Irish feminism has been 'hijacked' by these 'nationalist' women. Throughout the article Longley refers to 'nationalist' women as 'retarded' and 'tribal' (terms that can only be described as shockingly racist) rather than 'sisterly'. In this sense Longley places herself firmly in the radical/separatist (essentialist) camp calling for the sisterhood of feminism to rise above the 'tribalism' and 'backwardness' of Irish (but not British) nationalism.

In the current historical moment in Northern Ireland, it is essential to move beyond these positions. Instead a more thoughtful and open consideration of these different identity politics is imperative. This is particularly so as the image of woman has once again become a central site for the negotiation of national identity.[12] Whilst the mainstream productions cited at the beginning of this chapter do this in one way, there has also been an attempt to do this by remobilising a traditional set of assumptions on what determines the feminine and correct feminine behaviour. That is, women as loving, passive, humanitarian and caring, whose interests are primarily situated in the private space of home and family.

Such traditional representations of femininity have become central, in a series of Northern Ireland Office television adverts which were produced before the cease fires and only screened in Northern Ireland.[13] Formally they were adverts for the confidential phone line (set up to facilitate people reporting 'terrorist' activity). Such adverts are not new and have been on television in Northern Ireland since the mid-1970s. However, in 1993, a series of three adverts were produced which, in common with the mainstream film productions I have previously cited, broke with a long tradition of representing the paramilitaries, particularly the IRA, as psychopathic, and their actions as incomprehensible. Instead, they situated these men in their own communities and families, and depicted them as 'normal, everyday lads'. In effect, they began the process of de-demonising the terrorist. Moreover, by placing these men in family and community situations, they also acknowledged that the ideologies the various paramilitary groups represent were not separate and alienated from those of their 'communities' but rather receive varying degrees of support and recognition.

The producers of these adverts aimed to make the national allegiances Irish/British of these men unclear. In this respect, they worked against the dominant explanation of the conflict in Northern Ireland as a backward and incomprehensible battle between two religious factions – the two 'tribes' philosophy with Britain placed 'keeping the peace' somewhere in between.[14] This misrepresentation of the reasons behind the conflict was now displaced onto an equally problematic explanation – male violence. In these adverts everyone is a victim of terrorist violence, men because they can't help it and women because they have to suffer it. In these adverts violence is represented as an essentially male characteristic. Somewhat ironically, this connected them to an essentialist feminist position which maintains that one of the essentially 'bad' characteristics of masculinity is violence. In one of the adverts, a little boy is shown playing with a water pistol as two 'terrorists' arrive in a car to shoot his father. The equation between the boy, the toy, and natural male behaviour and the consequence of not controlling it, is made quite explicit. The national allegiance of the men – IRA, INLA, UVF, UFF – was intentionally ambiguous. Instead, it is their masculine violence and behaviour which is the problem to be resolved. The interpretation of the paramilitary violence being essentially masculine has the consequence of not only eliminating women from the 'problem' but also the solution.

However, in one of these adverts this 'national' obscurity is not maintained. In the advert titled 'Lady, Lady, Lady',[15] which was specifically directed at a female audience, the national 'difference' between the two male 'terrorists' is made explicit. This advert began with two marriage scenes, one Protestant, one Catholic, which intercut between one another as the men are saying their marriage vows. This makes it difficult to establish which couple is which, but none the less introduces the theme of a difference based on Catholic/Irishness,

Protestant/Britishness. Next we see a scene which appears normal and everyday – one of the men stands fishing. The other man then comes up behind him and graphically shoots him, moves to stand over him and shoots him twice more to make sure he is dead. This is followed by a series of shots which inter-cut between the two women, the wives of the 'terrorists' in their domestic space, doing the washing up, drying the dishes, lying alone in bed. The advert ends when finally they accidentally meet, smile and pass each other in a flower shop. A female voice-over then anchors the message of this advert:

> Two women, two traditions, two tragedies. One married to the victim of violence, one married to the prisoner of violence [accompanying which we see a shot of one of the husbands in prison], both scarred, both suffering, both desperately wanting it to stop. Don't suffer it. Change it. Call the confidential phone line.

The acknowledgement of the differences between these men operates to accentuate the sameness of the women; a number of dominant meanings of femininity are reconfirmed. It proposes that, in opposition to these 'naturally' violent men, women are by their very nature anti-violent, passive, peace-loving and humanitarian and their primary interests are love, marriage, home and family. Of course women in Northern Ireland desire 'peace', but to explain their desire through 'essential' female qualities is a particularly powerful ideological tool. As articulated by the female voice-over, the two women are ultimately the victims of violence, male violence, which they both desperately want to stop. In this advert they are situated as the peace-makers, a mythical space of female otherness which transcends these violent male struggles for 'national' identity.

This ideological positioning of women as essentially passive and anti-violent has also been central to certain types of feminism. Unfortunately this has worked to de-politicise women's desire and struggles for peace throughout the world. Chandra Talpade Mohanty challenges such essentialist interpretations of women's involvement in peace movements. She does this by making specific reference to a text by Robin Morgan (1984) in an edited collection of feminist essays, significantly titled *Sisterhood is Global: The International Women's Movement Anthology*. She criticises Morgan for promoting the idea that women have been involved 'in peace and disarmament movements across the worlds, because ... they desire peace (as opposed to men who cause war)' and 'Thus, the concrete reality of women's involvement in peace movements is substituted by an abstract "desire" for peace which is supposed to transcend race, class and national conflicts among women' (1992: 82).

In this advert women's desire for peace in Northern Ireland is not based on the need for real political, social, cultural and economic changes, which for Catholic/Irish women must address their place as a double Other. It is rather to be understood by their rejection of a male violence which does not represent them. This advert reaffirms some of the founding binary oppositions of patriarchal society: masculine/feminine, violent/passive, public/private, outside/inside and ultimately culture/nature. Whilst the men can represent national difference – their 'Otherness' – to each other, the women function in opposition to this. They can only represent their sameness as women and their Otherness to men.

In these recent adverts and the mainstream film and television productions noted above, women are represented as either a problem for 'male' struggle around national identity or they are positioned as outside of it. In them women's traditional femininity is reconfirmed, whereas masculinity, and a critique of its destructiveness and the need for it to change can now function as a base on which to form new allegiances. Consequently, in Northern Ireland these representations of women are working to reconfirm the place and authority of men to debate and resolve the 'problems' of national difference without them. If this analysis is correct, then we are seeing a number of popular cultural forms in which certain messages are working to separate women off from the debates around national identity. Ironically, this is being done through the acknowledgement of one type of feminism – an essentialising, radical feminism – and this has given such messages a validity they do not deserve.

If any progress on the question of national identity in Northern Ireland is to take place then the place of gender must be central to it (and I would maintain vice versa). For, as the feminist film-makers in Northern Ireland have revealed, the relationship between nationalism and feminism is a complex one, full of contradictions and contestations, but it is certainly not an irrelevant one. In its traditional patriarchal form, Irish nationalism has no space for feminism, and in its essentialising, radical form feminism has no space for the recognition of differences (including national) between women. What is required is an understanding of national identity and gender identity not as something inherent and essential but rather as socially and culturally constructed – 'imagined'. Then the potential for the creation of new 'imagined' identities which accommodate both desires for change and recognition would be possible.

In conclusion, it is important to state that I am not arguing for republican feminism. In fact, I am arguing for completely the opposite (though I do not doubt that because of the very powerful ideologically motivated coupling of nationalism and republicanism it will be interpreted that way). I wish to disengage nationalism, and its struggle for identity, from republicanism so that a much broader understanding of what Irish national identity might mean for women in Northern Ireland can be freely and openly considered without fear of intimidation or dismissal as 'extremist'.

Additionally, feminism needs to reject perceptions of female essentialism as a feminist strategy. Because if women continue to define themselves in this way they are ultimately placing themselves as the naturalised 'Other' to men. Moreover by continuing to define themselves only in relation to their sameness as women they exclude themselves from cultural and national struggles of difference. Ironically, this is also the position patriarchal culture gives them. Furthermore, if women are denied, or deny themselves, their sense of difference from other women this can have profound implications for a more pluralistic sense of identity. Women are not 'just' women: their subjectivity is made up of a number of complex and contradictory identities, all of which require both feminist investigation and consideration.

Acknowledgements

Thanks to Martin McLoone and Greg McLaughlin for their valuable comments on earlier drafts of this Chapter.

Notes

1. Exceptions are Loftus 1990; Rolston 1989.
2. Though this also has a tradition in films about the IRA, see, *Odd Man Out* 1947, *The Gentle Gun Man* 1952, *Shake hands with the Devil* 1959, *The Violent Enemy* 1969 and *Guest of the Nation*, 1935. For an excellent analysis of this see John Hill's 'Images of Violence' in (Rocket *et al.* 1988).
3. While Britishness is not hegemonic in the usual sense of the term, as it is contested by some sections of the community, it is hegemonic in its definition of 'common sense', the everyday and the 'normal'. For instance the school curriculum predominantly teaches British history, the English language etc., Union Jacks fly over official buildings, including state schools, some colleges of higher education, council buildings, police stations and even sports centres. British holidays are celebrated with St Patrick's Day still unofficially recognised. Attempts to integrate some forms of 'Irish' cultural representation are generally meant with hostility from the loyalist/British community. Red, white and blue graffiti is generally left untouched.
4. This is where the interpretation of both cultures being equally open to accusations of exclusiveness and sectarianism disintegrates, as argued by Butler 1993, 1994a and 1994b. It is important to recognise the extreme intolerance of the dominant British culture to the marginalised Irish culture.
5. However, this relationship is also one which needs to be understood, rather than simply condemned. In Northern Ireland it has been the Catholic Church which has supported and made space for the expression of Irishness in the face of opposition from the British government and the official culture of Britishness. Catholic schools taught/teach Irish history, culture and language, where the state schools did/do not. It financially supported and organised cultural events such as the GAA, Irish dancing and music, when the official state did/do not. This is not intended as a defence of the teachings and role of the Catholic Church but rather as a limited explanation of a much more complex relationship.
6. I have introduced the term Catholic because the two terms in the current 'Othering' in Northern Ireland are inextricably linked. To be Catholic is to be Irish and to be Irish is to be a Catholic, although in real life this is never so simplistic.

7. This silencing should not be taken lightly. To be identified as an Irish nationalist in Northern Ireland (including just being a Catholic) means that you can become a 'legitimate' target for various loyalist paramilitary organisations. It is not only films made by women which have suffered from the dominant coupling of 'Irishness/nationalism and republicanism (IRA)'. See Butler's (1993) review of Joe Comerford's film *High Boot Benny* (1993) and Bell's (1994) reply.
8. See McLoone 1990; Longley 1994b. In my teaching experience students' response to this documentary is predominantly positive, and female students are often shocked at their own lack of knowledge of the hidden history of female involvement in nationalism.
9. This difficulty is also an intentional element of the formal strategies of the film which refuse to situate Maeve as the positive heroine. There are, of course, other debates which are more concerned with identifying the experimental, anti-realist operations of *Maeve*, as opposed to the traditional, realist documentary form of *Mother Ireland*. Although this is not the specific concern of this article, it is nevertheless worth acknowledging, firstly, that feminist documentary film-makers have also been identified as employing different formal strategies to the dominant documentary form (see 'Real Women' in Kuhn 1982) Secondly, many feminists now recognise the importance of employing different strategies of representation for different purposes (see Juhasz 1994; Wolff 1990) in opposition to the concept of a 'politically correct' feminist form.
10. It is also interesting to note that the interview between Pat Murphy and Claire Johnston, which deals with such questions, was not included when the text was reproduced in the publication *Films for Women* (Brunsdon 1986).
11. For a clear discussion of the importance of locating the politics of experience and different senses of identity, see Moharty (1992).
12. The representation of women has been central to both the Irish and British nationalist/cultural identity struggles within Ireland both North and South. Anne Crilly's *Mother Ireland* investigates this as does Loftus (1990).
13. It is important to note that these adverts were withdrawn after the 1994 ceasefires and repeated following their breakdown.
14. During 1995 another set of adverts were produced which aimed to promote a cease fire 'feeling' – 'wouldn't it be great if it was like this all of the time' the punch line concludes. In these adverts the two tribes 'who couldn't get on' have now been replaced with the two traditions 'who cannot get on'. Once again the real inequality and discrimination experienced by the minority Catholic/Irish community in Northern Ireland is displaced onto an abstract 'human' misunderstanding about cultural differences and traditions.
15. In 1993 this advert won a gold award at the Irish International Advertising Festival.

CHAPTER 12

Modernising history: The real politik of heritage and cultural tradition in Northern Ireland

Desmond Bell

History, as we all know, is a fiercely contested terrain in Northern Ireland. The incommensurable character of nationalist and unionist narratives of history and identity provides the cultural dynamic of the current political conflict. Of any interpretative institution in Northern Ireland – museum, heritage centre or cultural traditions' exhibition – we can ask, 'Whose heritage is it celebrating?' This is a society well used to the partisan celebration of cultural identity, whether in Orange demonstrations or republican commemorations. How then does the heritage sector in Northern Ireland deal with the bitter fruits of Irish history? Can the production of a shared version of history through its heritage presentation play a part in reconciling the contemporary sectarian divisions which bedevil Northern Ireland society?

As David Brett (1996) has noted, in Northern Ireland the notion of heritage is closely allied with that of 'cultural tradition' and with a new approach to community relations. Culture and heritage are seen by the tutelary state[1] as potential vehicles of political reconciliation. State-supported activity in each area forms part of a distinctive political agenda concerned with fostering new structures of consensus *within* the constitutional status quo. The concepts of cultural tradition and heritage at work in 'official discourse' in Northern Ireland (i.e. the policy formulations and institutional practices of the Northern Ireland Office and its agencies) invoke a utopian sense of community and identity and a redemptive view of culture at odds with the realities of the ongoing sectarian conflict and with the machinations of the British state. In this article I explore the ideological role of the heritage and interpretation industry in reshaping our understanding of the past in Northern Ireland.

Over the last few years a number of new museums and interpretative centres have sprung up in Northern Ireland. These have been primarily concerned with presenting history for popular consumption rather than for academic dissection. This emergent heritage industry has been harnessed to tourist promotion and has attracted substantial public investment in an attempt to encourage growth in the service sector. In the immediate aftermath of the 1994 cease fire, tourism was identified as a major growth area in the Northern Ireland economy.[2] Indeed a boom in tourism was seen as the most tangible economic element of the proclaimed 'peace dividend'. Certainly tourist visits to Northern Ireland expanded dramatically in the period after the announcement of an end to hostilities.

From this time a concerted effort was made by the Northern Ireland Tourist Board in conjunction with Bord Fáilte (the Tourist Board in the Irish Republic) to sell Northern Ireland, particularly in the lucrative US and EU markets, as an integral part of a unified Irish tourist experience. This meant promoting Northern Ireland through a romantic rendering of its landscape (a marketing strategy already highly successful in the Republic (Bell 1995)). It also entailed a willingness on the part of tourist managers to engage with Irish history *within promotional and heritage discourses* in order to exploit the potential of museums and interpretative centres as recreational resources.

As Robert Hewison has argued, in the heritage centre history becomes reduced to 'a contemporary creation, more costume drama and re-enactment than critical discourse' (Hewison 1987). The heritage industry markets history to the recreational tourist as 'time travel' and in so doing abolishes the material past and historical time in favour of simulacrum and the stasis of myth. History is rescued from obscure texts and from pedantic historians. Through diorama (i.e. constructed scenario) and narrative emplotment is rendered as spectacle and fable. History made visible and accessible through its heritage presentation becomes a core element of the contemporary tourist experience.

Heritage in turn becomes a vehicle for communal self-definition in a period of rapid social change. The idea of heritage, as David Brett's observes, 'holds out the false promise that something can be preserved that will not melt away in air' (1996: 158). Brett, in the first serious study of the heritage industry in Ireland, *The Construction of Heritage*, argues that, '"heritage" is a product of the process of modernization which by eroding customs and expectations, forces us to re-articulate our sense of the past' (Brett 1996). I wish to suggest that this reconstruction of a popular sense of history in Northern Ireland can be seen as being closely involved with recent attempts to forge a new political settlement between the contending political factions in Northern Ireland around a pluralist agenda concerned with 'parity of esteem'.

Modernising history

Recently there has been a willingness on the part of some museum and heritage centres to tackle the recent history of political conflict in Ulster – we shall explore here the work of the Tower Museum in Derry. Contemporary curatorial strategies seem to be seeking to give voice on an impartial basis to each of the 'two main cultural traditions' in their presentation of the past.

The Tower Museum, which opened as the showpiece of the Derry City Council Heritage and Museum Service in October 1992, is clearly a new sort of interpretative institution. As its first Programme Organiser, Brian Lacey, noted,

> The aim was to establish a service which, unashamedly, could be both serious and popular at the same time and which would reconcile inside itself both the educational and 'touristy' dimensions of our work, without suffering any of the sense of schizophrenia or conflicts of interest, which nowadays afflicts the discourse between aspects of the museum world and the tourism industry.   (Lacey 1993: 57)

The museum, in line with other recently established heritage centres, is organised not around archive, historical object and scientific taxonomy but as a visitor 'experience'. This involves a chronological journey through a series of exhibits portraying the history of the city via various diorama, tableau and audio-visual presentations. (See Figure 12.1.)

Significantly, finance for the museum came primarily from public funds devoted to the development of tourism infrastructure. As Brian Lacey reveals, 'the Northern Ireland Tourist Board, who were advisers on the allocation of money for the project, were very unhappy about the the use of the word "museum" in the title' (Lacey 1993: 63). Presumably this was because they thought this might detract from its popularity as a tourist attraction. In the end the designers, the London-based Robin Wade and Pat Read Design Partnership, forged a compromise between touristic requirements and local demands that the new museum should honestly portray the difficult history and contentious recent past of the city and in so doing play a role in the reconciliation of the bitterly divided nationalist and unionist communities in Derry. As Lacey chronicles,

> From its establishment the (museum) Service had two main items on its agenda. By providing a range of visitor facilities we were to make a contribution to the economic improvement of the city through the development of its tourism infrastructure. Equally, we set out to make a contribution to cross-community mutual understanding and reconciliation.
>   (Lacey 1993: 57)

Accordingly the curators felt that it was appropriate, despite the reservations of the Tourist Board, that the museum should deal not only with the distant past but with 'the turbulent and controversial events of the last twenty five years'. Indeed this 'warts and all' portrayal of Derry's history was to win the museum a number of prestigious awards including a special commendation at the European Museum of the Year Award 1994. The judges praised,

> the great courage of the local authority (Derry City Council) in attempting to use the museum as a bridge between the political and religious factions in Northern Ireland, a function which it has fulfilled with conspicuous success.

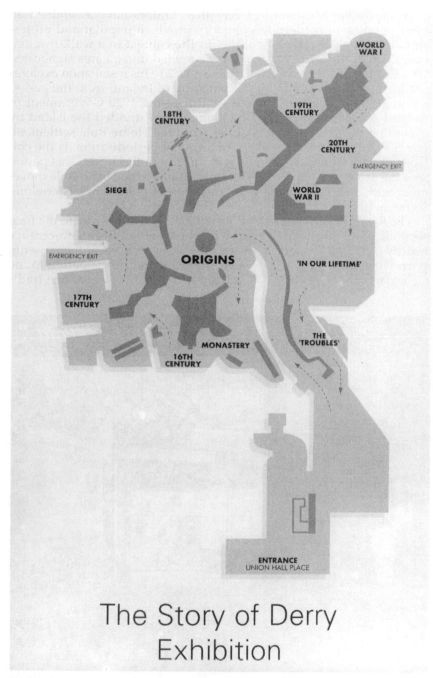

The Story of Derry
Exhibition

Figure 12.1 Tower Museum installation plan.

In the Tower Museum in Derry the curators have assembled an interpretation of modern Irish history in which popular and professional versions of the past collide. In the context of a walk-through exhibition of the history of the city we are led into an area signposted 'The Road to Northern Ireland'. (Figure 12.2.) This installation explores the historical background of the partition of Ireland from the period leading up to the first Home Rule Bill to the 1920 Government of Ireland Act, the legislation which effectively divided the island by excluding the six northern counties from the Home Rule settlement. For the curators the watershed, in terms of periodisation, is the collapse of nonconformist liberalism in the city in the 1880s. This period sees the growth of pan-Protestant opposition to the Home Rule movement with a corresponding reorganisation of politics in Ulster along sectarian lines.

The Road to Northern Ireland installation is the gateway to the final sections of the museum dealing with the troubled twentieth-century history of Derry. It stands between the earlier sections of the museum portraying the history of the town from the prehistoric period to the Georgian growth of the city – related through a common 'one tradi-

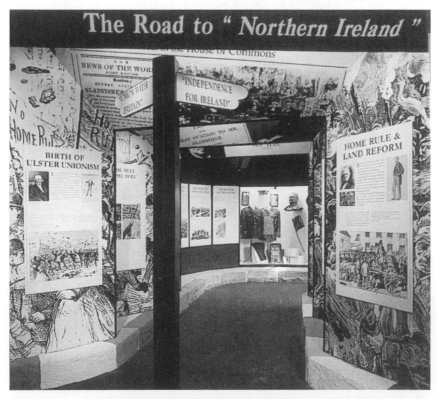

Figure 12.2   Road to Northern Ireland installation – entrance.

tion' narrative – and the latter sections dealing with the contemporary period. As such it is pivotal in establishing the curatorial parameters within which the highly contentious post-1965 period is explored. The Partition section of the museum leads us into an auditorium where we view a specially commissioned documentary film dealing with the Civil Rights period in Derry and its aftermath. Visitors leaving the auditorium pass through a final display area only recently constructed. The museum's latest exhibit presents a kaleidoscopic overview of Derry's recent history from 1965 to the present day, highlighting such events as the Civil Rights movement, Bloody Sunday, the Ulster Loyalist Workers' strike, the Hunger Strike and the current peace process (Figure 12.3.). We view a display of uniformed mannequins representing members of the IRA, the loyalist UDA, and the security forces (RUC and British Army). These figures are installed side by side in a number of exhibition cases, safely behind glass. Surrounding them is a display of various items of political literature and paramilitary paraphernalia from both republican and loyalist sources.

This installation is Northern Ireland's first public exhibition dealing with the contemporary troubles. The curators decision to 'arm' the IRA model in the exhibition with a real AK-47 Kalashnikov rifle previously used by the IRA plunged the museum into controversy in 1996 and led the RUC to seize the offending weapon and open an investigation into its legal status. Six months later the inclusion of an image of a masked republican gunman on the front cover of a promotional booklet for the museum led to further uproar (Figure 12.4.). Loyalist councillors demanded the withdrawal of the booklet. As DUP Councillor Hay was to ask, 'Is this the type of material we want on display in one of the main tourist attractions in the city?' Hay went on to suggest that, 'There must be some method of dealing with the history of the present in such a way that it does not offend anyone' (*Derry Journal*, 10 June 1997). The curators of the Tower Museum, together with other museum and heritage professionals in Northern Ireland, have of course been energetically searching for precisely such a method.

The striking 'Road to Northern Ireland' section of the history of Derry exhibition in the Tower Museum rehearses such a method. In this installation the single narrative structure through which Derry's history is related up to the 1880s gives way to a dual one portraying contending unionist and nationalist versions of history. On one side of the constructed road is an account of the events leading up to the Easter Rising from a nationalist perspective. On the other, loyalist opposition to Home Rule is portrayed by means of graphic panels simulating newsprint.

Set behind these panels on each side of the 'road' are a series of display cases containing nationalist and unionist political memorabilia – commemorative plates and postcards, sashes and paramilitary regalia portraying the political iconography of each movement. These displays, because of their location, only become visible after one has passed them and glanced back. They suggest a more jumbled and intimate, almost

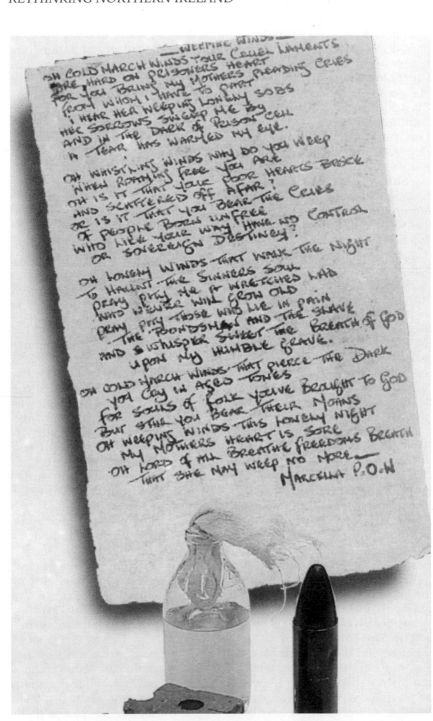

Figure 12.3 Prisoner's smuggled letter, petrol bomb and plastic bullet, part of 'The Troubles' installation.

Figure 12.4   Front cover of Tower Museum promotional brochure.

domestic, collection of historical memories reminiscent of a family china cabinet and its contents (this design feature may have been inspired by some of the partisan private collections of memorabilia such as the Apprentice Boys of Derry museum). These 'china cabinets' are installed on a separate plane from the main display panels. Their domestic and indeed intimate appearance contrasts with the bold graphic face and public language of the main panels. This collection of momentos suggests the complex assemblage of popular memory in Ulster. We are led to believe that out of these jumbled sources of cultural tradition the conflicting political identities of contemporary Ulster have been fashioned.

The floor of the installation takes the form of a narrow paved road flanked by decorated kerbs painted on one side in red, white and blue stripes and on the other in green, white and orange. This emblematic kerb design is instantly recognisable to those who know the 'mean streets' of Derry and Belfast, mirroring as it does the familiar territorial iconography of plebeian loyalism and its nationalist riposte. Here the intention of the exhibition designers is not to stake out the defensible boundaries of the sectarian ghetto but to signal again to the museum's visitors the complex interaction found in Ireland between popular senses of history and objective historical determination. History, we are reminded, is not only written in learned texts but inscribed on the ghetto's urban landscape and caught in the web of collective memory. In Northern Ireland gable end murals, graffiti, political posters parade a partisan but communally grounded sense of the past. History as myth, engendered in and through popular cultural practice, seeps into the pores of Ulster society. The curators of the Tower Museum seem to have abandoned the positivist sureties of Irish historiography which previously informed museum design. Instead, they have endorsed a more nuanced and multivocal account of the past. As Luke Gibbons (1996: 17) has argued,

> Understanding a community or a culture does not consist solely in establishing 'neutral' facts and 'objective' details: it means taking seriously their ways of structuring experience, their popular narratives, the distinctive manner in which they frame the social and political realities which affect their lives. Even the 'facts' themselves, where a communal mentality or world view is concerned, risk serious misunderstanding if their meaning is taken as self-evident.

Indeed the Tower Museum as a building is itself a testament to this dense interaction of history and myth. In Northern Ireland contemporary political sensibilities shape the presentation of history as heritage. The museum is located in a building known as the O'Doherty Fort, ostensibly named after one of the clans which ruled pre-plantation Derry and its hinterland. Despite its imposing late medieval rough stone façade and crenellations, the building is in fact a late 1980s construction (the tower was completed in 1986) and is a less than faithful

replica of an Ulster gaelic chieftains's tower-house keep. A more significant question for the citizens of Derry than the Tower's lack of historic
authenticity has been its siting. This is adjacent to Magazine Gate just
within the historic walls of Derry. These ramparts were erected in the
early seventeenth century during the settlement of Derry by London
merchant companies. The walls were designed as a bulwark against the
hostile native Irish displaced by the Protestant plantation of this part of
Ulster and have become a symbol of loyalist resistance to nationalist
encroachment. The tower on the other hand was commissioned and
built after a period when the unionist stronghold over political life in
Derry had been broken as a result of the civil rights struggle. As a
result of the subsequent political reform civic power shifted from a
Protestant oligarchy to an emerging Catholic middle class.

As archaeologists and historians have pointed out, there is little evidence that an original O'Doherty clan castle existed on the current
tower site in pre-plantation times. However, in the search for a suitable
location for the planned fort contemporary political sensibilities
tended to count for more than archeological and historical evidence.
The siting of the tower can be seen as a symbolic act involving a
reclaiming of the area by and for the natives. The building and siting of
the tower clearly represents an affirmation of nationalist identity in
post-Stormont Northern Ireland. In its bricks and mortar a myth of
origination is given concrete presence. As Brian Lacey notes, the
tower's construction,

> was viewed as symbolic, a positive indication that the remainder of the
> burnt-out historic city-core could be rebuilt, that the future in some way
> involved sorting out the complicated past, and that the nationalist present
> would need as much 'presence' as its unionist past.   (Lacey 1994: 28)

The decision to house the new municipal museum in the O'Doherty
Tower was a problematical one. The City Council had acquired the
tower from the Inner City Trust, an urban renewal voluntary group
associated with the dynamic community and civil rights activist Paddy
Doherty. The tower, built more as a contemporary folly rather than as a
public building, was totally unsuitable for use as a museum. In addition its close association with resurgent nationalism entailed a major
public relations challenge for a nationalist-controlled City Council
committed to healing sectarian divisions in Derry. The development of
the museum represented a curatorial challenge to respond to the multicultural aspirations of a new political order emerging in mid-1980s
Northern Ireland.

This new order was initially sketched in the New Ireland Forum
which floated the idea of joint British and Irish sovereignty over
Northern Ireland as a guarantee of the political rights of the two 'traditions'. Later it was given inter-governmental reality in the Anglo-Irish
Agreement. By now, however, the joint sovereignty concept had been
diluted and replaced with the more modest goal of achieving 'parity of

esteem' between the two communities. This proposed settlement, endorsed by both Dublin and London, was primarily concerned with incorporating the emergent Catholic middle class into a new political consensus around the majoritarian legitimacy of the Union and with delegitimising the militant republican struggle. Since the 1980s any serious commitment to structural reform of Northern Ireland on the part of the British government seems to have been replaced by a nebulous programme concerned with promoting multiculturalism. Within this new social contract the Catholic minority seems to being offered the right to participate in the cultural celebration of its Irishness in return for securing from its political representatives a degree of acceptance of the political status quo. Cultural relations have been ascribed a key role in sustaining this new 'social contract' for Northern Ireland.

The municipal authorities in Derry enthusiastically embraced this projected pluralist settlement with its talk of 'parity of esteem' between the 'two cultural traditions' in Northern Ireland. The museum, like a number of other heritage and public art projects sponsored by Derry City Council, was shaped by a municipal strategy which sought to present the city as an attractive tourist destination. Derry, it was felt, had the potential to be both a major heritage centre and a city where the two traditions could peacefully coexist in a rebuilt environment. From the late 1970s there was a sustained attempt to renovate the inner city with its Georgian streets and still intact walls, gates and bastions. The 1980s saw the development of a municipal strategy aimed at promoting Derry as a centre of cultural activity. The council actively supported the adventurous Orchard Art Gallery curated by Declan McGonagle and hosted the culturally innovative Field Day Theatre Company. In general the strategy was to distance Derry from the sectarian mire of politics in Northern Ireland by presenting it as a place apart. Derry would be the aspirant capital of the 'fifth province' which the intellectuals of the journal *Crane Bag* had postulated as a domain of the imagination. In the Maiden City pluralist thought could flourish outwith the partitions, prohibitions and polemics of contemporary Ireland.

The Tower Museum, despite early unionist opposition to the siting of the tower, soon seemed to gain a wide degree of acceptance within both communities in Derry. Its tourist potential in a city gearing itself up for heritage attractions became apparent. An approving visit and speech by Ian Paisley at the opening ceremony seemed to set the loyalist seal of approval for the venture.

In Northern Ireland curators and interpretation professionals have nervously sought to plot a consensual path between contending nationalist and unionist narratives of history. Indeed this concern became in many ways the core one for the curators of the Tower Museum. As Lacey reported, 'We consider the museum's major strength to be that it presents a highly contentious subject, the history of Derry, in an even handed manner' (Lacey 1996). Indeed curators were discovering that contemporary sectarian divisions could now even be alluded to in their exhibitions in so far as they could be rendered harmless through their heritage presentation as 'cultural tradition'.

Heritage and the tutelary state

There is, I would argue, an interesting parallel between the use of the concepts of 'cultural tradition' and 'reconciliation' within curatorial discourse in Northern Ireland's heritage industry and their employment within the community relations policy emanating from the Northern Ireland Office and its agencies. Many will find it strange that museums and interpretation centres should be involved in the business of community relations. But when they are, as is the case in Northern Ireland, this raises interesting questions both about the role of the state in the construction of heritage and about how particular interpretative orders relate to strategies of governance in ethnically divided societies.

Since the imposition of Direct Rule in 1972 the British state has systematically sought to portray the ongoing political conflict in Northern Ireland as being in essence one of 'deep rooted' sectarian division and 'mindless' violence. This official explanation of the troubles has permeated all aspects of the Northern Ireland Offices's activity. It is succinctly explicated in the research strategy document of the Office's Central Community Relations Unit published in 1991 in order to set out the government's approach to community relations.

> Northern Ireland remains a deeply divided society within which exist two separate groups with different political aspirations, religious beliefs, cultural traditions and social values. It is from this essential division that violence flows and political instability persists, with such heavy human and financial costs. (Central Community Relations Unit 1991)

Over the last twenty-five years the British state has sought to represent itself as an honest broker seeking to mediate between two ethnic traditions locked in an ancient struggle. From the perspective of Stormont Castle sectarian division has been seen as the cause rather than the effect of the political conflict. The role of the British state becomes one of seeking through its tutelary interventions to secure the conditions, cultural and political, for a pluralistic settlement of the current conflict within the constitutional status quo.

In the absence of any substantial political progress or agreement between the political parties in Northern Ireland, government attention has turned to a series of tutelary interventions aimed at addressing sectarian divisions and marginalising political dissent. Since the mid-1970s the state has underwritten a massive project of social pedagogy with the north's school children, teachers, community groups and social care professionals concerned with improving community relations within Northern Ireland. Through an impressive series of interventions in educational policy (Education for Mutual Understanding), in community work (via a generously supported Community Relations Council) and more latterly in arts and heritage activity (via the Cultural Traditions Group) the British state has sought to promote greater levels of understanding and tolerance between the north's polarised communities by encouraging the development of cross-community educational and cultural activity.

The early tutelary interventions focused on the possibility of reshaping social attitudes – particularly youthful ones. It was felt sectarianism and youthful involvement in paramilitary activity could be tackled by clearly-delimited, state-sponsored initiatives in the field of education and youth work. This approach was prevalent in the early years of direct rule, particularly under the last Labour administration, in power from 1974 to 1979. This correctional approach ended up psychologising and pathologising sectarianism, treating it as a structure of personal prejudice and communal failing based on ignorance and somehow related to a deficit in working-class culture. As I have argued elsewhere,

> this methodological approach reduces sectarianism to a pathology of individual sentiment. It conspires with 'official' definitions of sectarianism in deflecting attention from the political realm. At the same time, it scape-goats the working class child, or his/her culture, community and 'traditions', identifying these as the origin of sectarian conflict.   (Bell 1990: 149)

The last few years have seen the growth of a series of state-funded interventions in the area of community relations which have focused on a multicultural agenda. David Miller has traced the transition within official policy discourse from a 'cultural deficit' to a 'cultural tradition' approach to sectarian division. The term cultural tradition is now given a positive valency within community relations discourse. As Miller notes,

> Attempts as regulating relations between the two communities were joined, in the late 1980s by a focus on how the nationalist and unionist communities saw each other. Community Relations and Cultural Traditions work represents an attempt to enter the cultural sphere and to promote explorations of cultural identity with a view to fostering tolerance and understanding. Previously such work had been focused on emphasising the commonalities between nationalist and unionist, often leading to an unrealistic portrait of people working together. More recently tolerance of diversity and difference have come to the fore.   (Miller 1993a: 74)

The new object of government policy became to encourage the accommodation of communal divisions within a projected pluralistic settlement. The work of the Cultural Traditions Group has been one of the most sustained in this field. This organisation started off life as an academic discussion group under the aegis of the Institute of Irish

Studies at Queen's University, Belfast. However, it soon became assimilated into the Northern Ireland Community Relations Council as one of its sub-committees, with a budget provided by the Northern Ireland Office. Like its parent body the Cultural Traditions Group is formally independent of government but has a close relation with the Central Community Relations Unit at Stormont, the civil service body responsible for community relations policy. A characteristic of the group has been its ability to bring academics, civil servants, local politicians and community activists into a common forum.

James Hawthorne, the ex-Controller of BBC Northern Ireland who was to serve as the first Chairman of the new Community Relations Council (founded in January 1990) and who also played a leading role in the Cultural Traditions Group, identified 'cultural diversity' as a core theme in his opening address to the first conference of the group in March 1989:

> Community relations and cultural diversity cannot be separated. While the first is a problem, the second is surely an asset, provided its richness can be celebrated in non-threatening ways. There is much in common across the so-called 'community divide' but what remains separate is of value also.
>
> (Hawthorne, 1991: 2)

Hawthorne mapped out the core agendas of the new organisations:

> Community relations work is about helping people from the two sides to share activity in common without hatred and distrust. It assumes no political outcome but recognises that mutual respect and understanding are preconditions for any workable political solution. We have much to do to help create a climate in which cultural diversity and toleration can thrive.
>
> (Hawthorne, 1991: 2)

Earlier attempts to play down communal divisions and assertions of identity – formerly pathologised as 'prejudice' – were under the new multicultural agenda to give way to a sustained attempt to encourage the people of Northern Ireland, at all levels, to acknowledge and respect their differences, (Hawthorne, 1991: 2).

Heritage activity has been seen by the Cultural Traditions Group as a primary focus of its activities and the organisation has provided financial support and encouragement to a wide variety of local history, archival, heritage and commemorative projects across Northern Ireland. Schools have been encouraged by the Department of Education for Northern Ireland to introduce a common 'Cultural Heritage' curriculum to enable pupils to explore their own and their counter-religionists' culture. And as we shall see, the museum and heritage sector has sought to adopt an agenda of 'mutual understanding'.

This reconstruction of heritage in Northern Ireland as a vehicle for the promotion of communal reconciliation seems closely related to the tutelary activity being conducted by the British state under the banner of 'multiculturalism'. In part this eruption within curatorial discourse and practice in Northern Ireland of 'cultural tradition' and 'cultural diversity' talk has involved attempts to import a multicultural model of practice developed by the Community Relations Council in England to deal with relations between ethnic minorities and the 'host community' in inner city areas. The appropriateness of this model has been questioned by a number of commentators, not least because in Northern Ireland the host community (i.e. the Catholic Irish population that historically 'received' the Protestant settlers) finds itself now treated within the northern state as a marginalised ethnic minority! Having signally failed to eradicate sectarianism in the workplace, in housing or in communal relations (as the CRC has signally failed to tackle the problem of institutionalised racism in British society) the Northern Ireland Office has sought to reconfigure the unresolved political conflict within Northern Ireland around the key concept of 'cultural tradition'.

The heritage industry is expected to play its part in this ideological task by developing a curatorial strategy concerned with achieving 'parity of representational esteem' in the figuration of each community's historical experience. Thus, for example, the Ulster American Folk Park located near Omagh in County Tyrone, which commemorates a history of emigration from Ulster to the USA, was initially designed, as befits an institution that was the brainchild of Stormont civil servant Eric Montgomery, as a homily to Ulster Protestant virtue. David Brett calls the park 'a philosophical garden for a "Protestant tradition", figured and emplotted according to the symbolism of the (Pilgrim's) Progress'. As he points out, the park as originally designed 'is not neutrally Ulster-American in a geographic sense, but Ulster-Presbyterian-American in a confessional sense'. However, in response to the more pluralist spirit of the age the park has been forced to address the emigrant experience of the 'other tradition'. The curators have developed alongside their major installation dealing with the emigration passage of Thomas Mellon, the Ulster Protestant-born industrial baron, a parallel narrative dealing with the emigration story of John Joseph Hughes, also originally from the Omagh area, who went on to become Archbishop of New York. Catholic piety is to be celebrated alongside the pioneering spirit of the Protestant planter in a heritage presentation mindful of the need to cater for both 'cultural traditions'. This accommodation smacks of tokenism and, as David Brett notes, largely leaves unchallenged the curatorial organisation of the park as puritan pilgrimage and hymn to Protestant planter discipline. As he notes,

> There is small sense of the wretchedness that made the mass emigrations of the nineteenth century a matter of human survival and which were, of course, extensively Catholic and driven by economic necessity. This is a partial, and to say the least, an uncritical view of Ulster.   (Brett 1996: 118)

As history is 'modernised', that is cut adrift from critical enquiry and harnessed to both the community relations agenda and the heritage experience, notions of cultural identity and difference are becoming sanitised in a public discourse in part pluralist and in part touristic. Within this discourse culture is seen as redemptive and above politics. It is, or at least should be, in the words of Roy Foster, 'an imagination untrammeled by the spectre of power' (Foster 1989: 20) Cultural practice is effectively stripped of its political valency in a process which parallels the eradication of anti-imperialist dissonance from Irish history *in and through its heritage presentation*. The appeal of the heritage version of history is that it offers us the warm glow of nostalgia but at the price of collective amnesia. The difficult bits of history can simply be left out. The trouble is that in Ulster most of the main bits of history are difficult.

Heritage, then, revises history, rendering it as a tourist spectacle. Curators are expected to abide by the principle of 'parity of representational esteem' in their treatment of the past, a task that can most easily be achieved by sanitising history under a narrative of reconciliation. In effect the cultural industries have given popular efficacy to practices of historical revisionism long established within professional scholarship but lacking much purchase on the popular imagination. By historical revisionism I mean, in the Irish context, that intellectual movement which questions a nationalist-heroic narrative of Irish history either on the basis of empirical reservation or of postmodernist sophistry or, indeed, due to a profound political antipathy to nationalist ideology.

Postmodern revisions

The mid-1980s saw an explosion of critical interest in issues of collective identity and tradition in Ireland on both sides of the border. This preoccupation with identity and difference in part mirrored global concerns. The collapse of the old social solidarities spawned by industrial capitalism and the more general fragmentation of social life in the information age have, somewhat paradoxically, led to an intensification of both popular and academic interest in identity questions.

However, these postmodern currents have taken a particular form in Ireland. In Ireland postmodernist theory has been closely associated with a revisionist and, indeed, reactionary critique of nationalism (Bell 1993). The most vocal contributions to the debate on cultural identity have come from those seeking to revise nationalist historiography and political certitudes within a broader postmodern agenda. This is ostensibly motivated by a radical philosophical concern with the deconstruction of subjectivity and presence, but seems strangely congruent with a sustained campaign by the Irish and British governments to delegitimise and marginalise republican dissent. For example, the philosopher Richard Kearney, doyen of the new revisionist Irish Studies and influential court intellectual on both sides of the border, explicitly links his critique of nationalism to postmodern concerns:

> The translation of this textual strategy of deconstruction into political terms
> has, I will argue, radical consequences for our inherited ideologies. All total-
> izing notions of identity (imperial, colonial, national) are to be submitted to
> rigorous scrutiny in the name of an irreducible play of difference.
>
> (Kearney 1990)

A postmodern Ireland, he argues, will be a post-nationalist Ireland – a
'Europe of the regions'. Within this the efficacy of the nation state and
hence the relevance of national struggles will decline. The ongoing
revisionist attack on 'irredentist nationalism' in the name of secular
pluralism has of course material roots. No doubt this distancing of the
southern polity from the historic 'national question' expresses, as Edna
Longley acknowledges (Longley 1993), the aspirations of sections of
the country's intelligentsia and technocracy in the context of the
Republic of Ireland's integration into an expanding European
Community and into the global capitalist economy. The new pluralism
not only seeks to question nationalist moral judgements and territorial
claims regarding the North but to do this in the name of political modernisation and cultural liberalisation. Whether this revisionism
represents a new political maturity as Longley suggests, or, rather, a
naked pursuit of class interest is less clear. Either way this revisionist
spirit now abroad in the South clearly has import for political thinking
within Northern Ireland itself.

What I am suggesting here is that if we wish to understand historical revisionism as an ideological practice with purchase on popular
consciousness, rather than as an academic argument, then we must
turn our attention to the representations of history and culture found
in the heritage sector rather than in university textbooks. Within the
heritage industry historical revisionism meets popular culture around
a multicultural agenda complicit with the political status quo.

The Tower Museum, like a number of other interpretative centres,
has sought to acknowledge the 'right' of each of the two political communities to be adequately represented. The difficulty is that in
embracing the pluralistic agenda endorsed by the Northern Ireland
Office, the curators may have ended up unwittingly hypostatising the
very sectarian divisions that they undoubtedly abhor. The problem of
interpretative objectivity becomes reduced to the pragmatic goal of
achieving even-handedness in the representation of two reified traditions – a policy precept David Butler has labelled, in the context of a
critical analysis of broadcasting in Northern Ireland, 'balanced sectarianism' (Butler 1991a).

As Robin Wilson argued at the first Conference of the Cultural
Traditions Group,

> If we are talking about accommodating cultural traditions, we have got to be
> quite careful as to how we define that ... At its worst, however, it can be a
> straightforward accommodation of sectarianism. It can accommodate pre-
> cisely the notion that there are two monolithic traditions on this island, and
> it's crucially important that we distinguish the notion of accepting difference
> from the idea of praising diversity.   (Wilson 1989: 54)

Wilson, who was to make a joint submission with philosopher Richard Kearney to the Opsahl Commission, is here drawing an important distinction between *diversity* and *difference*. Unfortunately, he continues to use the concept of cultural difference in an essentially reified way. His emphasis is on toleration, on 'accepting difference' as a sociological given rather than on the constitution of difference in and through political struggle. As a result the radical import of the term is lost. Homi K. Bhabha in his book *The Location of Culture* has sought to draw a sharper more philosophically motivated distinction between the concepts of *cultural diversity* and *cultural difference*. He does so in order to question the platitudes of multiculturalism. Given the currency that multicultural discourse now has within Northern Ireland it may be instructive to consider his critique. For Bhabha, the concept of cultural diversity, now so central to race and community relations work in the western world, is a suspect one in so far as it is based on,

> – the recognition of pre-given cultural contents and customs; held in a time-frame of relativism it gives rise to liberal notions of multiculturalism, cultural exchange or the culture of humanity. Cultural diversity is also the representation ... of the separation of totalized cultures that live unsullied by the intertextuality of their historical location, safe in the Utopianism of a mythic memory of a unique collective identity. (Bhabha 1994: 34)

The concept of cultural difference, on the other hand, Bhabha argues, denies this essentialism. It is not concerned with the projection of an originary cultural tradition as the symbolic and textual standard against which other equally bounded traditions can be sociologically identified. Rather, it addresses the dynamic process by which cultural subjectivities are enunciated, a process riven with historical contingency and contradiction.

> Social differences are not simply given to experience through an already authenticated cultural tradition; they are the signs of the emergence of community envisaged as a project – at once a vision and a construction – that takes you 'beyond' yourself in order to return, in a spirit of revision and reconstruction, to the political conditions of the present. (Bhabha 1994: 3)

Cultural difference is the affirmation of value and authority with regard to a community's symbols and narratives. However much it may invoke the symbolic resources of the past it is born of present struggles. As such, Bhabha argues, the concept of cultural difference introduces,

> a split between the traditional culturalist demand for a model, a tradition, a community, a stable system of reference, and the necessary negation of the certitude in the articulation of new cultural demands, meanings, strategies in the political present as a practice of domination or, resistance. (1994: 35)

Bhabha is concerned in particular with the enunciation of senses of cultural identity and difference in the historical flux of postcolonial situations. For that reason the work of Frantz Fanon, dealing as it does with negritude and the cultural and political struggle against colonialism in Mediterranean Africa, is for him exemplary. Fanon recognises the power of tradition as a political resource employed by a subaltern people against a colonialism which has sought to denigrate and marginalise native cultures (Fanon 1986).

In the Northern Ireland context this anti-imperialist reading of cultural tradition entails, I would argue, a recognition that the 'two traditions' – i.e. unionism with its historic assertion of the privileges and power of the settler and nationalism with its ongoing resistance to British rule and imagining of a postcolonial 'new Ireland' – are not in any sense equal. The two traditions are not equal materially in terms of their access to political power. Nor are they in any sense equal on an ethical plane in terms of the moral worth of their respective claims. The loyalist demand to walk the Garvaghy Road and to parade in a triumphalist manner in Catholic areas is not the same sort of 'right' as that demanded by nationalist school pupils and adults in Belfast that they should be able to learn and be taught through the medium of the Irish language. The current attempt by Secretary of State for Northern Ireland Mo Mowlam, under pressure from unionist politicians, to treat Gaelic cultural activity in sport, music and language as equivalent to the explicitly sectarian demonstrations of the Orange Orders and to rationalise this position by reference to a rhetoric of respect for cultural diversity, shows how pernicious the simplistic application of multicultural logic can be when applied to Northern Ireland.

One of the speakers at the first Cultural Traditions conference held in 1989 was David Trimble, now leader of the Official Unionist Party. Trimble sternly warned the delegates of the dangers of attempting 'to integrate existing diversity'. He continued in a manner starkly at odds with the ecumenical spirit of the gathering,

> One should not try to blend together traditions that are essentially different. We may agree as to the extent of those differences, but there is little to be gained by trying to meld things together. Our object is to discuss how diverse traditions can be affirmed and enjoyed. We must not forget about affirmation, *for an attempt to prevent or inhibit that affirmation will simply create problems.*   (Trimble 1989: 25, my emphasis)

His address strikes a discordant note in the proceedings. But, in retrospect, it can be seen as prescient. Trimble complained about an asymmetry in the work of the Cultural Traditions Group and the treatment of what he calls 'Ulster–British culture' in relation to 'Irish Gaelic/Catholic culture' (his terms). He accuses nationalism of not fully recognising the existence of Ulster–British culture and seeking to assimilate it. For him,

This attitude is quite objectionable *and it does create difficulties for co-existence* between cultures when one culture is sometimes not prepared to recognise the existence of the other or engage with it on its own terms. Any form of co-existence must acknowledge the right of each culture to exist and perpetuate itself.   (1989: 48)

Some four years later in July 1995 David Trimble was to play a leading role in the loyalist confrontations with the police and the Catholic residents of the Garvaghy Road area in Portadown. Orange marchers tried to force their way through security force lines to defy a ban on parading in a nationalist area. The following year, and by now leader of a party which was by this stage playing a pivotal role in propping up the ailing Major government, he was instrumental in overturning a similar ban. After a three-day standoff between loyalists and the security forces at Drumcree Church the RUC caved in to political pressure and baton charged the Catholic residents of Garvaghy Road to clear a path for the Orange marchers to pass along a 'traditional' route. During the tense standoff at Drumcree loyalists interviewed by the British and world media were repeatedly to justify their actions in terms of the defence of cultural tradition and the preservation of their rights as an endangered identity.

Like the right in the USA, who have increasingly adopted and perverted the language of political correctness – of equal opportunity and of cultural diversity – in order to advance a reactionary programme to halt the legislative advances of ethnic minorities, loyalism has employed the rhetoric of multiculturalism to advance its historic triumphalist and sectarian objectives. It has taken its lead from Mr Trimble, patron of the Ulster Society, and exploited the opportunity offered to it by the misplaced pluralism of the cultural traditions lobby. At Drumcree loyalist intransigence made a mockery of the multicultural shibboleths of the liberal-pluralist state and revealed the political cowardice of the British state in Northern Ireland when confronted with the extralegal use of the unionist veto.

The whole notion of cultural tradition is, I would argue, a suspect one which should have no place in enlightened curatorial practice. Cultural diversity remains the buzz word in community relations circles in Northern Ireland. As a concept it is thoroughly integrated into the policy discourses of the tutelary state. Its humanistic privileging of a value-free viewpoint from which identitarian formations can be recognised in their diversity yet successfully integrated into a civic consensus, in effect, serves to marginalise radical affirmations of cultural difference of the sort that have been enunciated by the minority nationalist community in Northern Ireland in the course of its long struggle against the British state.

As Fanon acknowledges, the dynamic of liberation – and who can deny that the Catholic community in Northern Ireland has not been caught up in and indeed moulded by that dynamic over the past thirty years – entails new strategies of cultural engagement. The certitudes of tradition, of faith, fatherland and self-hood are called into question. As

Bhabha reminds us, for Fanon, 'The time of liberation is ... a time of cultural uncertainty, and most crucially, of significatory or representational undecidability' (1994: 35). The interpretative order involved in heritage presentation and in cultural tradition 'work' in Northern Ireland has unfortunately, as we have seen, been all too decidable. It has rested on notions of cultural diversity and of cultural tradition which assume that in Northern Ireland cultural difference is set in stone and that 'every signifier is spoken for' (Butler 1991b: 102).

In favour of representational undecidability as an interpretative principle

The 'Road to Northern Ireland' exhibition in Derry can be contrasted with another recent curatorial attempt to explore the interchange between, on the one hand, popular sensibilities and representations of Irish history and, on the other, professional assessment of historical evidence – Luke Dodd's interpretative installation for the Irish Famine Museum at Strokestown House in Roscommon. Like the Derry museum this involves an interesting interaction between site and installation. The museum is housed in the grounds and converted stables of the former ancestral home of the Pakenham-Mahons. This Anglo-Irish landed family originally came to Ireland after the Cromwellian settlement of Connaught. The Mahons found themselves in conflict with their Catholic tenants during the Great Irish Famine and Major Denis Mahon was murdered by one of his tenants in 1847. Surviving members of the family continued to live in the Palladian mansion in Strokestown Park until the 1950s. The house was later acquired by a local Catholic entrepreneur. Subsequently the Westward Trust, a local body, raised the funds needed to develop the museum as a commemoration of the Famine and its victims. As Niall Ó Ciosáin (1994: 24) notes,

> The narrative of the museum's location, therefore is emphatic: it is a story about inequality and exploitation. It describes poverty and starvation in precisely the place which did not suffer them, with the implication that the luxury of the big house depended on them.

As with the Derry museum the siting of the centre has a symbolic valency with a distinctive postcolonial character. With the departure of the historic landlord the 'big house' and its grounds have been yoked to a new cultural task – the illumination of the terrible events of the Famine. As the cover blurb of Stephen J. Campbell's accompanying historical publication opines, 'Strokestown Park now assumes a new and meaningful significance in an Ireland radically different to the one which originally produced it' (Campbell 1994). The Famine exhibition has been produced by a curator versed in contemporary art and cultural studies theory rather than by an academic historian. Indeed, playing with the tools of conceptual art, Dodd and his team strive to make a virtue out of historical indeterminacy. As the literary theorist Terry Eagleton has put it, the curators have produced, 'a postmodern museum in a Palladian setting, bereft of all central narrative' (cited in Ó Ciosáin 1994).

Luke Dodd and his collaborators seek to create 'a multi-vocal presentation' of the Famine. This requires going beyond the received sources that usually form the basis for a positivist historical narrative. They provide the visitor with a multilayered representation of the Famine as material event, historical memory and cultural trauma. This requires the curators to abandon a didactic approach to exhibiting history and to question the appropriateness of traditional empiricist historiography of the Famine, whether nationalist or revisionist. Despite the apparent ideological incommensurability of these approaches it could be argued that they in fact share a common starting point. Each seeks to arrive at a summary judgement on this watershed in Irish history based on a supposedly 'objective' assessment of texts, artefacts and conjecture. In the Famine Museum, as in the Tower Museum, the 'facts themselves' are contested in so far as they are seen as anchored in different communities of interpretation. In Derry the contest is between unionist and nationalist world views, in Strokestown it is between the radically incommensurable worlds of the Anglo-Irish gentry and of peasant agrarian resistance and between the production of historical evidence dealing with this period and postmodern scepticism regarding all truth claims. In each museum the visitor is invited to explore the framing of historical meaning, that is to say the production of truth as a historical process.

For, as the installations reveal, the 'historical evidence' available to us today is largely drawn from accounts of the time provided by the literate and political class of the period. The Famine Museum makes good use of the records of the Strokestown estate during the disaster but reveals these to be at best a partial view. Sources like these provide an invaluable insight into the mentalities of members of the English and Anglo-Irish ruling class who struggled to understand and respond to the Famine. But how then to represent the perspective of the dispossessed, the marginal, the victims of the Great Famine?

The exhibition includes a number of familiar engravings of Famine scenes from the *London Illustrated News,* images which are often held to possess photographic verisimilitude and to be an objective representations of the suffering of the cottiers during the Famine. The curators place these images among a number of other visual sources in painterly and photographic form. We confront a number of oil paintings of a highly stylised character representing Famine events (viz Daniel McDonald's Romantic rendering of the arrival of the Famine, *The discovery of the potato blight in Ireland* and Hayes, *An emigrant ship: Dublin bay at sunset*). We come across also a number of contemporary photographs of famine victims in Africa (one of which reveals a couple of predatory photographers focusing their cameras on an emaciated child). Through this curious counterposing of Victorian and contemporary images the curators point up the constructed nature of historical evidence in general and, in particular, the rhetorical character of visual representation. They also draw our attention to the imbrication of images in the patterning of power relations. The written and visual sources presented are revealed as having been enunciated within a particular historical formation of discourse and power. Within this the subaltern could find no voice of their own. The voice we do hear in the exhibition is a hesitant and whispered one. As we pass through the main famine exhibition room we hear relayed from concealed loudspeakers a multilayered sound track made up of voices recounting the murder of Major Mahon, administering the oaths of secret agrarian societies and relaying documentary traces of the Famine. This soundscape suggests that it is in the ephemeral and denigrated world of oral culture that the famine experience of the subaltern is to be found.

This sensitivity to the socially constructed nature of historical evidence and to the traces of power present in all textual and visual reportage is not as present in the Derry exhibition. The 'Road to Northern Ireland' exhibit, like Dodd's Famine installation, refuses recourse to an explicit dominant narrative purporting to deliver an objective judgement on events. However, here the similarities end. The Derry interpretative structure displays two and only two accounts of the same historical events. The evidential basis of these is not questioned. The steps to partition becomes a tale of two 'Traditions' unproblematically set in stone. The installation has a distinctive narrative topology. It offers us a preferred viewing point from which an ideal prospect can be gained of this section of the exhibition. This is clearly located in the narrow path between the two projected traditions on display, *and in a privileged position with regards them.* Here is located the tutelary space within which an ethic of 'balanced sectarianism' can be elaborated. The visitor is literally invited to occupy the middle of the road in a terrain clearly seen as contested. And just as the installation suggests a preferred reading of both Irish history and contemporary realities – a version of 'a plague on both your houses' – it also seeks to construct a preferred reader – a rational liberal subject versed in the pieties of pluralism (this is not to say that the exhibition may not have been read in a more partisan way by local visitors who may be inclined keep to their own side of the road and view 'the other side' from this position).

Significantly the sectarian road markings that give this installation its 'popular touch' stop as the exhibition corridor turns sharply to the right at a point in the chronological narrative which sees the visitor arrive at the First World War. The inference seems to be that in this period the sectional political differences so marked in Irish politics prior to 1914 were at least temporarily put aside as both unionists and nationalists flocked to the British standard to 'defend the rights of small nations', before the cataclysm of the Easter Rising irrevocably redrew the political boundaries. This seems to be a weighting of the historical evidence distinctly in the favour of a revisionist interpretation of the 1914-18 period. However, my concern here is less with the content of this historiographical judgement than with the visual structures employed.

The centrepiece of this section of the exhibition is an audiovisual display – a wall-mounted video monitor on which we view a short documentary film dealing with Derry and the First World War. Again this display is best viewed from the centre of the road and stands apart from the particularist nationalist and unionist narratives the visitor confronts up to this juncture. The film, which is on a constantly repeated loop, by and large conforms to the production conventions of a television documentary film – it is informationally led with a dominant narration overlaying the black and white archive footage of the First World War. The text seeks to enunciate the sort of historiographical authority characteristic of public service broadcasting. Indeed the independent film and video company that produced the film normally produce for the broadcast companies in Northern Ireland (BBC and UTV). As such this film and the longer one dealing with the civil rights period that visitors are invited to view in a specialist auditorium after having passed through the Road to Northern Ireland section, stands in marked contrast to the video installation found in the Famine Museum.

The latter piece, directed by film-maker Pat Murphy, departs significantly from the conventions of television documentary in its pacing, in the priority it gives to image over narration and in its strategy of visualisation. There is, of course, no archive footage of the Famine, no photographic record. In Pat Murphy's film the Famine is treated as an absent presence. Seamus Deasy's haunting images of an abandoned workhouse, a depopulated landscape, an empty sky are used by Murphy to good effect to suggest both the violence of the original event of the Famine and its subsequent impact on the Irish countryside felt to this day. The dislocation of image and narration which characterises the film encourages us to make meaning with these sources, to enter the frame of interpretation ourselves in order to produce an ordered sense of the past. The film, like the rest of the exhibition, demands, as Brett notes, that we *do* history rather than receive history as overinterpreted text. It opens out history as text to the vicissitudes of the present.

The Derry films provide a much clearer interpretative lead via their broadcasting style and traditional documentary narrative. The curators may have experimented with a bi-partisan narrative topology in the earlier part of the Road to Northern Ireland installation. However, they finally invite the visitor to occupy a single privileged, non-partisan, viewing position on Irish history. They further reinforce this distinctive specular structure-as-interpretative strategy by drawing, wittingly or unwittingly, upon the production conventions and accompanying consensual claims of British public service broadcasting. Public service broadcasting in Northern Ireland has developed a

highly refined editorial practice based on the dual strategy of project-
ing – often in the face of evidence to the contrary – an imagined public
formed around political moderation and civic consensus, and, on the
other hand, brokering a communication pact between political
extremes – a policy of 'balanced sectarianism'. We seem to have found
ourselves as visitors – as we do nightly in Northern Ireland as television viewers – to be the object of an impressive pedagogic intervention
directed at convincing us, whether tourist or native[3] that the political
problems of Northern Ireland are capable of resolution by securing
from the citizens of the region a commitment to cultural diversity and
to tolerance of each others' 'traditions'.

Notes

1. This term was first used by Jacques Donzelot (1986) to refer to the development of the nineteenth-century capitalist's state's activities in the social
   regulation of the lives of its citizens, particularly the working class, excer-
   cised via disciplinary institutions such as the school, prison and public
   health provision and via social policy interventions and social work practices focused on the family and the working class community.
2. In 1995 Northern Ireland had its best-ever year for tourism with a 16 per
   cent rise in revenue from visitors earned in that year. In the following year,
   in the context of a partial collapse of the cease fire, revenue decreased by
   £6 million, with 8 per cent fewer visitors coming to Northern Ireland
   (*Tourism Facts*, Northern Ireland Tourist Board, Belfast, 1997).
3. The evidence is that some 60 per cent of those who visited the museum in
   the first two years it was open were from Northern Ireland, with another
   10 per cent from the Irish Republic (figures from Tower Museum).

CHAPTER 13

What's wrong with multiculturalism? Liberalism and the Irish conflict

Bill Rolston

Introduction: culture, tradition and rhetoric

> 'I'm an Ulsterman, not an Irishman ... I don't jig at crossroads or play Gaelic football. We've got two races on this island'
>
> (John Taylor, quoted in *Beyond the Fife and Drum* 1995: 39)

There is a pervasive ideology afoot in the North of Ireland, which is so fashionable that it has become at least churlish to criticise it. It is recent in origin, dating no further back than the emergence of the 'troubles' three decades ago. During that time it has taken many institutional forms – from the Peace People through inter-church organisations to youth initiatives and community networks. It has also infused a number of state initiatives – the Community Relations Commission of the early 1970s, the Education for Mutual Understanding programme in schools in the 1980s and 1990s, the current Community Relations Council and its Cultural Traditions Group, and the recent peace and reconciliation funding initiative of the European Union. This ideology goes by a number of names, often interchangeable: community relations, cultural traditions, reconciliation. Its common theme is multiculturalism.

The influence of multiculturalism is evident in the extent to which it has colonised discourse on the conflict in Ireland. Its key words are 'diversity', 'tolerance', 'difference', 'integration', 'identity', 'culture' and 'tradition'. Those words are now used routinely by representatives of groups as diverse as the Royal Ulster Constabulary (RUC) and Sinn Féin, the Northern Ireland Office and the Catholic Church. As one example, take the response of David Trimble to criticisms of his support for the Orange Order marchers at Drumcree in July 1996. The RUC had blocked the passage of the Orangemen through the nationalist Garvaghy Road. But, after a five day standoff between hundreds of RUC officers and thousands of Orangemen, and widespread loyalist disruption throughout the North, the RUC succumbed to political pressure and pushed the marchers through despite nationalist opposition.

The previous July Trimble, then an aspirant for the leadership of the Ulster Unionist Party, had performed a victory dance hand in hand with Democratic Unionist Party leader Ian Paisley when the marchers had similarly reached the centre of Portadown. But in 1996, Trimble, now party leader, appeared the embodiment of reason.

> It's not just a matter of tradition, although tradition is important ... But it's more than just tradition. It's also the question of *affirming identity and culture* and demonstrating what you believe in and what you stand for. That's where the term comes from; that's why they're called demonstrations. The analogies that you should look at would be things like Fourth of July in the United States, Fourteenth of July in France. It is actually normal in most countries to celebrate and to affirm the national *identity* ... It is a normal event and ought to be regarded as a normal event. What is abnormal ... is the way in which a purely peaceful *affirmation of culture and identity* is then attacked by some people who go out of their way by quite some distance in order to do so. (*Talkback*, BBC Radio Ulster, 9 September 1996; emphasis added.)

This is a discourse which is not only different from that traditionally espoused by unionists, but also at variance with some of the utterances of others in Trimble's own party, such as deputy leader John Taylor, quoted at the beginning of this section.[1] Trimble's use of the fashionable discourse is less a measure of a transformed unionism than of the resonance of the ideology of reconciliation and community relations in contemporary popular culture.

Why has this ideology come to have such dominance, and why now? These are the questions at the core of this chapter. In summary, the answers are to be found in the importing into the North of Ireland, particularly in the 1980s and 1990s, of a liberal ideology which originated in the United States in the 1960s and was further developed in Britain in the 1970s. In urging the celebration of tolerance and diversity, this ideology became highly influential in policies derived in both societies to manage problems of race and class. Transferred to the North of Ireland, the liberal approach came to be seen as a solution to the deep-rooted sectarian divisions of the society. It emphasised 'two traditions' in an apparently faultless symmetry which ignores the power structures which emerged historically in Ireland and are in existence currently. History, colonialism, inequality, sectarianism are all reduced to relatively simplistic explanations which rest on social psychology, postmodernist discourse and wishful thinking.

The state and multiculturalism in the North of Ireland

> A society is enriched by difference and range of choice ... pluralism, openness to change and tolerance of diversity are more likely to provide a basis for mutual trust and resolution of conflict than insularity and protectiveness.
> (Hayes, 1993: 6)

It is important to stress at the outset the role of the state in the development of the multiculturalist agenda in the North of Ireland. The liberal response to the 'troubles', involving the key aspirations of 'peace', 'reconciliation', etc., was evident from the beginning. The state response was much more complex, involving a combination of reform and repression. Nor was the reform element always expressed in the 'culturalist' mode of urging 'reconciliation' and better 'community relations'. Despite early endeavours such as the Community Relations Commission (1969–74), the state's reform package was often more likely to be 'economistic' in form (see O'Dowd, Rolston and Tomlinson 1982) – that is, seeing economic reform as underpinning political stability.[2]

This is not to say that the multiculturalists were slow off the mark. From the beginning of the conflict they posited a relationship between schooling and the 'troubles', arguing that the schools were a key resource which could be used to further better community relations. Between 1970 and 1972 the Schools Project in Community Relations brought primary school children together at a 'neutral' venue (the Ulster Folk and Transport Museum) to encourage contact and communication. Following on from that, the Schools Curriculum Project, based at Queen's University, worked at introducing local studies into the primary school curriculum. The project ran from 1973 to 1978. Overlapping with this, the Schools Cultural Studies Project, based at the New University of Ulster between 1974 and 1980 and later from 1982 to 1984, sought to encourage better community relations through the introduction of a new subject in schools, Cultural Studies, rather than working through the existing curriculum (see Lambkin 1996: 67–70).

The culmination of this effort was the publication of *The Way Forward* by the Department of Education in October 1988 (DENI 1988). The department declared its interest in providing 'opportunities for pupils to gain awareness of aspects of history, culture and traditions which contribute to the cultural heritage of Northern Ireland'. Nor was this merely an academic interest. In providing such opportunities, schools would contribute to 'lessening the ignorance which many feel contributes to the divisions in our society' (cited in Lambkin, 1996: 76). The Education Reform (Northern Ireland) Order[3] in 1989 did more than express an interest. It established a Northern Ireland curriculum which is compulsory in all schools. There are six compulsory cross-curricular themes, two of which relate to the goal of engineering better community relations – Education for Mutual Understanding (EMU) and Cultural Heritage.

The emphasis in both these themes is on dispelling ignorance. Ignorance is taken to equal prejudice, and the reduction of prejudice is to be achieved through cross-curricular contact and knowledge. The Report of the Cross-Curricular Working Group on EMU (*Education for Mutual Understanding*, 1989), which was the basis of the Education Reform Order, spells this out in great detail. For example, one of the objectives of EMU is 'Understanding Conflict':

> By the age of 11 pupils should know about aspects of conflict within them-
> selves, between themselves and others, and about some approaches to its
> resolution. They should also know that conflict can cause personal suffering.
> (Cross-Curricular Working Group 1989: 14)

This is elaborated on for older pupils:

> By the age of 14, they should know about and have begun to understand the
> nature of conflict within the individual, the family, the peer group and the
> school. They should know about some of the reasons for conflict within
> Northern Ireland. They should understand that suffering can be caused by
> many things such as words, gestures, symbols and actions. They should know
> about a range of strategies for reducing conflict in different contexts. (p. 14)

It is only for pupils aged 16 that examining the nature of conflict rises
to the top of the list of goals; but even for this age group the emphasis
is on understanding 'that people affected by conflict can experience
differing emotions and reactions' and investigating 'measures which
can be taken to alleviate anger, fear and distress'. Throughout there is
an absence of emphasis on structural explanations of conflict and a
consequent over-reliance on social psychology.

For EMU the objective is to transform 'schools apart' (Darby and
Murray 1977) into 'schools together' (Dunn *et al.* 1984). The brief of the
Community Relations Council and its Cultural Traditions Group is
wider: as the problem is people apart, the solution is people together.

The roots of the state's sponsorship of this other arm of multiculturalism – Cultural Traditions – can be traced to 1983 and the formation of
the Two Traditions Group, a non-governmental, non-party political
discussion and lobby group. In 1988 the Central Community Relations
Unit of the Northern Ireland Office sponsored a series of meetings 'to
explore ways of promoting a better understanding of, and a more con-
structive debate about, our different cultural traditions in Northern
Ireland' (Crozier 1989: vii). Out of this came the Cultural Traditions
Group, which later became a sub-committee of the Community
Relations Council when it was established by the Northern Ireland
Office in 1990. Some of the original members of the Cultural Traditions
Group had previously been associated with the Two Traditions Group.

> The Cultural Traditions work of the Council aims to encourage a tolerance
> of diversity amongst the communities in Northern Ireland. It seeks to do
> this in part by supporting community projects which explore and debate
> questions of local identity and culture, and in part by helping to create
> resources which will stimulate that debate. (NICRC 1994: 23)

It hosts conferences and seminars, produces publications, and provides
grant aid to individuals as well as to organisations as diverse as the
RUC Historical Society and Glór na nGael.[4]

The work of the Cultural Traditions Group is underpinned by a theoretical rationalisation which is part social psychology, part social
work jargon and part postmodernist rhetoric:

It is the lack of sufficient information and understanding about each other's humanity, objectives, hopes and fears that limits political cooperation between communities. The work therefore concentrates on decreasing ignorance between communities and encouraging the development of empathy between conflicting individuals and groups.   (Fitzduff 1993: 7)

All the buzz words of postmodernism are apparent in the utterances of those associated closely with the Community Relations Council and the Cultural Traditions Group – 'tolerance', 'difference', 'diversity', and of course, the rejection of such essentialist notions as 'the nation':

Migrations and plantations, some voluntary, some forced, have ensured that none of us can ever return to a world of simple nationhood, where territory reflects a single group, with common language, ethnic background, cultural history, tradition, or even political aspiration.   (Fitzduff, in NICRC 1994: 10)

For his part, Hayes (1993) contrasts the relaxed tolerance of pluralism with the insecurity of its alternative. The words he uses repetitively are straight out of the postmodern lexicon: cosmopolitanism, difference, pluralism, tolerance, diversity, trust and self-confidence are contrasted with insularity, protectiveness, insecurity, failure of communication, lack of empathy, stereotyping, scapegoating and lack of trust. There is no doubt which terms are seen as positive and which negative.

The roots of multiculturalism: the USA, Britain and the concept of 'ethnicity'

Ethnicity was a tool to blunt the edge of black struggle, return 'black' to its constituent parts of Afro-Caribbean, Asian, African, Irish – and also, at the same time, allow the nascent black bourgeoisie, petit-bourgeoisie really, to move up in the system.   (Sivanandan 1983: 4)

The roots of multiculturalism are in the United States in the 1960s. The experience of urban riots and what was referred to as 'racial tension' led to a state response which managed to combine repression and reform. At the same time as the repressive policing of black ghettoes escalated and the Black Panthers were being removed through a sustained shoot-to-kill policy, federal, state and city governments, as well as philanthropic organisations, were inaugurating special programmes against poverty and for the improvement of 'race relations' (see Marris and Rein 1967). From the Ford Foundation's Grey Areas Programme, through the federal War on Poverty to the highly contested bussing policy in cities like Boston, liberals sought to defuse an explosive situation.

These policies were underpinned by the popular metaphor of the 'melting pot', the idea that, despite the diverse origins of the people who made up the USA, they could all unite under the common identity of 'American', sharing one culture. It was an ambitious and ultimately naive expectation. But for a while it had backing not merely from influential politicians such as Daniel Moynihan, but also from academia. As Bash (1979: 29) stresses, 'assimilation' became the 'reigning "theoretical" principle' in US sociology up to the 1970s. Its dominance, he hastens to add, was due neither to scientific rigour or theoretical sophistication; rather, sociological interest was determined by political ideology. While politicians sought to engineer the 'assimilation' of 'minorities', sociologists 'succumbed to the allure of social policy' (ibid.: 113) and provided spurious academic justification for the political project. 'Counterfeit sociology' (ibid.: 146) played a key role in the manufacture of the myth of the 'melting pot'.

By the end of the 1960s, it was clear that the ideal of the 'melting pot' was untenable as a result of the onslaught of urban rioting, endemic poverty and the articulate rejection of the ideal by Black and other activists. The liberal project switched at this point to prioritising the ideal of 'cultural pluralism'. And it was as such that the 'race relations' agenda was articulated in Britain. As in the USA, the response to the problem of riots and 'racial tension' in the inner cities was a combination of repression and liberalism. The former involved such measures as the curbing of Black immigration, and the increase of powers to the police to stop and search young, especially Black, men on inner-city streets. The state's liberal agenda involved sponsorship of such initiatives as the Institute of Race Relations, the Community Relations Commission (later the Commission for Racial Equality) and multicultural programmes in schools.

Underlying the liberal programme was the belief that poor race relations arose from cultural ignorance. The solution was therefore education, broadly defined. Discrimination came to be seen as individual or group prejudice, and not as exploitation. 'Race relations' were represented 'in terms of cultural relations ... and not in terms of power relations, least of all state power' (Bourne and Sivanandan 1980: 336).

As authors such as Bourne and Sivanandan have argued, this agenda often ignored the state's concurrent repressive policies towards Black people. Moreover, there was something deeply problematic in the underlying notion of 'education', which consists of explaining the beliefs and customs of 'ethnic groups' to White society. For 'just to learn about other people's cultures is not to learn about the racism of one's own' (Sivanandan 1983: 5).

Hence the opposition of critics such as Sivanandan to 'race awareness training' (RAT), a direct import from the USA, for its psychologism and its spurious notions of equality, especially its starting point that Whites too were harmed by racism. The multicultural agenda is instead understood as the rationalisation of a new stage of exploitation rather than the dawning of a new age of equality. For capitalism direct open exploitation of Black people qua Black people is passé. In its place is a system of class domination and inequality in which poor Blacks are relegated to the lower reaches of the working class. Multiculturalism is not an attack on inequality, but ultimately a justification of it. Where open discrimination is said to be gone and tolerance is in vogue, the Black poor have only themselves to blame. After all, there are now rich Blacks. The fundamental shift involved is 'from changing society to changing people, from improving the lot of whole black communities, mired in racism and poverty, to improving the lot of "Black" individuals' (Sivanandan 1985: 14).

Similar conclusions have been reached by critics of the multiculturalist project in British schools in the 1970s and 1980s (see Carby 1982; Lawrence 1982; Troyna 1992). The initial approach was assimilationist, seeing the Black child as lacking something – language, culture – and therefore needing help to avail of the benefits of mainstream education. Later there was a shift to a pluralist model which acknowledged that Black children did have a culture and abilities. But the articulation and formalisation of information about their culture was left in the hands of teachers. This ensured a weakening of the power of Black parents and the Black community to define their culture and history for their own children. Understanding factors such as institutionalised racism were never central in the multicultural approach; rather the emphasis was on discrimination as prejudice and on poor race relations as the result of lack of communication.

> Teachers involved in multicultural teaching maintained that they were improving the concepts of black children, providing positive images and alleviating disadvantage. This role confirmed the importance of the autonomy of their position, their need to be professionals, and displayed a liberal moral conscience of messianic proportions ... The parallels of missionaries following in the wake of armies of colonialism are more than metaphorical.
>
> (Carby 1982: 199)[5]

At the root of the argument of cultural pluralism was a concept which eventually came to take prominence in both academic and popular discourse: 'ethnicity'. Interestingly, the concept was a late arrival on the theoretical scene.[6]

Anthropologists quickly espoused the concept. But the enthusiasm was not universally shared. Marxists in particular were wary of a concept which prioritised culture over economics and power. Some, such as Saul (1979), did salvage the concept somewhat for the left; he argued that ethnicity in many African societies was an effect of neo-colonialism, and a useful tool for indigenous elites during the creation of postcolonial class societies. But others in the 'race and class' camp were less positive: 'A culture of ethnicity, unlike a culture of resistance, has no community and has no class' (Sivanandan 1985: 15).

Given the discovery and growth of multiculturalism in the North of Ireland, it was only a matter of time before 'ethnicity' began to take centre stage.

Interpreting 'the Northern Ireland problem': the rise of ethnicity

> The trend of the times is toward ethnic violence and separatism, so in this sense the fact that ethnicity is at the centre of the conflict in Ireland might be depressing, but should not be considered surprising or unusual (Hayes 1996: 9).

The conflict in Ireland since 1968/9 has spawned a vast literature. Whyte (1990) produced an epic survey of a huge swathe of this literature. He considered at length 'internal-conflict' interpretations (those which saw the root of the conflict as lying in internal relations and divisions within the North of Ireland) as well as structuralist (including Marxist) interpretations. Yet nowhere in the index to this extensive book does the word 'ethnicity' occur. Five years later, McGarry and O'Leary (1995) attempted an equally ambitious survey of the literature. They too examined external or exogenous explanations of the conflict – those which saw the Northern Ireland problem in the context of British–Irish relations, or imperialism, or irredentism – and internal or endogenous explanations – those which viewed Northern Ireland as a separate unit of analysis, independent of external influences. Their index cites references not only to 'ethnicity', but also to 'ethnic frontiers', 'ethnic groups', 'ethnic warfare', 'ethnicism' and 'ethno-nationalism'.

It was not merely that academic fashion had changed in the short period between Whyte's survey and that of McGarry and O'Leary. Global politics had been transformed. The Soviet system had collapsed. The Berlin wall was down. Protracted struggles in places like South Africa and Palestine appeared to be inching towards a political solution. Before, it had been possible to present the North of Ireland (along with the Basque country) as one of the few instances of an anticolonial war in a western European setting. Both left and right – the former positively, the latter negatively – could draw comparisons between the North of Ireland on the one hand and Vietnam, Nicaragua and Cuba on the other.

In this period a number of the key texts explaining the Northern Ireland conflict had been underpinned by Marxism; for example, Whyte (1983a: 15) pointed out, 'Of the eight best books on the history of Northern Ireland, four are by Marxists'. Not all of these Marxists espoused an anti-imperialist line. Some, such as Bew, Gibbon and Patterson (1979), followed a version of the 'internal conflict' approach, emphasising the indigenous factors in the northern conflict and the irredentism of the southern state. But Marxists, whether anti-imperialist or otherwise, were not drawn to 'ethnicity', a concept which seemed to rule out a class analysis (see Patterson 1992). The concept was an unfamiliar one to the historians, sociologists and political scientists who dominated the academic scene.

The anti-imperialist paradigm suffered a blow with the sudden change in global politics at the end of the 1980s. With the ending of the Cold War, the conflicts which came to the fore – Rwanda, Bosnia-Herzegovina, Azerbaijan, Kurdistan – were easily represented as 'ethnic', no matter how rooted they were in the structures of colonialism and global power, past and present. Moreover, many of these 'ethnic conflicts' were in Europe. Ireland, it seemed, was no longer unique; it could now be represented as just another 'ethnic frontier' in Europe.

Wright (1987), a political scientist, was one of the first to put the concept of 'ethnicity', and specifically the notion of 'ethnic frontiers', at the centre of analysis when he compared the conflict in the North with those historically in other European regions such as Prussian Poland and Bohemia under Austrian rule. Around the same time O'Sullivan (1986) presented the development of the Northern Ireland conflict in three stages of 'ethnic stratification'. Despite centring the concept in her analysis, she insisted that ethnicity alone could not explain the conflict, and that it was necessary to allow for the influence of class and state power.

Most researchers who gravitated towards the concept of ethnicity did not share this sense of the importance of history and of structure. Ethnicity, in fact, became a way of analysing the conflict with little more than a polite nod in the direction of imperialism, colonialism, state power and 'ethnic stratification'. Thus Wallis *et al.* (1986: 2) begin by stating: 'We do not propose to rehearse the historical background, which is well known. Suffice it to say that two distinct communities and identities have emerged in the north east of Ireland.'

Similarly Brewer (1992) acknowledges the role of colonialism, but only in so far as the past has produced the legacy with which people have to live in the present. 'The patterns of inequality in Northern Ireland were laid down long ago' (Brewer 1992: 354); history is thus background, rather than a substantive element in current conflict. To understand the present, the conceptual key is not 'history' but 'ethnicity':

> Sectarianism exists wherever religion marks the boundary between ethnic groups, and both represents (but also necessarily causes) the patterns of inequality by which society is stratified. (Brewer 1992: 358)

By the 1990s an internal conflict explanation resting on 'ethnicity' had become fashionable in academic circles. Thus Bruce (1994b: 30) could state confidently: 'I am arguing that the Northern Ireland conflict is an ethnic conflict and that religion plays an important part in the identity of the Protestant people.' Hayes (1996: 9), quoted at the beginning of this section, had no difficulty stating that 'ethnicity is at the centre of the conflict in Ireland'. And Darby (1995: 8):

> The Northern Ireland conflict will be described as an ethnic conflict ... the 'ethnic' definition is more suitable than other definitions which view it exclusively as a constitutional or religious conflict, or one based on economic, social or cultural inequalities. All of these are part of the problem, but none can claim exclusive rights to define it.

That prerogative, it seems, belongs to the over-arching concept of ethnicity.

Revising Irish history

> The depressing lesson is that history as conceived by scholars is different to what it is understood to be at large, where 'myth' is probably the correct, if over-used, anthropological term.   (Foster 1994: 144)

The 'internal conflict' approach was given a further boost by the revisionist school in Irish historiography. The roots of revisionism are in the 1930s, but it reached its zenith in the 1980s with historians such as Foster (1988) and Elliott (1989) and literary critics such as Longley (1994b). Journalists such as Eamonn Dunphy, Fintan O'Toole and Eoghan Harris popularised the approach in the southern media.

Ostensibly, the goal of revisionism is an objective account of history. That requires the immediate rejection of what is said to be the canon of Irish history (Shaw 1972), particularly as traditionally taught in Catholic schools North and South and institutionalised by the state in museums, monuments, aspirations and overall aura. This official Irish history is rejected as mythical and selective, glorifying bloodshed, sectarian in its treatment of unionism, and pseudo-religious in its vision of the unending struggle of the native Irish over seven or more centuries against British oppression.

The problems with revisionism are numerous and can only be summarised briefly here. Some relate to the debate on the nature of history. All historical memory is, in the anthropological sense, mythical; Ireland is no exception (see O'Dowd, this volume). Nationalisms throughout the world require their heroes, villains, myths and ideals. In acquiring these, they are often selective, choosing the heroes and myths which create and reinforce their view of their own identity.

More fundamental is the failure to acknowledge that nations do not go about the task of constructing themselves in isolation. This is particularly true of situations such as that experienced in Ireland, where the nation was imagined within the shadow of the colonial relationship to the British nation-state. Deane (1990: 9) sums this up succinctly:

> That is the characteristic of colonial and imperial nations. Because they universalize themselves, they regard any insurgency against them as necessarily provincial. In response, insurgent nationalisms attempt to create a version of history for themselves in which their intrinsic essence has always manifested itself, thereby producing readings of the past that are as monolithic as that which they are trying to supplant. They are usually, as in

WHAT'S WRONG WITH MULTICULTURALISM?

Ireland, under the additional disadvantage that much of their past has been destroyed, silenced, erased. Therefore, the amalgam they produce is susceptible to attack and derision.

Kiberd (1991: 16) makes a similar point: 'Nationalism on its own, unredeemed by other enriching ideals, was always doomed to be a replica of its imperial enemy.' In failing to recognise that all nations are social constructs, and that the nationalism of colonised societies in part mimics that of imperial societies, revisionism in Ireland implies that Irish nationalism is somehow unique, and uniquely culpable.

There are further problems with revisionism. In particular, its representation of the canon of Irish history is in fact a caricature. While it was true that what revisionists see as the offending version of Irish history was *taught* to school children in the South and, to a lesser extent, Catholic school children in the North, that was not the only history which was *remembered* and learned by people in the various classes and communities throughout Ireland. Moreover, while there was an official history in Ireland which had at times come close to the caricature, by the point revisionism had come to the fore, those times were long past. New readings of history were already being explored. The criticisms of the canon which were valid in the 1930s were by the 1980s tendentious. For example, there were those who were revising history in the light of the knowledge of colonial and neo-colonial experiences elsewhere, re-inventing Ireland as a society caught somewhere 'between first and third worlds' (Coulter 1994) and finding evocative resonances as a result. The revisionists did not welcome these commentators as colleagues, but judged them in effect to be little more than the new face of the old canon.

One of the commentators rejected by the revisionists, Declan Kiberd (1991), compares revisionism to similar phenomena in other former colonial situations, such as India (as captured in Salman Rushdie's *Midnight's Children*) and Latin America (as portrayed in Gabriel Garcia Marquez's *One Hundred Years of Solitude*). In these cases, and in Ireland as well, a post-colonial bourgeoisie comes to define its current cosmopolitan and modern identity by forgetting the past. As Kinealy (1995: 30) puts it, the 'key objective' of revisionism was 'to exorcise the ghost of nationalism from historical discourse and to replace it with historical narratives that persistently played down the separateness of the trauma and derided the heroes and villains of Irish history'.

She could have added that even more urgent was the exorcism not merely of old ghosts but also of current villains in the form of Irish republicans. Revisionism's rise is not coincidentally coterminous with the emergence of the 'troubles' in the North. The political programme at the root of revisionism involves rejecting republicanism and its analysis, disparaging any alternative analyses to revisionism by dismissing them as crypto-republican, and focusing on the unionists to the point of seeing them as the sole victims of political conflict. While there may be a certain symmetry in moving away from seeing nationalists as the sole victims, this substitution does as little to advance either under-standing or political solutions as the view it rejects. The over-riding concern was to avoid any historical topics (such as the Great Famine of 1845–9) which, it was argued, could lend ammunition to the IRA, and of course to attack anyone who failed to avoid those topics. Censorship was at the heart of the revisionist programme.

Revisionism had obviously a resonance in the North itself where myths are often said to be at the root of the conflict. From early in the 'troubles' there were indigenous commentators quick to see history as a major culprit in the emergence and continuation of violence. For example, Magee (1971: 6) summed up the position pithily: 'different ancestors, different anniversaries, different wars'. History in the North was represented not merely as a legacy, but also as a curse; thus Magee refers to 'two groups of people who were prisoners of history':

> Protestants and Catholics – unionists and nationalists, call them what you will – had a completely *unbalanced* view of the past, and, because of the manner in which their *mythology* had been acquired, had no knowledge at all of the historical basis of each other's point of view.
>
> (Magee 1971: 2; emphasis added)

The solution is to expunge history of its divisiveness, to devise a history which is not only more balanced, but also conducive to school children in the North seeing what they have in common and accepting the culture and traditions of the other side. The links between these views and the emergence almost two decades later of EMU are apparent. In short, this view of history fed into the ferment which was finally to present itself as multiculturalism. So, it is to the multicultur-alist project that we will now return.

Multiculturalism: What's the problem?

> The official position [is] that the underlying divisions in Northern Ireland are based in the mutual hostility of the two traditions and that, therefore, any well-intentioned person must be simply in favour of attacking sectari-anism. The virtue of this perspective is that it strongly implies that its opponents are in the business of fostering, or at least failing to challenge, sectarianism. (Miller 1993a: 76)

All of the strands considered above have come together in the multicul-turalist agenda for the North of Ireland: state initiatives such as EMU and the Cultural Traditions Group, influences from the USA and Britain, academic developments in relation to the Northern conflict and indeed more widely which rest on the concept of ethnicity, and on revi-sionism in Irish history. Given such wide-ranging origins, the project involves academics, cultural commentators, journalists, educationalists, politicians and policy-makers.

It is important to stress that, while there are undoubtedly elements of strategic planning involved, conspiracy is not the sole explanation of the existence of this agenda. The proponents of multiculturalism share an ideology; they move in a common universe of discourse. They share an agenda because they share a way of looking at the world. Moreover, they share also a sense of self-assurance; their way of seeing is so obviously contemporary and irreproachable that it is difficult to imagine any other way of viewing the world. Who would want to criticise such unassailably correct notions as 'tolerance' and 'reconciliation'? Yet a critical approach to this rhetoric and its underlying ideology is necessary. Such an approach may well end up rejecting not the words but the way in which they are used and the manner in which they have been monopolised, indeed hijacked. There are a number of deep-rooted problems in the multiculturalist approach as it is articulated by academics, policy-makers and others in relation to the conflict in the North of Ireland.

1. Psychologism

To begin with, the paradigm rests on socio-psychological explanations. Moreover, the psychology employed is often very basic:

> Much of what presents as inter-group or ethnic conflict is, I believe, determined by the self-perception of the groups concerned, their perception of others, and their preconceptions of others' view of them. Underlying most of these conflicts is a failure of communication, a lack of empathy and understanding which results in stereotyping and scapegoating, and a basic lack of trust.   (Hayes 1993: 10)

There is also often a level of imprecision involved in the use of psychological concepts; thus Darby (1995: 15, emphasis added), states that: 'Psychological factors, including real and *imagined fears*, are serious barriers to conciliation'. But there is no such thing as an imagined fear; all fear is real, even if the basis for it may be more or less realistic.

Pseudo-psychological explanations are at the base of many academic and popular accounts of the nature of sectarianism. The overall effect is to state or infer that the problem is all in the minds of those who have been raised in the North. Explaining sectarianism in this way is a neat avoidance of politics. To include politics in the picture is to be forced to consider the ways in which contemporary sectarianism derives from the colonial and post-colonial history of Ireland. Even among academics, this point is not always stressed, leading McVeigh (1995a: 622) to complain about 'the under-theorisation of sectarianism'. And as regards the state: 'sectarianism continues to be treated, within the policy discourses of the state, as a structure of personal prejudice and not as the result of an unresolved, post-colonial situation' (Bell, 1991: 89).

Brewer attempts to discover the similarities and differences between sectarianism and racism; for all the similarities, he concludes, there is a fundamental difference:

> Religion involves stereotypical not perceptual cues ... Phenotypical features require perceptual cues in order to mark differences. That is, they involve cognitive skills in perceiving cues of outward differences (the perception of differences in skin colour being the most obvious). Depending on a particular physical feature, such differences are correspondingly easier to discern and harder to avoid than those of religion.   (Brewer 1992: 360)

This is to impute a material reality to racism which goes far beyond its social origins. There is no racism apart from the culture which creates it, phenotypes notwithstanding. Racism, no less than sectarianism, is a social construct. Sectarianism is thus no less 'real' than racism, despite the apparent 'invisibility' of cues; conversely, racism is no less constructed than sectarianism, no matter how stark the differences in skin colour.

2. Denial/depoliticisation of history

The Irish are said to be 'prisoners of our upbringing' (Tanáiste Dick Spring, cited in *Irish Times*, 17 March 1993), urged on by 'ancestral voices' (O'Brien 1994); history is a 'burden' (Lyons 1979). The poet Gerald Dawe sums up the argument:

> The battles that are being fought out on the streets, and the language that we're using, concern ancient issues and don't really relate to the world as it is now.   (cited in *Beyond the Fife and Drum* 1995: 21)

Within this multiculturalist world view, in short, history is judged to be the ultimate psychological disorder. As Chris Ryder, one of the members of the Cultural Traditions Group, puts it: 'The obsession with the past on all sides is a sign of weakness and insecurity' (in *Shades of Orange* n.d.: 8).

There are three possible solutions to this problem. One is to avoid history altogether. Interestingly, this can even be done in the teaching of history as a school subject. Thus, the cultural traditions cross-curricular theme of the common curriculum of schools in the North of Ireland is so broad and the amount of time available to teachers so limited that, in reality, teachers pick and choose those topics, events and epochs to be covered. Thus, students from a unionist background can spend all their time considering the Battle of the Somme, while those in Catholic schools focus on the United Irishmen. In the name of mutual understanding each may never hear of the others' heroes.[7]

The second solution is to package history in such a way that any potential political sting in its tail is removed. The heritage industry is playing a key role currently in this depoliticisation of history (see Brett 1996; see also Bell, this volume). The process as it has affected one city, Derry, is acidly berated by Keenan (1993: 29):

They give us art, they give us craft villages, they give us a city and a culture that never existed, and they tell us: 'That is what you are and that is what your people were'. They cleverly throw back into our imaginations the very myths that sustained our grandparents' despairs. For the past two decades they have sought to force upon an entire community a set of values that is ostensibly decent, cultured and human, but is in reality an attempt to impose the complicity of quietude and passivity upon us ... There is no analysis, no meaning. History becomes a litany: all is significant and nothing counts in this mashing of our past.

The third solution is to insist that what people in the North are obsessed by is not history, but myth. The word is not used in the anthropological sense referred to earlier, but pejoratively. The antidote to myth is 'proper' history; this is why it is possible to contrast the 'use' and 'abuse' of history:

History can provide grievances for contemporary use, it can give an influential deterministic view of things and it can create traditions which weigh heavily on current events ... This phenomenon of course is found in many countries. Most societies use the past and myths about the past to a certain extent but some, including Ireland, seem to do so more than others.
(Walker 1996: 60)

Fanning (1994: 156) echoes these sentiments:

Nowhere else in the European, North American or antipodean democracies does the writing of twentieth-century history demand so constant a confrontation with mythologies designed to legitimise violence as a political weapon in a bid to overthrow the state.

3. Relativism

As a result of both psychologism and the attempt to depoliticise history, much of the literature of the multiculturalists is relativistic. Historical events, when they cannot be avoided in the narrative, must be presented in the least offensive way possible. A case in point is the plantation of Ulster:

The same territory was occupied by two hostile groups, one believing the land had been usurped and the other fearing that their tenure was constantly under threat of rebellion.
(Darby 1995: 9)

The reader is left wondering if the land had actually been taken from the natives and if the planters were actually under threat of native rebellion.

On a more contemporary note, one would be hard pressed to reach any conclusion on the debate which has been raging for the last few years about the Orange Order and its annual marches from reading the following account which appeared in the catalogue of a photographic exhibition on the Order sponsored by the Cultural Traditions Group. The text is by a member of the Group:

> Whether it personifies the colonnaded elegance of a mature, tolerant society, where civil and religious liberty is paramount, or is a rotten timber, sustaining the evils of bigotry and discrimination, depends very much on the individual viewpoint. (Ryder, in *Shades of Orange*, n.d.: 5)

It is this relativism which allows for the sponsorship under a cultural traditions label of monuments to the Orange Order. Thus, in 1995 Castlereagh Borough Council's community relations programme and the Central Community Relations Unit of the Northern Ireland Office paid for a monument commemorating the formation of the Orange Order at the Battle of the Diamond in 1795. Castlereagh councillor Patrick Mitchell (Alliance Party) objected on the grounds that it was a sectarian celebration of the killing of Catholics. The Mayor of Castlereagh, Grant Dillon (Ulster Unionist Party) stated: 'There may have been a certain amount of Catholics killed at the Diamond ... Those Catholics wouldn't have got killed if they hadn't decided to take the farmlands of the Protestants in that area.' And John Taylor, deputy leader of the Ulster Unionist Party and a Castlereagh councillor (unlike on a later occasion, quoted above), played the multiculturalist card: 'The Battle of the Diamond isn't a matter of triumphalism but about commemorating an event which had a momentous effect on the history of Ireland' (cited in *Irish News*, 23 September 1993). 'History' and 'culture' thus become panaceas, removing the action entirely from the real world of contemporary politics.

4. Reductionism

In other words, everything is cultural and culture is everything. There is no structural level. Colonialism, politics, triumphalism, institutionalised discrimination, state power – all are left behind when entering this multicultural world. When structure is referred to at all, it is usually only in relation to group dynamics.

For example, Hugh Frazer (formerly director of the Northern Ireland Voluntary Trust and later director of Combat Poverty in the South) and Mari Fitzduff (first director of the Community Relations Council) base their analysis of the North's conflict on three concepts: prejudice, intolerance and discrimination. Discrimination is defined as a denial of the rights of people or groups because they are different. Prejudice, it is argued, can be due to a 'personality structure', but more often is due to 'group mechanisms that engender defensiveness and hostility' (Frazer and Fitzduff 1994: 21). Given this analysis, the solutions to conflict are seen to be improved communication and understanding, and the promotion of tolerant acceptance of diversity of traditions and culture. As Fitzduff (1993: 7) puts it:

> The assumption behind 'Mutual Understanding' work is that it is the lack of sufficient information and understanding about each other's humanity, objectives, hopes and fears that limits political cooperation between communities.

5. Wishful thinking

There is an element of circularity in the above strategy for ending sectarian conflict: the problem is a lack of tolerance, the solution is more tolerance. There is also an element of wishful thinking which is apparent in other strategic statements from within the multiculturalist camp. Thus, the Opsahl Commission, which involved a major survey of a broad range of opinion in relation to the conflict, urged the following as one positive suggestion for progress:

> We encourage those church members in the Orange Order and other similar bodies to use their influence to persuade these organisations to consider imaginative alternatives – such as summer festivals – to marches along 'traditional' routes through areas which are now predominantly Catholic.
>
> (Pollak 1993: 121)

The Twelfth of July as Mardi Gras has been a minor but recurrent theme over the last three decades. While it may be experienced as such by some, there is no denying that marches on this day have led to numerous violent confrontations and deaths since the mid-1800s (see Boyd 1969). More recently, the confrontations between Orange marchers demanding their 'traditional right' to march through nationalist areas where they are not welcome – such as Garvaghy Road in Portadown, and Dunloy in County Antrim – have rarely been off the political agenda between 1995 and the present. In such a situation, wishing for more tolerance is naively idealistic. On the one hand, one is reminded of the statement of Archimedes, at once optimistic and unrealistic: 'Give me but one firm spot on which to stand and I will move the earth.' In one sense, there is no such place. On the other hand, perhaps because we are dealing with human society and not the laws of mechanics, all that is necessary to create such a place – according to multiculturalism – is to keep wishing for it.

6. Social engineering

In this sense, social engineering is at the heart of the multiculturalist project. Often the aim to change the world is articulated in almost messianic terms. Listen to Michael Longley, a member of the Cultural Traditions Group:

> Our aim should be to lift the community into consciousness and self-consciousness – the forming of a new intelligentsia, if you like – since it is the intellectual (and indeed the emotional) vacuum that makes room for violence. We are involved in cultural preparation, a constellation of conversions, to replace political belligerence with cultural pride.
>
> (cited in *Giving Voices*, 1994: 39)

Robin Wilson (a key force behind the Opsahl Commission) and Paul Nolan (director of the Workers' Educational Association in Northern Ireland) go further by suggesting practical ways in which to engineer this transformation. It is not enough, they argue, to leave integration to chance. There is a mechanism available to speed up the integration of housing areas, schools and workplaces. A major concern of funding bodies, they point out, is that projects they support help to further reconciliation. Most notably, in the aftermath of the cease fires of 1994, the European Union released £280 million in a 'peace and reconciliation' package. Yet, argue Wilson and Nolan, often there is little more than lip service paid to reconciliation in many of the programmes sponsored by the EU and other funding bodies. This should change; those projects which really deliver in terms of reconciliation should receive priority for funding:

> The bodies handling the allocation of substantial Eurofunds ... have every right to be rigorous in their demands upon applicants for support as to the content of their plans. The simple slogan should be: No Reconciliation, No Receipts. (Wilson and Nolan 1996: 17)

7. The 'two traditions' straitjacket

Finally, the ultimate irony is that the concentration on the notion of two traditions in everything from the day-to-day work of the Community Relations Council to the grand sentiments of the Downing Street Declaration actually masks diversity, albeit in the name of diversity. The days of building a supposed middle ground are in many ways gone and in its place is the emphasis on 'parity of esteem'. This formal equality aspired to involves always, and only, two players.

One effect of this is to overlook the real diversity and conflict within each 'tradition'; the moving accounts of people from Protestant and unionist backgrounds who have broken with their past – socialists, lesbians and gays, republicans, artists, and others – in Hyndman (1996) reveal starkly just how blunt the notion of 'two traditions' is. But the effects are even more widespread; the paradigm involves the creation of *two* traditions even where they clearly do not exist. Two examples in relation to the Irish language will illustrate this point.

In 1994, members of the Cultural Traditions Group noted their fears about the future of the Irish language: 'Members also took full account of fears that the language would eventually die if steps were not taken to save it' (*Giving Voices*, 1994: 25). Strangely, at this point there were 12 Irish-language primary schools (bunscoileanna) in the North, six in Belfast alone, as well as one secondary school (meánscoil) and numerous nurseries (naíscoileanna). These resources were provided without state funding, revealing the commitment of parents and communities to the language. In fact, the revival of the language in working-class areas of the North was one of the most remarkable cultural phenomena of the 1970s and 1980s. So, why should the Cultural Traditions Group have concluded that swift intervention was needed to save the Irish language?

The clue is in the Group's assertion that 'the language had unfortunately become associated with Republicanism in the eyes of many Protestants, which was a *distortion* of its *real* cultural significance' (*Giving Voices* 1994: 24; emphasis added). Substantial funding was therefore provided to set up the Ultach Trust 'to make classes available in areas in which people from the Protestant community will not feel threatened and to help create an environment in which they can comfortably learn and use the language' *(ibid.*: 25).

Thus, the communities where the revival of the language was organic were starved of state funding at the same time as funding was provided for people from communities where no such organic growth was being experienced. Thus was the chimera of symmetry created. The flaws in the argument are numerous: no effort is made to assess the substance of Protestant fears about the Irish language. Protestants had in fact been learning Irish, not merely in non-threatening venues such as the Ulster People's College, but also in the Shankill Women's Centre and in the prisons. Not everyone who had been learning the language was republican, although the vast majority did live in nationalist areas. And lastly, republicans had a right not merely to speak Irish but to interpret it as a potent symbol of their identity. The creation of the Ultach Trust implies that republicans had hijacked the language, as if somehow everything would be fine if proportionately fewer republicans were interested. The project is thus highly political in intent. This is not symmetry, but an exercise in attempting to depoliticise a cultural movement.

At the same time, the Cultural Traditions Group gives substantial financial support to the 'Ulster-Scot language' (see *Giving Voices* 1994: 27). Yet, there is very real doubt about whether such a language ever existed. The European Office of Lesser Used Languages concluded, after visiting Northern Ireland, that Ulster Scots was merely a dialect of standard English, presented as more for specific political reasons.

> The world was not made aware of its existence until the Ulster Scots Society was formed in 1994. In our trip to the Ards peninsula we failed to find a communal language other than English or to find an open Ulster Scots speaker ... It is difficult to think that the revival movement of Ulster Scots is a linguistic, non-political and cross-community one, like the Irish language movement.　　　　　(cited in *Irish News*, 1 September 1996)

While there is no doubt that unionism is experiencing an identity crisis, one aspect of which is the problem of defining what is specifically unionist about unionist culture, the 'two traditions' paradigm offers no solution to the problem. Instead, it pushes unionists into the ridiculous corner of having to come up with the equivalent of Irish where no such equivalent exists. Mimicry becomes a substitute for identity, and in the process lends credence to the fringes of unionism.

Meanwhile unionists are given no lead to search for their own hidden history and little encouragement to explore the nuances of contemporary unionist identity. Unionism continues to occupy the cultural cul-de-sac of marches and drums, the narrow ground of a history which rests on the recollection of two battles, the Boyne and the Somme. Where are the poems, songs and murals about other historical experiences of their ancestors – plantation, emigration, famine[8] – or the current experiences of many of their community – unemployment, women's experience?

Conclusion: culture, politics and resistance

It has been argued that current British policy at the cultural level in relation to the North of Ireland involves the equal depoliticisation of nationalism and unionism: 'Unionism is neutered to bright banners, bowler hats and Somme memorials; nationalism is reduced to whistle music, knitted sweaters, stout and turf fires' (Bruce, 1994a: 23). Butler (1994a: 24) refers to this policy as 'balanced sectarianism'.

Although this might seem a plausible argument, at closer inspection it proves inadequate to explain an important element in state cultural policy which derives ultimately from its differential relationship with Irish nationalism on the one hand, and Ulster unionism on the other. An adequate assessment of policy must acknowledge the history and effects of colonialism (see Ruane and Todd 1996: 178–203). It needs to recognise that the vibrancy of Irish nationalism in general and its republican strand in particular derives from a long experience of resistance. From their position of subordination, nationalists and republicans have more to say, more to dream, and can see themselves expansively as part of an international fraternity of subordinate groups resisting colonialism, imperialism and oppression. Unionism, on the other hand, because of its real or aspirational superiority, has more to lose, less to articulate,[9] and feels itself isolated in an increasingly unsympathetic world.

From the British state's point of view, the problem is that cultural policy which began by accepting this unequal situation would result in overwhelming support for nationalism and little scope for supporting unionism. Historically, Britain has always been more comfortable with a situation where unionist culture is in the ascendant, and there is little reason to believe that that position has changed radically: the British state cannot contemplate supporting a culture of resistance more than a culture of maintenance. The British state's fundamental ideological affinity is with unionism, for all its differences over details with actual unionists. It is extremely sympathetic to the cultural plight of unionism; it listens with sympathy to the protestations of those who argue on behalf of unionism that '"culture" is somehow seen as an activity that Catholics are inclined to go in for' and that 'anything cultural is possibly suspect and definitely a waste of time'.[10] Its response is to bolster selected elements of unionist culture out of all proportion to their influence in the North of Ireland.

At the same time its policies seek to depoliticise nationalist culture and in particular republican resistance. Despite the self-congratulatory rhetoric, cultural policy does not rest on equality. Far from being 'balanced sectarianism', this is akin to what Hickman (1995b: 17), speaking of other circumstances, refers to as 'incorporation', namely:

> the processes by which the state actively attempts to regulate the expression and development of the separate and distinctive identities of potentially oppositional ethnic groups, in order to sustain a single nation-state.

Hickman's conclusion relates to state policy towards the Irish in Britain in the last century, the effect of which was 'denationalisation'. She argues that a crucial tool in incorporation was the education system. It is not too far-fetched to see the parallels here; British state policy is focused on the incorporation of the potential and actual oppositional force of republicanism in the contemporary North of Ireland through a process of depoliticisation which involves not just the education system but the whole culture industry.

Notes

1. The other main unionist party, the Democratic Unionist Party, for its part is no stranger to the unreconstructed rhetoric of unionism. For example, in an otherwise sober and reasoned account of why the party was opposed to the Single European Act, there was a brief but telling return to DUP basics:

   Subsidiarity is a concept which was formulated for the Roman Catholic Church by Pope Pius XI ... Three quarters of the E.C. belongs to the Roman Catholic Church ... Never forget the Community as at present constituted is 187 million (78.5%) RC and 51 million (21.5%) Protestant. Kohl, Mitterrand and Delors, the main architects of Maastricht, are all faithful RCs.
   (DUP 1992: 7)

2. Richard Needham, while Economy Minister at the Northern Ireland Office, repeatedly stressed the economistic logic, that economic policy and reform was a key element in political strategy, including counter-insurgency. For example; 'It has to be in our interests ... for us to try to get more jobs in West Belfast ... that is the way in which we will reduce the terrorist menace, by making people economically independent from terrorism. That is the prime strategic objective of government' (*Newsbreak*, BBC Radio Ulster, 19 November 1989).
3. Under direct rule, Acts are created or amended for Northern Ireland through a system known as orders in council, rather than going through the normal stages of parliamentary debate and amendment.
4. Glór na nGael is an organisation which promotes the Irish language, in particular through providing classes for adults.
5. As Troyna (1992: 85) points out, even the successor to these programmes, anti-racist education, is often not much of an improvement. Racism is seen as 'immorality and ignorance rather than oppression and exploitation. Racism is invested with individualised not structural characteristics.' The focus is on 'white attitudes towards minority cultures'.

6. "'Ethnicity" seems to be a new term', state Nathan Glazer and Daniel Moynihan (1975: 1), who point out that the world's earliest dictionary appearance is in the Oxford English Dictionary in 1972. Its first usage is attributed to the American sociologist David Reisman in 1953' (Eriksen 1993: 3).
7. Information in this paragraph from well placed private source.
8. On the impact of the Famine on the Protestants of North-East Ireland, see MacAtasney 1997.
9. An interesting exception here is in relation to the cultural aspirations of some of those in the fringe loyalist parties, particularly the Progressive Unionist party (PUP). Gusty Spence, the Ulster Volunteer Force's (UVF) greatest hero and later instrumental in the revival of the PUP, learned Irish in prison and taught it to other UVF prisoners. Similarly, other ex-prisoners have been known to sing along to songs such as 'James Connolly' in the safety of conference venues abroad. The problem here is twofold: in attempting to define themselves as British-Irish, they have as yet been unable to create cultural practices which are identifiably and uniquely loyalist, and more immediately they have little scope to articulate this culture in the heartlands of loyalism.
10. The first quotation is from Ann Tannahill, publisher and former member of the Cultural Traditions Group (cited in *Giving Voices*, 1994: 13), and the latter from Libby Keyes, Community Relations Officer with Cookstown District Council (cited in NICRC 1994: 28).

Bibliography

Ackroyd, C., Margolis, K., Rosenhead, J. and Shallice, T. (1980) *The Technology of Political Control*, 2nd edn London: Pluto.

Adams, G. (1986) *The Politics of Irish Freedom*, Dingle: Brandon.

Adams, Gavin. (1995) 'Unionism, citizenship and Europe' in Aughey, A. *et al.* (eds) *Selling Unionism*, Belfast: Ulster Young Unionist Council.

Adamson, I. (1974) *Cruithin: The Ancient Kindred*, Newtownards: Nosmada Books.

Agnew, J. (1994) 'The territorial trap: the geographical assumptions of International Relations Theory', *Review of International Political Economy*, 1(1): 53–80.

Ahmed, L. (1992) *Women and Gender in Islam: Historical Roots of a Modern Debate*, New Haven and London: Yale University Press.

Alcock, A. E. (1995–6) 'Britain, Northern Ireland and the European Union', *Ulster Review*, 18: 24–6.

Althusser, L. (1970) *For Marx*, Harmondsworth: Penguin.

Althusser, L. (1971) *Lenin and Philosophy and other Essays*, London: New Left Books.

Amnesty International (1994) *Political Killings in Northern Ireland*, London: Amnesty International.

Ancram, M. (1995) 'Offering proposals, not tablets of stone', in *Northern Ireland Brief*, London: Parliamentary Brief: 5–6.

Anderson, B. (1983) *Imagined Communities: Reflections on the Origin and Spread of Nationalism*, London: Verso.

Anderson, B. (1992) 'The new world disorder', *New Left Review* 193: (3)–13.

Anderson, J. (1986) 'Nationalism and geography' in Anderson, J. (ed.) *The Rise of the Modern State*, Brighton: Harvester Press.

Anderson, J. (1988) 'Ideological variations in Ulster during Ireland's first Home Rule crisis: an analysis of local newspapers', in Williams, C. and Kofman, E. (eds) *Community Conflict, Partition and Nationalism*, London: Routledge: 133–66.

Anderson, J. (1994) 'Problems of inter-state economic integration: Northern Ireland and the Irish Republic in the European Community', *Political Geography*, 13 (1): 53–72.

Anderson, J. (1995) 'The exaggerated death of the nation state', in Anderson *et al.* (eds) *A Global World? Re-ordering Political Space*, Oxford: Oxford University Press.

Anderson, J. (1996) 'The shifting stage of politics: new medieval and postmodern territorialities?' *Society and Space*, 14 (2): 133–53.

Anderson, J. and Goodman, J. (1994) 'European and Irish integration: Contradictions of regionalism and nationalism', *European Urban and Regional Studies*, 1(1): 49–62.

Anderson, J. and Goodman, J. (1995) 'Regions, states and the European Union: Modernist reaction or postmodern adaptation?' *Review of International Political Economy*, 2(4): 600–31.

Anderson, J. and Goodman, J. (1996) 'Border crossings', *Fortnight*, No. 350, 16–17, May 1996, Belfast.

Anderson, J. and Hamilton, D. (1995) 'Why Dublin could afford a union', *Parliamentary Brief – Northern Ireland Special Issue*, Spring 1995.

Anderson, J. and Shuttleworth, I. (1994) 'Sectarian readings of sectarianism: Interpreting the Northern Ireland Census', *Irish Review*, 16, Autumn–Winter: 74–93.

Anderson, J., Brook, C. and Cochrane A. (eds) (1995) *A Global World? Re-ordering Political Space*, Oxford: Oxford University Press.

'An Orangeman' (1799) *Orange Vindicated, in a reply to Theobald McKenna Esq, with some observations on the new and further claims of the Catholics, as affecting the constitution and the Protestant establishment*. A new edition, revised and enlarged with notes, by the author, Dublin: printed by William McKenzie.

Arden, J. (1977) *To Present the Pretence: Essays on Theatre and its Public*, London: Eyre Methuen.

Arden, J. (1979) 'Rug-headed Irish kerns and British poets', *New Statesman*, 13 July: 56–7.

Arden, J. and D'Arcy, M. (1988) *Awkward Corners*, London: Methuen.

Arextaga, B. (1997) *Shattering Silence: Women, Nationalism and Political Subjectivity in Northern Ireland*, Princeton NJ: Princeton University Press.

Arthur, M. (1987) *Northern Ireland Soldiers Talking: 1969 to Today*, London: Sidgwick & Jackson.

Arthur, P. (1980) *The Government and Politics of Northern Ireland*, London: Longman.

Arthur, P. (1987) 'Elite studies in a "paranocracy": the Northern Ireland case' in G. Moyser and M. Wagstaffe (eds) *Research Methods for Elite Studies*, London: Allen & Unwin.

Ashcroft, B., Griffiths, G. and Tiffin, H. (1989) *The Empire Writes Back: Theory and Practice in Post-colonial Literatures*, London: Routledge.

Ashcroft, B., Griffiths, G. and Tiffin, H. (eds) (1995) *The Post-colonial Studies Reader*, London: Routledge.

Asmal, K. (1985) *Shoot to Kill? International Lawyers' Inquiry into the Lethal Use of Firearms by the Security Forces in Northern Ireland*, Cork: Mercier Press.

Aughey, A. (1989) *Under Siege: The Unionist Response to the Anglo-Irish Agreement*, Belfast: Blackstaff Press.

Aughey, A. (1990) 'Recent interpretations of unionism', *Political Quarterly*, 61(2): 188–99.

Aughey, A. (1994a)'Conservative party politics in Northern Ireland' in Barton, B. and Roche, P. J. (eds) *The Northern Ireland Question: Perspectives and Policies*, Aldershot: Avebury: 121–50.

Aughey, A. (1994b) 'Contemporary unionist politics' in Barton, B and Roche, P. J. (eds) *The Northern Ireland Question: Perspectives and Policies*, Aldershot: Avebury: 53–75.

Aughey, A. (1995a) 'The idea of the union' in Foster, J. W (ed.) *The Idea of the Union: Statements and Critiques in Support of the Union of Great Britain and Northern Ireland*, Vancouver: Belcouver Press: 8–19.

Aughey, A. (1995b) 'The end of history, the end of the union' in Aughey, A. *et al.*, *Selling Unionism*, Belfast: Ulster Young Unionist Council: 7–14.

Aughey, A. (1995c) 'The constitutional challenge' in Foster, J. W (ed.) *The Idea of the Union: Statements and Critiques in Support of the Union of Great Britain and Northern Ireland*, Vancouver: Belcouver Press: 46–52.

Aughey, A. (1995d) *Irish Kulturcampf*, Belfast: Ulster Young Unionist Council.

Aughey, A. (1996) 'Obstacles to reconciliation in the South', in *Building Trust in Ireland: Studies Commissioned by the Forum for Peace and Reconciliation*, Belfast: Blackstaff Press in association with the Forum for Peace and Reconciliation: 1–52.

Aughey, A., Adams, G., Burnside, D., Donaldson, J. and Harris, E. (1995) *Selling Unionism: Home and Away*, Belfast: Ulster Young Unionist Council.

Aunger, E. A. (1975). 'Religion and occupational class in Northern Ireland', *Economic and Social Review* 7(1): 1–18.

Bairner, A. and Sugden, J. (1993) *Sport, Sectarianism and Society in Divided Ireland*, Leicester: Leicester University Press.

Baldwin-Edwards, M. and Schain, M. A. (1994) 'The politics of immigration: an introduction', *West European Politics*, 17(3): 1–16.

Bambery, C. (1987) *Ireland's Permanent Revolution*, London: Bookmarks.

Bardon, J. (1992) *A History of Ulster*, Belfast: Blackstaff Press.

Barker, M. (1981) *The New Racism*, London: Junction.

Barker, S. (1998) 'Kelly into PR front line at Northern Ireland Office', *PR Week*, 27 February: 1.

Barth, F. (1969) *Ethnic Groups and Boundaries*, London: Allen & Unwin.

Barton, B. and Roche, P. J. (eds) (1994) *The Northern Ireland Question: Perspectives and Policies*, Aldershot: Avebury.

Bash, H. (1979) *Sociology, Race and Ethnicity: A Critique of American Ideological Intrusions upon Sociological Theory*, New York: Gordon & Breach.

Beckett, A. (1996) 'Lord Have Mercy', *Independent on Sunday Review*, 7 January: 8–11.

Belfast Telegraph, 24 November 1994.

Bell, C. (1996) 'Discrimination law: religious and political belief' in Dickson, B. and McBride, D. (eds) *Digest of Northern Ireland Law*, Belfast: SLS.

Bell, D. (1986) *Acts of Union: Youth Sub-culture and Ethnic Identity amongst Protestants in Northern Ireland*, Paper to the Sociological Association of Ireland, Annual Conference, April.

Bell, D. (1990) *Acts of Union: Youth Culture and Sectarianism in Northern Ireland*, Basingstoke: Macmillan.

Bell, D. (1991) 'Cultural studies in Ireland and the postmodernist debate', *Irish Journal of Sociology* 1: 83–95.

Bell, D. (1993) 'Culture and politics in Ireland: postmodern revisions', *History of European Ideas* 16(1–3): 141–6.

Bell, D. (1994) 'High Boot Benny – Stuck in a time warp or on the side of the angels', *Film Ireland* (No. 39): 36–8.

Bell, D. (1995?) 'Picturing the landscape: Die Grune Insel, tourist images of Ireland', *European Journal of Communication* 10 (1) March: 41–62.

Bell, G. (1982) *Troublesome Business: The Labour Party and the Irish Question*, London: Pluto.

Benn, T. (1989) *Office Without Power: Diaries 1968–72*, London: Arrow.

Beresford, D. (1987) *Ten Men Dead: The Story of the 1981 Irish Hunger Strike*, London: Grafton.

Bevins, A. (1996) 'The lion and the eunuch', *Observer*, 28 April.

Bew, P. (1995) 'Not yet passing the Corfu test', in *Northern Ireland Brief*, London: Parliamentary Brief: 33–4.

Bew, P. (1996) 'A nation proud, free and dull', *Spectator*, 21 August: 11–12.

Bew, P. and Patterson, H. (1985) *The British State and the Ulster Crisis: From Wilson to Thatcher*, London: Verso.

Bew, P., Gibbon, P. and Patterson, H. (1979) *The State in Northern Ireland 1921–1972*, Manchester: Manchester University Press.

Bew, P., Gibbon, P. and Patterson, H. (1980) 'Some aspects of national-ism and socialism in Ireland, 1968–1978', in Morgan, A. and Purdie, B. (eds) *Ireland: Divided Nation, Divided Class*, London: Ink Links.

Bew, P., Gibbon, P. and Patterson, H. (1995) *Northern Ireland 1921–1994: Political Forces and Social Classes*, London: Serif.

Beyond the Fife and Drum: Report of a Conference held on Belfast's Shankill Road, October 1994 (1995) Newtownabbey: Island Pamphlets.

Bhabha, H. (1994) *The Location of Culture*, London: Routledge.

Billig, M. (1995) *Banal Nationalism*, London: Sage.

Birnie, E. and Roche, P. J. (1995) *Economics Lessons for Irish Nationalists and Republicans*, Belfast: Ulster Young Unionist Council.

Birrell, D. and Murie, A. (1980) *Policy and Government in Northern Ireland: Lessons of Devolution*, Dublin: Gill & Macmillan.

Blackburn, R. (1995) 'Ireland and the NLR', *New Left Review*, No. 212: 151–5.

Bloch, J. and Fitzgerald, P. (1983) *British Intelligence and Covert Action*, Kerry/London: Brandon/Junction Books.

Bourne, J. and Sivanandan, A. (1980) 'Cheerleaders and ombudsmen: the sociology of race relations in Britain', *Race and Class* 21(4): 331–52.

Bowen, K. (1983) *Protestants in a Catholic State: Ireland's Privileged Minority*, Kingston, Quebec: McGill-Queen's University Press.

Bowyer Bell, J. (1996) *In Dubious Battle: The Dublin and Monaghan Bombings 1972–1974*, Dublin: Poolbeg.

Boyce, D. G. (1982) *Nationalism in Ireland*, London: Croom Helm.

Boyce, D. G. (1992) *Ireland 1828–1923: From Ascendancy to Democracy*, Oxford: Basil Blackwell.

Boyce, D. G. and O'Day, A. (eds) (1996) *The Making of Modern Irish History: Revisionism and the Revisionist Controversy*, London: Routledge.

Boyd, A. (1969) *Holy War in Belfast*, Tralee: Anvil Press.

Boyer, R. and Drache, D. (eds) (1996) *States Against Markets. The Limits of Globalisation*, London: Routledge.

Boyle, J. (1962) 'The Belfast Protestant Associations and the Independent Orange Order 1901–10', *Irish Historical Studies*, 13: 117–52.

Boyle, J. F. (1977) 'Educational attainment, occupational achievement and religion in Northern Ireland', *Ecomomic and Social Review* 8(2): 79–100.

Bradley, J. (1995) 'The two economies of Ireland: an analysis', in D'Arcy, M. and Dickson, T. (eds) *Border Crossings – Developing Ireland's Island Economy*, Dublin: Gill & Macmillan.

Bradley, J. (1996) *An Island Economy – Exploring Long-Term Economic and Social Consequences of Peace and Reconciliation in the Island of Ireland*, Forum for Peace and Reconciliation, Consultancy Studies No. 4, August. Dublin: The Stationery Office.

Brady, C. (ed.) (1994) *Interpreting Irish History: The Debate on Historical Revisionism*, Dublin: Irish Academic Press.

Brady, J. (1978) 'Pluralism and Northern Ireland', *Studies* 67: 88–99.

Breen, R. (1996) 'Who wants a United Ireland: Constitutional preferences among Catholics and Protestants' in Breen, R., Devine, P. and Dowds, L. (eds), *Social Attitudes in Northern Ireland: The Fifth Report 1995–6*, Belfast: Blackstaff.

Brett, David (1996) *The Construction of Heritage*, Cork: Cork University Press.

Brewer, J. D. (1991) 'The parallels between sectarianism and racism: the Northern Ireland experience', *One Small Step Towards Racial Justice: The Teaching of Antiracism in Diploma in Social Work Programmes*, CCETSW Education and Training Paper no. 8.

Brewer, J. D. (1992) 'Sectarianism and racism and their parallels and differences', *Ethnic and Racial Studies*, 15 (3): 352–64.

Brewer, J. D. (1994) 'The ethnographic critique of ethnography: sectarianism in the RUC', *Sociology*, 28(1): 231–44.

Brewer, J. D. with Magee, K. (1991) *Inside the RUC*, Oxford: Clarendon.

British and Irish Governments (1993) *Joint Declaration*, London.

British and Irish Governments (1995) *Frameworks for the Future – A new framework for agreement: A shared understanding between the British and Irish Governments to assist discussion and negotiation involving the Northern Ireland parties*, Government Publications, Belfast: HMSO.

Brooke, P. (1992) 'Politicians, soldiers and the place of the security forces', *Royal United Services Institute Journal*, April: 1–7.

Brown C. (1992) *International Relations Theory: New Normative Approaches*, Brighton: Harvester.

Brown, T. (1985) *The Whole Protestant Community: The Making of a Historical Myth*, Derry: Field Day.

Brubaker, W. R. (1990) 'Immigration, citizenship and the nation-state in France and Germany: a comparative historical analysis', *International Sociology* 5(4): 379–407.

Bruce, P. (1995) *The Nemesis File: The True Story of an SAS Execution Squad*, London: Blake Publishing.

Bruce, S. (1986) *God Save Ulster! The Religion and Politics of Paisleyism*, Oxford: Oxford University Press.

Bruce, S. (1987) 'The Northern Ireland conflict is a religious conflict', *Annual Meeting of the British Association for the Advancement of Science*, Belfast, 24–28 August.

Bruce, S. (1992) *The Red Hand: Protestant Paramilitaries in Northern Ireland*, Oxford: Oxford University Press.

Bruce, S (1994a) 'Cultural traditions: a double-edged sword?, *Causeway*, Autumn: 21–4.

Bruce, S (1994b) *The Edge of the Union*, London: Oxford University Press.

Brunsdon, C. (ed.) (1986) *Films for Women*, London: British Film Institute.

Buchanan, R. H. (1988) *Ulster: Exploring the Common Ground*, Canon Rogers Memorial Lecture, delivered at St Mary's College, Trench House, Tuesday 2 February.

Buckley, A. D. (1982) *A Gentle People: A Study of a Peaceful Community in Ulster*, Cultra Manor: Ulster Folk and Transport Museum.

Burnside, D. (1995) 'A positive unionism in Great Britain', in Aughey, A. *et al. Selling Unionism*, Belfast: Ulster Young Unionist Council: 15–18.

Burton, F. (1978) *The Politics of Legitimacy*, London: Routledge & Kegan Paul.

Butler, D. (1991a) 'Ulster unionism and British broadcasting journalism, 1924–89', in, Rolson, B. (ed.) *The Media and Northern Ireland: Covering the Troubles*, London: Macmillan.

Butler, D. (1991b) 'Broadcasting in a divided community', in McLoone, M. (ed.) *Culture, Identity and Broadcasting in Ireland*, Belfast: Institute of Irish Studies.

Butler, D. (1993) 'High Boot Benny', *Film Ireland* 38: 30–2.

Butler, D. (1994a) 'The study of culture in Northern Ireland, or "What's so bad about peace, love and understanding ?"', *Causeway* 27 Spring: 24–33.

Butler, D. (1994b) 'The study of culture in Northern Ireland Part II', *Causeway* 28 Summer: 50–5.

Butler, D. (1995) *The Trouble with Reporting Northern Ireland*, Aldershot: Avebury.

Cadogan Group (1992) *Northern Limits: Boundaries of the Attainable in Northern Ireland Politics*, Belfast: The Cadogan Group.

Cadogan Group (1994) *Blurred Vision, Joint Authority and the Northern Ireland Problem*, Belfast: The Cadogan Group.

Cadogan Group (1995a) *Lost Accord: the 1995 Frameworks and the Search for a Settlement in Northern Ireland*, Belfast: The Cadogan Group.

Cadogan Group (1995b) *Decommissioning*, Belfast: The Cadogan Group.

Cadogan Group (1996) *Square Circles: Round Tables and the Path to Peace in Northern Ireland*, Belfast: The Cadogan Group.

Caherty, T., Storey, A., Gavin, M., Molloy, M. and Ruane, C. (eds) (1992) *Is Ireland a Third World Country?* Belfast: Beyond the Pale Publications.

Cahill, G. A. (1970) 'Some nineteenth century roots of the Ulster problem, 1829–1848', *Irish University Review* 1(2): 215–37.

Cairns, D. and Richards, S. (1988) *Writing Ireland: Colonialism, Nationalism and Culture*, Manchester: Manchester University Press.

Callaghan, J. (1973) *A House Divided*, London: Collins.

Campaign for Free Speech on Ireland (ed.) (1979) *The British Media and Ireland: Truth, the First Casualty*. London: Information on Ireland.

Campbell, F. (1991) *The Dissenting Voice: Protestant Democracy in Ulster from Plantation to Partition*, Belfast: Blackstaff.

Campbell, S. (1994) *The Great Irish Famine: Words and Images from the Famine Museum Strokestown Park, County Roscommon*, Strokestown: The Famine Museum.

Canning, D., Moore, B. and Rhodes, J. (1987) 'Economic growth in Northern Ireland: problems and prospects', in Teague, P. (ed.) *Beyond the Rhetoric*, London: Lawrence & Wishart.

Canny, N. (1973) 'The ideology of English colonialism: from Ireland to America', *William and Mary Quarterly*, 3rd series, 30: 575–98.

Carby, H. (1982) 'Schooling in Babylon', in Centre for Contemporary Cultural Studies, *The Empire Strikes Back: Race and Racism in 70s Britain*, London: Routledge & Kegan Paul: 183–211.

Cardozo, N. (1978) *Lucky Eyes and a High Heart: The Life of Maud Gonne*, New York: Bobbs-Merrill.

Carmichael, S. and Hamilton, C. (1967) *Black Power: The Politics of Liberation in America*, New York: Random House.

Catterall, P. and McDougall, S. (1996) (eds) *The Northern Ireland Question in British Politics*, Basingstoke: Macmillan.

Central Community Relations Unit (1991) *Community Relations Research Strategy*, Belfast: Northern Ireland Office.

Clancy, P., Drudy, S., Lynch, K. and O'Dowd, L. (1995) 'Sociology and Irish society' in Clancy, P., Drudy, S., Lynch, K. and O'Dowd, L. (eds) *Irish Society: Sociological Perspectives*, Dublin: Institute of Public Administration in association with the Sociological Association of Ireland.

Clayton, P. (1995) *Settler Ideologies in Twentieth-Century Ulster: Persistence or Decline?* PhD thesis, Queen's University of Belfast.

Clayton, P. (1996) *Enemies and Passing Friends: Settler Ideologies in Twentieth Century Ulster*, London: Pluto Press.

Clifford, B. (1988) *Queen's: Comment on a University and a Reply to its Politics Professor*, Belfast: Athol Press.

Clulow, R. and Teague, P. (1993) 'Governance structure and economic performance', in Teague, P. (ed.) *The Economy of Northern Ireland – Perspectives for Structural Change*, London: Lawrence & Wishart.

Clutterbuck, R. (1981) *The Media and Political Violence*, London: Macmillan.

Cochrane, F. (1994) 'Any takers? the isolation of Northern Ireland', *Political Studies* XLII: 378–95.

Cohen, S. (1993) 'Human rights and crimes of the state: the culture of denial', *Australian and New Zealand Journal of Criminology*, 26(2): 97–115.

Colley, L. (1992) *Britons: Forging the Nation 1707–1837*, London: Pimlico.

Collins, M. (1995) *The Path to Freedom: Articles and Speeches by Michael Collins*, Cork: Mercier Press.

Commission for Racial Equality (1997) *The Irish in Britain*, London: CRE.

Committee on the Administration of Justice (1992) *Racism in Northern Ireland*, Belfast: CAJ.

Committee on the Administration of Justice (1996) *The Misrule of Law: A Report on the Policing of Events during the Summer of 1996 in Northern Ireland*, Belfast: CAJ.

Compton Report (1971) *Report of an Enquiry into Allegations against the Security Forces of Physical Brutality in Northern Ireland arising out of Events on the 9th August, 1971*, Cmnd. 4823, London: HMSO.

Compton, P. (1976) 'Religious affiliation and demographic variability in Northern Ireland', *Institute of British Geographers, Transactions* 1: 433–52.

Compton, P. (1991) 'Employment differentials in Northern Ireland and job discrimination: a critique' in Roche, P. J. and Barton, B. (eds) *The Northern Ireland Question: Myth and Reality*, Aldershot: Avebury: 40–76.

Connolly, C. (1995) 'Ourselves Alone? Clár na mBan Conference Report', *Feminist Review* no. 50, Summer 1995.

Connolly, S. J. (1992) *Religion, Law and Power, the Making of Protestant Ireland 1660–1760*, Oxford: Clarendon.

Connor, T. (1987) *The London Irish*, London: London Strategic Policy Unit.

Coopers and Lybrand and Indecon (1994) *A Corridor of Opportunity: A Study of Feasibility of Developing a Dublin–Belfast Economic Corridor*, Dublin, Report to IBEC/CBI (NI).

Cormack, R. and Osborne, R. (eds) (1991) *Discrimination and Public Policy in Northern Ireland*, Oxford: Clarendon Press.

Coulter, C. (1990) *Web of Punishment*, Dublin: Attic Press.

Coulter, C. (1993) *The Hidden Tradition: Feminism, Women and Nationalism in Ireland*, Cork: Cork University Press.

Coulter, C. (1994) 'Ireland: between the First and the Third Worlds', in Boland, E. *et al.* (eds), *A Dozen Lips*, Dublin: Attic Press.

Coulter, C. (1995) 'Feminism, nationalism and the heritage of the Enlightenment', in Foley *et al.*, *Gender and Colonialism*, Galway: Galway University Press.

Coulter, Colin (1994) 'The character of unionism', *Irish Political Studies* 9: 1–24.

Cox, M. (1997) 'Bringing in the "international": the IRA ceasefire and the end of the Cold War', *International Affairs*, 73(4): 671–93.

Cox, O. C. (1970) *Caste, Class and Race*, New York: Monthly Review Press.

Cox, W. H. (1989) 'A factory of books', *Parliamentary Affairs*: 42(3): 423–6.

Crawford, R. L. (1904) *Orangeism: its History and Progress. A plea for first principles*, Dublin: Official Guide.

Cross-Curricular Working Group (1989) *Education for Mutual Understanding: A Cross-Curricular Theme*, Report of the Cross-Curricular Working Group on Education for Mutual Understanding to the Parliamentary Under-Secretary of State for Education.

Crotty, R. (1986) *Ireland in Crisis. A Study in Capitalist Colonial Undevelopment*. Dingle: Brandon Books.

Crowley, N. (1993) 'Racism and the Travellers', *Anti-Racist Law and the Travellers*, Dublin: DTEDG, ICCL and ITM.

Crozier, M. (ed.) (1989) *Proceedings of the Cultural Traditions Group Conference, 3–4 March 1989*, Belfast: Cultural Traditions Group.

Culliton, J. (1992) *A Time for Change: Industrial Policy for the 1990s*, Report of the Industrial Policy Review Group, Dublin: The Stationery Office.

Cunningham, M. (1991) *British Government Policy in Northern Ireland 1969–89: its Nature and Execution*, Manchester: Manchester University Press.

Cupples, S. (1799) *Principles of the Orange Association stated and vindicated in a discourse delivered before the members of the Orange societies in Lisburn district July 12 1799*, Belfast: Doherty & Simms.

Curtice, J. and Gallagher, A. (1990) 'The Northern Ireland Dimension' in Jowell, R., Witherspoon, S., Brook, L. with Taylor, B. (eds), *British Social Attitudes: The Seventh Report*, Aldershot: Gower: 183–216.

Curtis, L. (1984a) *Ireland: The Propaganda War: The British Media and the Battle for Hearts and Minds*, London: Pluto Press.

Curtis, L. (1984b) *Nothing But The Same Old Story: The Roots of Anti-Irish Racism*, London: Information on Ireland.

Curtis, L. (1994) *The Cause of Ireland*, Belfast: Beyond the Pale Publications.

Curtis, L. P. (1971) *Apes and Angels: The Irish in Victorian Caricature*, Newton Abbot: David & Charles.

Darby, J. (1986) *Intimidation and the Control of Conflict*, Dublin: Gill & Macmillan.

Darby, J. (1995) *Northern Ireland: Managing Difference*, London: Minority Rights Group.

Darby, J. (1998) *Scorpions in a Bottle: Conflicting Cultures in Northern Ireland*, London: Minority Rights Publications.

Darby, J. and Murray, D. (1977) *Education and Community in Northern Ireland: Schools Apart*, Coleraine: Centre for the Study of Conflict.

D'Arcy, M. and Dickson, T. (eds) (1995) *Border Crossings. Developing Ireland's Island Economy*, Dublin: Gill & Macmillan.

Davis, C., Heaton, N., Robinson, G. and McWilliams, M. (1995) *A Matter of Small Importance? Catholic and Protestant Women in the Northern Ireland Labour Market*, Belfast: EOC for NI.

Deane, Seamus (1990) 'Introduction' to Eagleton, T., Jameson, F. and Said, E. *Nationalism, Colonialism and Literature*, Minneapolis: University of Minnesota Press.

Democratic Unionist Party (1992) *The Surrender of Maastricht: What it Means for Ulster*, Belfast: DUP.

De Paor, L. (1970) *Divided Ulster*, London: Penguin.

Department of Economic Development (1990) *Competing in the 1990s*, Belfast: Department of Economic Development.

Department of Economic Development (1995) *Growing Competitively: A Review of Economic Development Policy in Northern Ireland*, Belfast: Department of Economic Development.

Department of Education for Northern Ireland (1988) *The Way Forward*, Belfast: DENI.

Dewar, M. W. (1958), *Why Orangeism?* Belfast: Jordan.

Dickey, A. (1972) 'Anti-incitement legislation in Britain and Northern Ireland', *New Community* 2 (2): 128–133.

Dickson, B. (ed.) (1990) *Civil Liberties in Northern Ireland: The C. A. J. Handbook*, Belfast: CAJ.

Dickson, B. (ed.) (1993) *Civil Liberties in Northern Ireland: The C. A. J. Handbook*, 2nd edn, Belfast: CAJ.

Dixon, P. (1995) 'Internationalisation and Unionist isolation: a reply to Feargal Cochrane', *Political Studies*, 43 (3): 487–505.

Ditch, J. (1983) 'Social policy in "crisis"? The case of Northern Ireland' in Loney, M., Boswell, D. and Clarke, J., *Social Policy and Social Welfare*, Milton Keynes: Open University Press.

Donaldson, J. (1995) 'The U.S.A. effect' in Aughey, A. *et al.*, *Selling Unionism: Home and Away*, Belfast: Ulster Young Unionists Council: 19–25.

Donzelot, J. (1986) *The Policing of Families*, Basingstoke: Macmillan.

Dornbusch, R. and Edwards, S. (1991) 'The macroeconomics of populism', in Dornbusch, R. and Edwards, S. (eds) *The Macroeconomics of Populism in Latin America*, Chicago: University of Chicago Press.

Doyle, J. (1994) 'Workers and outlaws: unionism and fair employment in Northern Ireland', *Irish Political Studies* 9: 41–60.

Dunford, M. and Hudson, R. (1996) *Successful European Regions – Northern Ireland Learning from Others*, Research Monograph 3, Belfast: Northern Ireland Economic Council.

Dunn, S., Darby, J. and Mullan, K. (1984) *Schools Together?*, Coleraine, Centre for the Study of Conflict.

Eagleton, T. (1996a) *Heathcliff and the Great Hunger: Studies in Irish Culture*, London: Verso.

Eagleton, T. (1996b) 'The Hippest', *London Review of Books*, 7 March: 3+5.

Eagleton, T. (1996c) *The Illusions of Postmodernism*, Oxford: Blackwell.

Easthope, G. (1976) 'Religious war in Northern Ireland', *Sociology* 10: 427–50.

Edge, S. (1995) 'Women are trouble did you know that Fergus: Neil Jordan's *The Crying Game*', *Feminist Review* 50, Summer: 173–85.

Elliott, M. (1989) *Wolfe Tone: Prophet of Irish Independence*, New Haven and London: Yale University Press.

Ellison, G. (1997) Professionalism in the RUC: an Examination of the Institutional Discourse, unpublished PhD, Jordanstown: University of Ulster.

English, R. (1994) 'Cultural Traditions and Political Ambiguity', *Irish Review* 15: 97–106.

English, R. (1995) 'Unionism and nationalism: the notion of symmetry' in Foster, J. W. (ed.) *The Idea of the Union: Statements and Critiques in Support of the Union of Great Britain and Northern Ireland*, Vancouver: Belcouver Press: 135–8.

English, R. (1996) 'The same people with different relatives? Modern scholarship, Unionists and the Irish nation', in English, R. and Walker, G. (eds) *Unionism in Modern Ireland*, Basingstoke: Macmillan.

English, R. and Walker, G. (1996) (eds) *Unionism in Modern Ireland: New Perspectives on Politics and Culture*, Basingstoke: Macmillan.

Eriksen, T. H. (1993) *Ethnicity and Nationalism: Anthropological Perspectives*, London: Pluto Press.

European Court of Human Rights (1995) *Case of McCann and Others v. the United Kingdom*, judgement of 27 September 1995, Strasbourg.

Evans, P. and Pollock, E. (1983) *Ireland for Beginners*, London: Writers & Readers.

Evason, E. (1985) *On the Edge: A Study of Poverty and Long-Term Unemployment in Northern Ireland*, London: Child Poverty Action Group.

Evelegh, R. (1978) *Peace Keeping in a Democratic Society: The Lessons of Northern Ireland*, London: Hurst.

Fair Employment Agency (1983) *Report into the Non-Industrial Northern Ireland Civil Service*, December, Belfast: FEA.

Fair Employment Commission (1989) *Report of an Investigation into Queen's University*, December, Belfast: FEC.

Fair Employment Commission (1997) *Annual Report 1996–1997*, Belfast: FEC.

Fairweather, E., McDonough, R. and McFadyean, M. (1984) *Only The Rivers Run Free. Northern Ireland: The Women's War*, London: Pluto Press.

Faligot, R. (1983) *Britain's Military Strategy in Ireland: The Kitson Experiment*, London/Kerry: Zed/Brandon.

Falk, R. (1995) *On Humane Governance: Towards a New Global Politics*, Cambridge: Polity Press.

Fanning, R. (1994) '"The Great Enchantment": uses and abuses of modern Irish history', in Brady, C. (ed.), *Interpreting Irish History: the Debate on Historical Revisionism*, Dublin: Irish Academic Press.

Fanon, F. (1965). *Studies in a Dying Colonialism*, New York: Monthly Review Press.

Fanon, F. (1967) *The Wretched of the Earth*, Harmondsworth: Penguin.

Fanon, F. (1970a) *A Dying Colonialism*, Harmondsworth: Penguin.

Fanon, F. (1970b) *Toward the African Revolution*, Harmondsworth: Penguin.

Fanon, F. (1986) *Black Skin, White Masks*, intro. by H. Bhabha, London: Pluto.

Fanon, F. (1989) *Studies in a Dying Colonialism*, London: Earthscan.

Farrell, M. (1976) *Northern Ireland: The Orange State*, London: Pluto Press.

Farrell, M. (1980) *Northern Ireland: The Orange State*, 2nd edn, London: Pluto Press.

Farrell, M. (1983) *Arming the Protestants: The Formation of the Ulster Special Constabulary and the Royal Ulster Constabulary, 1920–7*, London: Pluto Press.

Feldman, A. (1991) *Formations of Violence: The Narrative of the Body and Political Terror in Northern Ireland*, Chicago/London: University of Chicago Press.

Ferguson, L. and McWilliams, M. (1994) 'The woman "other"', *Fortnight* 328: 24–5.

Fields, R. (1973) *A Society on the Run: A Psychology of Northern Ireland*, Harmondsworth: Penguin.

Fields, R. (1980) *Northern Ireland: Society Under Siege*, New Brunswick, NJ: Transaction.

Finlayson, A. (1996) 'Nationalism as ideological interpellation: the case of Ulster Loyalism', *Ethnic and Racial Studies*, 19(1): 88–112.

Fisk, R. (1983) *In Time of War: Ireland, Ulster and the Price of Neutrality, 1939–45*, London: Deutsch.

Fitzduff, M. (1993) *Approaches to Community Relations Work*, Belfast: Community Relations Council.

Foot, P. (1990) *Who Framed Colin Wallace?* Basingstoke: Macmillan.

Foster, J. W. (1994) 'Processed peace?', *Fortnight*, 326: 35–7.

Foster, J. W. (1995a) 'Why I am a unionist' in Foster, J. W. (ed.) *The Idea of the Union: Statements and Critiques in support of the union of Great Britain and Northern Ireland*, Vancouver: Belcouver Press: 59–64.

Foster, J. W. (ed.) (1995b) *The Idea of the Union: Statements and Critiques in Support of the union of Great Britain and Northern Ireland*, Vancouver: Belcouver Press.

Foster, J. W. (1996) 'Strains in Irish intellectual life' in O'Dowd, L. (ed.) *On Intellectuals and Intellectual Life in Ireland: International, Comparative and Historical Contexts*, Belfast and Dublin, Institute of Irish Studies & Royal Irish Academy: 71–97.

Foster, R. (1986) 'We are all revisionists now', *Irish Review* 1: 1–5.

Foster, R. (1988) *Modern Ireland 1600–1972*, London: Allen Lane.

Foster, R. (1989) 'Varieties of Irishness' in Crozier, M. (ed.) *Cultural Traditions in Northern Ireland: Varieties of Irishness*, Belfast: Institute of Irish Studies.

Foster, R. (1994) 'History and the Irish Question', in Brady, C. (ed.), *Interpreting Irish History: the Debate on Historical Revisionism*, Dublin: Irish Academic Press.

Frazer, H. and Fitzduff, M. (1994) *Improving Community Relations*, Belfast: Community Relations Council.

Fulton, J. (1991) *The Tragedy of Belief: Division, Politics and Religion in Ireland*, Oxford: Clarendon.

Gaffikin, F. and Morrissey, M. (1990) *Northern Ireland: The Thatcher Years*, London: Zed Books.

Gailey, A. (1987) *Ireland and the Death of Kindness: The Experience of Constructive Unionism 1890–1905*, Cork: Cork University Press.

Gallagher, T. (1987) *Glasgow: The Uneasy Peace*, Manchester: Manchester University Press.

George, A. (1991) 'The discipline of Terrorology', in George, A. (ed.) *Western State Terrorism*, Cambridge: Polity.

Gibbon, P. (1972) 'The origins of the Orange Order and the United Irishmen', *Economy and Society* 1: 134–63.

Gibbon, P. (1975) *The Origins of Ulster Unionism*, Manchester: Manchester University Press.

Gibbons, L. (1983) 'Lies that tell the truth: Maeve, history and Irish cinema', *Crane Bag* 17(2): 148–54.

Gibbons, L. (1996) *Transformations in Irish Culture*, Cork: Cork University Press.

Gibson-Graham, J. K. (1996) *The End of Capitalism (as we knew it). A Feminist Critique of Political Economy*, Oxford: Blackwell.

Giddens, A. (1989) *Sociology*, Cambridge: Polity.

Giddens, A. (1997) *Sociology*, 3rd edn, Cambridge: Polity.

Gill, S. and Law, D. (1989) 'Global hegemony and structural power of capital', *International Studies Quarterly*, 33: 475–99.

Gillespie, N. (1996) 'Employment, unemployment and equality of opportunity: an introduction' in McLaughlin, E. and Quirk, P. (eds) *Policy Aspects of Employment Equality in Northern Ireland*, Belfast, Standing Advisory Commission on Human Rights.

Gillespie, P. (1996) 'Britain in Europe: the politics of identification' in Gillespie, P. (ed.) *Britain's European Question: the Issues for Ireland*, Dublin: Institute of European Affairs: 75–106.

Giving Voices: the Work of the Cultural Traditions Group 1990–1994 (1994) Belfast: Community Relations Council.

Goodman J. (1996) *Nationalism and Transnationalism: the National Conflict in Ireland and European Union Integration*, Aldershot: Avebury.

Goodman J. (1997) 'The European Union: reconstituting democracy beyond the nation-state', in McGrew, A. (ed.) *The Transformation of Democracy? Globalization and Territorial Democracy*, Cambridge: Polity.

Gramsci, A. (1971) *Selections from the Prison Notebooks*, London: Lawrence & Wishart.

Gramsci, A. (1985) *Selections from Cultural Writings*, London: Lawrence & Wishart.

Greater London Council (1984) *Racial Harassment in London: Report of a Panel of Inquiry set up by the Greater London Council Police Committee*, London: GLC.

Green, A. (1995) 'The British Isles: a cliché for re-discovery', in Foster, J. W. (ed.) *The Idea of the Union: Statements and Critiques in Support of the Union of Great Britain and Northern Ireland*, Vancouver: Belcouver Press: 20–6.

Greenslade, R. (1996) 'True blue press turns orange', *Observer*, 19 May.

Gudgin, G. (1995) 'Peace beyond paper' in Foster, J. W. (ed.) *The Idea of the Union: Statements and Critiques in Support of the Union of Great Britain and Northern Ireland*, Vancouver: Belcouver Press: 104–6.

Gudgin, G. (1996) 'Job bias at work', *Unionist Review* 20: 20–1.

Gudgin, G. and Breen, R. (1996) *Evaluation of the Ratio of Unemployment Rates as an Indicator of Fair Employment*, Belfast: Central Community Relations Unit.

Gudgin, G., Hart, M., Fagg, J., D'Arcy, E. and Keegan, R. (1989) *Job Generation in Manufacturing Industry 1973–86: A Comparison of Northern Ireland with the Republic of Ireland and the English Midlands*, Belfast: Northern Ireland Economic Research Centre.

Guelke, A. (1988) *Northern Ireland: The International Perspective*, Dublin: Gill & Macmillan.

Hackett, C. (1995) 'Self-determination: the republican feminist agenda', *Feminist Review*, no. 50, Summer: 111–16.

Hall, J. A. (1993) 'Nationalisms: classified and explained', *Daedalus* 122 (3): 1–28.

Harris, E. (1995) 'Why unionists are not understood' in Aughey, A. *et al.*, *Selling Unionism*, Belfast: Ulster Young Unionist Council: 27–47.

Harris, R. I. D. (1991) *Regional Economic Policy in Northern Ireland 1945–88*, Aldershot: Avebury.

Harris, R., Jefferson, C. and Spencer, J. (eds) (1990) *The Northern Ireland Economy*, London: Longman.

Hartz, L. M. (1964) *The Founding of New Societies: Studies in the History of the United States, Latin America, South Africa, Canada and Australia*, New York: Harcourt, Brace & World.

Haslett, E. (1995) 'Historical injustices' in Foster, J. W. (ed.) *The Idea of the Union: Statements and Critiques in Support of the Union of Great Britain and Northern Ireland*, Vancouver: Belcouver Press.

Hawthorne, J. (1989) 'Chairman's Introduction' in Crozier, M. (ed.) *Cultural Traditions in Northern Ireland: Varieties of Irishness*, Belfast: Institute of Irish Studies.

Hawthorne, J. (1991) 'Living with our differences', *Community Relations*, no. 1: 2.

Hayes, B. C. and McAllister, I. (1996) 'British and Irish public opinion towards the Northern Ireland problem', *Irish Political Studies* 11: 61–82.

Hayes, Mark (1996) *Loyalism and the Protestant Working Class in Northern Ireland: Beyond Ethnicity?*, Southampton: Public Policy Research Centre, Southampton Institute.

Hayes, Maurice (1993) *Whither Cultural Diversity?*, Belfast: Community Relations Council.

Hazelkorn, E. and Patterson, H. (1994) 'The new politics of the Irish Republic', *New Left Review*, 207, September–October: 37–80.

Hazelkorn, E. and Patterson, H. (1995) 'Response to Porter and O'Hearn', *New Left Review*, no. 212: 148–51.

Held D. (1995) *Democracy and the Global Order: From the Modern State to Cosmopolitan Governance*, Cambridge: Polity Press.

Hennessey, T. (1993) 'Ulster Unionist territorial and national identities 1886–1893, Island, Kingdom and Empire', *Irish Political Studies* 8: 21–36.

Hennessey, T. (1996) 'Ulster Unionism and loyalty to the Crown of the United Kingdom 1912–1974' in English, R. and Walker, G. (eds) *Unionism in Modern Ireland: New Perspectives on Politics and Culture*, Basingstoke: Macmillan: 115–29.

Herman, E. and O'Sullivan G. (1989) *The 'Terrorism' Industry*, New York: Pantheon.

Hewison, R. (1987) *The Heritage Industry*, London: Methuen.

Hewitt, C. (1991) 'The roots of violence: Catholic grievances and Irish nationalism during the civil rights period' in Roche, P. J. and Barton, B. (eds), *The Northern Ireland Question: Myth and Reality*, Aldershot: Avebury.

Hickey, J. (1984) *Religion and the Northern Ireland Problem*, Dublin: Gill & Macmillan.

Hickey, J. (1986) 'Religion in a divided society' in Clancy, P., Drudy, S., Lynch, K. and O'Dowd, L., *Ireland: a Sociological Profile*, Dublin: IPA.

Hickman, M. (1995a) *Religion, Class and Identity: The State, the Catholic Church and the Education of the Irish in Britain*, Aldershot: Avebury.

Hickman, M. (1995b) 'The Irish in Britain: racism, incorporation and identity', *Irish Studies Review* 10: 16–19.

Hickman, M. and Walter, B. (1997) *Discrimination and the Irish Community in Britain: A Report of Research undertaken for the Commission for Racial Equality*, London: CRE.

Hill, J., McLoone, M. and Hainsworth, P. (1994) *Border Crossing: Film in Ireland, Britain and Europe*, Belfast: Institute of Irish Studies in association with the University of Ulster and the British Film Institute.

Hillyard, P. (1987) 'The normalisation of special powers' in Scraton, P. (ed.) *Law, Order and the Authoritarian State*, Milton Keynes: Open University Press.

Hillyard, P. (1993) *Suspect Community: People's Experience of the Prevention of Terrorism Acts in Britain*, London: Pluto in association with Liberty.

Hillyard, P. (1995) 'The Silence of the Lambs: British academics and the Northern Ireland Problem', paper for the biennial conference of the British Association for Irish Studies, University of Newcastle upon Tyne, September.

Hirsch J. (1995) 'Nation-state, international regulation and the question of democracy', *Review of International Political Economy* 2 (2): 267–84.

Hirst, P. and Thompson, G. (1996) *Globalisation in Question. The International Economy and the Possibility of Governance*, Oxford: Polity Press.

Hitchens, D., Wagner, K. and Birnie, E. (1980) *Closing the Productivity Gap*, Aldershot: Avebury.

Hockey, J. (1986) *Squaddies: Portrait of a Subculture*, Exeter: Exeter University Press.

Holland, J. and Phoenix, S. (1996) *Policing the Shadows: The Secret War Against Terrorism in Northern Ireland*, London: Hodder & Stoughton.

Holmes, R. (ed.) (1996) *A Vision for the Union: the Report of the Ulster Young Unionist Council*, Belfast: Ulster Young Unionist Council.

Holroyd, F. with Burridge, N. (1989) *War Without Honour*, Hull: Medium.

Hooper, A. (1982) *The Military and the Media*, Aldershot: Avebury.

Hoppen, K. T. (1989) *Ireland Since 1800: Conflict and Conformity*, London: Longman.

Horowitz, D. L. (1977) 'Cultural movements and ethnic change', *American Academy of Political and Social Science, Annals* 433: 6–18.

Hughes, M. (1994) *Ireland Divided: The Roots of the Modern Irish Problem*, Cardiff: University of Wales Press.

Human Rights Watch (1991) *Human Rights in Northern Ireland: a Helsinki Watch Report*, New York: Human Rights Watch.

Hutton, W. (1994) *Britain and Northern Ireland, The State We're In – Failure and Opportunity*, Belfast: Northern Ireland Economic Council.

Hutton, W. (1995) *The State We're In*, London: Jonathan Cape.

Hyndman, Marilyn (1996) *Further Afield: Journeys from a Protestant Past*, Belfast: Beyond the Pale Publications.

Irish Freedom Movement (1983) *An Anti-Imperialist's Guide to the Irish War*, London: Junius Publications.

Irish Times (1996) 'Editorial', 11 May.

Jackson, A (1989) 'Unionist history (i)', *Irish Review* 7: 58–66.

Jacobson, R. (1997) 'Whose peace process? Women's organisations and

Political settlement in Northern Ireland, 1996–1997', *Peace Studies Papers*, third series, Bradford: Department of Peace Studies, University of Bradford.

Jayawardena, K. (1986) *Feminism and Nationalism in the Third World*, London: Zed Books.

Jenkins, R. (1983) *Lads, Citizens and Ordinary Kids*, London: Routledge & Kegan Paul.

Jenkins, R. (1984) 'Understanding Northern Ireland', *Sociology*, 18 (2): 253–63.

Jenkins, R. (1986) 'Northern Ireland: in what sense "religions" in conflict?', in *The Sectarian Divide in Northern Ireland Today*, Royal Anthropological Institute of Great Britain and Ireland. Occasional Paper no. 41.

Jenkins, R. (1988) 'Discrimination and equal opportunity in employment: ethnicity and race in the United Kingdom' in Gallie, R. (ed.) *Employment in Britain*, London: Blackwell.

Jennings, A. (1988) 'Shoot to kill: the final courts of justice', in Jennings, A. (ed.), *Justice Under Fire: The Abuse of Civil Liberties in Northern Ireland*, London: Pluto Press.

Johnson, P. (1984) 'A bigot puzzled by all the fuss', *Guardian*, 13 June.

Johnston, Claire (1981) 'Maeve', *Screen*: 22 (44): 54–71.

Jordan, G. and Weedon, C. (1995) *Culture Politics Class: Gender Race and the Postmodern World*, Cambridge: Blackwell.

Juhasz, Alexandra (1994) 'They said we were trying to show reality – all I want to show is my video: The politics of the realist, feminist documentary', *Screen*: 35(2): 171–90.

Kabbani, R. (1989) *Letter to Christendom*, London: Virago.

Kaplan, E. Ann (1987) 'Feminist criticism and television' in Allen, Robert C. (ed.) *Channels of Discourse, Television and Contemporary Criticism*, London: Routledge.

Kearney, H. (1989) *The British Isles: A History of Four Nations*, Cambridge: Cambridge University Press.

Kearney, R. (1988) 'Introduction: thinking otherwise', in Kearney, R. (ed.) *Across the Frontiers: Ireland in the 1990s*, Dublin: Wolfhound Press

Kearney, R. (1990) 'Postmodernity, nationalism and Ireland', Paper to the Second International Conference of History of European Ideas, Leuven, Sept.

Kearney, R. (1997) *Postnationalist Ireland*, London: Routledge.

Keenan, S. (1993) 'Something in the air: Derry's revisionism in action', *Irish Reporter* 10: 27–9.

Kennedy, D. (1988) *The Widening Gulf: Northern Attitudes to the Independent Irish State 1919–1949*, Belfast: Blackstaff Press.

Kennedy, D. (1995) 'The realism of the union' in Foster, J. W. (ed.) *The Idea of the Union: Statements and Critiques in Support of the Union of Great Britain and Northern Ireland*, Vancouver: Belcouver Press: 27–36.

Kennedy, K. (1994) 'The context of economic development', in Goldthorpe, J. and Whelan, C. (eds) *The Development of Industrial Society in Ireland*, Oxford: Oxford University Press.

Kennedy, L. (1996) *Colonialism, Religion and Nationalism in Ireland*, Belfast: Institute of Irish Studies.

Kennedy-Pipe, C. (1997) *The Origins of the Present Troubles in Northern Ireland*, London: Longman.

Kiberd, D. (1991) 'The elephant of revolutionary forgetfulness', in Ní Dhonnchadha, Máirín and Dorgan, Theo (eds) *Revising the Rising*, Derry: Field Day.

Kiberd, D. (1996) *Inventing Ireland: The Literature of the Modern Nation*, London: Vintage.

Kiely, B. (1988) *Proxopera*, London: Methuen.

Kiernan, V. G. (1982). *European Empires from Conquest to Collapse, 1850–1960*, Leicester: Leicester University Press.

Kinealy, C. (1995) 'Beyond revisionism: reassessing the Great Famine', *History Ireland*, Winter: 28–34.

Kirby, P. (1997) *Poverty Amid Plenty – World and Irish Development Reconsidered*, Dublin: Trócaire and Gill & Macmillan.

Kitson, F. (1971) *Low Intensity Operations*, London: Faber and Faber.

Kitson, F. (1987) *Warfare as a Whole*, London: Faber and Faber.

Knobel, D. T. (1986) *Paddy and the Republic: Ethnicity and Nationality in Antebellum America*, Connecticut: Wesleyan University Press.

KPMG (1995) *The Social and Economic Consequences of Peace and Economic Reconstruction*, Dublin: Forum for Peace and Reconciliation.

Kuhn, A. (1982) *Women's Pictures: Feminism and Cinema*, London: Routledge & Kegan Paul.

Kuper, R. (1996) 'The many democratic deficits of the European Union', Paper given at European Consortium for Political Research Conference, Oslo, March–April 1996.

Lacey, B. (1993) 'The Derry Museum Service and the regeneration of the city', *Museum Ireland*, 3: 57–63.

Lacey, B. (1994) 'Conflicting opinions: understanding Derry', *Museums Journal*, August 1994: 28.

Lambkin, B. K. (1996) *Opposite Religions Still? Interpreting Northern Ireland after the Conflict*, Aldershot: Avebury.

Lawrence, E. (1982) 'In the abundance of water the fool is thirsty: sociology and Black "pathology"', in Centre for Contemporary Cultural Studies, *The Empire Strikes Back: Race and Racism in 70s Britain*, London: Routledge & Kegan Paul.

Lecky, W. E. H. (1916). *A History of Ireland in the Eighteenth Century*, London: Longmans, Green.

Lee, J. J. (1989) *Ireland, 1912–1985: Politics and Society*, Cambridge: Cambridge University Press.

Lee, J. J. (1997) 'Britain needs to learn that consensus politics won't work', *Sunday Tribune*, 13 July: 16.

Lee, R. (1992) 'Nobody said it had to be easy: Postgraduate field research in Northern Ireland', *Studies in Qualitative Methodology*, 3: 123–45.

Levin, P. (1997) *Making Social Policy: The Mechanisms of Government and Politics, and How to Investigate Them*, Buckingham: Open University Press.

Lichtheim, G. (1971) *Imperialism*, London: Allen Lane.

Liddle, J. and Joshi, R. (1986) *Daughters of Independence: Gender, Caste and Class in India*, London: Zed Books, New Delhi: Kali for Women.

Liechty, J. (1993) *Roots of Sectarianism in Ireland: Chronology and Reflections*, Belfast: Working Party on Sectarianism.

Lijphart, A. (1975) 'The Northern Ireland problem: cases, theories and solutions', *British Journal of Political Science* 5: 83–106.

Linehan, Hugh (1993) 'Getting out of jail', *Film Ireland* (no. 38) 12 Dec./Jan.: 14.

Lindsay, K. (1981) *The British Intelligence Services in Action*, Ballyclare, Co. Antrim: Dunrod Press.

Lipietz, A. (1992) *Towards a New Economic Order. Post-Fordism, Ecology and Democracy*, Oxford: Polity Press.

Litton, H. (ed) (1991) *Revolutionary Woman: Kathleen Clarke 1878–1972, An Autobiography*, Dublin: O'Brien Press.

Lloyd Report (1996) *Inquiry Into Legislation Against Terrorism*, Cm 3420, London: HMSO.

Loftus, Belinda (1990) *Mirrors: William III and Mother Ireland*, Dundrum, Co Down: Picture Press.

Long, S. E. (1972) *Folders on Ulster Matters*, Belfast: Belfast County Grand Orange Lodge.

Long, S. E. (1978). *The Orange Institution, by an Orangeman*, Belfast: Grand Orange Lodge of Ireland.

Longley, E. (1993) Submission to Opsahl Commission, reported in Pollak, A. (ed.) *A Citizen's Enquiry: The Opsahl Report on Northern Ireland*, Dublin: Lilliput Press.

Longley, E. (1994a) 'From Cathleen to Anorexia', in Boland, E. *et al.* (eds), *A Dozen Lips*, Dublin: Attic Press.

Longley, E. (1994b) *The Living Stream: Literature and Revisionism in Ireland*, Newcastle-upon-Tyne: Bloodaxe Books.

Loughlin, J. (1995) *Ulster Unionism and British Identity since 1885*, London: Pinter.

Lucy, G. (1996) *Stand-off! Drumcree, July 1995 and 1996*, Lurgan: Ulster Society.

Lustick, I. (1985) *State-Building Failure in British Ireland and French Algeria*, Berkeley: University of California Press.

Lustick, I. S. (1993) *Unsettled States, Disputed Lands: Britain and Ireland, France and Algeria, Israel and the West-Bank-Gaza*, Ithaca, NY: Cornell University Press.

Lyne T. (1990) 'Ireland, Northern Ireland and 1992: the barriers to technocratic anti-partitionism', *Administration* 68: 417–33.

Lyons, F. S. L. (1979) *The Burden of Our History*, Belfast: Queen's University.

McAllister, I. (1982) 'The devil, miracles and the afterlife: the political sociology of religion in Northern Ireland', *British Journal of Sociology* 33(3): 330–47.

McAllister, I. (1983) 'Political attitudes, partisanship and social structures in Northern Ireland', *Economic and Social Review* 14(3): 185–200.

Macardle, D. (1968) *The Irish Republic*, London: Corgi.

MacAtasney, G. (1997) *This Dreadful Visitation: the Famine in Lurgan/Portadown*, Belfast: Beyond the Pale Publications.

McAuley, J. (1994) *The Politics of Identity: A Loyalist Community in Belfast*, Aldershot: Avebury.

McAuley, J. (1997) '"Flying the one-winged bird": Ulster Unionism and the peace process', in Shirlow, P. and McGovern, M. (eds) *Who are 'The People'?: Unionism, Protestantism and Loyalism in Northern Ireland*, London: Pluto.

McBride, I. (1996) 'Ulster and the British Problem', in English, R. and Walker, G. (eds) *Unionism in Modern Ireland: New Perspectives on Politics and Culture*, Basingstoke: Macmillan: 1–18.

McCann, E. (1992) *Bloody Sunday in Derry: What Really Happened*, Dingle: Brandon Books.

McCartney, R. (1985a) *Liberty and Authority in Ireland*, Derry: Field Day Pamphlets 9.

McCartney, R. (1985b) *Northern Ireland Assembly Debates* 18 (4) [on the Anglo-Irish Agreement], 16 November.

McCartney, R. (1995) 'Sovereignty and seduction' in Foster, J. W (ed.) *The Idea of the Union: Statements and Critiques in Support of the Union of Great Britain and Northern Ireland*, Vancouver: Belcouver Press. 65–8.

McCartney, R. L. (1985) *Liberty and Authority in Ireland*, Derry: Field Day.

McCashin, A. (1996) *Lone Mothers in Ireland: A Local Study*, Dublin: Combat Poverty Agency.

McCashin, C. (1997) 'Secret SAS death squads killed IRA hitmen', *News of the World*, 15 June: 1–5.

McClintock, A. (1994) 'The angel of progress: pitfalls of the term "postcolonialism"' in Williams, P. and Chrisman, L. (eds) *Colonial Discourse and Post-colonial Theory*, Hemel Hempsted: Harvester Wheatsheaf.

McDonagh, O. (1983) *States of Mind: a Study of Anglo-Irish Conflict, 1780–1980*, London: Allen & Unwin.

MacDonald, M. (1986) *The Children of Wrath: Political Violence in Northern Ireland*, Cambridge: Polity Press.

MacDougall, S. (1996) 'The projection of Northern Ireland to Great Britain and abroad, 1921–1939', in Catterall, P. and McDougall, S. (eds) *The Northern Ireland Question in British Politics*, Basingstoke: Macmillan.

MacFarlane, A. (1978) *The Origins of English Individualism, the Family, Property and Social Transition*, Oxford: Basil Blackwell.

McFarlane, W. G. and Graham W. (1979) 'Mixed marriages in Ballycuan, Northern Ireland', *Journal of Comparative Family Studies* 10(2): 191–205.

McGarry, J. and O'Leary, B. (1995) *Explaining Northern Ireland: Broken Images*, Oxford: Blackwell.

McGill, P. (1996) *Missing the Target: a Critique of Government Policy on Targeting Social Need*, Belfast: Northern Ireland Council for Voluntary Action.

McGill, P. (1998) 'Out with the old', *Guardian Higher Education*, 24 March: vi.

McGrew A. (1995) 'World order and political space', in Anderson, J. *et al.* (eds), *A Global World? Re-ordering Political Space*, Oxford: Oxford University Press: 11–64.

McGuffin, J. (1974) *The Guineapigs*, Harmondsworth: Penguin.

McKernan, J. and Russell, J. L. (1980) 'Differences of religion and sex in the value systems of Northern Ireland adolescents', *British Journal of Social and Clinical Psychology* 19: 115–18.

McLaughlin, E. (1993) 'Women and the family in Northern Ireland: a review', *Women's Studies International Forum*, 16 (6): 553–68.

McLaughlin, E. and Quirk, P. (eds) (1996a) *Policy Aspects of Employment Equality in Northern Ireland*, Belfast: Standing Advisory Commission on Human Rights.

McLaughlin, E. and Quirk, P. (1996b) 'Targeting social need', in McLaughlin, E. and Quirk, P. (eds) *Policy Aspects of Employment Equality in Northern Ireland*, Belfast: Standing Advisory Commission on Human Rights: 153–86.

McLaughlin, Eugene (1996) 'Political violence, terrorism and crimes of the state', in Muncie, J. and McLaughlin, E. (eds) *The Problem of Crime*, London: Sage: 267–319.

MacLaverty, B. (1983) *Cal*, London: Jonathan Cape.

McLoone, Martin (1990) 'Lear's fool and Goya's dilemma', *Circa* 50: 54–8.

McLoone, Martin (ed.) (1991) *Culture, Identity and Broadcasting in Ireland: Local Issues, Global Perspectives*. Belfast: Institute of Irish Studies.

McNamee, E. (1994) *Resurrection Man*, London: Picador.

MacSwiney, T. (1964) *Principles of Freedom*, 4th edn, Dublin: Irish Book Bureau.

McVeigh, R. (1990) 'Racism and Sectarianism: A Tottenham/West Belfast Comparison', unpublished PhD thesis, Department of Social Studies, Queen's University, Belfast.

McVeigh, R. (1992a) 'The Undertheorisation of Sectarianism', *Canadian Journal of Irish Studies*, 16: 118–122.

McVeigh, R. (1992b) 'Racism and Travelling People in Northern Ireland', *SACHR 17th Annual Report*, London: HMSO.

McVeigh, R. (1994) *Harassment – It's Part of Life Here: The Security Forces and Harassment in Northern Ireland*, Belfast: Committee on the Administration of Justice.

McVeigh, R. (1995a) 'Cherishing the Children of the Nation Unequally: Sectarianism in Ireland' in Clancy, P., Drudy, S., Lynch, K., and O'Dowd, L. (eds), *Irish Society: Sociological Perspectives*, Dublin: IPA.

McVeigh, R. (1995b) *The Racialization of Irishness: Racism and anti-Racism in Ireland*, Belfast: CRD.

McVeigh, R. (1995c) 'The last conquest of Ireland? British academics in Irish universities', *Race and Class*, 37(1): 109–21.

McVeigh, R. (1997) 'Symmetry and asymmetry in sectarian identity and division', *CRC Journal*, 16: 5.

McVeigh, R. (1998) 'There's no racism here because there's no Black people: Racism and anti-Racism in Northern Ireland' in Hainsworth, P. (ed.) *Ethnic Minorities in Northern Ireland*, London: Pluto.

Madden, D. (1988) *Hidden Symptoms*, London: Faber and Faber.

Maddox, B. (1996) 'A fine old Irish stew', *New Statesman* 29 November: 21–2.

Magee, J. (1971) *The Teaching of Irish History in Irish Schools*, Belfast: Northern Ireland Community Relations Commission.

Maguire, M., Reiner, R. and Morgan, R. (1994) *The Oxford Handbook of Criminology*, Oxford: Oxford University Press.

Marris, P. and Rein, M. (1967) *Dilemmas of Social Reform*, London: Routledge & Kegan Paul.

Martin, J. (1982) 'The conflict in Northern Ireland: Marxist interpretations', *Capital and Class* 18: 56–71.

Mason, P. (1970) *Patterns of Dominance*, London: Oxford University Press.

Meaney, G. (1993) 'Sex and nation : women in Irish culture and politics' in Smyth, A. (ed.) *Irish Women's Studies Reader*, Dublin: Attic Press.

Memmi, A. (1990) *The Coloniser and the Colonised*, London: Earthscan Publications.

Millar, F. (1996) 'Tories get excited about "the Union" but without having the North in mind', *Irish Times*, 9 October.

Miller, D. (1993a) 'The new battleground? Community relations and cultural traditions in Northern Ireland', *Planet: The Welsh Internationalist* 102: 74–9.

Miller, D. (1993b) 'The Northern Ireland Information Service and the media: aims, strategy, tactics' in Eldridge, J. (ed.) *Getting the Message*, London: Routledge.

Miller, D. (1994) *Don't Mention the War: Northern Ireland, Propaganda and the Media*, London: Pluto Press.

Miller, D. (1995) 'The media and Northern Ireland: censorship, information management and the broadcasting ban', in Philo, G. (ed.), *The Glasgow Media Group Reader*, vol. 2, London: Routledge.

Miller, D. and McLaughlin, G. (1996) 'Reporting the peace in Ireland', in Rolston, B. and Miller, D. (eds), *War and Words: The Northern Ireland Media Reader*, Belfast: Beyond the Pale Publications: 421–40.

Miller, I. (1988) *Research Supported by the Economic and Social Research Council, 1987 Supplement*, London: ESRC.

Miller, R. (1986) 'Social stratification and mobility' in Clancy, P., Drudy, S., Lynch, K. and O'Dowd, L. (eds) *Ireland: A Sociological Profile*, Dublin: Institute of Public Administration.

Mitchell Report (1996) *Report of the International Body on Arms Decommissioning*, Belfast/Dublin: The International Body.

Mjøset, L. (1992) *The Irish Economy in a Comparative Institutional Perspective*, Dublin: National Economic and Social Council.

Modood, T., Berthoud, R. and others (1997) *Ethnic Minorities in Britain: Diversity and Disadvantage*, London: Policy Studies Institute.

Mohanty, C. T. (1992) 'Feminist encounters: locating the politics of experience' in Barrett, M. and Phillips, A. (eds) *Destabilizing Theory: Contemporary Feminist Debates*, Cambridge: Polity Press.

Montgomery, E. (1959) 'Nomenclature – are we Irish, Northern Irish or Ulster?', Memorandum for the Cabinet Publicity Committee, 17 April, PRONI CAB 9F/123/72.

Moore, B. (1990) *Lies of Silence*, London: Bloomsbury.

Moore, C. (1995) 'How to be British?', *Spectator*, 21 October: 2–5.

Moore, J. (1991) 'The Labour Party and Northern Ireland in the 1960s', in Hughes, E. (ed.) *Culture and Politics in Northern Ireland*, Milton Keynes: Open University Press.

Moore, R. (1972) 'Race relations in the Six Counties: colonialism, industrialisation, and stratification in Ireland', *Race* 14: 21–42.

Morgan, A. (1980) 'Socialism in Ireland – Red, Green and Orange', in Morgan, A. and Purdie, B. (eds) *Ireland: Divided Nation, Divided Class*, London: Ink Links.

Morgan, R. (1984) 'Planetary feminism: the politics of the 21st century' in *Sisterhood is Global: The International Women's Movement Anthology*, New York: Anchor Press/Doubleday.

Morgan, R. (1989) *The Demon Lover: On the Sexuality of Terrorism*, London: Methuen.

Morris, M. (1992) *Ecstasy and Economics*, Sydney: EM Press.

Mullan, D. (ed.) (1997) *Eyewitness Bloody Sunday: The Truth*, Dublin: Wolfhound Press.

Munck, R. (ed.) (1993) *The Irish Economy: Results and Prospects*, London: Pluto Press.

Munck, R. and Hamilton, D. (1993) 'Alternative scenarios', in Munck, R. (ed.) *The Irish Economy: Results and Prospects*, London: Pluto Press.

Munck, R. and Hamilton, D. (1994) 'A disintegrated economy', *Fortnight*, January.

Murray, B. (1984) *The Old Firm: Sectarianism, Sport and Society in Scotland*, Edinburgh: Donald.

Naidoo, J. (1989) *Tracking Down Historical Myths*, Johannesburg: AD Donker.

Nairn, T. (1977) *The Break-Up of Britain*, London: New Left Books.

Nairn, T. (1988) *The Enchanted Glass: Britain and its Monarchy*, London: Radius.

Nairn, T. (1997) *Faces of Nationalism: Janus Revisited*, London: Verso.

Nandy, A. (1983) *The Intimate Enemy: Loss and Recovery of Self under Colonialism*, Delhi: Oxford University Press.

National Council for Civil Liberties (1993) *Broken Covenants: Violations of International Law in Northern Ireland – Report of the Northern Ireland Human Rights Assembly*, London: NCCL.

National Economic and Social Council (1989) *Ireland in the European Community: Performance, Prospects and Strategy*, Report 88. Dublin: NESC.

Neal, F. (1988) *Sectarian Violence, the Liverpool Experience 1819–1914, an Aspect of Anglo-Irish History*, Manchester: Manchester University Press.

Nelson, S. (1975) 'Protestant "ideology" considered: the case of discrimination' in Crewe, I. (ed.) *The Politics of Race*, London: Croom Helm.

Nelson, S. (1984) *Ulster's Uncertain Defenders*, Belfast: Appletree Press.

New Ireland Forum (1984) *Report*, Dublin: The Stationery Office.

Newsinger, J. (1995) 'British security policy in Northern Ireland', *Race and Class* 37(1): 83–94.

Niven, R. (1899) *Orangeism as it is and was. A concise history of the rise and progress of the institution, with appendix. Also papers relating to an investigation by Royal Commission held at Castlewellan, into the occurrences at Dolly's Brae on the 12th July, 1849*, Belfast: Baird.

Northern Ireland Community Relations Council (1994) *Fourth Annual Report*, Belfast: NICRC.

Northern Ireland Economic Council (1989) *Economic Strategy: Overall Review*, Report 73, Belfast: NIEC.

Northern Ireland Economic Council (1990) *Economic Assessment: April 1990*, Report 81, Belfast: NIEC.

Northern Ireland Economic Council (1992) *Inward Investment in Northern Ireland*, Report 99, Belfast: NIEC.

Northern Ireland Economic Council (1995a) *Through Peace to Prosperity*, Occasional Paper 3, Belfast: NIEC.

Northern Ireland Economic Council (1995b) *The Economic Implications of Peace and Political Stability for Northern Ireland*, Occasional Paper 4, Belfast: NIEC.

Northern Ireland Growth Challenge (1995) *Northern Ireland Growth Challenge: Interim Summary for Progress*, Belfast: NIGC.

Northern Ireland Information Service (1995) *Building on the Peace in Northern Ireland*, 2nd edn, Belfast: Northern Ireland Information Service.

North Report (1997) *Report of the Independent Review of Parades and Marches*, Belfast: The Stationery Office.

Nutt, K. (1993) 'Time for a real change', *Fortnight*, no. 320: 42–3.

O'Ballance, E. (1981) *Terror in Ireland: the Heritage of Hate*, Novato, CA: Presidio Press.

O'Ballance, E. (1989) *Terrorism in the 1980s*, London: Arms and Armour.

O'Brien, C. C. (1994) *Ancestral Voices: Religion and Nationalism in Ireland*, Dublin: Poolbeg.

Ó Ciosáin, N. (1994) 'Hungry grass: the new Famine Museum at Strokestown House', *CIRCA*, no. 68: 24–7.

O'Clery, C. (1997) *The Greening of the White House*, Dublin: Gill & Macmillan.

O'Connell, M. (1993) *Truth the First Casualty*, Eire: Riverstone.

O'Connor, F. (1993) *In Search of a State: Catholics in Northern Ireland*, Belfast: Blackstaff.

O'Donnell, R. and Teague, P. (1993) 'The potential and limits to North–South economic co-operation', in Teague, P. (ed.) *The Economy of Northern Ireland – Perspectives for Structural Change*, London: Lawrence & Wishart.

O'Dowd, L. (1990) New Introduction to Memmi, A. *The Coloniser and the Colonised*, London: Earthscan Publications.

O'Dowd, L. (1991a) 'The States of Ireland: some reflections on research', *Irish Journal of Sociology*, 1: 96–106.

O'Dowd, L. (1991b) 'Intellectuals and political culture: a unionist–nationalist comparison', in Hughes, E. (ed.) *Culture and Politics in Northern Ireland*, Milton Keynes: Open University Press, 151–73.

O'Dowd, L. (1995) 'Development or dependency? State, economy and society in Northern Ireland', in Clancy, P., Drudy, S., Lynch, K. and O'Dowd, L. (eds) *Irish Society: Sociological Perspectives*, Dublin: Institute of Public Administration.

O'Dowd, L. (ed.) (1996a) *On Intellectuals and Intellectual Life in Ireland*, Belfast: Institute of Irish Studies.

O'Dowd, (1996b) 'Intellectuals and intelligentsia: a sociological introduction' in O'Dowd, L. (ed.) *On Intellectuals and Intellectual Life in Ireland*, Belfast: Institute of Irish Studies.

O'Dowd, L., Rolston, B. and Tomlinson, M. (1980) *Northern Ireland: Between Civil Rights and Civil War*, London: CSE Books.

O'Dowd, L., Rolston, B. and Tomlinson, M. (1982) 'From Labour to the Tories: the ideology of containment in Northern Ireland', *Capital and Class* 18: 72–90.

O'Hearn, D. (1995) 'Global restructuring and the Irish political economy', in Clancy, P., Drudy, S., Lynch, K. and O'Dowd, L. (eds) *Irish Society: Sociological Perspectives*, Dublin: Institute of Public Administration.

Ohmae, K. (1990) *The Borderless World*, London: Collins.

O'Leary, B. (1997) 'The Conservative stewardship of Northern Ireland, 1979–97: sound-bottomed contradictions or slow learning?', *Political Studies* xix, 663–76.

O'Leary B., Lyne T., Marshall J., Rowthorn, B. (1993) *Northern Ireland: Sharing Authority*, London: Institute for Public Policy Research.

O'Leary, B. and McGarry, J. (1993) *The Politics of Antagonism: Understanding Northern Ireland*, London: Athlone Press.

Oliver, J. (1978) *Ulster Today and Tomorrow*, London: PEP.

O'Malley, E. (1989) *Industry and Economic Development. The Challenge of the Latecomer*, Dublin: Gill & Macmillan.

O'Malley, E. (1992) 'Problems of industrialisation in Ireland', in Goldthorpe, J. and Whelan, C. (eds) *The Development of Industrial Society in Ireland*, Oxford: Oxford University Press.

O'Neill, S. (1994) 'Pluralist justice and its limits: the case of Northern Ireland', *Political Studies* XLII: 363–77.

Orange Institution (1813) *A Slight Sketch, with an Appendix containing the Rules and Regulations of the Orange Societies of Great Britain and Ireland*, Dublin: Charles.

Orange Institution (1885) *Ritual of Introduction to the Orange Order*, Dublin: Forrest.

Orange Institution (1891) *Index to Principal Resolutions, Addresses etc. June 1881 to December 1890*, Dublin: Forrest.

Orange Institution (1902) *Ritual of Introduction to the Orange Order*, Armagh.

Orange Institution (1916) *Laws and Ordinances adopted December 15th 1915*, Belfast: Grand Orange Lodge of Ireland.

Orange Institution (1963) *Centenary Official History 1863–1963*, Belfast: Universal Publishing Co.

Osborne, R. D. (1981) 'Equality of opportunity and discrimination: the case of religion in Northern Ireland', *Administration* 29(4): 331–55.

O'Sullivan, K. S. (1986) *First World Nationalisms: Class and Ethnic Politics in Northern Ireland and Quebec*, Chicago: University of Chicago Press. Oxford: Blackwell.

Paisley, R. (1992) 'Feminism, unionism and "the brotherhood"', *Irish Reporter*, no. 8, fourth quarter:

Pat Finucane Centre (1996) *In the Line of Fire*, Derry: Pat Finucane Centre.

Pat Finucane Centre (1997) *For God and Ulster: An Alternative Guide to the Loyal Orders*, Derry: Pat Finucane Centre.

Patterson, G. (1992) *Fat Lad*, London: Chatto & Windus.

Patterson, H. (1980a) 'Independent Orangeism and class conflict in Edwardian Belfast: a re-interpretation', *Royal Irish Academy* 80 (1): 1–28.

Patterson, H. (1980b) *Class Conflict and Sectarianism: The Protestant Working Class and the Belfast Labour Movement 1868–1920*, Belfast: Blackstaff.

Patterson, H. (1982) 'Paisley and Protestant politics', *Marxism Today* 26(1): 26–31.

Patterson, H. (1992) 'The debate on Northern Ireland', *Science and Society*, 56(4): 467–74.

Percival R. (1996) 'Towards a grassroots peace process', *Irish Reporter* 22, June: 59–62.

Phillips, P. T. (1982) *The Sectarian Spirit: Sectarianism, Society and Politics in Victorian Cotton Towns*, London: Toronto University Press.

Philo, G. and Miller, D. (1998) *Cultural Compliance: Dead Ends of Media/Cultural Studies and Social Science*, February, Glasgow: Glasgow Media Group.

Phoenix, E. (1994) *Northern Nationalism: Nationalist Politics, Partition and the Catholic Minority in Northern Ireland, 1890–1940*, Belfast: Ulster Historical Foundation.

Pollak, Andy (ed.) (1993) *A Citizens' Inquiry: the Opsahl Report on Northern Ireland*, Dublin: The Lilliput Press.

Poole, M. A. (1982) 'Religious residential segregation in urban Northern Ireland', in Boal, F. W. and Douglas, J. N. (eds), *Integration and Division: Geographical Perspectives on the Northern Ireland Problem*, London: Academic Press: 281–308.

Portadown News, 10 October 1969.

Porter, M. (1990) *The Competitive Advantage of Nations*, Basingstoke: Macmillan.

Porter, N. (1996) *Rethinking Unionism: an alternative vision for Northern Ireland*, Belfast: Blackstaff Press.

Porter, S. and O'Hearn, D. (1995) 'New Left Podsnappery: the British Left and Ireland', *New Left Review*, no. 212: 131–47.

Pringle, D. (1985) *One Ireland, Two Nations: A Political Geographical Analysis of the National Conflict in Ireland*, Letchworth: Research Studies Press.

Price, J. (1995) 'Political change and the Protestant working class', *Race and Class*, 37(1): 57–69.

Przeworski, A. (1995) *Sustainable Democracy*, Cambridge: Cambridge University Press.

Purdie, B. (1990) *Politics in the Streets: The Origins of the Civil Rights Movement in Northern Ireland*, Belfast: Blackstaff Press.

Queen's University (1993) *Second Report on Equal Opportunities*, Belfast: Queen's University.

Quigley, G. (1992) 'Ireland – An Island Economy', Text of speech to the Confederation of Irish Industry, Dublin, 28 February.

Reed, D. (1984) *Ireland: The Key to the British Revolution*, London: Larkin Books.

Rennie, J. (1996) *The Operators: On the Streets with 14 Company – The Army's Top Secret Elite*, London: Century.

Rex, J. (1986), *Race and Ethnicity*, Milton Keynes: Open University Press.

Reynolds, L. (1995) 'Feile an phobail: an exercise in cultural expression', *Ulster Review* 18: 27–8.

Roberts, D. A. (1971) 'The Orange Order in Ireland: a religious institution?', *British Journal of Sociology* 22(3): 100–36.

Robinson, P. (1982) 'Plantation and colonisation: the historical background', in Boal, F. W. and Douglas, J. N. H. (eds), *Integration and Division: Geographical Perspectives on the Northern Irish Problem*, London: Academic Press: 19–47.

Roche, P. J. (1994) 'Northern Ireland and Irish nationalism – a unionist perspective', *Irish Review* 15: 70–8.

Roche, P. J. (1995) 'Northern Ireland and Irish nationalism', in Foster, J. W. (ed.) *The Idea of the Union: Statements and Critiques in Support of the Union of Great Britain and Northern Ireland*, Vancouver: Belcouver Press.

Roche, P. J. and Barton, B. (1991) (eds) *The Northern Ireland Question: Myth and Reality*, Aldershot: Avebury.

Roche, P. J. and Birnie, J. E. (1995) *An Economics Lesson for Irish Nationalists and Republicans*, Belfast: Ulster Unionist Information Institute.

Roche, P. J. and Birnie, J. E. (1996) 'Irish nationalism: politics of the absurd', *Unionist Review* 20: 13–15.

Rockett, K., Gibbons, L. and Hill, J. (1988) *Cinema and Ireland*, London: Routledge.

Rogers, E. (1881) *The Revolution of 1688, and the History of the Orange Association of England and Ireland*, 5th edn, Belfast: W. and G. Baird.

Rolston, B. (1983) 'Reformism and sectarianism: the state of the union after civil rights' in Darby, J. (ed.) *Northern Ireland: The Background to the Conflict*, Belfast: Appletree.

Rolston, B. (1989) 'Mothers, whores and villains: images of women in novels of the Northern Ireland Conflict', *Race and Class* 31(1): 41–57.

Rolston, B. (ed.) (1991a) *The Media and Northern Ireland: Covering the Troubles*, Basingstoke: Macmillan.

Rolston, B. (1991b) 'Containment and its failure: the British State and the control of conflict in Northern Ireland', in George, A. (ed.), *Western State Terrorism*, Cambridge: Polity.

Rolston, B. (forthcoming) 'Social research and political conflict' in Bell, R. (ed.) *A Troubles Collection: The Northern Ireland Political Collection and the Study of the Conflict*, Belfast: Linenhall Library.

Rolston, B. and Miller, D. (1996) 'Introduction' in Rolston, B. and Miller, D. (eds) *War and Words: The Northern Ireland Media Reader*, Belfast: Beyond the Pale.

Rolston, B. and Tomlinson, M. (1988) *Unemployment in West Belfast: The Obair Report*, Belfast: Beyond the Pale Publications.

Rose, R. (1971) *Governing without Consensus: an Irish Perspective*, London: Faber and Faber.

Rosenberg J. (1994) *The Empire of Civil Society*, London: Verso.

Rowthorn, B. and Wayne, N. (1988) *Northern Ireland. The Political Economy of Conflict*, Oxford: Polity Press.

Royal Ulster Constabulary (1997) *Conditions of Access to the RUC for Research Purposes*, Force Research, Management Support Department, RUC, October.

Ruane, J. (1992) 'Colonialism and the interpretation of Irish historical development', in Silverman, M. and Gulliver, P. H. (eds) *Approaching the Past: Historical Anthropology Through Irish Case Studies*, New York: Columbia University Press.

Ruane, J. and Todd, J. (1996) *The Dynamics of Conflict in Northern Ireland: Power, Conflict and Emancipation*, Cambridge: Cambridge University Press.

Ryan, M. (1994) *War and Peace in Ireland: Britain and the IRA in the New World Order*, London: Pluto.

Ryder, C. (1991) *The Ulster Defence Regiment: An Instrument of Peace?* London: Methuen.

Sabel, C. (1996) *Local Partnerships and Social Innovation*, Paris: OECD.

Said, E. (1983) *Covering Islam*, London: Routledge & Kegan Paul.

Said, E. (1993) *Culture and Imperialism*, London: Chatto & Windus.

Said, E. and Hitchens, C. (eds) (1988) *Blaming the Victims: Spurious Scholarship and the Palestinian Question*, London: Verso.

Saul, J. S. (1979) 'The dialectic of class and tribe', *Race and Class* 20(4): 347–72.

Savage, D. C. (1960) 'The origins of the Ulster Unionist Party 1885–6', *Irish Historical Studies* 12: 185–208.

Schlesinger, P. (1980) 'Between sociology and journalism' in Christian, H. (ed.) *The Sociology of Journalism and the Press*, Sociological Review Monograph, 29, University of Keele.

Schlesinger, P. (1991) *Media, State and Nation*, London: Sage.

Schutz, B. M. and Scott, D. (1975). 'Natives and settlers – comparative analysis of the politics of opposition and mobilisation in Northern Ireland and Rhodesia', Monograph, *Series in World Affairs* 12 (M2): 1–67.

Shades of Orange (n. d.) Belfast: Cultural Traditions Group.

Shaw, F. (1972) 'The canon of Irish history: a challenge', *Studies*, 61, Summer: 115–53.

Sheehan, M. (1995) 'Fair employment: an issue for the peace process' *Race and Class*, 37(1): 71–82.

Sheehan, M. and Tomlinson, M. (1996) 'Long-term unemployment in West Belfast' in McLaughlin, E. and Quirk, P. (eds) *Policy Aspects of Employment Equality in Northern Ireland*, Belfast: Standing Advisory Commission on Human Rights.

Sheehan, M., Munck, R. and Hamilton, D. (1997) 'Political conflict, partition and underdevelopment of the Irish economy', in O'Day, A. (ed.) *Political Violence in Northern Ireland: Conflict and Conflict Resolution*, Westport, CT: Greenwood Publishing Group.

Shirlow, P. and McGovern, M. (eds) (1997) *Who are 'The People'?: Unionism, Protestantism and Loyalism in Northern Ireland*, London: Pluto.

Singleton, D. (1982) 'Housing a divided community: the paradox of reform in Northern Ireland', *Housing Review*, 31(3): 77–81.

Sinn Féin (1994) *The Economics of a United Ireland*, Dublin: Sinn Féin.

Sinn Féin (1997) *Putting People First – The Role of the Community in Economic Development*, Policy Review and Development Department, Discussion Document, Dublin: Sinn Féin.

Sinn Féin (no date) *The Ulster Defence Regiment: The Loyalist Militia*, Dublin: Sinn Féin Publicity Department.

Sinn Féin/SDLP (1988) *Sinn Féin/SDLP Talks*, Belfast, Sinn Féin.

Sinnott, R. and Davis, E. E. (1981) 'Political mobilisation, political institutionalisation and the maintenance of ethnic conflict', *Ethnic and Racial Studies* 4(4): 398–414.

Sivanandan, A. (1983) 'Challenging racism: strategies for the '80s', *Race and Class* 25(2): 1–11.

Sivanandan, A. (1985) 'RAT and the degradation of black struggle', *Race and Class* 26(4): 1–33.

Sluka, J. (1989) *Hearts and Minds, Water and Fish: Support for the IRA and INLA in a Northern Ireland Ghetto*, Greenwich, CT: JAI Press.

Smith, A. D. S. (1981) *The Ethnic Revival in the Modern World*, Cambridge: Cambridge University Press.

Smith, A. D. S. (1986) *The Ethnic Origins of Nations*, Oxford: Blackwell.
Smith, D. and Chambers, G. (1991) *Inequality in Northern Ireland*, Oxford: Clarendon Press.
Smyth, C. (1994) *Queen's University Belfast and the Fair Employment Crisis*, Belfast: Dept of Politics, QUB.
Smyth, M. (1972) *Battle for Northern Ireland*, Belfast: Belfast County Grand Orange Lodge.
Solomos, J. (1988) *Black Youth, Racism and the State*, Cambridge: Cambridge University Press.
Stalker, J. (1988) *Stalker*, Harmondsworth: Penguin.
Statewatch (1991) 'Reforming the UDR?' *Statewatch* 1(4): 3–4.
Statewatch (1992) 'Brian Nelson' *Statewatch* 2(2): 4–5.
Statewatch (1993a) 'Collusion and Britain's Irish policy', *Statewatch* 3(4): 12–13.
Statewatch (1993b) 'Matrix-Churchill and Public Interest Immunity', *Statewatch* 3(3): 14–15.
Statewatch (1994) 'MI5/MI6 – Trick or Treat?' *Statewatch* 4(1): 7–8.
Statewatch (1995a) 'Bloody Sunday Documents Missing', *Statewatch* 5(6): 18–19.
Statewatch (1995b) 'The Stalker Affair', *Statewatch* 5(3): 17–19.
Statewatch (1996) 'Law and Orange Order', *Statewatch* 6(4): 15–17.
Stewart, P. (1991) 'The jerrybuilders: Bew, Gibbon and Patterson – the Protestant working class and the Northern Ireland state' in Hutton, S. and Stewart, P. (1991) 'The jerrybuilders: Bew, Gibbon and Patterson – the Protestant working class and the Northern Ireland state', in Hutton, S. and Stewart, P. (eds), *Ireland's Histories: Aspects of State, Society and Ideology*, London: Routledge.
Stringer, P. and Robinson, G (1991), *Social Attitudes in Northern Ireland*, Belfast: Blackstaff Press.
Sutton, M. (1994) *Bear in Mind These Dead: An Index of Deaths from the Conflict in Ireland 1969–1993*, Belfast: Beyond the Pale Publications.
Taylor, P. J. (1991) 'The English and their Englishness: "a curiously mysterious, elusive and little understood people"', *Scottish Geographical Magazine* 107 (3): 146–61.
Taylor, R. (1987) 'The limits of Liberalism: the case of Queen's academics and the "Troubles"', *Politics*, 7(2): 28–34.
Taylor, R. (1988a) 'Social scientific research on the "Troubles" in Northern Ireland: The Problem of Objectivity', *Economic and Social Review*, 19(2): 123–45.
Taylor, R. (1988b) 'The Queen's University of Belfast: the liberal university in a divided society', *Higher Education Review*, 20 (2), Spring: 27–45.
Thatcher, M. (1995) *The Downing Street Years*, London: HarperCollins.
Todd, J. (1987) 'Two traditions in unionist political culture', *Irish Political Studies* 2: 1–26.
Tomlinson, M. (1993) 'Policing the new Europe: the Northern Ireland factor' in Bunyan, T. (ed.) *Statewatching the New Europe: A Handbook on the European State*, London: Statewatch: 87–114.

Tomlinson, M. (1994) *25 Years On: The Costs of War and the Dividends of Peace*, Belfast: West Belfast Economic Forum.

Tomlinson, M. (1995a) 'Can Britain leave Ireland? The political economy of war and peace', *Race and Class* 37(1): 1–22.

Tomlinson, M. (1995b) 'Imprisoned Ireland', in Ruggiero, V., Ryan, M. and Sim, J. (eds) *Western European Prison Systems: A Critical Anatomy*, London: Sage: 194–227.

Tomlinson, M. (1995c) 'Fortress Northern Ireland: a model for the new Europe?' in Clancy, P. *et al* (eds) *Ireland: a Sociological Profile*, Dublin: Institute of Public Administration.

Tomlinson, M. (1997) 'Whose law and order? Facing up to Northern Ireland', *Criminal Justice Matters*, no. 26: 20–1.

Treasury, (1996) *Expenditure Plans and Priorities: Northern Ireland, The Government's Expenditure Plans 1996–97 to 1998–99*, Cm 3216, London: HMSO.

Trimble, D. (1989) 'Address to conference', in Crozier, M. (ed.) *Proceedings of the Cultural Traditions Group Conference, 3–4 March 1989*, Belfast: Cultural Traditions Group.

Trimble, D. (1996a) 'Address to Ulster Unionist Party Annual Conference', 1996, *Irish Times* 21 October.

Trimble, D. (1996b) 'Building blocks for the Union', in R. Holmes (ed.) *A Vision for the Union: The Report of the Ulster Young Unionist Council*, Belfast: Ulster Young Unionist Council: 26–32.

Troyna, Barry (1992) 'Can you see the join? An historical analysis of multicultural and antiracist education policies', in Gill, D., Mayor, B. and Blair, M. (eds), *Racism and Education: Structures and Strategies*, London: Sage: 63–91.

Urban, M. (1992) *Big Boys' Rules: The Secret Struggle Against the IRA*, London: Faber and Faber.

'Veritas' (1813). *Letters written in England, in August 1813, explaining the Rise, Progress and Principles of the Orange Institution, in Ireland. With additional notes*, Dublin: Tute.

Von Tangen Page, M. (1996) 'The inter-relationship of the press and politicians during the 1981 Hunger Strikes at the Maze Prison' in Catterall, P. and McDougall, S. (eds) *The Northern Ireland Question in British Politics*, Basingstoke: Macmillan.

Wainwright, D. and Miller, I. (1986) *Research Supported by the Economic and Social Research Council 1985*, London: ESRC.

Wainwright, D. and Miller, I. (1987) *Research Supported by the Economic and Social Research Council 1986*, London: ESRC.

Walker R. B. J. (1993) *Inside/Outside: International Relations as Political Theory*, Cambridge University Press, Cambridge.

Walker, B. (1990) 'Ireland's historical position – "Colonial" or "European"?', *Irish Review* 9: 36–40.

Walker, B. (1996) *Dancing to History's Tune: History, Myth and Politics in Northern Ireland*, Belfast: Institute of Irish Studies.

Waller, P. J. (1981) *Democracy and Sectarianism; A Political and Social History of Liverpool 1868–1939*, Liverpool: Liverpool University Press.

Wallerstein, I. (1974) *The Modern World System I: Capitalist Agriculture and the Origins of the European World Economy, 1600–1750*, New York: Academic Press.

Wallerstein, I. (1980) *The Modern World-System II: Mercantilism and the Consolidation of the European World-Economy, 1600–1750*, New York: Academic Press.

Wallis, R. (ed.) (1975) *Sectarianism, Analyses of Religious and Non-religious Sects*, London: Owen.

Wallis, R., Bruce, S. and Taylor, D. (1986) *'No Surrender': Paisleyism and the Politics of Ethnic Identity in Northern Ireland*, Belfast: Department of Social Studies, Queen's University.

Ward, M. (1983) *Unmanageable Revolutionaries*, London: Pluto Press.

Ward, M. (1990) *Maud Gonne: Ireland's Joan of Arc*, London: Unwin Hyman.

Watson, P. (1978) *War on the Mind: The Military Uses and Abuses of Psychology*, London: Hutchinson.

Watson, P. (1980) *War on the Mind: The Military Uses and Abuses of Psychology*, rev. edn, Harmondsworth: Penguin.

Weber, M. (1930) *The Protestant Ethic and the Spirit of Capitalism* (trans. Talcott Parsons), London: Allen & Unwin. First published in German in 1904.

Weeks, J. (1997) 'The golden thread of intelligence is bringing terrorists to heel', *Police* XXIX(5): 6–8.

Weitzer, R. J. (1990) *Transforming Settler States: Communal Conflict and Internal Security in Northern Ireland and Zimbabwe*, Berkeley: University of California Press.

Whyte, J. (1983a) *Is Research on the Northern Ireland Problem Worthwhile?*, Belfast: Queens University.

Whyte, J. (1983b) 'How much discrimination was there under the Unionist regime?' in Gallagher, T. and O'Connell, J. (eds) *Contemporary Irish Studies*, Manchester: Manchester University Press: 1–35.

Whyte, J. (1990) *Interpreting Northern Ireland*, Oxford: Clarendon Press.

Wichert, S. (1991) *Northern Ireland Since 1945*, London: Longman.

Widgery Report (1972) *Report of the Tribunal Appointed to Inquire into the Events on Sunday, 30th January 1972, which Led to Loss of Life in Connection with the Procession in Londonderry that day*, London: HMSO, HC 220.

Wilkinson, P. (1986) *Terrorism and the Liberal State*, 2nd edn, Basingstoke: Macmillan.

Wilkinson, P. (1996) 'Report of an investigation into the current and future threat to the UK from international and domestic terrorism . . .', *Inquiry into Legislation Against Terrorism* (Lloyd Report) vol. 2, Cm 3420, London: HMSO.

Wilson, B. D. (1997) 'Requests for access to the RUC for research purposes application procedure', letter to Professor Brian Bates, Head of Research, Queen's University, 2 October.

Wilson, R. (1996) *Reconstituting Politics*, report no. 3, March 1996, Democratic Dialogue, Belfast.

Wilson, R. (1989) contribution to debate reported in Crozier, M. *Proceedings of the Cultural Traditions Group Conference, 3–4 March 1989*, Belfast: Cultural Traditions Group.

Wilson, R. and Nolan, P. (1996) 'No reconciliation – no receipts', *Fortnight*, September: 16–17.

Wilson, R. M. (1989) *Ripley Bogle*, London: Andre Deutsch.

Wilson, R. M. (1993) '1989' in *21 Picador Authors Celebrate 21 Years of International Writing*, London: Picador.

Wilson, R. M. (1996) *Eureka Street*, London: Secker & Warburg.

Winter, J. (1997) 'Preface' in Mullan, D. (ed.) *Eyewitness Bloody Sunday: The Truth*, Dublin: Wolfhound Press.

Wolff, J. (1990) 'Reinstating corporeality: feminism and body politics' in *Feminine Sentences: Essays on Women and Culture*, Oxford: Polity Press.

Wollstonecraft, M. (1992) *A Vindication of the Rights of Women*, London: Everyman.

Working Party on Sectarianism (1993) *Sectarianism: A Discussion Document*, Belfast: Inter-Church Centre.

Wright, F. (1973) 'Protestant ideology and politics in Ulster', *Archives Européennes de Sociologie* 14: 213–80.

Wright, F. (1987). *Northern Ireland: A Comparative Analysis*, Dublin: Gill & Macmillan.

Wright, F. (1990) 'Is Northern Ireland Britain's Algeria?' *De Gaulle et son siècle, Journées Internationales*, paper F086, 19–24 November. Paris: UNESCO.

Wright, J. (1990) *Terrorist Propaganda*, Basingstoke: Macmillan.

Yorkshire TV (1993) *First Tuesday – The Forgotten Massacre*, 6th July.

Index